A PLACE TO LIVE

Other books by Wolf Von Eckardt

MID-CENTURY ARCHITECTURE IN AMERICA *(editor)*

THE CHALLENGE OF MEGALOPOLIS

ERIC MENDELSOHN *(Masters of World Architecture series)*

LIFE FOR DEAD SPACES *(with Charles M. Goodman)*

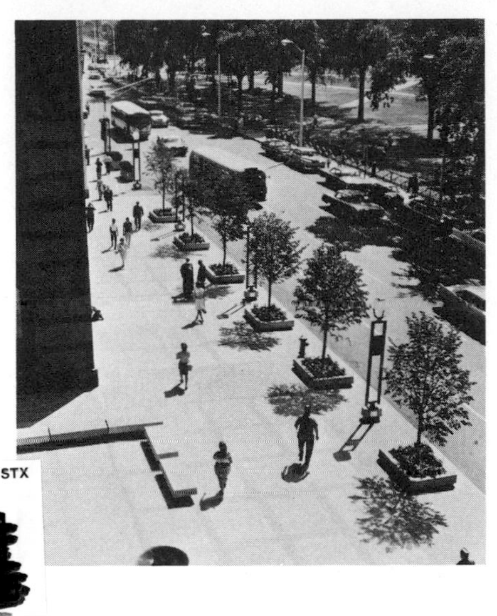

A PLACE TO LIVE

THE CRISIS OF THE CITIES

by WOLF VON ECKARDT

FOREWORD BY
AUGUST HECKSCHER

A SEYMOUR LAWRENCE BOOK
DELACORTE PRESS, NEW YORK

LIBRARY OF CONGRESS CATALOG CARD NUMBER: 67-20653
MANUFACTURED IN THE UNITED STATES OF AMERICA
FIRST PRINTING

DESIGNED BY *Larry Kamp*

Grateful acknowledgment is made to the following for permission to reprint the material from the works cited below.

AIA Journal: for "Brasìlia—Symbol in the Mud."
American Heritage Publishing Co., Inc.: for "The Bauhaus," originally published in *Horizon*, November 1961.
Harper's Magazine: for "The Case for Building 350 New Towns," originally published December 1965.
The Sterling Lord Agency: for excerpts from The Phantom Tollbooth by Norton Juster. Copyright © 1961 by Norton Juster. Reprinted by permission of The Sterling Lord Agency.
New American Library: for excerpts from The Individual and the Crown: A Study of Identity in America by Hendrik M. Ruitenbeek.
The New Republic: for "Urban Renewal and the City."
Saturday Review: for "The Age of Anti-Architecture" originally published January 23, 1965.

Contents

VI. THE NEW COMMUNITY

Foreword

by AUGUST HECKSCHER

Administrator of Recreation and Cultural Affairs, New York City

Some time ago my friend, Wolf Von Eckardt, asked me whether I would write an introduction to his book. I consented, somewhat rashly (not having seen the book) but knowing that everything he writes about architecture is lively and sensible. Now that I have been able to read the galley proofs I am more than pleased by my original decision.

A Place to Live is a surprising achievement, bringing together as it does so much seemingly diverse material, and relating it all to a consistent point of view. The reader will find here excellent journalism, the touch of the practiced essayist, an often rigorously critical spirit, historical perspective and a solid substructure of humanistic values. The book speaks of architecture in a way that architects and planners will find refreshing, and that the lay reader will find novel and revealing. It makes comprehensible the divergent styles and strains within a highly important sector of modern life, one that in the years ahead may be decisive in determining the quality of life upon this planet.

So great, indeed, is likely to be the influence of architecture upon our lives—architecture understood in the broadest terms to include planning and concern for the total environment—that one stands almost appalled at the responsibilities which lie upon this one profession. A comparatively short time ago it was enough that the architect have the skill to design individual buildings, elegant or utilitarian as the requirement might be. Now he conceives and lays out cities and regions, and thinks in terms of man's philosophy and his ultimate values. It is essential, therefore, that good architectural critics be developed—and Mr. Von Eckardt is one of the best of them. It is essential, too, that the public at large be able to understand fully what the architect is trying to do.

If I were writing a book, instead of merely writing the introduction to one, I would call it *The Limits of Architecture*. I would want to talk about the possibilities of architecture in re-making our world, and, as a result, re-making men's ideas and behavior. I would also want to talk about limits in a more exact sense—the point beyond which architects cannot go without presuming to do the work of statesmen—and even of gods. There is an idea abroad today that almost any problem can be solved by good design—an idea that is quite often true, but one that could lead us into a fatal neglect of other tasks and disciplines. It seems unfair to architects to expect them to tell us how truly rational and humane creatures should want to live, when they should be able to content themselves with providing the form and structure through which accepted values can be expressed.

The architect, as this book makes plain, is not only a builder, however; he is also an artist, and as artist he carries the burden of prophesy and the compulsion to tell us what the good life is. Like the contemporary painter or writer, he must determine the subject matter of his art, not merely make more beautiful and relevant a body of knowledge and faith that has come down to him. No architect worth his salt today will forgo the responsibility of helping to shape and modify the program which he embodies in structure. Yet in determining the program, he risks entering into fields where he can have only intuitive knowledge, and where he is tempted into an unsettling kind of pride.

But I am not, as I said, writing a book, and my own task is limited to introducing the very good one which Mr. Von Eckardt sets before us. His tone is cheerful, though his judgments of the contemporary world are somber; he leads us toward hope, though only after having brought us through some very stony lands. He is not polemical or wedded to any narrow dogmas. And he speaks about the great issue of our time: how we may still manage to shape an environment—inevitably an urban environment—which answers to man's fundamental needs for sharing, for aloneness, for common celebrations and private joys, as well as for such fundamental things as breathable airs and potable waters. He is a guide well worth following through the often unexpected twists and turns of his theme.

Prologue: The Crisis

Ever since, millions of years ago, man got tired of roaming the grasslands and settled down, he has sought to give his dwelling some amenity and personal distinction. It seems a strong urge essential to civilization.

At boarding school, when I was about nine years old, we were forbidden to clutter the dormitory with anything of our own, not even with pinups which soldiers are allowed over their bunks. It must have bothered me. On a sudden impulse I cleaned out a shelf of my locker next to my folding bed, lined it with colored paper, fastened some picture postcards inside, and put up a display of pretty stones and some other pathetic little items I was fond of. Every time I opened the locker I would admire this humble altar to my individuality. It did wonders for my morale.

One day some bully caught me at it. He made a snide remark, and I did something I've never since had the courage or inclination to do. I hit him. He soon got much the better of me, which is probably why I remember my first, vague discovery that a good place to live must have identity, *a sense of place*.

This much may be quite obvious to anyone who has hung his own pictures and draperies on his four walls to make them his own. But we spend only part of our lives in our homes. Most of us no longer work, play, worship and obtain the things we need, or think we need, to keep body and soul together on the homestead. We live in communities, much as I lived in the boarding-school community.

What may seem less obvious is that our urban and suburban neighborhoods, too, need a sense of place to be meaningful to us, to give us a sense of belonging, to give each individual a sense of his place in a bewildering cosmos.

Much has been said and written about the increasing ugliness and inefficiency of our present urban environment. It accounts, I believe, for the current malaise of our society.

We discuss this malaise mostly in social, political and economic terms. Architecture and city planning—which is, or should be, one and the same, since city planning and urban design is really architecture on a large scale—is mentioned only when the discussion gets down to aesthetics. Since the advent of the industrial age, which enthusiastically yields old human values to new machine demands, aesthetics are thought of mainly as "beautification," and are not very high on the list of the problems that beset our environment.

That, I submit, is where we have gone wrong.

In the past, as you will readily concede when you look at old buildings and old towns, people quite naturally gave free reign to the urge to give their place to live some amenity and personal distinction. As building the place became more complex and specialized, we seem to have lost that instinct. In all the hassle about our dismal urban condition—about housing, recreation, transportation, governmental confusion, crime, education, water, air and land pollution, and the ghettos—we tend to forget, in fact, that what we are really talking about is our place to live.

The quality of that place determines the quality of our life. And if we now discover that despite our high standard of living, our standard of life leaves much to be desired, it is precisely, I believe, because our place to live—the communities and neighborhoods in our cities and suburbs—is largely a mess.

Since we no longer live in caves, our communities consist of architecture. It is not their only ingredient, since man does not live by shelter alone, but it is an essential one.

True, architecture is the product of social, political, and economic conditions or, as Mies van der Rohe has put it, "the will of the epoch translated into space." But in the end the architect is also an artist of sorts and as such, like all artists, a lonely man. He can draw at best on the collective wisdom of his profession when, confronting that empty paper on his drafting board, he starts translating that "will of the epoch."

Architecture today is, I fear, in a state of crisis. And that crisis has contributed, to a larger extent than is generally realized, to the urban mess. Architecture has failed to respond to the needs of our time and the varied requirements of its surroundings. It is shouting in isolation. Lacking a sense of place in time and space, it fails to give our environment a sense of place.

And this is so, I hold, because our architecture has betrayed the original tenets of the twentieth-century architectural revolution.

All this may sound a bit abstract. But as you read on, I hope to make clear both the nature of the crisis in architecture and the nature of the kind of place to live for all sorts of people with all sorts of inclinations—the kind I believe we all need and want. It is a place that at once expresses and stimulates the individuality and creativity of every person.

A crisis, of course, is a turning point—for better or worse. I am optimistic. We can, I am sure, already see that the crisis in architecture is a turning point for the better. There is evidence that, as in the past, architecture can create such places in modern terms. And much as my dormitory locker did when I got through with it, these places are bound to do wonders for the morale of the people who live in them.

That, at any event, is what this book is about. In the first part I deplore how most of our architects help destroy rather than create the sense of place in our cities and suburbs. The second part reviews the noble ideals of the early Moderns who attempted to marry art and technology to create a truly livable environment in a technological age. This is followed by an account of the betrayal of these ideals in the midcentury battle of styles.

In the fourth part I turn to urban design, its predominant traditions and their still lingering influence. Fifthly I survey how current architectural wisdom has affected our efforts to renew American cities. And finally I discuss the more recent humanistic approach to community architecture and speculate how this approach when served by our developing technology might shape a better city to come.

Needless to say, much of what I criticize, argue and plead is criticized, argued, and pleaded by a good many others. I only present for what librarians call "the general reader" and in a personal summary and context what various experts are starting to say in scattered and various ways.

Better still, there is also a growing number of architects such as, among others, Walter Netsch with his campus for the University of Illinois in Chicago or William Conklin with his design of the Virginia New Town, Reston, who are already translating this epoch's desperate urge for a new humanism into buildings, neighborhoods, and towns.

This is not a visionary book. It points to a new turn in man's old urge to give his dwelling place some amenity and personal distinction—the urge, to use Aristotle's phrase, not merely to come together in cities to live, but to stay to live the good life.

I. A SENSE OF PLACE

The illustrations in this book were
selected and placed to give the reader a
quick visual impression of what the text
discusses. Their precise identification
along with the picture credits,
will be found on page 415.

1. Shouting in Isolation

There is today, as city planner Edmund N. Bacon has said, "an appalling lack of image of what the American city may become." And this, I submit, is largely the failure of modern architecture.

We are now, with our urban renewal and demonstration programs, beginning reluctantly to spend some money and energy on the improvement of our place to live. But we don't have a clear concept how we want to live, how we want our houses, neighborhoods, and cities to develop physically, where and how we will live and work, and how these areas will relate to each other and to nature.

"A plan," says Bacon, "based on these realities must be the starting point—the framework within which social, political, and economic interactions necessary for the creative development of an urban society can occur."

Bacon, it happens, came up with such a plan for giving a distinctive new look to his old home town, Philadelphia. As a result the necessary interactions did occur. They occurred not so much because the people and leaders of Philadelphia were persuaded by his proposed traffic patterns or economic statistics. They were intrigued by a three-dimensional model of proposed new buildings, streets, and malls that was created back in 1947. More than 385,000 Philadelphians, including all the school children, went to see a vision of "A Better Philadelphia" which Vincent G. Kling, Oskar Stonorov, and others had designed and which Willo von Moltke and others later refined and improved. What intrigued them was, in the end, an aesthetic vision, a physical concept, something people could see and identify with. It was architecture.

Having achieved something of an aesthetic consensus, Bacon and his planners managed to get things done in Philadelphia. It was the first American city in recent years to rebuild its downtown center. And although other cities have followed, there is as yet little vision of what our architecture ought to be and to do for us. We do not quite trust it—at least not enough to accept the physical plan as the starting point and framework within which social, political, and economic interactions can occur. In fact, it often seems that we are so far from having one that, unless a Bacon appears, we don't even realize how badly we need it.

Many city planners argue that design, architecture, and aesthetics should be the least of our worries. The impediments to livability, they say, are problems that politics, economics, science, and technology must solve. Their own contribution to the solution is devoted mainly to urban fortune-telling. They prophesy endlessly sprawling megalopolises and ecumenopolises—vast expanses dotted with honeycomb megastructures pierced by radarmatic speedways rising in Daliesque landscapes and populated by happy robots who do not talk but communicate with each other by video phone and computer.

This might be harmless fun if they didn't tell us that these flights of fancy into nightmarish visions of the noncity of tomorrow will cure the ills of today. They won't.

It is true, of course, as the future-tellers maintain, that technology is changing the world and that we must live with change. But man has not changed. He still breathes, eats, and makes love in hopelessly old-fashioned ways. He still wants to roam the fields and woods and swim in lakes and rivers. He still yearns to live with the tribe and be part of its rites and activities. And he still wants to give his place to live that personal distinction, that something that makes him feel he belongs.

The early Modern movement in architecture understood this. Although its International Style glass boxes are in bad repute today, this revolution had all the right ideas. It foresaw, indeed it anticipated, most of the urban problems that plague us today. One can make the case that Le Corbusier in his *Toward a New Architecture* proposed to avoid the Watts riots some forty years before they happened.

With great idealism the Functionalist crusaders, as someone has called them, declared that a marriage of art and technology, performed in the spirit of social concern, would bring forth a new aesthetic. It was not to be a "style," though that is what it turned out to be, but a clean, honest, and wholesome new shape of all man-made things that would bring about a clean, honest, and wholesome new *Wohnkultur,* as the Germans call it, a new culture of living. Everything, from the cup from which we drink to the city in which we live, was to be functional in a scientific and technological sense, and thus everything from coffee in the morning to a spree on the town at night was to be a happy and meaningful experience in a new world of science and technology.

They have created a great many works of art, such as Walter Gropius' Bauhaus at Dessau, Mies van der Rohe's Barcelona Pavilion, and Le Corbusier's Villa Savoye at Poissy near Paris. These buildings did, indeed, hold the exciting promise of at once expressing and shaping a changing way of life in a new age of relativity and relative values. This had a profound influence on our current architecture, but not a pervasive one.

Today, a generation later, these buildings are still considered avant-garde museum pieces, interesting experiments outside the main stream of our culture. The promise of the new architecture to "bring beauty and unity into the chaos of our time," as Gropius defined its mission, has remained unfulfilled. The new architecture has preciously little influence on our way of life. It has not given our place to live the personal distinction that would make us feel at home and happy and creative in it.

This is not to say that today's architecture itself is not creative. We live in a wonderfully exciting, a most energetic time. Our architecture, like our art, reflects this excitement and energy. But it has lost its direction.

You can't have direction if you don't have a goal. Architecture today moves, as always, with the major currents in art. Today's art, in turn, because it is frustrated by the complexity and relativity of the world, seeks meaning not in what it presents, but in the "process" of presentation and in innermost personal experience. This is often beautiful and is a part of our time, but not all of it.

If architecture is to give that something extra to the cave, as it should, it has to concern itself with more than monuments for the few. I am not arguing that every architect should henceforth design nothing but public housing projects. But neither should architects have strayed as far as they did from the original aims of Modern architecture. The essence of the Gothic was its religious spirituality. The essence of the Renaissance was enlightenment. The Modern pioneers saw that we have entered an age of social awareness. Our own inventiveness has forced us to acknowledge that we all, as Adlai Stevenson put it in his last speech, "travel together, passengers on a little space ship, dependent on its vulnerable supplies of air and soil."

The reason our architecture appears to have lost this awareness, it seems to me, is that the twentieth-century architectural revolution has floundered on three enormous failures:

The first was the failure to fully harness modern technology—one of its basic objectives. Just watch the primitive methods, compared to, say, the automated production of an automobile, by which even a daring skyscraper, let alone a simple house, is still being built. Consider how many new roofs, let alone bathrooms, still leak until they are patched and patched again after much pleading with reluctant contractors. Just think how silly it is that we still haven't found a simple way to hang a picture on the wall of a modern house without breaking either the plaster or the nail and that we still have to repaint our interiors every three years at growing expense. As architect Raymond Reed has observed, medicine has increased our longevity, and agriculture has dramatically increased productivity and value, while architecture has reduced productivity and increased prices. Our great-grandfathers paid for the family home in three years, and though we live in an age of technological production, we are lucky to qualify for a thirty-year loan. The majority can afford it. But two affluent decades after the depression and the war, almost a quarter of the nation is still ill housed. We have supplied far more people with good automobiles and television sets, than with good homes.

The second failure was the failure to provide historic continuity. Modern architecture began, in the words of Henri van de Velde, one of its godfathers, as "a revolt against the falsification of forms and against the past . . . a moral revolt." In their zeal to start from scratch, the first modern architecture schools, under the influence of the Bauhaus, prohibited the teaching of architectural history for fear of corrupting their students. When the modern movement threw out the bath water of dishonest eclecticism, it also threw out—or tried to for too long—the child of man's cultural heritage. It forgot the psychological assurance that familiar, traditional forms give us. People want a house to look like a house and a church to look like a church. There was, however, nothing in the Villa Savoye to tell a good shoemaker in

Poissy that this odd box on stilts is a place to live, let alone more comfortable than his traditional one.

Functionalism in architecture has lately been replaced by a resurgence of Expressionism. The terms, I'll admit, are arbitrary, though convenient. In a tentative way, I'll try to sort things out a little later in this book. A serious appraisal of our current architecture will obviously have to wait until the construction fences are down and the dust has settled. Only then can we intelligently label new forms or win at the fascinating detective game of the art historians about who influenced whom and why.

But it is not too early to state that whether or not we'll ever settle on a generally accepted architectural style for our time, we should at least have some sort of visual harmony and order. Architects and city planners all talk about it. But the new, undisciplined abstract Expressionism or the kitsch of buildings gift-wrapped in grilles is no more apt to lead to it than the old overdisciplined glass box Functionalism. Neither respects tradition and the continuity people seek in their place to live.

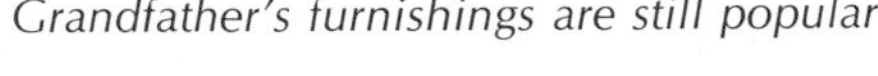

Grandfather's furnishings are still popular

The two failures of twentieth-century architecture have combined to spawn a third—the failure of modern architecture and design to gain genuine popular acceptance. Even today Americans, who always seek to employ the latest scientific methods in their work and the latest gadgets in their homes, would still let out a howl of indignation if a Villa Savoye or a Ronchamp chapel were to be put in Scarsdale.

Surely the Greeks never thought Doric columns and entablatures controversial, certainly not a full generation after they first appeared. Although some conceited twelfth-century Italians thought pointed arches "barbaric and Gothic," the style was soon accepted as perfectly natural and dominated everything from handwriting to cathedrals. Thomas Jefferson designed Monticello and the University of Virginia in a Classic Roman style, because that was the thing to do at the time, and no one questioned it. He thus could apply his energies and ingenuity to designing it well to respond to specific needs.

You need only look at all those "Colonial" or split-level Cinderella Cape Cod Ramblers in our suburbs, not to speak of the hideous, eclectic interior furnishings in even the most modern apartment buildings, to see that "Modern" is not the accepted style of our time. It is hardly what most people in America today identify with.

This is not just because people have abominable taste, as architects and architecture critics, including myself, would often have it. Taste is a fickle thing that is all too easily seduced by fashion which, in turn, is easily manipulated. Modern architecture and what it stands for has simply never struck a chord with enough people to determine our visual culture. It has not, so far at least, produced a demonstrably better mousetrap. Nor—and this seems to me even more important—does it satisfy our yearning for historic continuity and a sense of place, the ingredients of order and culture.

The crucial test, says James S. Ackerman, Harvard's Fine Arts chairman, "is the architect's sense of tradition and invention." By tradition he means, "the inescapable continuity of the work of today with that of the past without which nobody could even draw a plan or communicate his ideas to a foreman, much less make a comprehensible building; it is the vital life stream of architecture that protects our environment from chaos." Invention is "the injection into that stream of a fresh substance which at best blends with and enriches it, and becomes part of the tradition of tomorrow. The designer is not wholly free to select his tradition, because it is not his alone; it belongs to the culture as a whole, and if he mistakes its nature, his work sooner or later is revealed as arbitrary and without meaning. Consequently he is not wholly free in his invention either, because an innovation that does not emerge from and blend with tradition is an artificiality that forever shouts isolation."

In their isolation our architects have hurried from Functionalism to historicism, mysticism, arty self-expression and vain exhibitionism. Some of their buildings, such as Louis Kahn's medical laboratories at Philadelphia, although hard to understand, are moving and challenging. Some possess innovations that promise to enhance the repertoire of good architecture. Most, however, are only titillating or ingratiating and this has suddenly made their architects public heroes. Architects are more fashionable today than ever in the history of their profession. But the popular architectural stars, such as Edward Durrell Stone, Paul Rudolph, Minoru Yamasaki, or Charles Luckman, and all their instant imitators, create mostly arty sensations that, with all their fanciful sculptural dressing, trimmings, and grilles, vie with each other for attention like stunt shows at a county fair.

True, a decade or two ago we demanded more richness and exuberance. But the trouble with these performances is not exuberance or lack of talent. They are narcissistic and antisocial. Like prima donnas they hog the urban show, refusing to restrain themselves in the company of older architecture. The Swiss art historian Sigfried Giedion, a devout missionary of Modern architecture in its beginnings, calls these structures "playboy architecture . . . an architecture treated as playboys treat life, jumping from one sensation to another and quickly bored with everything." This playboy architecture must take a share of the blame for turning our urban environment into a chaotic county fair on a continental scale.

Why worry? Who says it's bad? One man's monstrosity may be another man's Taj Mahal. But is it? One need not argue taste as long as there are accepted cultural standards. But how can there be standards if there is not even much public interest in what the public interest is? This is where we are somewhat in a vicious circle. For lack of aesthetic and cultural standards we condone bad taste on a scale that disrupts our environment. The disrupted environment, in turn, makes us all the more indifferent toward arriving at standards.

A good many critics and picture-magazine editors applaud playboy architecture for offering new sensations, vaguely hoping that the building will at last please us enough to set a new trend. We all rejoiced when we first saw the pictures of Ed Stone's New Delhi Embassy, its grilles lyrically reflecting in a placid pool. This helped turn it into a cliché. For what we forgot is that architectural design is so intimately tied in with the community and our complex life, that a lasting new expression of taste can rarely be original or individual. Original expression of valid good taste is such an extraordinary accomplishment that in past periods only a very few have succeeded or even tried.

We have little to hope from the Pan Am Building, for instance. It straddles Park Avenue in New York, virtually on top of Grand Central Station, conspicuous only for its unseeming bulk and disregard of its surroundings. This hundred-million-dollar slab is two blocks wide and fifty-nine stories high. That makes it the world's largest of the crop of so-called investment buildings, erected by speculators to yield rent profits. It blocks the vista of Park Avenue, an important American street which was beginning to assume a consistent architectural style and thereby a pleasing harmony.

Ed Stone's mammoth John F. Kennedy Center for the Performing Arts in Washington, D.C., a New Delhi Embassy of giant proportions that disastrously crowds a lovely riverfront, is a monument to our fetish of giganticism. It stuffs an opera house, a theater, a concert hall, and a movie house to boot into one huge building. The questionable assumption is that corporate culture is more efficient and, ergo, better for you than culture on a human scale. It isn't. It is only inefficient and bewildering and entering those huge portals will reduce a man to an ant.

Character assassination

Paul Rudolph's much acclaimed parking garage at New Haven visually busts a whole city block. His Massachusetts State Service Center withdraws from its three surrounding Boston streets and violates their harmony and integrity.

Charles Luckman dumps his ugly, illiterate fifty-story Prudential Tower amidst the gentle old houses of Boston's Back Bay for no purpose other than to dwarf John Hancock, Prudential's rival, and the only result is the tragic ruin of Boston's long cherished skyline.

An architecture born of social concern has largely turned from professionalism to commercialism. Boston's Prudential, to single out one example, seems to me somewhat like an act of character assassination —the character many generations of Americans have given their city.

2. Between the Dollar and the Dream

It takes two to produce a building. There is the architect and there is always a client who insists on further congesting an already congested downtown area, on wrapping all the performing arts in a Byzantine grille, on building a massive temple to store automobiles, or on dwarfing his competitor. That client, of course, is no less confused than the rest of us—caught as we are in a binge of bewildering change. It is also always the architect who defends his folly, not with the understandable argument that he must eat, but with some philosophic rationalization that compounds the confusion.

One of the difficulties is that architects, like most of us, are so inundated with floods of information that they have become illiterate and know little about history. Not knowing where they have been, they can hardly know where they are or where they are going. They have no sense of place in time.

Though the architects have let us down, we must admit that we have also let down the architects. We haven't given them much of a chance. An orderly and livable place to live in must be planned, designed, and controlled. We must accept this as a necessity of modern civilization, much as we accept traffic lights, compulsory typhus injections, and crop controls. Though few of our designers and architects are really good, they are, as a profession, at least as efficient as our traffic engineers, medical doctors, or agricultural experts. Yet, according to the most optimistic guesstimates, less than a quarter of all that is built in this country, and only 5 per cent of our houses, are designed by aesthetically trained professionals. We now have planning commissions in most cities. None of them has been given authority to engage in other than abstract exercises that everyone quarrels about. In Germany city planners are called *Städtebauer,* or "city *builders,*" not planners. We must, I think, come to that. Too much of our planning is an abstract exercise with little or no influence on what is actually built.

Most building in America just happens, and it happens very badly. We let it happen very badly not so much because we are powerless (after all, we *do* protect children from typhus and whooping cranes from extinction), but because we still have only vague and indifferent notions about what—in terms of modern life and our uncertain aesthetics—we expect the great architecture of great cities to be. Some people actually want to abolish cities altogether.

In the past the fact that so much building went on without the blessing of professional designers alarmed no one but possibly the professionals themselves. The residential folk architecture around the temples and cathedrals was picturesque enough, even if it was often rather unsanitary and inflammable.

Today, design or no, we are about to build as much again in one generation as we have built in our entire history. We are urbanizing one million acres every year—the equivalent of a whole new Chicago. It's time we knew where we are going. While architects and city planners must lead in expression, in giving form to our emerging concepts of how we ought to live, the concepts must be ours.

This order, I fear, cannot be created by reckless and rugged individualism, though where a fundamental order exists, individual expression within that order is not only desirable but vital. We live, if you'll pardon the truism, in a mass culture, which simply means that everything that is done, for good or bad, is done on a vastly larger scale than ever before. This calls for vastly larger responsibility on the part of those who are doing it, and more collective guidance on the part of those it is done to. It didn't much matter in the past if some Punch and Judy show in the other end of town gave nightmares to the children in the audience. Put such a show on television and it becomes a concern of society. It didn't much matter if someone built himself a coach whose brakes didn't work. Turn out millions of unsafe cars, each with the power of 250 horses, and everybody is in trouble.

In our political system safeguards against wicked television shows or dangerous automobiles do not rely exclusively or even primarily on the police power of the state. They rest largely on the business acumen of large enterprises that must be responsive to their customers or go broke. In most of our endeavors today large corporations with their concentration of finance, talent, research, and other resources meet our needs and create new ones in the name of progress. There are public regulatory agencies and the checks and balances of competition, but, on the whole, the corporations are pretty enlightened. Whatever else it is, this is surely the epoch of large corporations.

In building, however, we still have mostly a chaotic agglomeration of wicked shows, produced by a multitude of small men with small minds. They see open land and the city as a huge quarry to be mined for quick profit. In the name of free enterprise we give them far more license than we would ever give car manufacturers, airlines, or broadcasters. As a result, as clients in an epoch that should build what it stands for, we could hardly do worse.

We are beginning to care a little more now than did our parents, who could always move farther west when things got too messy. The last generation let the industrial revolution overrun our cities, their waterfronts, and surroundings with its factories, railroad tracks, warehouses, slums, grime, and decay. This generation is stuck, struggling to get out from under these mistakes without having fully learned from them. We still act as though we had infinite space to overrun. In most enterprises that affect the public welfare, we have rejected the fuzzy economic laissez-faire liberalism of Adam Smith, but in building our environment, which affects the public welfare most decisively, we still hang on to the doctrine.

The majority of our federal programs heavily favor narrow private interests, and those that don't—for example, public housing—are deliberately kept puny. It started in the New Deal which believed, probably rightly at the time, that the government must prop up the homebuilder and mortgagor to get the ailing economy going again. The economy has long been doing quite well, but the theory hangs on. Housing legislation still equates the welfare of the building industry with the public welfare. Government home financing regulations take a banker's glass-eye view, favoring property values over human values. It is, as housing expert Charles Abrams points out, not surprising, therefore, that low-income families were all but forgotten until the war against poverty came along. The urban renewal program tends to favor downtown business: housing for the poor is replaced by corporation palaces and luxury apartments. The highway program favors the automobile and heavy construction industry. No wonder that in public transportation we are the most underdeveloped country in the industrialized world.

On the local scene building codes are devised not only to protect the public against poor construction, fire, crowding, and insufficient sanitation. Most of them also protect our reactionary building-trade unions and building manufacturers against the technological advances of the twentieth century. They are written and upheld not to give us economical, well-functioning buildings but giant featherbeds of brick and stone. In the city of Philadelphia you could not, until just a few years ago, construct curtain-wall buildings. The building code did not permit it. It was said to have been upheld mainly by the political power of John B. Kelly, Princess Grace's father, whose construction company specialized in masonry.

Real estate taxes penalize improvements and thus encourage land speculation and slum lords. Fly over any city in the country and you will see large patches of land close to the city covered with nothing but weeds or weedy, barely used structures. This land is kept out of the market for speculation, and urban development is forced to skip and jump over it and push further out into the countryside. Out there, land may be cheaper, but roads, sewers, school buildings, and other services are, of course, more expensive. The speculator who holds on to needed land until the price soars up is rewarded by the tax collector for not "improving it." We have found ways of curbing the exploitation of child labor and some of our other natural resources. We still consider land sacrosanct private property and treat it as a commodity to get rich with.

Our zoning is obsessed with rigid segregation of land use and income groups. It carefully sets aside the areas where we may shop, work, amuse ourselves or meet other people spontaneously—as though these things were not part of living. Within the residential areas zoning establishes a caste system more rigid than any that ever prevailed in India. There are high-income neighborhoods and middle-income neighborhoods and the ghettos for the poor. It's all devised to protect property values, not human values.

It is comforting to know that the zoning laws prevent the construction of some hideous gas station right next to my house. On the other hand, it might be rather convenient to be able to get gas for my car

Every so often you find a good client

without having to drive three miles away. There must be some solution other than a hideous station or none at all. It has rarely occurred to anyone in this country that even a gas station could be attractively designed and unobtrusive. No one has effectively gone to work on the problem.

Tapiola, the wonderful New Town in Finland, has a most attractive gas station right in the neighborhood to prove that architects can do it. Here, no one has really challenged them. Good architecture needs good clients.

Every so often you find a triumph in unexpected places. Along U.S. Route 50, not far from Washington, D.C., I recently discovered what at first glance seemed to be a beautiful new art museum. It turned out to be the offices and warehouse of Capitol Car Distributors, the regional Volkswagen dealer. The fact that a lot of people in their region thought small, enabled Capitol's president, Alan M. Dix, to think big—and elegant. Here was a man who really cared.

Dix cared about the color and texture of all the exposed little pebbles in his concrete panels. About the sculptured lines of his columns. The play of shadows created by the louvers. The handsome forecourt that gives his building's palatial facade distance and dignity. Most of all, and most importantly for his employees and the people driving on

Highway 50, he cared about the trees on his thirty-three acre site. He kept so many of them standing, in fact, that from the road, you barely see how much he cared about every detail. Under the trees he put lush landscaping—flowering shrubs and green lawns and a reflecting pool with a waterfall. His building, which is as handsomely elegant inside as out, stands in a park instead of a parking lot. That, for a commercial place along this, or any other U.S. highway, is rare indeed.

The greatest surprise of my unexpected discovery was that Mr. Dix employed architects who had before not been conspicuous for outstanding design. The feat, it seems, was largely the work of a good client.

There are others, of course. Some investors try to do better than squeeze every penny of rentable space out of their office or apartment buildings. But even if the developer, in our fragmented and fragmentary building industry, cares enough to build, say, a handsome apartment house, there is not much he can do about the quality of the school the children of his tenants attend or the park they play in. The same is true of the suburban homebuilder who may put up a hundred lovely houses. Often, he doesn't have the resources to put the overhead wiring into the ground where it belongs, or even to build sidewalks. Whether the houses are lovely or not, they don't add up to a really good place to live.

Paradoxically, only the large, anonymous investment appears to be able to protect small, personal values. The really big entrepreneur, backed by the really big chain department store, will encourage a number of small businesses, which provide individual service and specialties, to open shop in his large shopping center.

A close friend, a lady who lives alone, stuck it out in a New York slum apartment until very recently. The worst of her experience was not the noise on the streets, though she was wakened one night by a shrill female voice shrieking, presumably at a cop, "I may be a whore but I am not a prostitute!" Nor was it the stench in the hall, the ailing elevator or the chronic midwinter breakdowns of the heating and hot-water system. It was the Kafkaesque search for the ever-changing landlord, who, even when finally tracked down, had a way of receiving complaints with much the same sublime indifference with which the Grand Canyon receives a pebble thrown into it by a child.

When she finally moved out, she moved, to my slight dismay, into one of those superblock slabs that New York's urban renewal has wrought and that Jane Jacobs and I heartily disapprove of. It is an ugly human filing cabinet and disrupts the neighborhood as well as the cityscape. My friend, however, has clean halls, a well-functioning heating system, and a lovely balcony with a view of Central Park. What's more, if anything goes wrong she need only call the ever courteous and attentive manager, who is always on duty, and the trouble is eliminated within hours. The place, you see, is owned and operated by a large corporation which has its "image" at stake.

The anonymity and indifference of the small-businessman builders and owners of our places to live is not confined to the poor. Suburbanites, too; are complaining that their new dream nests still lack a final coat of paint or have water gathering in the yard or a bathroom door that doesn't fit. Their biggest gripe, reported the real estate editor of the Washington *Post*, "is that new owners can't find anyone interested in their complaints. 'We can't get the builder, and the selling agent has lost interest,' one caller said."

The big boys, entrepreneurs like William Zeckendorf—though, unfortunately, he seems to have overreached himself—or the Reynolds Metals Corporation, Alcoa, and others, have, on the whole, produced far better architecture and better new neighborhoods than the multitude of small developers with their limited interests and resources. The most promising places to live in America, such as the New Towns of

Only big clients can help create urban order

Reston in Virginia, Columbia in Maryland, or Valencia in California, are the result of large-scale investments by large corporations such as Gulf Oil or the John Hancock and Connecticut General Life insurance companies. There are encouraging signs that other big corporations are becoming interested in housing and community building. Only big clients, it seems, are able to commission comprehensive architectural design to help create urban order. Others can do it only with help from the federal government.

The basis of urban order, we are beginning to see, is the preservation and creation of a sense of place. Its current destruction or omission is not only an aesthetic loss. It has, I believe, a great deal to do with the uncertain state of our mental health and our standard of life.

3. Identity Returned

When caveman first felt the need, long before I did, to turn his place into something more than shelter and painted things he was fond of on the wall, he brought art into the world. The urge to give one's place personal identity is not only a motivation for individual and collective self-expression. Identity is not only what man wants to give his habitat. It is also what his habitat gives man.

Erik H. Erikson, the eminent psychologist, speaks of the "mutual significance" of man's identity and the world around him. Man's greatest urge, he says, is to give identity to this world, so that the world, in turn, can give identity to him. The most important ingredient of this mutuality, he adds, is continuity.

We don't know whether caveman also hit bullies who came and sneered at his paintings and threatened to destroy these symbols of his identity. As soon as history was recorded, it recorded that this sense of place, symbolized by such things as monuments, flags, and songs, evoked such strong loyalties in people that they continued to go to war to defend it.

While we often condemn such aggressive tendencies, at least in others, we actually consider this loyalty a great virtue. This probably stems from the fact that home, town, city, and country, being the place where we have often lived for generations, returns to us the sense of accumulated identity our forebears have lavished on it. We focus most of our memories, dreams, thoughts, and aspirations on it. In a cold, impersonal cosmos, it therefore gives us a sense of belonging, of being part of something we can understand and part of a place where we fit in and are needed.

This loyalty is, of course, essential to make our collective habitat work politically. Despite our diverse and often divergent personal interests, it holds us together somehow and keeps us from slitting each other's throat more often than we do.

Not long ago it was widely assumed that identity and loyalty were rooted only in the land a man and his family owned as their own real property. Jefferson, for instance, thought that only landowners would have the right motivation for taking part in public affairs. We no longer hold this view. Although we still require that a person must have resided for some time in a community before he can vote or run for office in it, we no longer care whether he owns or rents his residence.

Property, as August Heckscher has pointed out, has to a large extent become abstract and impersonal. "It does not tell you anything of a man's mind and spirit if you learn that he has sold his General Motors stock and bought International Business Machines. Even the most tangible goods are not so much possessed as consumed: they are acquired and disposed of, leaving behind no trace, neither taking the character of their owner nor imparting anything of themselves to him. And as for owning a plot of earth, it now means less and less. New roads are pushed through near by. Housing developments surround it. The view, the very air, is cut off. A man's home is no longer his castle when the total environment is altered unrecognizably."

"What the individual requires, therefore," says Heckscher, "is not a plot of ground but a *place*—a context within which he can expand and become himself."

My locker altar, the cave paintings, most people's living rooms, the village church steeple, the Piazza San Marco, or New York's skyline all demonstrate that the sense of place, like the flag, is visible and must manifest itself visibly before we can feel and experience it. In the end it is architecture which expresses it with all of Erikson's "mutual significance."

Just how architecture does this is difficult to say. Old places seem to have it more often than new ones. You can walk for hours in some old parts of town—Washington's Georgetown, Boston's Beacon Hill, the French Quarter of New Orleans, or the old parts of San Francisco, for

An old street returns what generations gave

instance, not to speak of the Ile de la Cité in Paris or of Venice—and still be fresh and ready for more adventure. Walk in other places and a severe drain on your energy soon makes you look for a taxi. In cities that supposedly herald the shape of the future, such as Los Angeles or Brasilia, you don't even attempt to walk.

"There is no there there," reported Gertrude Stein after she was shown—I believe it was Oakland, California. It doesn't much matter where it was. Oakland or Oklahoma City, urban America is much the same. If you do much traveling in America, it is easy to forget just where you are when you step out of your hotel in the morning. From coast to coast vast, gray urbia and vast, green suburbia, rich man's luxury highrise or poor man's public housing project are alike in their anonymous sameness. With rare exceptions, there is no there there. There is no there there at all.

This is disturbing not only as a matter of appearance. In 1964, close to an apartment house in Kew Gardens, a gray but by no means unpleasant middle-class suburb of New York City, twenty-eight-year-old Catherine Genovese was murdered on the street early one morning. She was stabbed several times by a man who took half an hour to kill her. As you may recall reading, thirty-eight people living on that street admitted having heard her screams. Several watched the murder from their windows. Not one bothered to call the police. No one, newspaper reporters were later told, wanted to get involved. The anonymity of the place, I am sure, has a good deal to do with this apathy. Who wants to be involved with row upon row of gray apartment slabs? Yet without involvement with the stage set you remain a mere spectator of the drama that takes place in it.

Vast, gray urbia came first. It was bad enough that in the industrial revolution cities just grew and grew, row upon row of houses and tenements. They broke Aristotle's rule that a city, to be a good place to live, ought to be large enough to encompass all its functions but not too large to interfere with them.

Then, with affluence and the automobile came green suburbia. They gave the white middle class the means to flee the city and move into suburban miniature manors on diminutive country estates, sprawling farther and farther out. The fact that people are spread so far apart also dangerously dissipates the quality of urban life—the life seven out of ten Americans lead today.

One penalty we pay is precious time. In the eighteenth century it took man ten minutes to get from the outskirts to the center of his city. In the nineteenth century it took twenty minutes. Today, despite the fact that we own vehicles capable of transporting us at a hundred miles per hour, it takes, on the average, forty minutes. The trouble in suburbia is not only that it takes all that time to get downtown, but that people must mobilize all of 250 horsepower whenever they want to buy a pack of cigarettes or have a drink in the warm conviviality of a tavern. This makes the suburbanite almost as deprived as the slum dweller. The irritated restlessness of the itinerant suburban child, forever being dragged along on mother's far-flung errands, can be as pathetic as the sad eyes of a slum child. Even the affluent two-car family can no longer spontaneously do as it wants. Johnny cannot attend his Boy Scout meeting or Jane her dancing lesson while Dad is at work and Mother out shopping. How often do any of them get to a theater? Or worse, how often do any of them meet people of different income, color, or persuasion? How many affluent Americans can experience the wealth of culture and civilization that cities are built to offer—not vicariously on television but in their heart and soul?

Gray urbia and green suburbia are now caught in the blender of unprecedented economic boom and out comes metropolis, a vast urbanized area that is, for the most part, neither city nor suburb. It has none of the advantages of either and all the disadvantages of both. The white affluent middle class, which used to give the city stability, moves out and, sped by federal superhighways and mortgage insurance, spreads the unsightly manifestations of its wealth all over the countryside. Poor in-migrants from the country, sped by farm mechanization, which is

Man's greatest urge: A place where he belongs

aided by federal subsidies, move in and spread the diseases of their poverty all over the city.

While we're very democratic about spreading blight, we are very careful not to mix people. What not long ago we fancied was about to become a truly classless society has segregated rich and poor in its zoning system. Democracy in America, it seems, stops at the office or factory gate. On the job we frown at class distinctions. At home we insist on sticking strictly to our own class. Our residential areas are considered exclusive private clubs. The "wrong" kind of people are kept out because the "right" address, of course, is as much, or more, of a status symbol than club membership.

There is, as a statistical fact, more racial segregation today in our residential housing pattern than there was two decades ago. Even as race segregation begins slowly to break down, economic segregation remains, because middle-class Negroes don't want to live next to poor people either. A typical example of that occurred not long ago when well-to-do liberals of both races jointly opposed a public housing project in Hyde Park-Kenwood, the rehabilitated neighborhood around the University of Chicago. "Black and white shoulder to shoulder against the lower classes," quipped comedian Mike Nichols.

All this has been abundantly noted, analyzed, and lamented. We cannot help but see, as we drive along our superhighways, that city and country have blurred and that the result is ugly. We smell the pollution of our lakes and rivers, and our eyes smart from the pollution of our air. We know that children are not safe on the street even amidst the high-priced Cinderella homes. It is evident that neighborhoods and communities are overrun and dissolving and with them the established order they represent. We dread megalopolis, the growing together of several metropolises—or conurbation, as the British call it—which is already occurring along the Atlantic seacoast from Boston to Washington and in the Ruhr basin of West Germany. That, of course, is what "beautification" is all about.

The term scares me a little. It helps, of course, but our real problems are not solved by sprinkling wildflower seeds along highways, getting rid of automobile junkyards, billboards, overhead wiring, smog and water pollution alone—important as all this is. Nor will the planting of azaleas in neglected old city parks, or even the creation of new ones, cure our urban malaise. The new "City Beautiful" movement, if that is what is emerging, must be more than a revival of Thoreauvian ideals about birds and bees.

In fact these ideals have contributed to a phenomenon that has been little noticed in all this: It is not only the countryside that has been suburbanized but the city as well. The freeways, with their exorbitant space demands, the setbacks that disrupt the harmony of the street, the whole, almost obsessive emphasis on "open space" within the city, further blur the distinction between the suburbs and downtown. The idea is that cities are too crowded and must be opened up. Our recent architecture and urban design are opening up to excess. The result is that, much like abstract expressionism in painting and sculpture—which I have nothing against if it is good—this fashion in city planning abstracts the city. It deliberately and somewhat rebelliously replaces familiar images with willful, intuitively designed, though highly rationalized, forms. They create a jumble of high and low. Buildings jut out or stay back and are placed at odd angles. You have to negotiate needless distances to get from one place to the next.

The sameness in our cities is not the result of monotony, however, but of too much disharmonious variety. Their problem today is not, as the conventional wisdom would have it, that they are too crowded, but that they are too spread out, not that overall, urban densities are too high, but that they are too low. This raises havoc with the urban ecology.

Ecology is a relatively new word, denoting the interdependence of all things. We apply it mainly to the wondrous balance of nature which may not be disturbed with a chain reaction of consequence. Rachel Carson has helped us to understand this, pointing out, for instance, that when you poison insects you may also kill the birds that feed on them and that reckless chemical warfare on nature will silence it. A classic case was the enormous proliferation of Arizona's Kaibab deer in the twenties. Wolves, puma, and its other natural foes were eliminated by well-intentioned men who meant to protect the deer. The Kaibab, their numbers unchecked by the predators, increased from four thousand to a hundred thousand in less than twenty years. All edible greenery on the range suffered, but the deer themselves suffered most grievously of all. In one hard winter sixty thousand starved to death. The rangers had to take over the role of the wolves, step in with their guns and kill until there were no more deer than their food supply could sustain.

In the city, which is also very much a living organism, endless variables are equally closely and mutually interrelated. In fact, it is really redundant to speak of an urban ecology because the word, coined almost a hundred years ago by the German zoologist Ernst Haeckel, who spelled it *Oekologie,* derives from the Greek *oikos,* which means "house" or "a place to live."

Today, as has been said often enough, the urban ecology is badly disturbed. We fail to give our places to live sufficient love and attention. There is therefore often too little they can return to us.

4. Watts

"It is interesting, if not useful, to consider where one would go in Los Angeles to have an effective revolution of the Latin American sort," wrote architect Charles M. Moore, dean of the Yale School of Architecture, recently. "Presumably, that place would be in the heart of the city. If one took over some public square, some urban open space in Los Angeles, who would know? A march on City Hall would be equally inconclusive. The heart of the city would have to be sought elsewhere. The only hope would seem to be to take over the freeways, or to emplane for New York to organize sedition on Madison Avenue; word would quickly enough get back."

I happened to read this on the same summer day of 1965 when Los Angeles *did* have a revolution, but not of the operetta kind. For days a vicious, nihilistic riot raged in the Watts district. It had happened before—in the sordid slums of Harlem, on Chicago's South Side and in some other ghettos. Now everyone was shocked that it should happen in the benign and relatively tolerant California climate, on streets that are shaded by palm trees and lined with outwardly presentable little houses. We wondered why California Negroes should act so much more violently than Negroes in the South and just at a time when, with the passage of voting rights legislation, civil rights had made another decisive step forward.

The difference, I submit, is one of setting. The deep South is not yet urbanized. The towns are relatively small. The oppressed Negroes live in communities where people by and large still know, communicate with, and mean something to each other. Leadership can and does develop. And it can and does rally the Negro community to disciplined, nonviolent protests and marches on city hall which is within walking distance and in the heart of a town which is also theirs. Once arrived, the marchers can physically confront what their leaders now like to call "the white power structure." Despite the abstract term, the people, some of them sadistic fanatics, are real enough. Every child can see, experience, and know what it is all about. This, it would seem, accounts largely for the admirable discipline of the civil rights movement in the South. Even under extreme stress and provocation, a miserable little city like Selma, Alabama, having retained the physical setting of a *civitas* of sorts, has also retained that setting's historic civilizing function.

Watts, in contrast, is a segment of that endless, formless urban mess which, like a stranded jellyfish, rots in the California sun. The conspicuous consumption flaunted under the gaudy skyscrapers of Wilshire Boulevard only emphasizes the conspicuous vacuity under the palm trees of this peculiar suburban slum. There is much in both to suggest the American dream turned nightmare: free, bold enterprise reaching for the sky along the "miracle mile," and an absurd remnant of the suburban ideal in Watts.

So, even in *reductio ad absurdum,* the American dream is not for all Americans to share. That distant "miracle mile" isn't for the people of Watts to take pride in, and three and four large families are crowded into the little suburban houses. Yet, they did not, I gather, riot for civil rights or even to protest their poverty. They did not set out to die for a cause.

The McCone Commission, investigating the causes of the riots, found unemployment the most distressing of a number of problems facing the Negroes of Los Angeles. In addition, the voters of California had just reinforced their ghetto walls by passing Proposition 14 which repealed the fair housing act, the attitude of the police was regarded by Negroes as hostile, and public transportation in an area where only 14 per cent of the people own cars was woefully inadequate.

What it all added up to was the sickness of the cities, and a desperate boredom that moved the people of Watts to killing and death.

Their frustrations, loneliness, and search for identity just simply exploded.

The problem in Watts, then, is not quite Charles Moore's problem that there is no place in Los Angeles to take a revolution to. The problem is that there isn't even a place for a decent revolution to jell. There is, in contrast to the South, no staging area, no leadership, no community, no accessible city hall, and no visible power structure. It's all just a Kafkaesque, nightmare abstraction which went bang, like that.

I wonder whether there would have been a riot in Watts if somewhere between those freeways and under those palm trees there had been a town square, a center, a kind of *agora* such as Fresno has recently created on its Mall; some focal point where people can spontaneously get together and in the encounter somehow find out who they are and what they hope to make of their lives.

This is not to say that architecture and city planning alone, without economic improvement and social justice, can solve the problem. Poverty and race discrimination are worse in the South. In Watts, it would seem, the two only aggravated a disease that is rampant not only in our dark ghettos but all over town, all over our lily-white suburbs, and all over the urbanized world, including the Communist countries. Among its early symptoms are school dropouts, leather jackets, switch blades, gang warfare, dope addiction, wifeswapping parties, alcoholism, and TV dinners. In its milder forms it is the disease that keeps the psychiatrists busy.

Nor do I claim that antisocial and self-destructive behavior is a modern invention. There was a lot of drinking and fornication and all the rest in ye goode olde towne. TV dinners are a fine way to eat your cake and watch David Brinkley, too. Conscientious sociological studies prove that a lot of people are perfectly happy in Levittown if they have two cars and enough room in the house to get away from the kids' TV.

Perhaps we indulge in too much deploring. The current fashion of calling society sick is, I suspect, a way of feeling sorry for ourselves because, like every other generation, we've got a few problems. But since we can now flick a switch when it gets a little warm in the room and, abracadabra, it becomes cool, we also, somehow, expect that we can match the invention of the air conditioner with some kind of social conditioner to convert cool nonconformists, teenagers, and other troublesome elements into warm mediocrities. Some behavioral scientists, as they call themselves, actually talk about "social engineering." It hasn't worked so far. Many of us turn into crybabies when such silly expectations are disappointed. Like hypochondriacs who keep taking their temperature, we keep taking more useless and expensive psycho-sociological studies.

Yet we cannot deny a malaise. There are, even in Levittown, an undue number of people who find it hard to cope with the world. The increase of crime and other unpleasantnesses is out of proportion to the population increase. The fever of rapid urban change and growth creates most uncomfortable rashes. Many a man who has everything enjoys nothing, not even the hedonistic fruits of relaxed moral standards or the syrupy "understanding" and indulgence of bad behavior which Sigmund Freud has inadvertently brought into the world. Juvenile delinquents who used to wear a mischievous grin now sport a desperately bored poker face. They are not enjoying their delinquency one bit.

The trouble seems to be not that people are out for more kicks but that they enjoy them less. Perhaps that is the essence of the urban malaise. Exurbanite, cliff dweller, and slum dweller alike, once afflicted by this malaise, lack the ability to feel emotion and experience life. They attempt to escape their inner emptiness and feeling of insufficiency by various means—from staring indiscriminately at television all day to less harmless pursuits. They seem constantly on the run, driven by anxiety, like men who have lost their shadows and are trying desperately to retrieve them. What man has lost is his sense of identity.

This is no startling revelation. It has been said in various ways by various observers for some time now. Hendrick M. Ruitenbeek, for instance, writes in his *The Individual and the Crowd* that "in the old-fashioned inner-directed society, the individual . . . could identify with his community if only because he could rarely escape from it. Thus fixed, the community itself could develop a more differentiated form, often in esthetically satisfying architectural form. . . . The individual in transitional or other-directed societies lacks superego support for his identity. Consequently, he tends to seek identity through identification with a shifting group of his peers, whether these be classmates, fellow workers, or neighbors. Such shifting groups can provide only pseudo-identification, however; and the independence that characterizes an achieved individual identity can be attained only with the utmost difficulty. Rather than face himself, the individual submits to that lack of privacy which, again, seems so striking a characteristic of American life. Unfenced yards, picture windows, open-plan houses characterize a kind of life where the bathroom affords the only privacy generally respected (or indeed generally desired). In their search for identification, Americans involve themselves in so many organizations and groups, other than the frequently all-embracing corporation in which they work, that they often seem overwhelmed by the sheer weight of demand on their time.

"Nevertheless, it cannot be said that the sense of belonging is on the increase in our society, as many observers say they believe; on the contrary it has declined and continues to do so. Modern man is losing any genuine sense of belonging because he finds it difficult to identify himself with the multitude of social roles he has to play. Current popular emphasis on belonging and 'togetherness' signifies a longing rather than an achievement; something desired, not something possessed. When Housman wrote:

I a stranger and afraid
In a world I never made

he was prophet, as poets are apt to be. Feeling alone in an alien world is now the emotional property of Everyman."

Unemployment in Watts, Harlem, or the South Side, I might add, burdens this emotional property beyond the breaking point. These insights, however, have come from psychiatrists and have thus concerned themselves with the individual in all his complexity. They have taken the place where he lives, the chaos in the modern urban environment, more or less for granted, content to accept the malaise as the product of "civilizational pressures" not susceptible to change. Beyond individual psychotherapy for the rich and social work for the poor—recently escalated into a "war against poverty"—we only study and deplore the matter, hoping that if we study and deplore long enough everybody will wake up some fine morning radiating mental health, well adjusted and responsible.

It has been all but completely overlooked that the shadow of human identity is cast by the light of human community. Community, in turn, except in its most abstract sense, relates to its physical setting as the soul relates to the body. A community with which to identify and from which to receive identity cannot very well exist without its buildings and locus, the physical place which this mutuality creates.

Such places can be and are now being designed and built. It begins with the house or apartment that, in its arrangement of rooms and spaces, provides us the right balance between being together with others and being alone. Both are necessary to make community, even family community, meaningful. It is amazing how often, in our homes and apartments, the need for individual privacy is overlooked. A German psychiatrist recently noted that our roads in America are jammed with large cars with only one occupant. He reprimanded his American colleagues about this waste. Car pools, he said, could reduce rush hour traffic by a quarter or even a third. He received what he thought was a surprising answer. The morning and evening drive to work, his American colleagues told him, are often the only moments in the day when the hardworking American male can be by himself.

The same right balance between private spheres and public spheres is needed in the community. A good community is not necessarily a chummy place where everyone knows everyone. It is a place where the experience of community—a walk to catch some air and to see some people and things—is always at hand. Only such a palpable, physical community, I should think, can create the standards against which mental health must be measured. Only a tangible community can give us a tangible order which is what we are supposed to adjust to and be responsible about.

Having overlooked the vital importance of the physical environment—in plain words, the importance of the architecture of houses, neighborhoods, and cities—psychiatrists and behavioral scientists have little to say about its planning and building. They offer a lot of advice on how to make love, friends, and responsible citizens, but none on the right kind of setting for making them. Psychiatrists, sociologists, ministers, social workers, and others who professionally deal with people rarely get together with architects and city planners, at least not until very recently. When they do, mostly at special academic convocations, the discussions are mostly that—academic. Their chief accomplishment is to enrich the already obscure gobbledegook of the planners with a choice new phrase or two in sociologese.

Most books and dissertations on the city and various aspects of the urban environment—with few exceptions such as the works of Victor Gruen and Lawrence Halprin—content themselves mainly with a diagnosis rather than a proposed cure of the urban condition.

This is fine—proper diagnosis is the premise for proper therapy—unless the two are confused, which all too often they are. I suspect that much of this obsessive analyzing of what went wrong and where and why doesn't help as much to put things right as the analysts like to think it does. I doubt that going through life blaming one's parents for one's woes really makes one a better or healthier person. I doubt that all these studies, telling us that traffic is really as bad as we know it is or that slums are really as unhealthy as they appear to be, help solve the problem of the automobile or low-income housing.

The obsession with retrospective research is understandable. The holocaust has been so drastic that we want to know what hit us. In trying to find out, we use the methods of science, which are to observe and describe rather than to evaluate, in order to come to valid conclusions. This works well with the antics of chromosomes. It is less than infallible in human affairs, quite simply because the behavioral scientist is caught up in humanity every bit as much as the rest of us. He, too, must rely on intuition which is better nourished by passionate concern rather than by statistical measurement. It is nice to know the precise velocity of the holocaust. What the scientists and behaviorists must help us to know is how we can again become the masters of our urban fate and how, for that matter, we can muster our collective will to do so. For surely we have the means.

5. Rediscoveries

There is cause for optimism. A ferment of new thought and social criticism about our environment has seized the country and bubbled to the very top of political leadership in an amazingly short span of time. President Johnson, as pragmatic a leader as any we've had in our history, talks not only about securing the blessings of wealth, power, or military security but also, in the wake of John F. Kennedy's inclination, "the needs of the spirit." He has offered a federal program on "natural beauty" and called a White House conference on it. He has pleaded that the nation "think, work, and plan for the development of entire metropolitan areas . . . to put the highest concerns of our people at the center of urban growth and activity."

John Kenneth Galbraith was perhaps the first to point out that *The Affluent Society* is wanting. Michael Harrington confirmed this with shocking specifics in his book on poverty in the United States, *The Other America.* Other writers quickly followed Harrington's explorations of the slums and ghettos which our wild building binge had left behind.

Rachel Carson's *Silent Spring,* a passionate and well-documented book on the disastrous effects of chemical insecticides, similarly opened the nation's eyes to a grave new threat. Peter Blake charged that God's own country is turning into *God's Own Junkyard*. His admirably brief and immoderate tract showed us in words and pictures the mess that billboards, junked cars, overhead wiring, roadside stands, and other ugliness are making of our landscape and cityscape. It was not the only charge of its kind, but it helped focus public concern and indignation. Interior Secretary Stewart L. Udall, surely as sparkling in his intellectual as in his political grasp, explored a new conservation ethic, as he calls it, in *The Quiet Crisis*. Recent books by Lewis Mumford, Jane Jacobs, William H. Whyte, and Jean Gottmann directed our attention to the staggering problems of rapid urbanization that began to point to new solutions.

No idea is ever entirely the work of one man or one group. It is fed by many arteries and capillaries, visible and hidden. But once the right time and the right writer or writers burst it out of semiawareness, the fresh stream of an idea can suddenly flood away even deeply rooted conventional wisdom, immerse the thinking of others, and cause whole areas of activity to bloom with new creation. Often we never realize just whence the stimulation came.

The bibliography of the Great Society is not made up of the works

The fever of rapid change often brings rashes

of entrenched experts and specialists. The credentials of its authors are not certificates of a scientific "discipline" or profession in the field they have chosen to write about. Michael Harrington, Lewis Mumford, Rachel Carson, Jane Jacobs, and William Whyte are merely "writers," journalists in the best sense.

We need the experts and the technicians. But we also need, as Gropius has said, "more search and less research." Most of all we need men of creative determination to build an environment that is socially just, chemically pure, aesthetically endurable, and technically efficient, an environment that will above all, as President Johnson has put it, "create and preserve the sense of community with others which gives us significance and security, a sense of belonging and of sharing the common life."

This appears to be the basic issue for most people. The majority of Americans—including some prominent Modern architects—prefer to live in old houses and old neighborhoods. Even those who live in modern houses and hang paintings of our time in their living rooms are apt to furnish those living rooms in the style of their parents and grandparents. If they can afford it they live in the old, mostly Victorian houses of Georgetown in Washington, D.C., Beacon Hill in Boston, Society Hill in Philadelphia, Telegraph Hill in San Francisco, or Greenwich Village and Brooklyn Heights in New York.

In fact, wealthy people often put up with considerable inconvenience for the sake of character, charm, and quaintness. Many Georgetown houses, for instance, are incredibly small. Most of them are not, as good Georgetowners often believe, Federal or Georgian, but Victorian. They often measure not more than eighteen or twenty feet in width, have halls and stairs on which two people can barely pass each other, five or six small rooms on three stories, only one bathroom, a tiny kitchen, and a paved backyard the size of a postage stamp. Yet at great expense people restore and cherish these simple builders' houses with touching devotion and turn them into instant heirlooms. They pay prices for them that would easily buy a modern villa with push-button everything.

This is not to say that *all* old houses are small or inconvenient or that the blessings and innovations of modern houses are confined to push-button gadgets. In addition to character, an advantageous location, and pleasant grounds with mature trees and gardens, many old buildings also have spacious interior arrangements, a convenient layout or, as architects call it, a sound "logic of spaces." They often have high ceilings and thick, soundproof walls. Modern houses have the ad-

It's art. But where do you put the furniture?

vantage of gadgets, built-in heating, cooling and furnishings, interior layouts designed for living without servants and, with their glass walls and glass sliding doors, a new, enchanting indoor-outdoor relationship. Well-designed modern houses have character too, or at least a distinctive quality. But living in them doesn't always come naturally at first. It takes the right *Weltanschauung*. It becomes an article of faith. An international-style house, in its studied and pristine simplicity, calls for the studied and pristine life of a Zen Buddhist monk rather than the living habits of our culture with its penchant for hoarding and clutter. The glazed facades of Mies van der Rohe's middle-income town houses at Lafayette Park in Detroit are superb works of art. But where do you put the furniture?

Since the people who live there are not willing to give up their davenports and commodes for the sake of Mies' art, they place them against the glass wall. That ruins much of its aesthetic effect.

I talked about this with Mies, who is, with his clear and simple unpretentiousness, a most endearing person to talk to. He smiled, not a smile of disdain but one of almost shy helplessness. "*Ja,* that, I'm afraid, is a matter of education," he said at last. He seems to feel that placing furniture against a glass wall somehow violates good manners,

Are we as Puritan and virtuous as all that?

and I suppose it does. It is also not only a matter of the psychological yearning for continuity Erik Erikson speaks of, but also of economics. People have inherited those davenports and commodes or sometimes made an adventure of getting them at an auction, and if the unsightly backs of these pieces mess up the elegant austerity of Mies' design, that's too bad for Mies. They wouldn't want to swap these possessions for equally elegant and austere modern furnishings even if you paid them money into the bargain.

Shown Philip Johnson's famous glass house at New Canaan, a lady exclaimed, "Oh, but I wouldn't want to live here!"

"Nobody has asked you, madam," Johnson shot back.

The problem isn't entirely a private affair between Johnson, a bachelor, and his visitor. Like Mies, Johnson and all good architects seek validity. Modern residential architecture, however, never really invited us to live with it. It preached that we ought to. It remained an exclusive cult, demanding a superior morality. It appealed, as Russell Lynes has pointed out, to the virtues of modesty, clean living, and disdain for what we call vulgar display. As it turned out we were never as Puritan as we fancied ourselves to be. Most of us never quite wanted to live in three-dimensional sermons, and Johnson himself, for instance, quite openly deserted the cult for his own elegantly sensual, hedonistic, and eclectic historicism. What it comes down to is, I believe, that new aesthetics or not, we find the cold, machine-made simplicity of this sermon uncomfortable. Despite the Modern movement's early romantic adulation of technology, we really want to get away from the machine and what looks machine-made.

The preference for old houses has been a tremendous boon to the historic preservation of buildings and, more recently, to the beginning preservation of our cities. It has led to our rediscovery of the need for a sense of place.

It isn't mere fashion. The preference for old houses, old furniture, and "period" interiors is not confined to the sophisticated and well-to-do. Those who can't afford to buy and remodel old houses build "genuine replicas" or think they do. More accurately, the speculative builders, well aware of public tastes, build the "Colonial Cinderella Ramblers" for them. They build them in used brick, or brick that is made to look used, and clutter them with dormers behind which no one sleeps, columns that support nothing, stable lanterns that light no stables, and other insults to genuine tradition. The "genuine replica" furniture is mass produced with the "antiqued" finishing applied and the worm holes drilled in. We wrap television sets in Chippendale consoles. What all this boils down to is not a fleeting whim but a full-scale counterrevolution against modern design.

The salesmen of modern houses and apartments feel compelled to cram their sales models with historic associations. Once the prospec-

A masquerade without wigs and candles

tive buyer has entered the contemporary doorway, he is quickly led to escape this troubled age into the presumably more comfortable past of valances, Queen Anne and Chippendale with a phony Early American cradle thrown in for patriotism.

The word is "traditional." More often than not it means that fluttery decorators concoct a riotous mishmash of different traditions, totally foreign to both themselves and their clients. You find a hapless Queen Anne cocktail table visually kicked about by Louis XIV, while some Jacobean piece seeks refuge under the sumptuous ruffles of yards and yards of drapery spilling out from under a gilded wrought-iron valance.

The model apartment in a brand new, modern luxury apartment house I visited recently sported wedding-cake icing on the much too low dining-room ceiling, a miniature Hall of Mirrors, more mirrors on a somewhat bothersome structural column in the living room, a non-structural, arched Romeo and Juliet colonnade in the master bedroom, picture wallpaper with Piranesi motives, and all kinds of Louis This or or That bric-a-brac, and a lush display of artificial flowers.

Nowadays there is little left of the Puritan morality that Russell Lynes long ago thought modern austerity might perhaps appeal to. In fact, when the Rue des Gourmets restaurants inside the glass-box, modern New York Hilton hotel opened not long ago, their designer, William Pahlmann, proudly advertised his feat to the trade, full page, under the headline, "This story begins in a bordello."

This antimodern reaction is not entirely harmless. The damage is not only a matter of taste. Again, it touches on the fundamental issue of identity. For by escaping into phony replicas of the past we escape facing what it is we stand for and who and what we are. A farmhouse is distinct because it includes the barn and the stables. A motel built in 1965 that is made to look like a Colonial farmhouse is not only an expression of vulgar illiteracy. It is also phony because there are no animals in the "stable," the occupants don't wear wigs or read by candlelight, and its design refuses to include an honest expression of television and other real needs and wishes of the people in it. A community design that apes Colonial Williamsburg is a failure because its identity conflicts with but does not include the presence of the automobile and other realities of our time.

The problem is not new. Goethe wrote some 150 years ago to Eckermann: "I cannot approve of furnishing entire rooms in an imitated style and of living in the surroundings of a bygone period. It is always a kind of masquerade which, in the long run, does not bode well, but will rather have a detrimental influence on the people who indulge it. For it stands in contradiction to the living days into which we are born and emanates from an empty and hollow attitude and mentality which is thus confirmed. Upon a gay winter's evening one might well attend a masquerade dressed as a Turk, but what, alas, would we think of a person who would show himself in such disguise all year around? We would assume either that he is crazy or, at all events, disposed to become so."

As sculptor Richard Lippold put it, "The truly creative man has faith in his time." Bordello interiors and fake Colonial Williamsburg facades display a sad lack of such faith, and the escape into historic ostentation, such as shown by the Sam Rayburn House Office Building in Washington, is not only an escape into bad taste. It is also, in no small measure, a failure to meet creatively the natural need of people to feel truly at home with their creations and the things they want and love.

If this reaction has brought us much deplorable fakery, it has also boosted the preservation of the genuine. Not long ago Philip Johnson, for instance, who in the thirties helped bring the International Style to this country, literally walked a picket line to save the very eclectic, very Beaux Arts Pennsylvania Station in New York. Twenty years earlier he would undoubtedly have been delighted to join the wrecking crew.

What seems to have happened is that the sophisticated Washingtonians who first discovered the charms of the Negro slums of Georgetown also discovered the architectural charms of historic architecture in general, and began to fight the wrecking balls to preserve it. Since Georgetowners tend to be very influential people, the whole preservation movement gained in significance. Georgetown, I dare say, is the foremost recruitment area for the officers and board members of the National Trust for Historic Preservation.

It became no longer a question of whether or not George Washington had slept in a building. The building itself became important, even the humble landmark. At first only Federal or Colonial seemed to count because this, oddly, was somehow considered more American than later styles. Now the architectural preservationists extend their passion—usually with more zeal than actual effect—to more recent creations as well. Thanks largely to the efforts of Interior Secretary Stewart L. Udall, the Trust recently even took an important *modern* building under its protective wing. It saved Frank Lloyd Wright's intriguing little Pope-Leighey House in Virginia from the highway bulldozers and placed it in restored splendor on the Woodlawn estate near

Mount Vernon. Frank Lloyd Wright would have chuckled at the irony of it all—but the relocation was well done and the house is a pleasure to visit.

What's more, the Georgetown idea spread. Much to the surprise of the city planners and housers, who initially wanted to tear down everything that didn't meet their bureaucratic definition of decent, safe, and sanitary dwellings, people spontaneously began to dislodge the poor from old city neighborhoods all over the country and restore the neighborhoods. The same trend is evident in Europe.

It is not only old houses people want to live in, but old neighborhoods. What attracts them, however, is not address, charm, and history alone. Old Williamsburg has all of this and candlestick makers in wigs to boot. Yet people don't move to Georgetown, Beacon Hill, Hyde Park, Kenwood, or Greenwich Village to live in a museum.

They move there because these places—like most human settlements before the industrial revolution—have relationship and identity in their architectural design. "Relationship," says the English critic Ian Nairn, "means making the parts of the environment fit together. Identity is the recognition and enhancement of the specific needs and qualities that make one place different from another." If you have that in a neighborhood or town, you can relate to and identify with it.

An important element here, I believe, is wholeness. You don't feel fully at home in any fragment of a house—bedroom, dining room, or study. You feel at home in a house or apartment as a whole. You do so because it is the place where you sleep *and* eat *and* enjoy your privacy as well as, if you'll pardon that horrible word, your togetherness. It is, furthermore, the place where you hang your favorite pictures on the wall and express your personality in the way you arrange things.

In the same way an old town, in contrast to modern subdivisions or rigidly zoned residential areas, constitutes a community as a whole. We know that it does because our eyes can survey and our legs can conveniently negotiate its completeness. We see the center with its church steeple and city hall and marketplace. We see the park or riverfront where we go for a breath of fresh air. We see where people work and where they shop and play. You see, almost at a glance, how you, yourself, fit into a discernible order of things. Place is defined. You can sense it.

We seek this subconscious assurance from a town just as in a building we seek the assurance that it will stand up. A structure makes us uncomfortable if we can't somehow see or sense what supports it. Ex-

Ancient lessons newly applied

pressing the structure is by no means an architectural whim but, I believe, a psychological necessity of good design.

There are, and should be, surprises—a sudden vista or some unexpected structure. Yet the order, identity, and relationship declare themselves. The important streets with the important people and stores are wide. The less important ones are narrow. You can tell whether a square is a market or a ceremonial place or both. If you get attuned to this order, you don't really have to know the town or the language to find a pharmacy, say, or a good restaurant. The plan has its built-in logic, and there is always a church steeple or some tower to orient you.

The wholeness of a town includes its people. We subconsciously want to be assured not only of the presence of the pharmacy or restaurant but also of the pharmacist, the cook, the waiter, and washer of dishes. We want to know who is going to launder our shirts. A complete town that contains a variety of people with a variety of incomes engaged in a variety of activities is never dull. There is always life, and the bustle also means greater safety than we find on our deserted downtown streets at night. We find here security and significance because, in Lewis Mumford's words, man "in all his cumulative historic richness, his regional individuality, his cultural complexity is in the center of the picture. He plays his part as a dramatist, scenic designer, actor, and spectator in the unfolding drama of life."

We are beginning to rediscover this.

6. Jane Jacobism

The drama of urban life, as Mumford acclaims it, has no script. A city is a place where anything can happen, which is as good a reason as any why architecture and city planning should save and not destroy it.

I experienced the delight of city living one memorable evening, shortly after we had moved to a charming Victorian street near Dupont Circle in the heart of Washington. My wife announced that she had forgotten to take the meat out of the freezer. Dinner would be at least an hour late. Back in the suburbs this might have been a minor tragedy as I tend to get irritable when hungry.

That evening I suggested we walk over and try a promising looking Spanish restaurant four or five blocks away. The restaurant, it turned out, kept its promise with a superb *paella* which the proprietor washed down with cool Spanish wine that he literally poured down our throats from a *porron,* or Spanish flask.

We left feeling nearly as spirited as the flamenco dancers who entertained at dinner. At home we found our daughter, Marina, listening to the radio, entranced in a concert of Elizabethan music that had just started. The concert, we learned, originated from the Phillips Collection. Since that delightful gallery is just down the block from us, there seemed no sense staring at the loudspeaker. We walked over, found seats, and could look at as well as listen to Christiane Van Acker, which is pure delight on both counts. The Belgian mezzo was accompanied on the lute by Michel Podolski, her husband.

In the intermission the people sitting in front of us turned out to be our friends, Alan and Lois Fern, whom we had not seen for some time. Alan informed us that he had parked his car right in front of our house. He was a bit hesitant, however, about stopping in for a drink after the concert. Mademoiselle Van Acker and M. Podolski, his house guests, he explained, would surely be tired after the performance.

He was wrong. With very little persuasion the musicians came and kept bubbling with charming vitality in our living room until well after two in the morning. We learned much about the lost music of the time of Mary Tudor, the *air de cour* from Mary Stuart to Louis XIV and England's golden age of lutenist song writers which they had discovered in the libraries they visited on their tours all over the Western world. The frozen steak had prompted a most enchanted evening. Marina, who studies music, was particularly fascinated by the interesting guests we had suddenly brought home in the middle of the night. It could hardly have happened in a suburban subdivision.

Nor is the opportunity for such spontaneous encounters, for stimulation and a rich and varied cultural and social life the only advantage of the truly urban way of life.

There are the specialty shops—our Greek delicatessen around the corner, the grocery two blocks away where they know us and stock our favorite cheeses, and our indispensable French butcher. There is Mr. Warsaw at the liquor store who, in addition to good Beaujolais, provides cash, if need be, after the bank is closed. There is a sauna in a nearby hotel to perk us up. All this and much, much more is within walking distance, as is Rock Creek Park and the enchanting Dumbarton Oaks gardens for our Sunday strolls. Out in suburbia we had to drive for at least half an hour to find a place to walk and even then we always had to return to where the car was parked, which is a bore. Our suburban street had $35,000 houses but no sidewalk.

As Jane Jacobs had pointed out in her *The Death and Life of Great American Cities*, all these advantages of the old neighborhoods, yes, even of the slums, count even heavier for the poor. For the grown-ups, particularly the elderly, there is the social life of the street to watch and become part of and the gossiping on the stoops. For the children

"The city is the people"

there are always new worlds to explore and that unique and irreplaceable youth center—the corner store.

The old city neighborhood offers security in different ways. Being huddled together within the wholeness of a town gives people much the same sense of protection and belonging as though there were still a medieval wall to offer real protection. This sense of security takes the tangible form of credit in the small neighborhood stores. The grocer downstairs might also watch the baby for you for a while. Or you can leave the key to the apartment with him for a relative who might want to get in while you are out.

There are always, as Jane Jacobs observed, a thousand eyes on the street—the eyes of storekeepers, bartenders, vendors, stoop sitters and mere passers-by. "The public peace—the sidewalk and street peace," she writes, "is not kept primarily by the police, necessary as the police are. It is kept primarily by an intricate, almost unconscious, network of voluntary controls and standards among the people themselves, and enforced by the people themselves. In some city areas—older public housing projects and streets with very high population turnover are often conspicuous examples—the keeping of public sidewalk law and order is left almost entirely to the police and special guards. Such places are jungles. No amount of police can enforce civilization where the normal, casual enforcement of it has broken down."

The problem of insecurity, says Mrs. Jacobs, "cannot be solved by spreading people out more thinly, trading the characteristics of cities for the characteristics of suburbs." Almost prophetically, writing five years before Watts exploded, she points to Los Angeles as an example. "It has virtually no districts compact enough to qualify as dense city areas. Yet Los Angeles cannot, any more than any other great city, evade the truth that, being a city, it *is* composed of strangers not all of whom are nice. Los Angeles' crime figures are flabbergasting."

Idolatry of the old, particularly the old slums of the poor, can go too far. Jane Jacobs, however, has made not just a valuable, but a positively decisive contribution to modern city planning philosophy, and she has the sparkling wit to temper her intensity. While the planners plotted to destroy old neighborhoods for the abstract blessings of decent, safe, and sanitary superblock projects, she walked the streets of Greenwich Village in New York, North End in Boston, and Back-of-the-Yards in Chicago to find out what people there really needed and wanted. They need and want, she perceptively reported, the same virtues in a place to live as the people who made Georgetown sophisticated. They only need them more. This was important to know.

Some admirers of Mrs. Jacobs, however, have made of this discovery an orthodox Jane Jacobism which is just as blind and stupid as the doctrinaire superblock planning wisdom ever was. The virtues of cozy old buildings and streets should not blind us to the horrors of rats. The advantages of concentrating people should not lead us to condone crowding large families into one room. For every grocer in the old neighborhoods who gives credit to a poor family there is many an absentee slumlord who doesn't. The slumlords, in fact, hold their tenants in the grip of a terror matched only by that of the landlords in Charles Dickens' London of a hundred years ago. When, inspired by Mrs. Lyndon B. Johnson's "beautification" efforts, the people in a Washington, D.C. slum neighborhood recently got together and started to spruce up and plant their front yards, the landlords promptly shut off the water. Worse than this deed, to me at least, was that the victims of these Scrooges pleaded with reporters not to get the story into print for fear of angering their landlords into further reprisals.

Rats, slumlords, stench, and frustration are the other side of the romantic coin of Jane Jacobism which, in a strange alliance of liberals and reactionaries, has mounted a crusade against the federal urban renewal bulldozers. At its best, this crusade keeps charging the drab old windmills of public housing projects built before the Kennedy administration reformed public housing's architectural design. At worst, it represents the same profit-greedy interests that turned the romantic old neighborhoods into slums in the first place.

7. Creative Response

The challenge now, it would seem, is to combine the virtues of the old with a creative response to the new – to build places to live that have both a sense of place and up-to-date plumbing. This is the new and constructive departure for a realistic modern architecture. Or, perhaps, not a departure so much as a renewed pursuit of what modern architecture's Functionalist crusade had originally set out to do.

"Let us turn our backs on fantasy and Utopia both and confront reality," wrote Patrick J. Quinn, professor at the architecture school at Berkeley, in a manifesto written jointly with his colleagues Charles M. Moore, Donald Lyndon, and Sim van der Ryn. "Although we have pretended to let art remarry science, we carefully maintain them in separate corners of the mind, to the detriment of both. . . . We flatten magnificently sculpted land for homes, and yet build artificial hills on the roofs of city garages. Clearly we are caught somewhere between the dollar and the dream, each of which is an evasion of the real issue."

The real issue, Moore states in the same manifesto (published in the autumn 1962 issue of *Landscape*), is that "we are in urgent need of understanding *places* before we lose them, of learning how to see them and to take possession of them.

"It seems evident, to people who study such things, that birds sing not for the joy of the morning or the beauty of the season but in order to take possession, to establish acoustically the limits of their domain. The Chinese more ponderously achieved the same sort of demarcation with their Great Wall. But, since men are subtler than birds, they long ago elevated this act of taking possession into an art, by abstracting the act."

We can, a good many architects like Quinn and Moore now say, revive this art to build our places to live. August Heckscher is right when he writes that a sense of place "cannot be bought; it must be shaped, usually over long periods of time, by the common efforts of men and women. It must be given scale and meaning by their love. And then it must be preserved. It must be saved from changes that are too rapid, and from the kind of invasions that alter its essential character."

True. The Piazza San Marco, for instance, most often cited as superbly expressing the genius of place, was not the expression of one genius. It was indeed shaped over a period of nearly a thousand years, beginning with the eleventh-century Byzantine Basilica to the Fabbrica Nuova, which was built by order of Napoleon in 1810, and the campanile which was rebuilt at the beginning of this century.

This does not mean that we must give up in humble despair and wait another thousand years for another Piazza San Marco to emerge. Some planners advocate such despairing laissez-faire and call it "organic growth." Cancer is organic growth, too.

The argument against determined community building is that "we can't play God." For what, then, has God given us the ability to shape our environment, to harness fire and water and even to rocket off into outer space? Surely not to let greedy speculators, blinder-clad highway engineers, and vicious slumlords foul our land for ourselves and our children. Nor does democracy absolve us of the responsibility to determine what our objective and values should be and to act on this determination. The right to determine the shape of our environment by democratic means is the real freedom at stake.

Another argument is that Americans have turned into nomads who never settle down long enough to care. The Census Bureau tells me that one in five American families moves every year. Perhaps they would move a little less often if the places they found were really worth caring for. As to the four million Americans who live in trailers, or "mobile homes," as the industry now calls them, don't they prove precisely that despite all their moving they want the continuity of their same four walls? The challenge here, it seems to me, is to build them attractive trailer courts.

A Piazza San Marco of our time

We may not have created a Piazza San Marco in our time, but we *have* built Rockefeller Center in New York and Constitution Plaza in Hartford and the Village Center of Reston, and we can be proud of them. We may not have a place as livable as Rothenburg ob der Tauber or Colonial Williamsburg surely were, but we have beginnings of such livability in La Clede Town in St. Louis.

The worst we can do is despair. Architecture, to be sure, is in a bad way. There are also many architects who are beginning to see this and who know that the answer to bad design is never no design but better design. Some have already proven, it seems to me, that the will of this epoch is more than confusion and narcissistic self-expression.

Some time ago I visited Eero Saarinen's chapel at M.I.T., surely an uncompromisingly modern building. I found an elating peace, a wonderful sense of inner exaltation in this quietly dramatic space. I was quite annoyed when I heard a group of children racing noisily down the glass corridor that leads to the round, brick chapel. I feared not only for my contemplation but also for the tripod of my camera.

The instant these kids came to the threshold of the chapel they hushed. The calm light streaming down Harry Bertoia's screen on the simple altar and flickering on Saarinen's undulating brick walls struck them to silence. They tiptoed about for a while, obviously feeling the powerful sense of the place. Soundlessly they departed. As soon as these unaccompanied little boys and girls got out into the corridor again they joyfully resumed screaming, teasing, and chasing each other.

There is such sense of place from which to gain an awareness of being alive in La Clede Town, a project of gay and perhaps somewhat overly cute town houses for families of moderate income. Chloethiel Woodard Smith has designed it in an effort to recreate the neighborly qualities of old neighborhoods, complete with "Ma and Pa" stores whose owners live upstairs, a laundromat where women can meet and gossip as by the old town well, and a real, honest to goodness pub—the Jane Jacobs kind of thing. As I wandered around I encountered a most attractive, teen-age Negro girl and was at once guiltily abashed about the somewhat too libidinous smile with which I appraised her. But she smiled right back. "Do you like it here?" she chirped gaily.

A middle-aged gent with a camera would scarcely have held as spontaneously pleasant and, for me, informative conversation with a strange girl in the Negro ghetto where she presumably had lived before. With her free and unselfconsciously self-aware attitude, more than with her bubbling tales of community life in La Clede, my new friend confirmed that Mrs. Smith has succeeded in creating the atmosphere she set out to create.

Striving to create such sense of place will not endow architects and city planners with a miracle cure for the ills of an emerging mass society in the throes of explosive urbanization. It might help them not to evade the problem with pretty, pretty buildings or fight it by cursing people, poor taste, and automobiles and hurling witty insults against whatever else it is they don't like. The answer of the M.I.T. Chapel or La Clede Town was an architecture rooted in realism and inspired by social concern.

This concern begins with the place of each individual thing we build in the community, for communities, not only housing, freeways, corporation palaces, subdivisions, projects, and whatnot, are what we ought to create. The single building alone can no longer meet our needs. Before the industrial age, as Charles Burchard has pointed out, the family house was a self-contained unit in which great-grandparents, grandparents, parents, and children all lived together and toiled together to support their family unison. They even spun and wove to

The old neighborhood spirit re-created

produce the clothing. They bore their children there and cared for the sick and aged there.

Today these functions have all exploded into the community. Children are educated away from the home, together with other children. Father goes away to work, and mother travels out of the home for the family's food and clothing. So it goes.

As Burchard put it, "It is just as important that the walk of the child from home to his school be no less safe, efficient and pleasant than his walk from his bedroom to the morning breakfast table in the home." We all accept design standards for homes which make sure that we don't have to stumble through the plumbing to get to the dining room. We now must accept as equally important design standards which rule out crossing highways on the way to school.

The New Towns both in Europe and the United States have recognized this, and the best of them are good communities with a strong sense of place. In designing these communities their architects have found themselves retracing the more gradual development of the old medieval towns. As William Pereira, who is designing several New Towns in California, has put it, they see the challenge of the future "as an opportunity to make history anew."

Vitally necessary as New Towns are to bring social and physical order into our urban environment, they are only part of the task. It is easy to start well from scratch out in the open country. It is more difficult, but also, perhaps, even more important, to rebuild and rearrange our existing cities and suburbs so as to create true neighborhoods and real communities. This means a shift in emphasis away from the old cure-all of "slum clearance," which has only pushed the slums around from one end of town to another. Rather than taking housing away from the people in the slums, we would give them buildings and places to extend their lives—community, cultural, and social-service centers, playgrounds for the young and little parks for the old.

With this concept foremost all else falls into place. Instead of destroying communities with freeways, our transportation arteries would define and strengthen communities. Instead of segregating people and their activities, we would move towards residential democracy and integrate both people and public places. We would thus provide equal access for everyone to the things that make for urban livability—parks, public transportation, entertainment, culture, and commerce.

As we thus restructure cities and suburbs with social concern, we will find that the individual building assumes a higher purpose than immediate profit for its owner. We will find that the meaning of architecture is in its response to its place—its place in nature, its place in the community, and its place in the whole urban ecology.

The first generation of Modern architects has failed in this because it disregarded continuity. The second generation—which has often given up being Modern and contents itself with being merely "contemporary"—has failed us even worse because it tried to deceive us. It claims to go to bat for beauty, as Ed Stone has put it. Like press agents, the playboys of architecture contrive to create an "image" instead of establishing an identity. The beauty, however, is mostly cosmetic. The image is not an identity because true identity is always inclusive. It includes the "image," if you will, the needs and desires of others, the reality of the world we live in, and the things that are in it.

We need and desire art. It is an important thing in the reality of our world. From architecture, unless our place to live is to be either chaotic or recklessly engineered, we have to expect even more than art, whether it is the art of Mies or of Paul Rudolph, of the first or the second generation of Moderns.

Some time ago, in the course of one of those discussions of professional ethics, Howard Shaw admonished his fellow members in the American Institute of Architects: "Be a gentleman if you can, but for God's sake be an architect!" Now that we can presume all architects to be perfect gentlemen I would amend this phrase to read: "Be an artist if you can, but for God's sake be an architect."

For in the span of only a decade, the art of architecture has already amply explored the extremes. Consider Mies' Crown Hall, at the Illinois Institute of Technology, and Rudolph's Art and Architecture Building at Yale.

Crown Hall distills architecture to its absolute essence—enclosed space, universal space. Mies began with his precise, unadorned steel trusses from which his large, low-slung glass box is suspended, seemingly to lift it out of the ground. This sparse steel cage is as light, as refined, as elegantly proportioned as he could make it and still hold the large expanse of glass. His form is the purest geometry that will accommodate the function without interference. Its function? Do not functions change with increasing frequency nowadays? Mies asked himself. Is it possible to predict how architecture might be taught in twenty or forty years? The only function one could be sure of, Mies decided, was the function of utmost flexibility. He created nothing but a loft.

You enter Crown Hall by a wide flight of steps placed classically

Intellectual purity . . .

. . . versus emotional self-expression

and symbolically in the center of each long side of the building. A straight walkway leads directly and unmistakably to them. Behind the glass doors you find yourself in a huge, unobstructed room, 120 by 210 feet, where, separated only by temporary, low partitions, all the school's various activities take place. Only the industrial design department, along with the toilets and other services, has been relegated to the basement. The basement has windows at grade level which is the little trick that makes the building appear to be pulled out of the ground by those girders that span the roof.

The loft has its drawbacks. If a student moves his chair, you hear the squeak throughout the hall. But most conversation is muffled because the only sound-reflecting surface is the ceiling, eighteen feet above. With the whole wide world around you behind the glass walls, there is nothing in particular to distract you from your work. If you can read in the park, one critic observed, you can read in Crown Hall.

If Crown Hall is extreme architectural purism, the Art and Architecture Building is almost absurd architectural Expressionism. Audacious in scale, color, and texture, a tweedy, rough concrete, it culminates an interesting progression up New Haven's Chapel Street, past Eggerton Swarthout's massive Romanesque palace and Louis Kahn's quietly dignified Art Gallery. It is Art with a capital A, a work of sculpture, and if you could get it down to size, it would make a fascinating exhibit along with, say, the early Cubist work of Jacques Lipchitz, in any respectable art gallery.

The entrance, as an irreverent Yale student has put it, "can be found by pacing off a hundred steps on York Street from the corner and turning left." After mounting two flights of stairs and avoiding three false entrances and a drop of thirty feet straight ahead, you can enter the main building through a glass door which opens on a blank wall. Just before you hit the wall, turn right and step down into a pit. This is the big central hall of the building around which all else revolves.

You can also find the small, dingy lobby and take an elevator to the seven floors above and two floors below. The floors are but fleeting way stations in a vertical maze of some thirty-six different levels and a horizontal labyrinth of interlocking spaces of different sizes, shapes and heights.

At times, as you walk through the complex cement bowels of the structure, you are oppressed by ceilings so low you fear they will scrape your head. At other times, suddenly forced to look down from seemingly unguarded heights, you fear acute vertigo. There were, at the time of my visit, no directional signs. The shared distress of planned confusion, like natural disasters, seems to bring out the best in fellow man. The students and secretaries who work in this brooding ruin are conditioned to be helpful. Repeatedly relying on their directions, I negotiated several corners, up-and-down steps, dark passages lit by rows of open light bulbs so placed they often singe your ears (and no doubt provide free bulbs for all the student rooms at Yale) and marched —there was no other way—bravely through a seminar session held in an open hall to get to the tiny cage where the faculty member I came to see has his office. Another step and I might have crashed down fifty feet through the glass wall which contains him, his chair, and his desk.

To work in this designed disorder with its contrived mystique of fixed and interlocking spaces, the students have to add to it with improvised partitions, papers taped to the huge glass windows to keep out the glare, and all kinds of other clutter. Some rooms are rarely, if ever, used, because they are small shrines adorned with plaster casts and not really usable. Crown Hall may have no more privacy than a public park. The Art and Architecture Building has no more privacy than a New York subway at rush hour and far more distractions.

Both are undeniably art, but as a work of architecture that responds to its human purpose, that includes you and me and the conditions of our time, I found Walter Netsch's campus for the University of Illinois at Chicago more reassuring. Here, the architecture, one might say, has merged the art of Mies and the art of Rudolph. It is pure and Classic, almost a pristine expression of structure. It is also, with its bold, sculptural forms and stark play of light and shadow, brawny and emotive. It has all the drama of an exciting stage set. More importantly, the complex of pleasingly arranged buildings, dominated by a broad-shouldered tower, adds up to an efficient environment, a "micro-city," as Netsch calls it, that is built for people and advances where the familiar Chicago left off. Symbolizing the continuity, Hull House mansion, an old structure where Jane Addams founded a pioneer social settlement, has been preserved and harmoniously integrated in Netsch's new urban design.

Netsch, of the Chicago office of the large architectural firm, Skidmore, Owings, and Merrill, did not brood about the mystique of space. With a scientific mind he began by analyzing the functioning of a modern, downtown university. He found it wasteful of motion, space, and money to cling to the traditional departmental structures such as separate "physics" or "social science" buildings, each with its own classrooms, laboratories, faculty and administrative offices. Instead, he

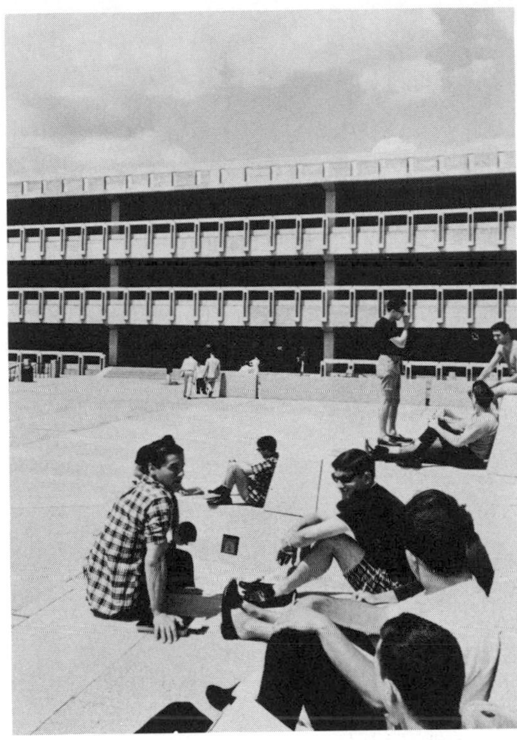

The heart: A paved plaza with classrooms below

designed each of the fifteen buildings on the thirty-four acre site to serve a function, rather than a department.

The heart of his campus is a paved plaza surrounding a sunken amphitheater that seats 2,500. Here everything comes together. This open space is always full of life. On each of the plaza's four corners is a differently shaped exedra, a circular, hollow mound that serves as a sheltered, outdoor meeting place. It was fun to watch the goings-on in these casual enclosures from the nearby library. In one of them was a group of students arguing and gesticulating as students might have argued and gesticulated four hundred years ago on the University Square of Heidelberg, which is now a parking lot. In another, a dozen or so girls were practicing a cheerleading ritual. From up where I was this scene had some of the hilarity of a silent movie.

This plaza is actually a roof. Beneath it are the lecture halls used by all academic departments. Surrounding this "great court" are the other buildings which, like ripples in a lake, become larger the farther away they are. The two largest house all the engineering and science laboratories. Others house classrooms, the library, student union, and so on. All the faculty and administrative offices, as well as seminar rooms

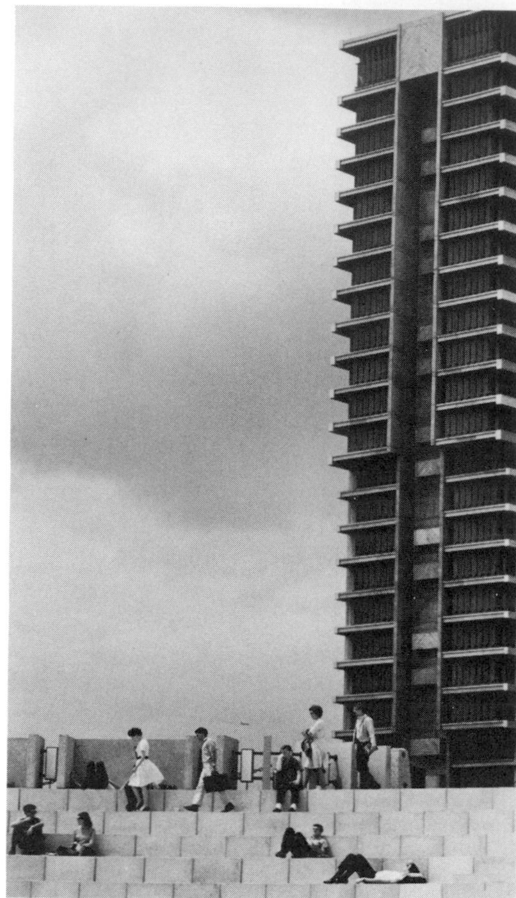

A gutsy tower for administration

for groups small enough not to crowd the elevators, are in the tower, a giant that stands almost defiantly on massive stilts.

All these buildings are connected by elevated walkways on the second-story level and with the central plaza. Here the students walk fast from building to building. They walk all the faster in Chicago's icy winter winds which can make these walks very unpleasant. The elevation of the walkways, however, reduces stair climbing because it provides split-level access. It also enlarges the handsomely landscaped ground space where students amble leisurely and where there are sitting areas. All cars are banned from the campus, but both parking and the subway are easily accessible.

Here, then, is a clear and ingenious organization and design. It serves what Netsch calls "social communication," since, for once, students and faculty of different disciplines rub elbows and have the opportunity to exchange ideas. It was also less expensive and easier to build since it is obviously more efficient to put all the laboratories with their elaborate plumbing together. Finally, the concept simplifies circulation; it is easy to get around.

Varied in its bold, simple forms, in part rough-cut granite, in part coarse concrete, the campus has a strong, yet almost casual unity. All these buildings are muscular structures of concrete and brick and dark, deeply framed slits of glass that occasionally get into the way of the view. The buildings exude confidence, however, and have an appealing directness about them. Like athletes in action, they seem absorbed only in what they are doing, unconscious of the observer. Nor are they the least dressed up. Dress would only get in their way. Though in some ways these buildings, like Rudolph's Art and Architecture

Cars are banned and students walk fast

Building, are also at first a bit startling, we understand their game at first glance. As at the Air Force Academy, which Netsch also designed, we have visual order. No one can deny Congress Circle's considerable merits as a work of art. But this time it is the art of architecture, a creative response to the needs of a big-city university today.

There are other, though not enough, examples of recent architecture that is responsible because it responds to human needs—the kind of design we need to bring order and creative livability into our chaotic, ever-changing surroundings.

Though he came up with an almost revolutionary new approach to the physical organization of a university campus, Netsch says, "I hope this is the last nineteenth-century campus we ever have to design." He is thinking of a more scientific approach to architecture, of a single system, rather than the assembly of divergent components; total unity, rather than a collection of individual buildings that are "objects."

After thousands of years of conceiving buildings in essentially the same manner, we seem to be moving towards a new phase, new concepts of building in an exploding urban society. We are beginning to see what has been called Instant Cities, Megastructures, and Platform Cities of Babylonian scale. There is no doubt that we can engineer them. To make the Instant Cities into pleasant new towns, the Megastructures into livable communities in the sky, and the Platforms into something more than human ant hills, our architects are beginning to conceive of them as more than abstract monuments. Like Walter Netsch, the best of them remember history and man's ancient urge to give his place to live some personal distinction—a sense of place.

II. ART AND TECHNOLOGY

1. "Architecture or Revolution"

It was a motley crowd, unkempt and unruly, that flocked to Weimar in the spring of 1919: boys in the blue shirts and leather shorts of the youth movement, girls from the art academies and craft shops, and men pushing forty in the battered uniforms of the Kaiser's defeated army. All of them were poor. The hunger and halfhearted revolution of Germany's last, bitter World War I winter still lingered. The daily fare was turnips and turmoil.

But these hopeful bohemians cared little for the new constitution of Germany's first, short-lived republic that was just then being written in Weimar. They were attracted by a ringing proclamation announcing the opening of a new school, a new training laboratory of art, architecture and design. It was called *Staatliches Bauhaus Weimar*, State House for Building.

"The ultimate goal of all visual arts is the building," the proclamation said. "Together let us conceive and create the new building of the future which will unify architecture *and* sculpture *and* painting in one form and which will rise one day toward heaven from the hands of a million workers as a crystal symbol of a new faith."

On the cover of the modest four-page leaflet, outlining the curriculum, was a woodcut by Lyonel Feininger. It showed a cathedral in the rays of three stars that symbolized a threefold intention: To break "the pretentious class distinction . . . between craftsman and artist," to achieve a new unity of art and technology, and to thereby conceive and create a new social architecture that was to build a better world for modern man.

Walter Gropius, who founded the Bauhaus, had drafted this program while he served as an officer on the battlefield of Namur. It was decisively advanced by Mies van der Rohe who directed the Bauhaus in its last two years before the Nazis closed it early in 1933.

The essence of this program was also the passionate credo of Charles-Edouard Jeanneret, better known as Le Corbusier. Although not directly connected with the Bauhaus, Le Corbusier stated its idea most succinctly, perhaps: "The machinery of society, profoundly out of gear," he wrote in his famous tract *Vers Une Architecture Moderne* in 1923, "oscillates between an amelioration of historical importance and a catastrophe. . . . Building is at the root of the social unrest today. . . . Machines will lead to a new order both of work and of leisure. Entire cities have to be constructed, or reconstructed, in order to provide a minimum of comfort, for if it is delayed too long, there may be a disturbance of the balance of society. . . . We are dealing with an urgent problem of our epoch. Nay, with *the* problem of our epoch. . . .

"Architecture or revolution."

Through the Congrès Internationaux d'Architecture Moderne, or CIAM, which Le Corbusier helped found in 1928, this gospel spread across the entire world. Along with the Bauhaus, it helped change the shape of just about everything built or designed "from the coffee cup to city planning," as Mies put it.

It was not a new style for coffee cups, buildings or cities—"International," "Bauhaus," "CIAM" or otherwise—that these environmental revolutionaries sought. "The Bauhaus was an idea . . . only an idea has the power to spread that far," said Mies. "A 'Bauhaus Style,'" Gropius has written, "would have been a confession of failure and a return to that devitalizing inertia, that stagnating academism which I had called into being to combat. Our endeavors were to find a new approach . . . which would finally lead to a new attitude toward life. The Bauhaus has helped to restore architecture and design of today as a social art."

The first CIAM statement put it similarly. The aim of the organization, said the paper handed out to its charter members at Sarraz castle in Switzerland, was ". . . to place architecture in the proper, that is economic and sociological, context." In the end, it was Le Corbusier again who summed it up best. "The 'styles' no longer exist," he wrote. "They are outside our ken. . . . All the values have been revised. There has been a revolution in the conception of what architecture is."

The essence of this conception, to brave a summary, was that, now that the machine was about to produce everything man-made around us, everything must be designed. The design should be "functional," a much debated word which, stripped of emotional associations, I take to mean simply (a) a scientific approach to meeting human needs and (b) an honest expression of the technology employed.

In theory this is still the basic conception of modern architecture. In practice it hasn't worked out. It remains a promise, at best a prophesy.

Gropius and his Bauhaus, Mies and Le Corbusier have, nevertheless, altered our concepts of the design of everything "from the coffee cup to city planning." Although they have *not* achieved a true marriage of art and technology and although they have *not* brought about an aesthetic consensus that would give our man-made environment visual harmony, they have irrevocably stated these goals. That was their revolutionary step forward.

Much of what the Bauhaus and CIAM proclaimed had been said before. The American sculptor Horatio Greenough said "form follows function" before Louis Sullivan said it, and long before it became a controversial slogan. Walt Whitman and others had chanted about the promise of the machine age. All the important movements and experiments in art had their forerunners in the avant-garde ateliers of Paris.

Nor was there anything radically new in the building technology which influenced the aesthetic concepts more than the actual techniques employed by Gropius, Mies, and Le Corbusier. Sir Joseph Paxton, in 1850, had built his Crystal Palace in London entirely of prefabricated iron components and glass. William Le Baron Jenney in Chicago, in 1883, though he was not really aware of it, had built the first steel skeleton structure, the Home Insurance Building, which led to curtain wall construction. Louis Sullivan and the Chicago School had begun to shape this new construction method towards a new aesthetic, though their skyscrapers were still encrusted with Art Nouveau or eclectic decorations.

Ornament, too, had been proclaimed "a crime" before the first

World War. It was no accident that the Austrian Adolf Loos made this pronouncement after his visit to the United States in 1893 where he saw the work of the Chicago School from which Frank Lloyd Wright was to emerge. All of this decisively influenced the German *Werkbund* which brought forth Gropius and Mies and inspired Le Corbusier.

It was after the war that the leading *Werkbund* artists and architects formed their militant Novembergruppe in Berlin, an avant-garde group that put Mies in charge of the architectural exhibits. Significantly, it took its name from the month, in 1918, of the German revolution.

In the end the Bauhaus proclamation in Weimar and *Vers Une Architecture Moderne* in Paris derived their ardor from the incredible intensity of the moment in history in which they were written. All of this ferment—the new social awareness, the new art, the new technology—had simmered under the surface before. The artillery shells of World War I suddenly burst the crust of Victorian complacency, and it all erupted like a volcano. Its ashes still fertilize the soil of most of our cultural endeavors.

The Second World War somehow never had this explosive effect. It was already part of a new era, not its beginning. It was of the first war that architect Eric Mendelsohn wrote: "As few before us, we felt the meaning of living and dying, of end and beginning—its creative meaning in the midst of the silent terror of no-man's land and the terrifying din of rapid fire."

This new awareness, this new urgency of the creative meaning of technological and political change, put all the previous ferment into a more passionate, burning focus.

Before the First World War Loos had still written, "I revel in the chaos of the time." After the war Gropius said, "The chaos of the time insulted me!"

The threat of chaos seemed serious now. An established order had crashed in what the art historian Egon Friedell has called "the collapse of reality." The world of comfortable absolutes had worn thin even before Einstein told us that the universe is infinite and everything is relative, and before Freud stated that human behavior stems from far more than rational, conscious thought.

Under the impact of this new knowledge the artist found it—and often still finds it—well nigh impossible to depict a reality which no longer exists. The architect, too, felt he had to search beyond previously conventional representation of classic absolutes.

The struggle was on to find not a new style but new laws of design,

"Creative meaning in the midst of silent terror."

laws strong enough to withstand "the collapse of reality" and the recognition that, as Paul Klee wrote in 1921, "for the whole there is no right or wrong since it lives and develops through the interplay of forces, and in the universe, too, good and evil finally act together productively."

No one, except perhaps a Zen master, could have written these words even a decade or two earlier.

2. *Gesamtkultur*

Before World War I, around 1910, Gropius, Mies, and Le Corbusier had all three apprenticed in the office of Peter Behrens in Berlin.

Gropius, born in 1883 in Berlin, was the son of an architect and grew up in a family which combined the best of Prussian devotion to duty and discipline with the strong liberal bent and artistic inclination of German upper-middle class families. Tall and handsome, he wears his great idealism with the restrained dignity of an old-school cavalry officer. He is the patient pedagogue, the synthesizer of ideas. Nothing is "either, or" for him, he has often said, it is always "and."

Ludwig Mies—he added his mother's surname, van der Rohe, when he became an architect—born in 1886 in Aachen, was the son of a bricklayer who also ran a small stonecutting shop. Mies has often laughingly boasted that he never received any formal architectural education. He learned to draw when he designed stone ornaments. He learned construction working with a furniture designer. A somewhat stocky man, he never likes to talk much and appears gruff. But he is a most warmhearted man. Nor is he really shy. He seems, in an earthy sort of way, a simple man who is much too secure within himself to strain to project an image of himself into a hectic and complicated world. He wants to create, as I see it, an image, not of his personality, but of architecture.

Le Corbusier, born in 1887 in La Chaux-de-Fonds, not far from Geneva in Switzerland, died in 1965. He came from a watchmaker family and made a cult of his Gallic personality. By ancestry the Jeannerets are French, descendants of the Albigenses, heretics of the south of France in the twelfth and thirteenth centurics who fanatically opposed the Roman Church despite severe and prolonged persecution. Most of them were reserved and somewhat suspicious by nature. Though Charles-Edouard Jeanneret assumed the name Le Corbusier from another branch of the family, the somewhat fanatical and suspicious hereditary trait seems to have stuck. Wearing thick, horn-rimmed glasses, Corbu, as his friends called him, would remind you of nothing so much as an excitable raven.

Behrens was at the time the chief architect of a giant electrical corporation, the Allgemeine Elektrizitäts Gesellschaft, or AEG, and designed a number of remarkable, newly functional yet still monumental factories for it, notably the Berlin Turbine Factory of 1908. He also designed just about everything else for AEG, from turbo-engines to light fixtures and from exhibits to letterheads. AEG was probably the first large industrial organization to be concerned with what today we call the "corporate image." The idea of such comprehensive design was advocated by the movement called Deutscher Werkbund of which Behrens and later Gropius and Mies were prominent leaders and which Le Corbusier had been sent to study by the Art School of Chaux-de-Fonds.

The Werkbund, I would say, stood at the beginning of Modern architecture in its ideological sense. It was here that "the revolution in the conception of what architecture is" began.

The Werkbund, in turn, begins with the arts and crafts movement of William Morris and John Ruskin in England. Morris revived craftmanship with all its medieval connotations in romantic protest against industrial production. The Werkbund, however, felt that craftsmen should not oppose the machine but take it over.

What impressed Hermann Muthesius, a trade attaché at the German embassy in London from 1896 to 1903, were the new houses, the furniture, the sanitary ware and household utensils these English craftsmen had created, rather than their mystic philosophy. On his return to Germany he advocated that German artists and craftsmen do likewise, not in their attics and workshops, but by working with big industry and commerce in the new factories.

With typical, high-flown Teutonic perspicuity, Muthesius lectured on "The Spiritualization of German Production." In 1907, in Munich, he founded the Werkbund, not only to promote industrial design but as a great moral cause. Its early members and leaders included the most illustrious names in German architecture at the time, all of them idealistic young Turks. Among them were, in addition to Gropius, Mies, and Behrens, Hans Poelzig, Ernst May, Hans Scharoun, Otto Bartning, and Ludwig Hilberseimer.

Big industry responded with surprising enthusiasm and promptly hired designers and architects. English art historians, notably Reyner Banham, had reason to hint that it was all a conspiracy to beat the British competition in the world market. Competition always motivates industry, of course. But whatever motivated its financial sponsors, the ranks of the new German movement were primarily interested in low-cost housing and *Zweckbau*, architecture for a social purpose, which is hardly an export item. There was more to the Werkbund than German nationalism.

At the time, everywhere in the Western world, Ruskin's antimachine romanticism had given way to an equally romantic adulation of the machine. "We cannot but think all good machinery is graceful, also the line of the strength and the line of the beauty being one," wrote Oscar Wilde. Other poets and writers—particularly Émile Zola and Walt Whitman—began to be carried away by the promise of industrialization. To the unlikely audience of Daughters of the American Revolution in Chicago, Frank Lloyd Wright stated in 1904 that the machine "is now grown to the point that the artist must take it up, no longer in protest. Genius must dominate the work of the contrivance it has created. This plain duty is relentlessly marked out for the artist in this, the Machine Age. He cannot set it aside, although there is involved an adjustment to cherished gods, perplexing and painful in the extreme, and though the fires of long-honored ideals shall go down to ashes. They will reappear, phoenix-like, with new life and purposes."

Though they did not hear this panegyric across the ocean, the artists and architects of the Werkbund set out in much the same spirit to design buildings of all kinds, new furniture, household appliances, even blankets, window displays, and typography. Attacking the root problem of effective, rational industrialization, they advocated the standardization and modular coordination of industrial products so that all manner of parts and pieces would fit together.

The Werkbund architects, in fact the whole Modern movement, kept preaching, searching, and designing to achieve standardized, modular production of building components, in particular. Rationalization of the building industry became a foremost article of faith, demanding the development of uniform component parts according to spatial and structural measurement. "One must organize the building of apartment houses after the example of the automobile fabrication," demanded Bruno Taut. The demand is still echoed today. Yet, hundreds of noble experiments later, particularly in America, it is still nothing more than another one of those good but perhaps a little impractical ideas.

German industry did, however, beginning with World War I, adapt industrial standardization for a number of other products with its Deutsche Industrie Normen, or DIN. To the envy of American printers, all paper in Germany, for instance, has standard sizes. Printing presses, bookbinding machinery, and desk drawers and other containers are made to fit. The postage stamp is the smallest unit. Quadruple it and you have a postcard. Quadruple *that* and you have the standard business letter sheet and so on up to the billboard poster. There is little waste. Different lines, DIN-A, DIN-B, etc. assure all the variety of sizes you could hope for. Instead of calling your printer for stationery 8½" by 11" you simply tell him to make it DIN-A 4 and you know it will fit all desk drawers you buy in Germany. One of the few similary standardized items in America is the thread of electric light bulbs.

The Werkbund considered industrial standardization as more than an expedient. It was a matter of passionate *Weltanschauung* and to lead to a new aesthetic, variously but most frequently labeled *Die Einheit der Funktion*, or the unity of function. This new functionalism, in turn, was to give us a new *Gesamtkultur,* a total new culture. The gist of this culture was to be architecture, the new environment. The man-made environment was to be not a mere matter of houses, factories and roads, but, as Gropius put it, "an ethical force."

"The ideal dwelling," said Taut, "has nothing to do with aesthetics, but only with ethics. The practical and ethical become a unit, and therefore the new dwelling becomes completely beautiful."

Muthesius held that "only through standardization can we recover the general significance which architecture had in times of a harmonious culture."

In Germany, in the years before the first war, much of capitalist industry shared this dream for a brief, fleeting moment, much as Soviet Communism, even more fleetingly, flirted with it in the late 1920's. The Imperial German government also backed the movement and established an office for Muthesius in the Prussian Department of Commerce. This was the time when, not only in Europe, big industry built housing and company towns for its workers—Krupp's projects near Essen, for example, and Kohler Plumbing's town, Kohler, Wisconsin, American Steel and Wire's Fairfield in Alabama, and U. S. Steel's Gary in Indiana. This was also the period when the London authorities commissioned Frank Pick to design the still exemplary stations, trains, signs, and symbol of the London subway. Industry was concerned with planning and building and, often beyond that, with all aspects of environmental design. It was an era of high expectations and the Werkbund idealism was an expression of the general social optimism.

No one, perhaps, personified this better than Walther Rathenau, one of the great, if perhaps least known geniuses of our time. He was a philosopher, industrialist, and statesman. In addition to being on the board of about a hundred enterprises, he directed the AEG, which employed Behrens and which his father had founded.

Though a most successful capitalist, Rathenau was a fervent believer in economic as well as political democracy. He prophesied that the equalization of property and income would come about through mass production and mass consumption. World War I pulled him onto the political stage. At its beginning, foreseeing the threat of the British blockade of Germany, he organized the stockpiling of raw materials which enabled his country to hold out as long as it did. At the war's end he became involved in the preparation for the Treaty of Versailles. Soon after he attempted to bridge the gulf between labor and the middle class by founding a new Democratic Party and the gulf between Germany and the Allies by advocating a United States of Europe that would include a Russia reconstructed by the joint efforts of victors and vanquished. He was Germany's foreign minister when, in June 1922, bullets and hand grenades of right-wing fanatics killed him at the age of fifty-five on his way to his office in Berlin.

In his role as a Maecenas of responsible industrial design, Rathenau equaled Italy's Adriano Olivetti of typewriter fame and America's Walter Paepcke of the Container Corporation of America. As with these two, design was not only a matter of consumer appeal or efficient production, but an expression of a sense of responsibility for visual culture, in fact, *Gesamtkultur* in the ethical, moral sense that the Werkbund had in mind.

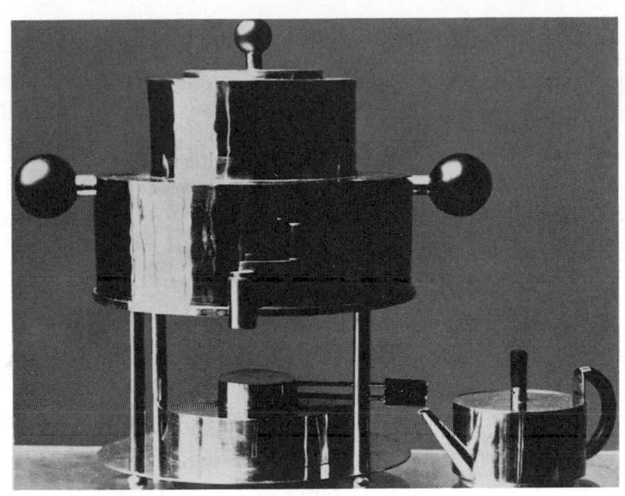

3. Spiritual Samovars

The Rathenau murder was one of far too many on the streets of Germany, denoting the turmoil into which design was expected to bring order and harmony. While the politicians talked bravely about peace and a new, democratic beginning, homeless, disillusioned officers and noncoms talked revenge and sowed their seeds of reaction and counter revolution.

Yet there was also the glow of high hope on the faces of artists and intellectuals in the cafes and unheated studios. Wedged between the Kaiser's fall and Hitler's rise—the fabulous twenties—was an extraordinary burst of creativity, a new search for values, and it was most intense, perhaps, in Germany. Thomas Mann, Rainer Maria Rilke, Franz Werfel, and others pursued it in literature, Emil Nolde and Oskar Kokoschka in painting, Wilhelm Lehmbruck and Ernst Barlach in sculpture, Arnold Schoenberg and Kurt Weill in music, Max Reinhardt and Erwin Piscator in the theater, Ernst Lubitsch and Josef von Sternberg in film. All art surged forward to new horizons.

All this helped make the Bauhaus into what art historian Nikolaus Pevsner called "the paramount center of creative energy in Europe."

When Hitler covered Germany with his deadly shroud, much of that creative energy was transferred to the United States. Gropius came to

Harvard in 1937 and trained a whole new generation of architects not only in his own classroom but also with his great influence on architectural training elsewhere. Mies taught at the Illinois Institute of Technology which he also, in part, built. Laszlo Moholy-Nagy, another important Bauhaus man, who died in 1946, launched a "New Bauhaus" in Chicago which later merged with IIT where Hilberseimer also teaches. The Bauhaus painter Josef Albers first taught at Black Mountain College and then at Yale. The graphic designer Herbert Bayer went to work for Paepcke's Container Corporation and guided much of the design, teaching, and searching that came out of Paepcke's cultural sparkplug in Aspen, Colorado. Marcel Breuer became one of America's foremost architects. There are several others.

It all began when Gropius was suddenly ordered out of the trenches of World War I to an audience with the Grand Duke of Weimar. The Duke wanted to know if he would take over Weimar's Grand Ducal Arts and Crafts School which, in 1906, Henri van de Velde, also a Werkbund leader and architect, as well as a painter, had founded and designed. The succession could not be effected until the carnage was over. By that time Gropius signed his contract with the Provisional Socialist Government of the new Republic of Sachsen-Weimar-Eisenach. On his insistence the arts and crafts school was merged with the Weimar Academy of Fine Arts across the street. Under the new name, the Bauhaus remained an institution of the state, which accounts largely for much of the political troubles it encountered throughout its existence.

At the beginning the new school had only forty or fifty students. There was no tuition fee. Like the faculty, most of the students lived in whatever quarters they could find in town. For those who could not afford the rent, Gropius got the authorities to provide a free dormitory. He also obtained some land on which the students raised produce for their inexpensive canteen, a vital necessity in those hungry days. "I never knew how some of them made it," said Gropius later.

No one rushed to the drawing boards to design that "Crystal palace of a new faith." Shivering in overcoats in winter, the Bauhaus students were, in those first Weimar years, instructed by both a craftsman and an artist. Gropius' idea was to train their hands and eyes simultaneously. What more than anything else sparked the tremendous influence the Bauhaus was to have on all modern design was the remarkable teaching staff that handled the training, often in chaotic ways.

Johannes Itten, an eccentric painter from Zurich and a genius as an art educator, invented the famous six months' "basic course," which

Moholy-Nagy and Albers later perfected. Itten called it "the big house-cleaning of the mind," and his students called it "the purgatory." The idea was to cleanse the student of all preconceived notions about art and design, particularly the despised "academy" approach. Itten would ask the students to explore the various possibilities of contrast by drawing such contrasts as smooth-rough, fluid-solid, still-moving, large-small. He would teach them to discover the "feel" of materials and texture before they would investigate how the textural qualities could be represented, and would seek to develop their sense of color, touch, and space. He would suddenly require the rapid assembly of collages made from odd objects. All this, though today practically standard procedure in art schools around the world, was new and revolutionary at the time. It was the backbone of the Bauhaus system.

From there students would move on to the printing shop which Lyonel Feininger co-directed, take ceramics with sculptor Gerhard Marcks, or proceed to weaving, metal work, stained glass, mural painting, or Oskar Schlemmer's famous theater workshop. When the professorial Kandinsky arrived in 1922, he took over stained glass from Paul Klee who first went on to teach weaving and then metal work. Here Klee, as one irreverent student put it, helped turn out "spiritual samovars and intellectual doorknobs." Eventually, these two "hallway masters," as the students were apt to call them because they were seen more frequently in the corridor than in their workshops, also offered courses in straight art and art theory. These courses led both men to formulate their fascinating, if esoteric and abstract, philosophical essays—Klee's *Pedagogical Sketchbook* and Kandinsky's *Punkt und Linie zu Flaeche* (Point and Line to Plane).

In the first chaotic Weimar years the Bauhaus produced astounding and often still exciting sculptures, murals, collages and paintings; Marcel Breuer's first cubic and clumsy wood furniture; Josef Albers' stunning, abstract glass windows; Herbert Bayer's posters and typography; Oskar Schlemmer's ballet costumes and stage-set experiments; an array of expressionist chess sets, light fixtures, coffee urns and silverware, tapestries, bookbindings, kinetic paintings produced by electric light; spectacular kites that would fly over the sedate little town; tumultuous costume parties; a first-class student band producing a Dadaist kind of jazz; a crazy men's suit, consisting of a kind of Cossack blouse and funnel-shaped corduroy trousers that Johannes Itten tried to promote; a great deal of excitement among Central Europe's artistic and intellectual elite—but really no architecture to speak of.

There was talk, incessant, passionate talk, about architectural form

America's new forms excited the Bauhaus

and purposes. The fundamental premise, of course, was that Ruskin was all wrong when he said that "ornamentation is the principal part of architecture." Ornament, as Loos had said, was tantamount to crime. The new architecture, it was generally agreed in line with whatever it was that everyone advocated as Functionalism, was to express the structure. Here the thesis of the French architect and architecture historian Eugène Emmanuel Viollet-le-Duc provided much philosophical underpinning.

Viollet-le-Duc, in 1840, was put in charge of preserving France's great Gothic cathedrals and restored many of them, including Notre Dame in Paris. Some people charged that he restored them to shapes that they had never possessed. Be that as it may, he made the largely valid discovery that the Gothic arches, spires, and flying buttresses were not some capricious creative invention. They were not, he asserted, only an artistic expression of deep religious feeling, but resulted from "the necessity of the structure." Everything in Gothic architecture, he said, was arrived at by the logic of engineering. If you wanted to display the newly invented stained glass in a stone structure—and stone was the most available and most lasting building material in France at the time—the openings had to be pointed arches to stand up. Walls thus pierced had to be reinforced with flying buttresses to absorb the downward thrust of the weighty roof. He persuasively carried the theory into just about every detail of Gothic structures. He carried on a long, polemic feud with the dominant École des Beaux-Arts which taught that you start with a concept of what the building ought to look like—some style of the past—and then figure out how to construct it and accommodate the human activities it is to shelter.

Structural necessity or no, architects, at the Bauhaus or anywhere else, never got very far away from an image of the end product of building, a vision of its ultimate form, which is determined not so much by its structure as by the imagination.

Forms that much excited the people at the Bauhaus were the great barns, silos, and grain elevators in America's Midwest, not only because they were spontaneous, utilitarian structures of unique, strange beauty, but also, I suspect, because the distant continent, seemingly so free of repressive traditions, held a peculiar romantic lure.

From that continent also came pictures of boldly assertive new houses, houses designed for the prairie, that no longer boxed formal rooms into some kind of facade but represented dynamic compositions of interlocking volumes and masses and contained, under low-slung, sweeping, horizontal roofs, a variety of spaces flowing into one another—the new architecture of Frank Lloyd Wright.

Wright, although at that time hardly known in his own country, was much in vogue among European architects ever since, in 1910 and 1911, Ernst Wasmuth, the Berlin publisher, issued two volumes of his early work. This was followed, in 1925—still some years before anything about or by Frank Lloyd Wright was published in America—by a handsome collection in the Dutch publication *Wendingen* of plans, drawings, and photos with tributes to Wright by several Americans and Europeans.

Frank Lloyd Wright's genius—a strong influence

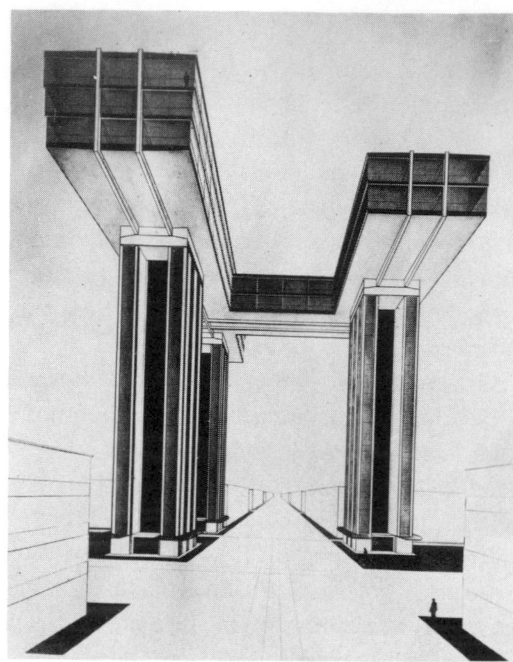

Lissitzky—abstract architecture on paper

From Russia, too, had come new, much discussed influences with an immediate bearing on architecture: Suprematism and Constructivism. It began in 1913 when Casimir Malevich, who had struggled with Cubism, acting on sudden impulse, dropped all "disturbing elements" from his picture, and all that remained was the simple geometric form—a black square on a pure white surface. Not long thereafter, joined by El Lissitsky, he ventured linear, three-dimensional designs, a kind of abstract architecture on paper and canvas. Lissitsky, in fact, stated that this was to be the *Umsteigestation von der Malerei zur Architektur*, "the transfer point from painting to architecture." Constructivism was further extended by the brothers Naum Gabo and Antoine Pevsner, who were later to become sculptors. Led by Vladimir Tatlin, Constructivism became for a moment the dominant style of the Bolshevist revolution in Russia. Trotsky encouraged it. In 1921 Lenin began to frown on this art form as unsuitable for proletarian mass propaganda. The fact that Kandinsky was thereafter appointed to the Bauhaus and that Malevich visited there, caused Hitler and his followers to charge the Bauhaus with *Kultur-bolschewismus*, cultural Bolshevism.

The Bauhaus issued a German translation of Malevich's book, *The Non-objective World,* first published in Moscow in 1915. The school never denied the unquestionable influence of Constructivism on its architecture and industrial art, particularly on the efforts of Moholy-

Nagy. Gropius, for reasons he has never convincingly explained, has consistently and vehemently denied the at least equally important influence of de Stijl, a parallel, though more disciplined, development in Holland. De Stijl began with Piet Mondrian and his ever more simple geometric patterns. Theo van Doesburg, painter, sculptor, and architect, took it from there and, assisted by many talented architects, notably Johannes Oud, joined forces with Mondrian to develop a new industrial, technological, and architectural style of "functional purity." *De Stijl* was the name of the group's magazine.

The de Stijl idea was that by reproducing, in effect, Mondrianlike paintings on a large, three-dimensional scale, the laws of aesthetically balanced composition of contrasting horizontals and verticals would coincide with the laws of steel-beam construction. Their aim was an architecture of antinature (a notion that obsessed Mondrian to such a point that he professed to be unable to eat within the sight of trees), in which the tyranny of nature would be supplanted by a purely man-made harmony in which art and life could be happily reunited.

Doesburg was much interested in the Bauhaus and may well have had ambitions to take it over and make it de Stijl's *Congregatio de Propaganda Fide,* much as Pope Gregory XV established the Propaganda in 1622 to spread the true faith. One day in 1923, apparently uninvited, Doesburg appeared in Weimar to do missionary work for his de Stijl movement. Asymmetrically balanced red, blue, and yellow rectangles soon blossomed forth at the Bauhaus, and for a while it looked, indeed, as Schlemmer noted, that the students would proclaim de Stijl's Mondrian their Allah and van Doesburg his prophet. "This Dutchman," Schlemmer wrote of van Doesburg in his diary, "so fervently wants

Van Doesburg took it from Mondrian

architecture that painting, inasmuch as it does not reflect it, doesn't even exist for him. He is a most articulate advocate of his ideas, so that the Bauhaus students are much attracted, particularly those who search for architecture, which was, they say, the central promise of the Bauhaus which it still owes them."

The students were right. Gropius' idea was that only graduates of four years of design work, a state-issued journeyman certificate in hand, would be allowed in his "research department," where architecture was both taught and practiced. At Weimar this part of the program was never realized. Times were bad, and most of Gropius' own architectural work remained on paper. An exception was the remodeling of a theater in nearby Jena and an experimental house, Am Horn, built for the first public Bauhaus exhibition in 1923. Oddly enough, it was designed by the painter Georg Muche. Or was it odd – considering that most architectural talk and ideas at the time came from painters? At any rate, Am Horn, to judge from the pictures, appears as a rather pathetic affair. It had a large, square living room in the center with all the other rooms around it. The living room, which like a railroad concourse had to take all the traffic, was somewhat higher than the rest of the house to give it light through clerestory windows. The house was furnished with Marcel Breuer's wood furniture and all kinds of other student work. "Three days in Weimar," quipped a critic who reviewed the exhibition, "and you don't want to see another square for the rest of your life."

The students did. Though van Doesburg was not allowed to lecture at the Bauhaus, he held a private course in a nearby hall and the students cut class to hear him talk about more squares and theories. It provoked quite a crisis at the Bauhaus. In the end, van Doesburg was somehow or other eased out of town. He angrily proclaimed from Paris that the Bauhaus "is thoroughly rotten inside, and whatever little good there may be in it is simply a dilute extraction from de Stijl."

Van Doesburg's attack, however, was mild compared to those by the Nazis, who were rapidly becoming stronger, particularly in Weimar. When they cut his budget by two-thirds, Gropius closed the Bauhaus in Weimar in 1925 and accepted an offer to move it, lock, stock, faculty, and students, to Dessau. Here a progressive mayor, Dr. Fritz Hesse, promised a more favorable climate and provided the money for a spanking new building.

4. A New Building

The Bauhaus that Gropius built in Dessau in 1926 was, in a way, a synthesis of everything that had been ventured and discussed in the ferment of the talkative Weimar years.

A white reinforced concrete and steel structure with large glass areas, it is an asymmetrical composition of workshops, lecture rooms, dormitories, and classrooms for the associated Dessau Trade School. Each of these functions is clearly expressed and treated differently, yet logically related. The complex, spanning a road, is forged into a harmonious, lively, and rhythmic unity. The road, by the way, wasn't there before. Gropius put it there—symbol, perhaps, of a motorized age.

Yes, as has often been said, the building shows some de Stijl influence, not, as van Doesburg had feared, in a "dilute extraction," but in a disciplined, rational refinement. There are also other influences. You can, in the strong horizontal lines, cantilevers, and window ribbons, discern something of Frank Lloyd Wright. The large glass wall which encloses the three-story workshop wing, probably the first glass-curtain wall of such size, might well have been inspired by Constructivist abstractions, as, carried even further, Mies' consistent purism is.

If Gropius had produced a new synthesis of much that was tried and built at the time, that is precisely what he has always aimed for. All his life he preached "synthesis," pulling all the best ideas together. That was why, at Weimar, he had condoned the constant struggles, open and clandestine, though they had caused much turmoil. That is why most of his work (though not the Bauhaus Building) is done in collaboration with other architects. In fact, his firm in Cambridge does not bear his name but is called "The Architects' Collaborative."

Gropius, as well as Modern architecture, had attained fame before the Bauhaus Building. With Adolf Meyer, Gropius had helped point to the new direction with his Fagus Works, a shoe-last factory in Alfeld an der Leine. It was not, as it seems, a steel-frame building such as Sullivan had pioneered with the Carson, Pirie, Scott department store in Chicago. The bulk of the Fagus Works consists of masonry load bearing walls. Its novelty is in the new concept of form. The mass is dissolved and dematerialized by the round, much photographed, glass staircase at the corner.

Again with Adolf Meyer, Gropius repeated the same idea in the different form of the office building for the 1914 Werkbund exhibition at Cologne. Both these buildings, at least on the grainy photos that remain, look rather like ugly ducklings and seem utterly dated today.

The Bauhaus Building, however, which the East Germans have re-

A new concept: the mass is dissolved by glass

A three-dimensional manifesto, clean and unadorned

cently restored, still appears totally modern. It is no longer some groping or merely provoking avant-garde challenge, but a clear and still valid statement of twentieth-century architecture. Here, full blown and almost all at once, was the three-dimensional manifesto of what was later to be called the International Style.

It looked all smooth, clean, polished, and unadorned, as though every part had been produced by a machine and the whole assembled on a conveyor belt. It wasn't. It was all shaped and built in the same manner in which materials had been shaped and buildings been constructed for a hundred years or more.

The workshops and masters of the Bauhaus helped equip and furnish the new building. Every thoughtful detail, fixture, and furnishing contributed to the claim of a total new visual order.

This had its effect on the work of the school. Much calmer and more purposeful, though with undiminished artistic verve, it settled down to business. The curriculum was thoroughly revised, and several Weimar students, notably Herbert Bayer, Marcel Breuer, and Josef Albers, now became instructors. The Bauhaus soon derived a considerable income from its industrial and graphic designs sold to industry for mass production. Much of the low-cost furniture—which largely inspired what you see today in Knoll and Herman Miller display rooms—chinaware, light fixtures, and particularly wallpaper became so popular that some manufacturers would advertise the Bauhaus Style—a term still used at times. A style, however, was far from the minds of those who worked at the Bauhaus. They did not simply package industrial products for sales appeal as so many American "stylists" do. After thorough study of production processes, they sought to bring technical and functional requirements into harmony with aesthetics.

And, at last, an architecture department was added, headed by the Swiss Hannes Meyer. He was joined by Hilberseimer, who had written an influential book on city planning. The emphasis was on practical training and low-cost housing.

The Bauhaus had, however, brought its innate state of political crisis along to Dessau. The right-wing attacks also increased. Gropius resigned, and Hannes Meyer took over. Meyer didn't think much of fine art, which infuriated the painters, particularly Kandinsky. He made no bones of his leftist political views which brought the rightist attacks to a frenzy. Gropius has later written that Meyer "was a treacherous character, which I did not recognize early enough. I believe that Hannes Meyer's inner downfall was his denying art as such. It narrows the field, if the rational point of view is made the only factor."

Howard Dearstyne, an American student at the Bauhaus who knew Meyer well, thought him immature rather than "treacherous." Meyer's letters of protest after his dismissal are, as if to prove it, ebullient diatribes. In all his writings and quite astute architecture he seems to have believed in much of the same things Gropius believed in, only fanatically more so. Gropius' sharp reaction to Meyer's "denying art as such" only proves that, like the rest of his fellow pioneers, he is first and foremost an artist rather than a functionalist designer.

Meyer went to the Soviet Union and later to Mexico where he did very creditable work. He died in Switzerland in 1954 and now seems to be the hero of the successor of the Bauhaus in Germany, the Hochschule für Gestaltung in Ulm.

According to his biographer, the Swiss architect and Ulm teacher Claude Schnaidt, Meyer was embroiled in the raging controversy between two implacably opposed groups of architects in the Soviet Union at the time. The urbanizers held that the socialist city ought to be something like Ebenezer Howard's Garden City, a comprehensively planned, compact New Town of limited size. It was to be entirely collectivized. Everyone was to eat in the same huge canteen. The disurbanizers opposed orderly communities on a human scale. They favored an even distribution of the population all over the country along the major highways, with each family living in its own, private, mass-produced house. America's sprawling suburbs come uncomfortably close to this ideal.

Stalin ended the argument in 1932. The turning point was probably the international competition for the Palace of the Soviets in which a number of interesting modern schemes had been submitted, the most exciting one by Le Corbusier. They were all rejected and an imitation Italian Renaissance palace was erected instead. Henceforth, decreed Stalin, all planners and architects had to belong to only one organization and practice "Soviet Realism," a mawkish, pompous, archaic, pseudo-classic architecture, adorned with flattened out columns and heroic statuary of high-breasted maidens and tractor drivers. Even Soviet atomic reactor plants—to judge from the models of them shown in a Soviet exhibition in New York a few years back—were made to look like Classic temples. A long way from Malevich's Constructivism, Soviet Realism was to respect national traditions and be the answer to the material and spiritual needs of the proletariat. Stalin didn't seem to realize—or did he?—that the national traditions were not those of the various nationality groups within the Soviet Union but of the Imperial Romans.

Hitler shared Stalin's taste, though he streamlined his Roman temples a little. Official Washington also tended dangerously towards this style, to wit, the Smithsonian History and Technology Building. The Sam Rayburn House Office Building, built 1955 to 1965 and designed by the Philadelphia firm of Harbeson, Hough, Livingston, and Larson under the supervision of Capitol Architect George Stewart, isn't even streamlined. It looks like nothing so much as the epitome of Soviet Realism, the Palace of Culture in Warsaw, Stalin's gift to the Poles and twentieth-century civilization.

At any event, in 1930 Mies van der Rohe took over the Bauhaus and made it primarily an architecture academy. The brown tide of Nazism soon engulfed this, like all other worthy institutions in Germany. In September 1932, Mies moved the school into a deserted telephone factory in Berlin and tried to run it as a private institution. The Nazis soon moved in. Stormtroppers surrounded and searched the school building and planted the swastika flag on its roof. Mies was not about to let them get away with it. He had a lengthy talk with Alfred Rosenberg, the Nazi's "cultural" leader. Mies told me he baffled Rosenberg, who ranted about modern design, by pointing out that the mighty Nazi happened to be sitting behind a modern desk. The idea of industrial design—the aims of the Werkbund—suddenly appealed to Rosenberg. "Perhaps we ought to have a school like this," he said.

He consented to let the Bauhaus continue provided Hilberseimer, who was considered a security risk because he had once signed some civil liberties petition, was fired. Mies laughed, which again baffled the Nazi, and left.

The faculty was delighted about the apparent stay of execution. There were drinks all around. Then Mies announced: "Now *we* are going to close the Bauhaus!"

5. "Less is More"

Most people tend to equate Modern architecture with glass boxes and then complain about them (as I did some pages back). Glass boxes are practically synonymous with Mies.

Mies, however, is a very great architect and, no doubt, the most architectonic of them all. He gave us a straightforward, systematic approach to architecture that others can follow, and for a while most architects did. He doesn't mind that at all. His only regret is, he told me, that most of those who design in his manner do it so badly.

Mies' architecture is so teachable because, while, as a group, the Modern pioneers changed the concept of what architecture is, Mies got down to fundamentals. He restated in modern terms the concept of what *building* is. He was, in the twenties, as romantically idealistic about the social potentials of a new architecture as any of the Werkbund group. He still is, though forty years later he feels that "we cannot expect too much, we should not talk so big." But he is also, and always was, more concerned with the individual building than with the environment. A good German craftsman, he insists on sticking to his craft.

"Social architecture? What is that?" he asked when I talked with him recently. "The sociologists fight among themselves. If anyone will tell us architects what people need, we'll tell them how to build it. We can only reflect what civilization and what culture we have."

I suggested that one trouble might be that architecture has not come up with low-income housing to meet social needs. Mies thought this a wrong premise. "Needs are the same for everyone," he said. "Everyone wears the same clothes and drives the same kind of car. Architecture must come up not with social housing but with the right housing."

Yes, but is his housing "right"? I asked. Isn't it cold and impersonal? "What does cold mean?" he laughed. "You can have cold milk or warm milk. But you can't have a cold or a warm architecture! Nor can you have a personal architecture. Architecture is impersonal. If it isn't, it is arbitrary, as it often is. I don't want five cent social architecture, but a responsible architecture that is valid for everyone."

I ventured that the architecture of the individual building alone was probably only part of the problem. The problem was the sum total of buildings, the challenge of city planning. "Well, city planning is not my field," said Mies, not with annoyance or belligerence, but matter-of-factly. "Why don't you see Hilberseimer?"

Mies admits that his undisguised use of steel and glass and the building methods these dictate to him are "in glaring contrast to our traditional conception of architecture." But he believes, as he wrote recently, "that it would be possible to . . . harmonize the old and the new in our civilization. Each of my buildings was a statement of this idea and a further step in my search for clarity." He seeks clarity in a precise display of the structure, "well formed and comely in the nude," to use Louis Sullivan's wonderful phrase.

The old, the tradition, Mies hoped to harmonize with, is Classicism. Unlike Le Corbusier, who visited Greece early in his life and became enraptured by the glorious play of light and shadow, by the emotional impact stirred up by the Acropolis, Mies, while still working with Behrens, discovered the pristine Classicism of a then little noted building in Berlin—the Neue Wache, a monumental little guardhouse on Unter den Linden, the ceremonial avenue of Prussian kings.

The Neue Wache was designed in 1815 by Karl Friedrich von Schinkel, a painter as well as an architect. His Classicism was sentimental, part of the Greek Revival in the post-Napoleonic period, which was not so much concerned with what the original Greek Classicism was, but with what this period of rising middle-class wealth, culture, and enlightenment thought it ought to have been. After painting picturesque stage sets with Gothic constructions, he became a "rationalist" architect in the employ of Frederick William III of Prus-

Schinkel: logic, clarity and elegance

sia. He was also capable of building most handsomely a cast-iron Gothic shrine as a war memorial.

What Mies—and, since then, his followers—admired Schinkel for, however, was the pure and architectonic clarity of all his design. The Neue Wache resembles a Classic temple only faintly. Pediment and columns are only suggested in that squarely simplified, geometric porch set against a square stone block with two big slabs on either side. The building is a study of contrast, unified by extraordinary logic and conveying a great sense of simple elegance. This elegance is achieved with exquisite proportions and refined detailing. "God is in the details," Mies has often said.

For Mies, Schinkel represented enough of the "old in our civilization." To seek harmony with his Classicism was sufficient, probably because Mies considers it timelessly valid and not merely a recurring ideal in the ebb and flow of aesthetic philosophy. Here was a way out of stylistic confusion, particularly of the mannerist, entangled decorative forms of Art Nouveau that were still so much in vogue when Mies began. He never looked any further into the past. It has never bothered him much whether or not buildings are in harmony with the existing cityscape. "When Gothic structures appeared in Romanesque cities, they were viewed as intruders, too," he told me. I later found that this amazingly consistent man had written the same sentence, almost verbatim, forty-one years earlier. Mies feels that ours is a new epoch, and

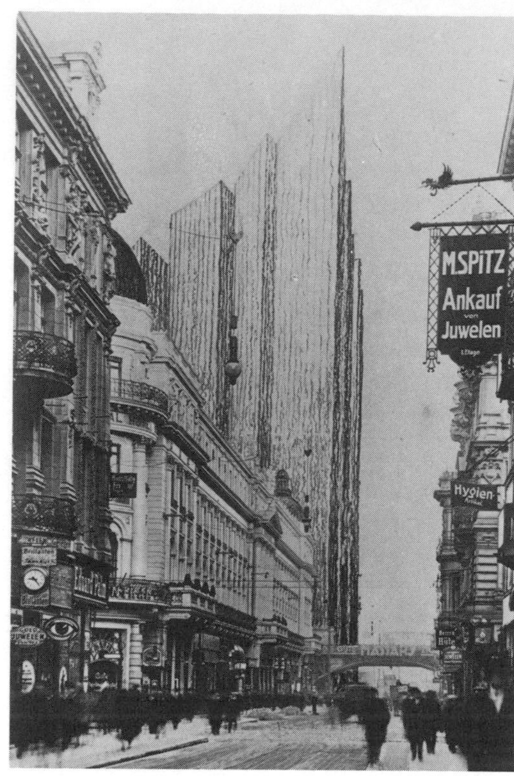

Nothing could be more glass

history holds no answers for him. "We must start to think for ourselves," he said, "and try to follow reason, not grand ideas. We must build again in a reasonable way."

The reasonable way to him was "to free the practice of building from the control of the aesthetic speculators and restore it to what it should exclusively be: building." It was as simple as that.

Building begins with building materials. In the enviably unhurried, simple, systematic way of a good craftsman, Mies set out to investigate what glass and steel, brick and concrete had to offer. But none of these design studies were actually built.

In 1920, for a competition, he designed a twenty-story steel and glass office building on a triangular site along Berlin's downtown Friedrichstrasse. No building could be more glass. Only the steel skeleton, the "bones," as Mies put it, set back inside the uninterrupted glass "skin," and, way inside, the elevator core, were solid. All else was transparent. He explained that, to him, the great beauty of a skyscraper revealed itself best during construction. "Only then," he wrote, "does the gigantic steel web seem impressive. When the outer walls are put in place, the structural system which is the basis of all artistic design, is hidden by a chaos of meaningless and trivial forms. When finished these buildings are impressive only because of their size." To keep his skyscraper impressive, he made its skin transparent. Transparency, of course, is the essential nature of glass.

Another idea that recurs throughout Mies' work is that the skin-and-bones construction would keep the interior space entirely unobstructed and thus completely flexible within the module of his structure. It was, as he has put it, "universal space" which the occupants could subdivide and use with complete freedon as whim and changing needs dictate. Only such interior freedom, he feels, can produce a really valid architecture, because it would be independent of any given use or purpose, an architecture for all purposes and all time.

The Friedrichstrasse Office was designed for a triangular site. This led Mies to give his glass tower a prismatic shape which some critics considered somewhat "expressionistic." Mies said he placed the glass

Frank Lloyd Wright updated on a Mondrian floor plan

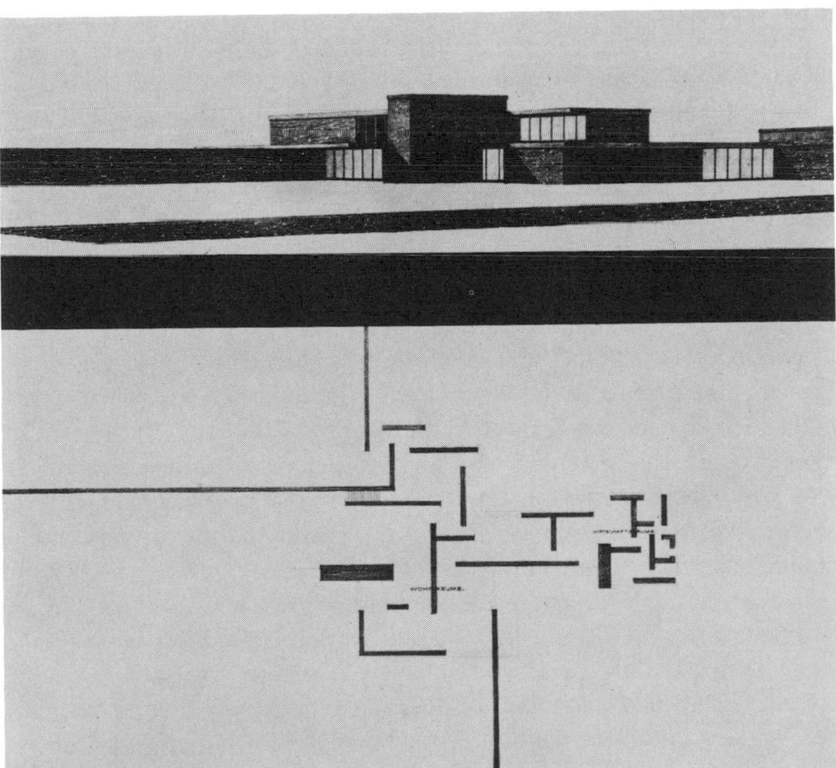

walls at slight angles to each other to avoid the monotony of overly large glass surfaces. The important property of glass, he pointed out, is the play of reflections and not the effect of light and shadow as in solid buildings.

His study of light reflections, done on a model he hung outside his office window, led him to a second glass skyscraper design of curvilinear form. Again, he was not out for anything original or startling. He only sought to exploit the potentials of glass and create something meaningful with them. Forty-six years later a building very much like it is rising on Chicago's Lake Shore Drive—a seventy-story apartment building. Its architects, George D. Shipporeit and John C. Heinrich, former associates of Mies, readily concede that Mies' 1920 project inspired it.

From glass—and numerous charcoal sketches of glazed surfaces—he proceeded to brick. His Brick Villa of 1923 approaches a complete unity of outdoors and indoors by extending three of the four load-bearing walls beyond the skin of the enclosure into the garden. This principle had been pioneered by Frank Lloyd Wright, although Wright has often obscured it with fussy, ornate details. As Peter Blake has pointed out, Mies, with his great gift for the essence of things, brought "Wright up to date and made him modern!"

The following year, 1924, Mies turned to concrete. Concrete, which the Italian master engineer Pier Luigi Nervi has called "molten stone," is, of course, a plastic material. It is poured into forms and wants to be used in free, sculptural ways. Nervi later perfected a plastic, sculptural architecture where skin and bones are one and can, with the laws of tension rather than gravity alone, span huge spaces.

Mies stuck to his rectilinear forms with his Concrete Villa. He made it *look,* however, as though the whole had been cast in a single mold. Into this molded shape he cut out his window openings at will. This building, too, is a somewhat Wrightian composition of contrasting and interlocking cubes, and one wonders how completely free Mies actually was from aesthetic speculation, whether, for that matter, anyone is ever really free of visual associations. Yet, if the glass skyscrapers couldn't be more glass and the brick villa couldn't be more brick, this villa was certainly concrete to the core. Again Mies had proved, at least on paper and to his own satisfaction, that each material, properly used, dictates its own aesthetic.

So far, Mies had actually built only a few houses, and none of them, presumably due to the caution of his clients, fully embodied his ideas. The only notable design he actually built before the Weissenhof Exhibi-

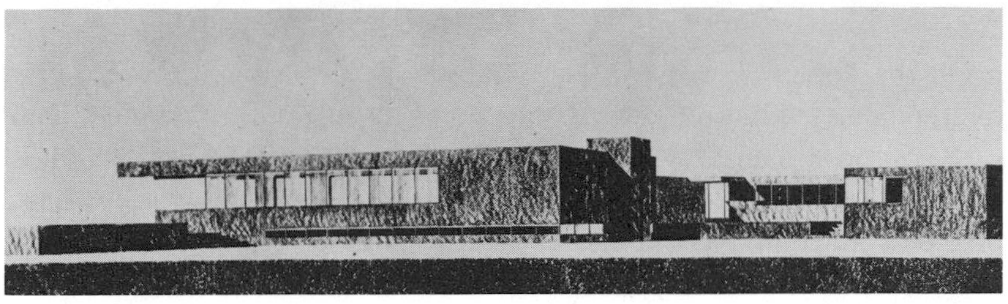

Finally Mies turned to concrete

tion made him famous was a memorial for Karl Liebknecht and Rosa Luxemburg, two Communist leaders who were assassinated by the Nazis. When Hitler came to power, he had it promptly destroyed, but it was not an overwhelming loss. The rather forbidding cubist brick composition—actually, a thick wall treated as a free standing relief—showed little more than that Mies knew how to handle this material. He is not a sculptor.

The great, sad loss to the world, however, is that Mies' Pavilion for the 1929 International Exhibition in Barcelona has disappeared. For here, in one little jewel of architecture, was all the refinement, elegance, and beauty that Mies and the "will of our epoch" could muster. It was dismantled after the exhibition closed and was presumably shipped back to Berlin. There were various treasure hunts and during the American occupation many German officials were grilled as to its whereabouts. At one time a lady from Idaho called Mies in Chicago and claimed she had found it. She wanted Mies to put it up in her garden. Mies just laughed.

The Barcelona Pavilion began with a telephone call to Mies from someone in the German Ministry of Commerce. The Reich was distressed, the man said, to learn that the British and French planned to have exhibits at Barcelona. He thought the Germans ought to have something, too. Could Mies design a pavilion in a hurry? The budget was 180,000 Reichsmark. Mies said he would try.

On a raised platform, 175 by 56 feet, paved with travertine, he built what is, by near unanimous acclaim, the purest work of art which architecture so far achieved in this century. Incorporating most of Mies' ideas, it consisted basically of a thin, flat roof supported by eight slim, chromed steel columns of cruciform section. Totally independent of this purest of pure structures was an open composition of free standing walls of rich materials—honey-colored golden onyx, green Tinian marble, and frosted glass. An onyx block, a little more than ten feet high and split twice, determined the height of the pavilion.

On the floor plan these walls look like nothing so much as a Mondrian painting. They make a chaste and beautiful pattern and served no other purpose than to define a flow of spaces. As in the Brick House, some walls continued out from under the roof onto the terrace where, on either side of the pavilion, they enclosed outdoor spaces, each with a pool of different size. In one of the pools was a sculpture of a dancing nude by Georg Kolbe.

Inside there was nothing but a low table, six stools of steel and white leather, and two of the now famous Barcelona chairs. "Only after the building was practically completed," Mies told me, "did we realize that the King of Spain, Alphonso XIII, would probably want to sit down if he visited the pavilion. That's why I rather hurriedly designed the chair." That chair turned out to be a masterpiece of twentieth-century design. Today there is hardly an office reception room with any aspiration to modern elegance without a pair of King Alphonso's chairs. This may be the closest we have come to a Functionalist visual culture. Only in Mies' own office—a big loft in a dingy, old building in Chicago—is the leather delightfully battered and worn.

Much has been made of the way the Kolbe statue stood, sheltered by onyx walls, in one of the Barcelona pools. This, it is said, is an example of a unique integration of art and architecture seldom achieved

Universal space

in our time. It is. The truth is also, as Peter Blake has related, that Mies originally wanted a Lehmbruck figure for this spot. When this proved impossible to arrange, he took a taxi to Kolbe's studio on one of his last days in Berlin before leaving for Barcelona and borrowed the best substitute he could lay his hands on.

Mies himself agrees with everyone else that the pavilion is his finest work, largely because he had complete freedom of design and didn't have to clutter it up with exhibits.

Beyond its repose and the experience of moving through a sequence of spaces, this great masterpiece of what set out to be a "Functional" architecture, had no function at all.

6. A Machine to Live In

In the years after the First World War, Le Corbusier amused his friends by riding his bicycle around Paris in a derby hat and infuriated everybody else by calling a house a *machine à habiter*, a machine to live in.

The statement, of course, is rooted in the whole machine idolatry and technological expectation of the Modern pioneers. Le Corbusier, least of all romantic, poetic Corbu! did not mean that we should all become robots and inhabit some artless, soulless, mechanical space capsule.

He thought, rather, as his words explained better than his later architecture, that a house, to offer man a creative life, ought to be conceived, designed, and produced in the same rational manner in which automobiles and airplanes are conceived, designed, and produced. He felt that the tradition-bound, irrationally designed and constructed houses and tenements in the city frustrated the promise of the new age.

"Man of today is conscious, on the one hand, of a new world which is forming itself logically and clearly, which produces in a straightforward way things which are useful and usable [he wrote in *Towards a New Architecture*]. On the other hand, he finds himself, to his surprise, living in an old, hostile environment.

"This framework is his lodging; his town, his street, his house or his flat rise up against him, useless, hinder him from following the same path in his leisure that he pursues in his work, hinder him from following in his leisure the organic development of his existence, which is to create a family and to live, like every animal on this earth and like all men of all ages, an organized family life.

"In this way, society is helping forward the destruction of the family while she sees with terror that this will be her ruin."

Could this not be one of the more astute analyses of the underlying causes of the riots in Watts, of the frustration we are watching with terror in all our slums and ghettos?

Surely today, as we pile study upon study of the sociological, psychological, and biological aspects of housing, we are at last beginning to search for a rational approach. As we call in electronic computers to help us bring method into the present madness of nondesigning our environment, should we not concede that a house is, or should be, a *machine à habiter*?

Look, for instance, at the heating and cooling machinery in the modern home, particularly the homes usually depicted in our Better-Homes-Beautiful magazines which ranted most noisily against Le Corbusier's dictum. Consider all the kitchen gadgets, from the useful refrigerator which revolutionized shopping—and thereby helped disintegrate our communities—to the convenient eye-level stove whose heat energy is piped in from afar, to the fanciful electric carving knife. The institutional advertisements are full of the more or less alluring attic-to-basement communication devices and automatic, electronic remote control kitchens of the future.

Yet, when it is proposed that we apply modern technology to design and construct the shell for all this, there is still much emotional resistance. Obviously neither the engineering mind nor its extension, the computer, can furnish the house with a soul or give it creative inspiration. That calls for just that—creative inspiration.

But when it comes right down to it, Le Corbusier brought far more new inspiration to social architecture than we have yet been able to absorb. When he died in August 1965, while swimming off the French Riviera under the Mediterranean sun he loved, he left enough provocative ideas for at least another generation of architects to work on.

Gropius, the somewhat mystical aristocrat of the intellect, and Mies, the master craftsman of building, are essentially architects of steel and glass, materials that demand geometric precision. Le Corbusier is an architect of concrete, the plastic material that can be formed at will.

The two Germans, brought up in chill, cloudy climates, think of architecture as man-made shelter with nature and gardens a much respected antithesis. Corbu's outlook was Mediterranean. He was much preoccupied with sun, shade, and cooling breezes. He strove to submerge and tame nature and to bring it into his buildings and cities.

Gropius and Mies want nothing as much as order and harmony—the neat, square, and harmonious order of Central European fields and meadows covering gentle hills with their quilt pattern of forests without underbrush, and the harmony of clean towns with well-swept sidewalks, which the Germans call *Bürgersteig,* or burghers' walk. Le Corbusier's vision is imbued with the vitality of Mediterranean *con*fusion—the tumultuous fusion of man and a harsh, arid earth, of azure seas clashing with jumbled rocks. It includes irregular patches of vineyard wrought from steep hillsides, and the *con*fusion of densely clustered, stony, Mediterranean towns, with their odorous, littered lanes laboriously winding between the forbidding privacy of high, whitewashed walls.

The decisive experience in Corbu's life seems to have been his journeys to Italy, Greece, and the Balkans, with their landscapes where nature is for man not spiritual repose but relentless struggle. "The city," he wrote later, "is man's grip on nature. It is a human operation directed against nature." He was to make his Visual Arts Center in Harvard, for instance, a grand operation against the very nature of the Harvard Yard.

His creative home always remained in landscapes where beauty is not man-made order but rests in the very invincibility of all this tumul-

The Harvard Yard confused . . .

tuous confusion. He was to make his shapes at Ronchamps and Chandigarh bizarre and his concrete *brut,* as brutally raw as volcanic rocks under the sun. Schinkel saw the Acropolis in Athens as expression and example of a sheltering, ready-made order that men need only emulate and abide by. To Le Corbusier it was, as it is to art historian Vincent Scully, not shelter at all, but built to stir men "to a recognition of the facts in relation to which they must act themselves." The judges of Chandigarh surely must assert their action in their Palace of Justice.

In the eyes of such natives of temperate zones as Lewis Mumford, Corbu's buildings seem often inhuman. But man was always the measure of Corbu's work—frugal, Mediterranean man. His mistake was to confuse Harvard for Chandigarh. Corbu demanded the same *Gesamtkultur* which Gropius demands. So did other social thinkers such as Jean Jacques Rousseau, Saint-Simon, and Charles Fourier, who inspired him.

Nor did Corbu ask of others what did not satisfy himself. He lived in a modest apartment on the Rue Nungesser et Coli in Paris, and all he created all over the world emanated from the same somewhat messy studio at 35 Rue de Sèvres. Though he had attained world fame and a good income by 1952, he built himself a summer cabin at fashionable Cap Martin on the French Riviera that is no more pretentious than a hermit's hut—or common Mediterranean dwelling. He was proud of it and thought it most comfortable. In it he accommodated what he considered all human housing needs in 170 square feet. There were two beds and chairs for living, a table and bookshelves for work, a wash basin and toilet for hygiene, and storage in the double ceiling for suit-

. . . with Chandigarh?

cases and all other cumbersome, cluttering possessions. For Corbu, as the art students of Harvard and others learned, the joys of life were not a matter of material luxuries.

Le Corbusier became acquainted with reinforced concrete in 1908, while working with Auguste Perret, the pioneer in the structural use of this material. At the time the very thought of building with "molten stone" was literally laughed out of school. A structural engineer who began a lecture on the subject at the dominating École des Beaux-Arts at the time never managed to make himself heard above the derisive hilarity of the young gentlemen architects.

Perret, in his famous apartment house at Rue Franklin in Paris and other buildings, used concrete much like other architects in those days began to use steel, for simple and square post-and-beam construction. It was not until 1922, at his beautiful church of Notre Dame in Le Raincy, that he put concrete to work to give him the structural and sculptural freedom the material is capable of.

Le Corbusier, too, in his earlier work, used concrete in rectangular compositions. But it was not because he failed to recognize its plastic possibilities, but because he was immersed in the rectangular world of the Cubists. Much as the Modern pioneers disclaimed any style, there was, of course, always some art style or other, elevated to a *Weltanschauung,* to dominate their architectural thought. Le Corbusier, we must remember, had begun to paint. He worked with the painter Amédée Ozenfant, with whom he published the essay "After Cubism" and the magazine *L'Esprit Nouveau.* The "new spirit" to follow Cubism, the two proclaimed, called for even more extreme Cubism, the precision, hardness, and smoothness of machine products. Le Corbusier's buildings at the time, too, were precise, hard, smooth, and square.

They were, however, much more than three-dimensional paintings. Corbu was always architecturally inventive. In September 1914, for example, the war had devastated entire villages in Flanders and Le Corbusier—not involved in the war because of his Swiss nationality—proposed how they might be quickly and cheaply rebuilt. He devised a structural reinforced concrete framework consisting of six columns supporting three slabs—floor, second story, and roof—and a cantilevered staircase, which could all be poured on the site from simple, standardized forms. The exterior envelope and the interior partitions consisted of prefabricated, mass-produced parts that could be assembled to suit the owner. He called it the Domino House.

He soon followed up the idea with a succession of far more sophisticated houses, only a few of which were actually built. They all explored the design of a system of standardized components for industrial mass production. Large plants, he predicted in 1923, will be able to solve the housing problem. Dwellings, urban and suburban, will be "enormous and square-built and no longer a dismal congeries." They will be beautiful, too, "with the vitality that the artist's sensibility can give to its strict and pure organism."

Forever issuing manifestoes, Corbu now proclaimed "The Five Points of a New Architecture": *pilotis*, or stilts; roof gardens; a free interior plan liberated from load-bearing walls; long ribbon windows; and a "free" facade.

Pilotis, he proclaimed, are "a solution to the great sickness of our present-day cities." Instead of sinking the house into the dark, humid earth, he would lift it above the ground into the air. The garden or public outdoor space thus continues under the house. The roof garden, furthermore, would replace the greenery, sunshine, and air the house takes from the ground. Le Corbusier had technical, as well as sentimental and human reasons for it. His beloved concrete tended to crack under the strain of contraction and expansion. A good protection, he found, was moist sand. So why not grow grass on it and have trees, shrubbery, and flowers as well?

Today there is hardly a skyscraper in our cities that is not built on stilts or that pretends to be. More often than not, however, the open

Concrete as raw as volcanic rocks in the sun

ground space is greedily filled up again for profitable private use right to the building line. A splendid idea is turned into a meaningless visual cliché.

The roof garden, an equally splendid idea, has so far rarely been taken up in America. On the roof of the Unité in Marseilles, Le Corbusier has built a delightful playground for children, complete with wading pool. On the same roof there is also an open air theater. It had been done before, of course. But in recent years, in America we are just timidly beginning to design our apartment house roofs for people to use.

Two other results of what he called his "assiduous and stubborn research" were not included in Le Corbusier's five points. One appeared first in 1922 in his design for the Citrohan Houses (an invented name, deliberately similar to "Citroën," the automobile), to symbolize his hope for assembly-line production. It was the two-story living room, a studiolike affair, a delight America's suburban builders imitated much later in their "split-level ramblers." The other was his proposal, also as early as 1922, to stack complete two-story houses above and next to each other into a large apartment building. The central corridor was to be a kind of street from which, at regular intervals, you turned into open, two-story patios, a private garden for each family. In the garden is the "house."

This concept, again largely realized in the Unité, seems an obvious solution to the problem of housing people densely in the city and yet give each family its own private share of fresh air and outdoor living. It seems rather incomprehensible that Corbu's *villas superimposées,* the stacked houses of 1922, are also now only at the very beginning of their development and popular acceptance.

As was the case with Mies, all these ideas remained largely on paper at the time. This made the impatient Le Corbusier ever more cantankerous. He became openly bitter in 1927, when his entry in the international competition for a League of Nations building in Geneva won the first prize—only to be ultimately rejected on the idiotic grounds that it was drawn in the wrong kind of ink. This design, too, was prophetic. Here were the stilts, the roof gardens, and garden terraces to make work more pleasant in the office wing; an assembly hall designed for good acoustics; horizontal and vertical circulation and communication within the complex; and rational access for automobiles and provisions for parking them.

The rejection of the design scandalized modern artists, architects, and intellectuals all over Europe and drew them together. In 1928, at

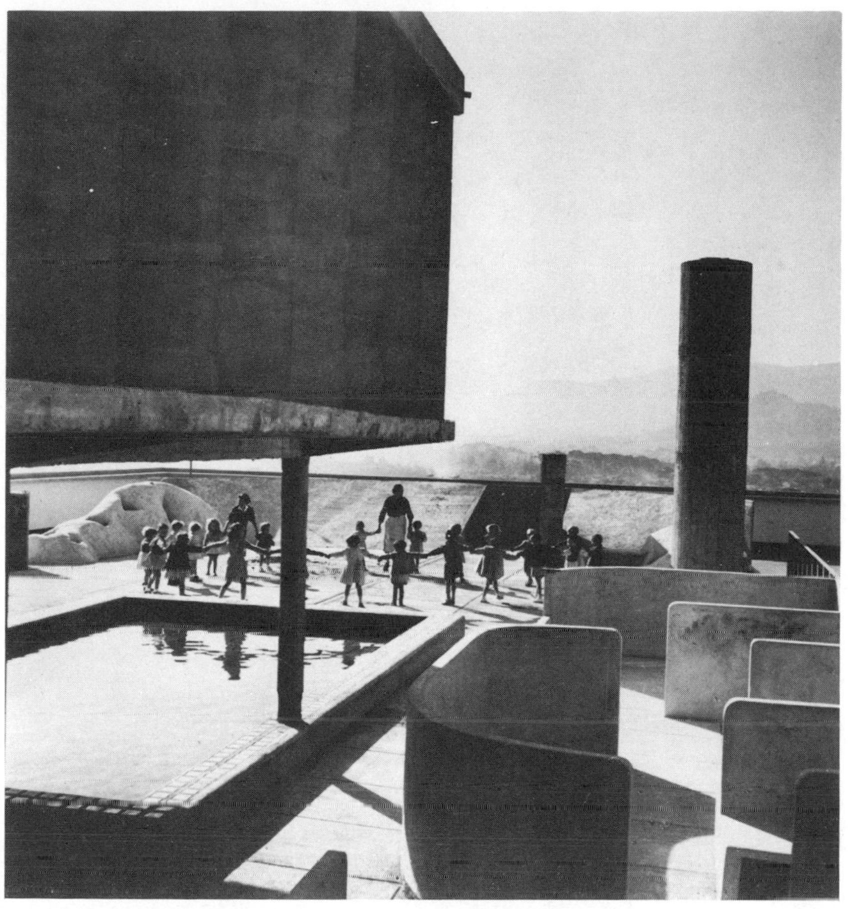

What the house takes, the roof returns

the instigation of Le Corbusier and Sigfried Giedion, Madame Hélène de Mandrot called a meeting of architects at her castle at La Sarraz in Switzerland. It became the first *Congrès Internationaux d'Architecture Moderne,* a world-wide movement combating the academies with its often dogmatic but highly influential proclamations on architecture and city planning.

CIAM dissolved itself in a quagmire of internal hassles at its tenth Congress at Dubrovnik thirty years later. In these three decades it did a great deal of constructive work, committed a great many errors, and helped to radically change our places to live.

Yet, though practically every Modern architect in Europe was present, CIAM's first meeting at La Sarraz had numbered barely three dozen people.

7. Weissenhof

All the ideas of the Modern movement in architecture up to that time culminated in 1927 in one big demonstration project—the Weissenhof community near Stuttgart. The exhibition was sponsored by the Werkbund, and Mies, then its vice-president, was in charge.

"The problem of the modern dwelling," he announced, "is primarily architectural, in spite of its technical and economic aspects. It is a complex problem of planning and can therefore be solved only by creative minds, not by calculation or organization. Therefore, I felt it imperative, in spite of current talk about 'rationalization' and 'standardization,' to keep the project from being one-sided or doctrinaire."

Mies invited sixteen of Europe's leading architects, among them Gropius and Le Corbusier (who at once picked the very best site of the lot). All the buildings were to be moderate in cost. Most were single family houses, and a few were small apartment buildings—thirty-three units all told. Mies refrained, however, from laying down any rigid program that might interfere with free expression, though he couldn't resist one stipulation: All buildings had to have flat roofs!

Mies knew that a good place to live is not merely an accumulation of efficient expediencies or mechanical gadgets. He planned Weissenhof as a community, hoping, for instance, to separate automobiles from people. The authorities at Stuttgart, however, much like the authorities responsible for Washington's Southwest forty years later, thought this much too daring and advanced. After all, they argued, the houses would have to be sold after the exhibition. So the usual road pattern for the usual motor traffic and parking prevailed.

Mies' site plan succeeded, nevertheless, in giving the variety of architectural efforts a remarkable unity. The tight cluster is arranged along an S-curved road along the side of a hill and appears more spacious than it is. Every house has a view. The composition is dominated by Mies' own four-story apartment house, undoubtedly the best of its kind built in Europe at the time. It was of simple, steel-framed construction, finished in white stucco, topped with sheltered roof gardens, and given distinction by meticulously proportioned window ribbons. With movable partitions Mies arranged the interior layout of each of the twelve apartments differently to suit the wishes of the occupants.

Aside from the sleeping compartments, Le Corbusier's two houses also offered much pleasant livability. Both were based on potentially standardized building components. Both provided a logical and convenient progression from entrance to kitchen to dining room and an enormous living room, the hub of all family activity and a spatial event with wonderful views out into the open. Both, with their patios under

Flat roofs were obligatory

the stilts and roof gardens, fused indoor and outdoor living. In one house the living room was two stories high with a low-ceiling dining area. The bedrooms above opened into a hall. In the other house the sleeping compartments, much as those in a sleeping car, could be closed off with a movable partition at night and opened to add to the size of the living room during the day. This preoccupation with flexibility was quite typical and succeeded, of course, in cutting the expense. The rub is lack of privacy.

Gropius displayed his concern with industrial prefabrication. His two houses at Weissenhof were designed of lightweight metal skeletons on a modular grid of one square meter, enclosed with asbestos cement panels lined with cork tiles. Everything in them was designed for low-cost mass production. Neither house was much to look at, but both seemed remarkably serviceable and no prefabricated house since has gone far beyond this demonstration. Any large manufacturer might have gone into assembly line production with it. What was lacking, even in the impoverished Germany of the time, was a clear need to put up with the austerity of the house. That was, it seems, also the difficulty the General Panel Corporation encountered in 1945, when it attempted to manufacture a similar Gropius design in the postwar United States.

Their austerity was also, I would judge, the reason the other Weissenhof houses did not establish themselves with the common man, though they did, almost instantly, become the vogue with the European intelligentsia. There was surely enough variety, what with the concepts of Gropius, Mies, and Le Corbusier now echoed by the Dutch architects J. J. P. Oud and Mart Stam, the Belgian Victor Bourgeois, and the German Hans Scharoun. But variety or not, the new style—and a style it obviously was, despite disclaimers—was too far removed from the nostalgic dreams of the middle class—dreams of pitched roofs, shutters, and roses on picket fences—to be much of a success with them. Only the very rich commissioned luxurious villas—such as the Tugendhats commissioned Mies to build them his famous Barcelona Pavilion-like house at Brno, Czechoslovakia—in the manner conceived for a new industrially produced social architecture. Sophisticates who were not as rich contented themselves with the new furniture shown at Stuttgart—notably Marcel Breuer's and Mart Stam's tubular seating, and Mies' cantilever chair. These, too, were intended for the assembly line—but sell today as virtually hand-made status symbols for several hundred dollars apiece.

Weissenhof was followed up by some other industrial design exhibits, notably the Werkbund show in Paris in 1930, where Marcel Breuer and Herbert Bayer were particularly well received. Barely three years later Hitler was in power and his Nazis circulated pictures of Weissenhof showing Arabs on camels. This graphic fake was followed by architectural vandalism. To overcome the "Bolshevist depravity" of this "Arab Village," the Nazis put pitched roofs on its houses. Allied bombers nearly completed their destruction. The Bonn Republic, however, has recently reconstructed Weissenhof.

But only the style, not the spirit of its architecture survived. As Douglas Haskell, the astute former editor of *Architectural Forum*, put it, "form alone remains of the great upheaval." It is one of the great ironies of our culture that the architecture of the Novembergruppe, the "crystal symbol" of social awareness, was to be fully embraced only in the crystal palaces of big, capitalist corporations.

Nothing like Weissenhof has ever been attempted again anywhere, with the exception of Interbau in Berlin in 1957, an international exhibition of housing and construction where leading architects from fourteen countries designed thirty-five buildings, primarily high-rise apartment houses for nearly seven hundred families, to rebuild the totally destroyed Hansaviertel, Berlin's most elegant downtown residential area. (This time, Le Corbusier even insisted that he be given a spectacular site far away from the project.) The United States contribution,

A useful retrospective of modern architecture

Hugh A. Stubbins' handsome Congress Hall (nicknamed the "pregnant oyster") is also outside the Hansaviertel.

Compared to Weissenhof, which heralded things to come, Hansaviertel is rather like a retrospective of Modern architecture, although we could use such an exhibition in America today. It could provide an enormous incentive for a much needed new and creative technical and social approach to housing and community building. Some foundation, city, or, perhaps, the federal government should sponsor such a demonstration of where our social architecture stands and might go. Outstanding architectural designers, engineers, city planners, and, perhaps, sociologists might be invited to come forward with their most advanced ideas for a model community with model buildings and facilities. There should be none of the usual shackles to inventiveness and daring—no building codes, zoning regulations, market studies of consumer preferences, or voluminous government restrictions. The purpose would be to challenge the design professionals and stir up the building industry, the large industrial corporations, and, most of all, the general public.

What few demonstrations we have lately had in this country of "the house of the future" have been either gimmicks or purely commercial enterprises, usually a combination of both. They advance or advertise specific materials or products, such as plastic, plywood, electrical gadgets, and so on. The model houses at the New York 1964-65 World's Fair were perfectly dismal displays of crass hucksterism and abominable taste. The "Traditional House," designed by Merton S. Barrows, was nothing, more or less, than the cute and anachronistic pseudo-something-or-other brick and gabled roof cottages with electrically lit kerosene stable lamps and shutters that didn't shut, which you see all over Suburbia USA. Edward Durrell Stone's "Modern House," with its industrialized, *nouveau riche* styling, was only a rather pretentious status symbol, whose improvement over the cluttered and impractical "Traditional House" was only that it was simply bigger and gaudier. In the Formica House, the exploration of midcentury good taste in America was illuminated by gushy music, automated stage lighting, and a taped sermon on the virtues of plastic.

Even the more serious experimental homes, built annually for the past few years by the National Association of Home Builders, though useful in their way, are badly handicapped by a parochial mentality. These houses test only what cautious building manufacturers have developed, not what might be technically possible or socially desirable. The Home Builders, quite naturally, only want to know what *they*, not modern technology and design, might offer that an uninformed public is willing to buy. Since the home builders do quite well with what they are producing today for the vast middle-income market, there is no great desire on their part to bother much about their product. Low-income housing, urban sprawl, all the social aspects of our places to live are not burning concerns to them. In fairness, though, I should add that the Home Builders Association has recently conducted searching and candid symposia on these problems.

It took until 1967 before we saw meaningful technological experiments in housing on this continent—Habitat 67 at Montreal and a government sponsored study of prefabricated low-income apartments, town houses and garden apartments at Reston, Virginia. Neither are on the scale of Weissenhof and Hansaviertel, despite America's equally desperate need to reduce the cost of housing construction.

We started out with that ideal when America's first large-scale urban renewal project was launched in Southwest Washington, in the shadow of the Capitol. The initial hope was that the dismal alley dwellings there were to be replaced with housing that was not to cost more than seventeen dollars per room per month. This ceiling had to be removed in 1959, however, because it turned out that, federal urban renewal assistance or no, even enlightened, liberal developers with savvy just couldn't do it. Our architecture and building industry are unable to provide decent housing at moderate cost and profit without subsidies. As in most other urban renewal projects, the slums were replaced with luxury housing and none of the displaced low-income Negroes were able to return.

Nor, unless Habitat and the Reston experiment finally pave the way, are we apt to see any startling change in the essential design of houses or apartment buildings over what was presented at Stuttgart forty years ago. The appearance has changed somewhat, largely, as we shall see further on, under the influence of the Expressionist resurgence. But Charles M. Goodman's luxury town houses at Reston, for instance, built in 1965, look much the same as Le Corbusier's moderate-income house at Weissenhof, though Goodman's arrangement of interior spaces isn't nearly as daring and interesting. On the whole, all that is different is that the austerity of 1927 has been replaced by affluence, more often than not ostentatiously. Today's good, Modern, residential architecture, such as there is, is more ingratiating, if you will, less self-consciously avant garde. That is all to the good. We now omit some too drastic, too Spartan, too "architectural" innovations and ideas which people simply do not want. Le Corbusier's sleeping-car compartments and galley, for instance, were immediately ridiculed at Stuttgart, despite his protestations that no one minds being squeezed into bed on trains going sixty miles an hour. But neither, it turned out, did anyone want to pay a mortgage day after day in order to play choo-choo train night after night.

8. Market Resistance

The Nazis at Weissenhof are not the only ones who put pitched roofs on modern buildings. Our homebuilders today do the same thing in effect when they put "Colonial" pediments over glass and aluminum doors. Both confirm Le Corbusier's complaint, back in 1923, that "the right state of mind does not exist" for producing a modern house that looks like a modern house.

"Everybody, quite rightly, dreams of sheltering himself in a sure and permanent home of his own," Le Corbusier wrote. This dream, he charged, "provokes an actual state of sentimental hysteria." Though, as so often, he overstated the case, he was, and is, right. Nostalgic sentiment tends to win out over good taste in residential architecture far more often than in monumental, commercial, or industrial building design. Most of us are apprehensive about living with the offsprings of a courtship of art and technology. In fact, if you consider Buckminster Fuller's Dymaxion House and early vintage prefabs, most of them do look like bastards.

But it was not only "sentimental hysteria" and certainly not for lack of trying that most attempts at factory-produced houses have failed so far.

The idea is not to stamp entire houses out like so many automobile bodies. It is, rather, to avoid as much costly time and labor-consuming handiwork as possible on the often frozen or rainy building site. To this end, the parts are turned out in factories under controlled conditions by skilled workers who can employ large machines and don't have to waste time moving from job to job. To make the whole thing worthwhile, the trick is to turn out the components in sufficient quantity and large enough for simple assembly, yet not too large to make shipping and handling difficult.

The idea is quite old. As far back as 1624 the English brought a prefabricated, panelized wood house to this country for use by a fishing fleet. This house was taken apart, moved, and reassembled many times. In fact, many of America's early settlements contained prefabricated housing. The California Gold Rush of 1849 was a good market for the prefabricators and so were the Civil War army camps. Many of the precut wood houses in America's history were supplied by mail order establishments; Sears, Roebuck alone sold 110,000 in forty years. Special railroad rates were established for portable houses around 1870. Grosvenor Atterbury, a New York architect, offered houses built of precast, hollow-core concrete as early as 1910.

One of the leading prefabricators before the Second World War, however, was the German firm Christoph and Unmack, which shipped panels for barracks of all kinds all over the world. Out of this firm came Konrad Wachsmann, a brilliant architectural engineer and the foremost pioneer of modern industrialized building. His efforts, now carried on at the Building Research Institute of the University of Southern California in Los Angeles may still yield us more rational ways of providing shelter.

Lately Wachsmann's research has been pursuing some of the engineering concepts originated by Buckminster Fuller, the inventive techno-philosopher (or techosopher, as he might say, with his penchant for inventing words). His ingenious igloo, a shelter machine that puts any "machine for living in" Le Corbusier ever dreamed of to shame, combines, he says, a dynamic approach to construction with maximum efficiency and is thus "dymaxion." The thing can be built out of light metals, plastic, or even cardboard and is all of one piece. It consists of a dome made of octagonal or tetragonal supports which reduce all structural stresses to tensions along geodesic principles. It's light enough so helicopters can move it about, an amazing stunt to behold. Fuller designed his biggest bubble yet, a dymaxion dome, twenty-two stories high, for the U. S. Pavilion at the 1967 International Exposition

Dynamic approach with maximum efficiency

at Montreal. It is handsome as an exhibit building. But for practical purposes of living his dome never got off the ground.

The prefab Wachsmann and Gropius presented to a group of American government officials in 1943 seemed to promise greater acceptance. With government encouragement the General Panel Corporation was founded and its product, though made mostly of wood, since metal was needed for the war, much resembled that designed by Gropius at Weissenhof. All you needed was a hammer to put it together, largely with specially designed metal clips, and a pair of pliers to take it apart again if you wanted to move it elsewhere. A later four-room model was to be fabricated in twenty minutes at a cost of $150 and erected in thirty-eight man hours. In 1947 General Panel opened a plant in Burbank, California, in the hope of producing ten thousand houses a year for $4,585 each, minus the land.

By this time about a hundred house prefabricators had set up shop in the United States, encouraged mainly by war demands. Of over one and a half million houses and barracks erected in army camps, overseas military bases, war production plants, and atomic centers or shipped to allies abroad, two hundred thousand, or one-eighth, had been factory produced. There was good reason to believe that millions of dreamhouses would now shortly roll off the assembly lines, awaiting only white picket fences and rose bushes to turn the postwar housing shortage into a veteran's dream come true.

In January 1946 President Truman summoned Wilson Watkins Wyatt, ex-mayor of Louisville, to the White House. By May of that year, under Wyatt's direction, bold new ideas for a national housing strategy had been drawn up and submitted to Congress as the Veteran's Housing Emergency Act. Mass-produced prefabs were to be a vital part of this strategy. Industrialists like Henry J. Kaiser and the leaders of Douglas Aircraft, Beech Aircraft, and other large corporations were consulted. Labor unions had pledged their full support. It was decided to put prefab production more or less into one basket—the Lustron Corporation of Ohio, which turned out a serviceable, enamel-coated steel house. In the end, Lustron, indeed, laid an egg.

The main trouble with industrialized building production, it seems, is lack of adequate capital. Lustron itself could muster only $840,000 in private equity. The federal government's Reconstruction Finance Corporation first lent it $15½ million and later, after much Congressional hassle, another $15 million. The company said it needed a total of $50 million.

The Lustron story has never been fully told. Even 50 million dollars, it appears in retrospect, would not have been enough to break the vicious circle of inadequate technical and market research, which led to an inadequate production system and product, to disappointing sales, and to an inadequate dealer and distribution organization, all of which resulted in inadequate capitalization. By 1951 Lustron was out of business.

It was one thing, as Burnham Kelly, now dean of architecture at Cornell, points out in his *The Prefabrication of Houses*, to start flooding the world with millions of automobiles. They were new and exciting and can do a lot more than horses did. It was another to attempt the mass production of houses. A prefab house is still a house which is nothing new or exciting at all. It doesn't do a thing a conventional house can't do better, except that it might be cheaper. That, however, is precisely what also makes it suspect. During the war, to speed the housing of war workers, the government lowered building standards and used substitute materials. The public's idea of a prefabricated house was prejudiced by the result.

What's more, all the entrenched, vested interests ganged up on the prefabs. Building-trades unions often refused to put them up. Why, the things are designed and built without any lathering and plastering in them, protested William J. McSorley, general president of the Wood,

Wire, and Metal Lathers International Union, American Federation of Labor. "We believe that all houses that are erected for the purpose of housing human beings should be lathered and plastered in a proper manner, so as to protect sanitation and health of the inhabitants."

For fear of competition the friendly neighborhood lumberyards refused to sell materials to prefab manufacturers or act as distributors. Many banks refused to make loans to prefab purchasers. Government bureaucrats often supported this opposition. Philadelphia officials of the Federal Housing Administration insisted on a pitched roof to assure "those essential esthetic qualities and visual appeal which are necessary to assure continued marketability."

Emboldened by this victory, the disorganized building industry rose to meet the challenge itself. Assisted by federally insured mortgages but with primitive methods and mostly conventional and poorly designed houses, it wrought a near miracle. Between 1947 and 1964 it produced an average of 1½ million housing units a year. The post-war housing shortage was replaced by today's sprawling suburbia. Not even 5 per cent of it is designed by architects or functionally planned.

Efforts at prefabrication continue, but on a socially insignificant scale. In 1964 there were some thirty-six prefab manufacturers in the country who produced about 212,000 units, a little over 22 per cent of all the private single family housing starts that year. None are really inexpensive. The most attractive and probably most livable prefab is the Techbuilt house designed by Carl Koch. In its clean, rational design it is the most direct descendant of the Modern movement. Its great advantage is that with many different models and sizes it offers a truly architecturally conceived house without the architect's fee. It is the ideal vacation house because a Techbuilt dealer will put it up in any remote spot.

Techbuilt demonstrates that the idea of an efficient system of standardized units which all fit together continues to hold great promise. The British employ it to a limited extent, not so much for houses which people seem to want tailor-made, but for larger buildings, notably schools and apartment houses. Even in Britain rationalization doesn't go far enough to be as economical as it might be. Ideally, the system must start at the point where the metal is smelted or the tree is cut to make the most rational use of materials. It must include all doorknobs and plumbing fixtures—everything that goes into a building. Even the simple, streamlined Lustron house had no less than seven thousand parts!

Sponsored by the Ford Foundation's Educational Facilities Labora-

The Techbuilt House—sensible and livable

tories, twelve California school districts have recently jointly developed a coordinated system. Together they promised the product manufacturers that at least twenty-two schools would be built to make it worth while to adopt it. As Josephy White of Inland Steel, one of the manufacturers involved, put it, "A relationship was established between the needs of people and existing industrial technology." It involves the architect, he added. "Without him the potential of industry as an enlightened productive force may never be fully realized."

Yet, while the architects and housing experts were halfheartedly looking about for ways to produce more housing at lower cost by factory methods, four million Americans, as of 1966, lived presumably quite happily in totally prefabricated homes. The fact that these homes were on wheels made them suspect. A good many communities, in fact, still regard "mobile home" parks as slovenly and corrupting gypsy camps and ban them from their residential areas. Some of these parks, however, are far better landscaped and designed and offer far more amenities—such as underground wiring, swimming pools, playgrounds, community halls and laundry centers—than most conventional subdivisions.

The people who live in what used to be called trailers, says the Mobile Home Manufacturers Association, have higher incomes than the national average, more formal education than the average conventional home owner, and fewer children than the single home family.

Far from being gypsies, they only take advantage of the best housing bargain available in the country today. Today's mobile homes are as spacious as comfortable apartments. The "double wides"—two trailers parked parallel to each other and joined—include up to 1,440 square feet of living space, divided into two or three bedrooms and one or two bathrooms. They have all the gadgets including, of course, gas, oil, or electric heating and air conditioning. They come completely furnished in Early American, French Provincial, Oriental, Mediterranean, traditional or contemporary decor, including draperies, lamps, carpeting—with automatic dishwashers and garbage disposals extra—for a retail price of three thousand to twelve thousand dollars, or about ten dollars per square foot. They are sold and financed like a car. The average price of a conventional builder home, by comparison, is about fourteen dollars per square foot without furnishings.

This bargain is possible because mobile homes are produced like automobiles on the assembly line—engineered and built as a cube with the sidewalls vertical webs and the floor and roof the top and bottom flanges. Structurally they are much stronger than conventional houses built on the site because they are engineered to withstand the stress of highway transportation. In the larger plants a complete mobile home, finished down to the last kitchen drawer and light bulb, comes off the assembly line every fifteen minutes.

They are, of course, ugly ducklings, because the width of the basic cube is limited to twelve feet, the maximum allowed by most states for movement on the highway. What's more, their manufacturers strive to express their mobility with streamlined forms and the kind of "styling" we associate with speed. In fact, however, the success of this billion dollar industry rests not so much on the mobility as on the economy of its product.

It is estimated that 85 per cent of the larger mobile homes use their wheels for only one trip—from the factory to the first site. If their owners move they usually sell the thing and buy another one at their new location.

This discovery prompted one manufacturer, Redman Industries, to take the wheels off, design the trailer as a small house with a slightly slanted roof and picture windows fronting a sizable redwood porch and sell it as a "leisure home." It is quite livable, handsome, and solid. You can buy it for less than five thousand dollars retail. And all you have to do is prepare the foundation—concrete piers are recommended

—and get the water pipes, sewer drains, and utility lines ready. The dealer will cart the thing to your site on his own axles which he takes back again and install the house, it is claimed, with only four men in one day.

This factory-produced "leisure home," first introduced in December 1966, in turn, prompted the federal government to give a $200,000 research grant to the Reston Foundation, which operates the public facilities of the Virginia New Town, to study the application of the idea for permanent low cost housing. Reston's architects, Whittlesey, Conklin and Rossant, hope to come up with some two hundred town houses, garden apartments, and high-rise units by treating the factory-produced cube as a modular unit which can be combined or stacked in various ways.

Habitat 67, the experimental housing project at the 1967 International Exposition at Montreal, is built on a similar principle. Its designer, the brilliant Moshe Safdie, however, also attacks the problem of housing people closely together while giving them private gardens and safe open space for the children to roam.

Safdie casts his basic modular housing cube in a nearby shed. The floors, ceiling, windows, doors, plumbing, wiring, other mechanical equipment, and all the rest—85 per cent of all that is needed—are installed on the ground. The concrete boxes are then lifted by gigantic cranes into a kind of honeycomb, a self-supporting structure, in which they combine into "villas in the sky." The shape of the structure resembles an open, elongated pyramid, somewhat broken up to let light and air into the inside. The roof of the house below forms the terrace garden—each seventeen by thirty-eight feet—for the one above. They are planted with shrubbery and small trees that are centrally watered and fertilized.

On the inside of the pyramid every second floor is a "street in the sky" to lead you into the house. It widens at intervals to make room for small playgrounds. On the ground Safdie envisions community centers, schools, churches, shopping and all the rest.

The Montreal fair project realizes but the first phase of Safdie's design, which calls for a thousand units, an entire Levittown on one-tenth of the land area. The Canadian authorities had money only for one hundred and sixty "villas" of varying size, some of them with two stories. This small population did not make the construction of the community buildings on the ground economically feasible. What's more, Habitat's houses are still rather expensive. The investment in the concrete casting equipment, the expensive cranes, design and

Concrete boxes form "villas in the sky"

tooling for complete, prefabricated bathrooms and kitchens and other things is made, however. If this is amortized in the second phase of Safdie's design, the cost per unit should be brought within reach of moderate income families. That, with nearly a quarter of this nation still ill-housed—not to speak of the desperate housing needs elsewhere in the world—is an important promise.

Both Redman's attractive "leisure home" and Habitat 67 prove already that a rational building system need not lead to uniformity and monotonous communities. A brick, after all, is prefabricated, yet brick buildings can be monotonous or richly varied, their design can make for a prisonlike housing project or a Colonial Williamsburg. It all depends on the skill of the designer. A good, flexible, integrated building system, somewhat like a more complex, adult Erector set, could free the architect of the burden of cumbersome routine details to use his creative talent where it counts.

Variety and good design do not mean that the architect, as he does now, virtually has to invent the wheel all over again every time he gets a commission to design a home.

9. ". . . Mainly in America"

There had been some Modern architecture in the United States before Philip Johnson, with the help of Alfred H. Barr, Jr., organized a Department of Architecture at New York's Museum of Modern Art in 1932. But Americans knew and saw little of it until this propaganda center of the new style began to enlighten them.

Like Mies, Gropius, Breuer, Moholy-Nagy, and the rest, its harbingers had also come from Europe. Eliel Saarinen, Eero's father, arrived in 1923 from Finland. Richard Neutra landed here that same year from Austria. William Lescaze had come in 1920 from France, though he was born a Swiss.

The elder Saarinen was the only one of the three who had already been famous in Europe. His daring entry in the international competition for the Chicago Tribune Tower had won him second prize, $20,000, and an invitation to build a new career on the new shores. He brought with him the modern concepts of design and architecture which had begun to seethe in Europe. Here, there was only Frank Lloyd Wright, regarded as an eccentric rather than a prophet in his own country, so that it fell largely to the elder Saarinen to pave the way for the arrival, fifteen years later, of Gropius and Mies. He could do so all the better because he seemed far less revolutionary than he actually was. He practiced and taught Functionalism and honest expression of structure not as a belligerent *Weltanschauung* but as an intrinsic element of his art. In Helsinki there had never been, as there was in Berlin, the tense and tortured sense of outrage at a world and time out of joint, nor a messianic urge to set it right. Finland is an outpost of European culture which can enjoy and advance the fruit of the heartland's artistic ferments without suffering them.

With such Northern detachment, but by no means without intensity, Eliel Saarinen could design buildings in this country that were Modern without giving offense to tradition. He could bring Carl Milles and his gay, sensuous statues to Cranbrook, the new art school near Detroit which he built and directed, and no one in the stolid Midwest was particularly shocked. People enjoyed the beauty and freshness of both buildings and statues and forgot their novelty and modernity. They responded to the stark discipline and utter directness of the elder Saarinen's architecture because it was readily understood. It appeared not as an intellectual experiment but as something natural—all the more so because Saarinen brought from Finland a love of earthy, natural materials, mainly brick and stone.

More Modern than the still somewhat Art Nouveau Cranbrook were

Eliel Saarinen—a palatable modern

Eliel Saarinen's movingly simple churches, notably Christ Lutheran Church in Minneapolis. One of his most significant contributions, perhaps, was the Crow Island School, at Winnetka, Illinois, built in 1940 in collaboration with Perkins and Will. A spreading, one-story building of inexpensive brick, it separated different age groups in four wings, each with its own outdoor play area. The classroom units were L-shaped with a work area in the short side and the classroom itself in the long side. The space and the movable furniture permitted informal grouping, and the orientation made the most of natural light. Each classroom let the children directly out into the open and its generous windows included the world beyond. The light, cheerful, economical, and functional building helped set the pattern for thousands of suburban schools to come.

Neutra had briefly worked for Eric Mendelsohn in Berlin. On his arrival in this country he first spent a few months in New York detailing Gothic ornaments and then went on to Chicago. It had long been the object of his romantic dreams, nourished by what he had read of Louis Sullivan and Frank Lloyd Wright. He was disappointed when, as he emerged from the dark smoke of the Illinois Central terminal, "the prairies were not immediately visible." Nor could many architects even tell him just who Louis Sullivan was. He called, he relates in his

Neutra's "health house," a Modern pioneer

memoirs, on the embittered, forgotten, alcoholic, and ailing master. At Sullivan's funeral, shortly thereafter, he met Frank Lloyd Wright. "It was just like suddenly seeing the unicorn or some other fairy tale figure one has been searching for behind the rainbow," Neutra recalled. Wright, too, was broke and unappreciated. He invited Neutra to visit him in Taliesin. An American friend advised the young immigrant not to take his innocent young bride into "such a den of iniquity."

Neutra got his start first with the large architectural firm of Holabird and Roche, then with Frank Lloyd Wright, and, in 1926, teamed up with Rudolph M. Schindler, also a Taliesin alumnus, in Los Angeles. California, at the time, proved more receptive than any other part of the country to Neutra's superbly elegant and rational houses in the new manner. His "health house," as he called it, for Phillip Lovell, built in 1927 to 1929 on a steep slope with Los Angeles' Griffith Park hills as a backdrop, was as Modern as anything Mies or Le Corbusier built in Europe at the same time. In its inventive construction—a steel casement fabricated in sections and enclosed with glass and thin concrete and balconies suspended by slender steel cables from the roof frame—it was, if anything, more advanced. Neutra applied his great technical interest and deep social concern to schools, hospitals, and housing projects. The aesthetics of the International Style soon caught up with him, but he long kept his lead with his ingenious solutions to the specific problems of the site and the people for whom his buildings were designed. He fell behind when, in the mid-fifties, no longer a pioneer, he was tragically seized by the disease of excessive personal vanity. The quality of his work seemed to decrease in direct proportion with his appetite for publicity. His earlier houses, however, came to terms with the demands of modern living far better than those of most.

The most spectacular harbinger of Functionalism on these shores—incredibly, at Philadelphia, the most conservative center of the conservative East—was the Philadelphia Savings Fund Society Building, designed in 1929 by William Lescaze and George Howe. With its interplay of masses and the window ribbons that continue around the corner, it was, to some extent, Gropius' Bauhaus Building turned into a skyscraper. But it had many original features as well. Though no one would call it graceful, PSFS had character and interest. Even today it doesn't appear the least bit dated or self-consciously Modern.

But there was practically nothing publicly known about the architectural goings-on in Europe until Henry Russell Hitchcock reported

Philadelphia's PSFS still looks up-to-date

on them for *Architectural Record* in 1928. Professor James Marston Fitch of Columbia carefully checked the back issues of architectural magazines not long ago. The only reference to the Functionalist movement, he found, was to one of its planning conferences in Amsterdam in 1924. American architects, and the editors who served them, were, it seems, fully absorbed with the problem of applying the lessons of the École des Beaux-Arts to the growing pains of American cities. Despite Frank Lloyd Wright's sermon to the Daughters of the American Revolution, Europe's machine romanticism never really touched us here. Children of the machine age, we took the machine for granted. In a wide-open continent, there seemed not the slightest danger that mass production would pose a problem to a still wide-open culture. And when, at last, the virtues of a machine-age architecture were touted, it was not by engineers or a Henry Ford, but by a young man who was then a student of classic philology at Harvard.

The student, Philip Johnson, son of a well-to-do lawyer at Cleveland, had by chance come across that celebrated Hitchcock article. Shortly thereafter he journeyed to Germany to see the new architecture for himself and met Mies at the Bauhaus. With Hitchcock he collaborated later on the book that defined and labeled the International Style. With Mies, whom he helped bring to this country, he collaborated on its greatest landmark, the Seagram Building. That was not, however, until Johnson had gone back to Harvard in his forties for a degree in architecture, which turned the historian into practitioner. He was probably the only architecture student ever to build, rather than draw, his master's thesis. The resulting house in Cambridge was, for a while, almost as much of a conversation piece as his later glass house at New Canaan. Though he studied mainly with Marcel Breuer, Johnson was, in those days, more Miesian than Mies.

Philip Johnson has the means to be financially independent and the gumption to be intellectually independent. He moves in what some call "society," which is his brevet to move influential people along with the changing seasons of advanced taste. But he prefers to circle high above the smart set, rather like a falcon above a bevy of mice, to shoot down only for prey. He thus descended upon Mrs. Phyllis Bronfman Lambert, the daughter of Seagram's president, for instance, to secure the commission for the Seagram Building for Mies.

Johnson delights in his quick-on-the-draw erudition, and will flash you a sly, expectant smile to see if some outrageously shocking assertion has hit home. It inevitably has. As long on learned sophistication as he is quick with his wit, his aim is devastating. Only politeness restrains his impatience with a world full of insufferable dullards and he usually keeps his tongue in cheek. But he is not cynical. You may wonder what he is doing in long, ponderous meetings on public housing and the social obligations of architecture, he, the hedonist who built himself an expensive miniature pavilion in a garden pond at New Canaan, a delicate marble whim that serves no purpose other than his enjoyment. What's wrong with enjoyment? Why shouldn't public housing tenants also enjoy the pleasure of good architecture?

When the Functionalist crusaders arrived in the late thirties, they did not make their impact immediately felt on the American cityscape. Gropius' and Marcel Breuer's first houses at the time were rather timid statements, obliging and bewildered, like most immigrants. Their impact, and it was revolutionary, was on the architecture schools: Gropius and Breuer at Harvard, Mies and Moholy-Nagy at Chicago. The war soon interfered with the actual construction of their lessons.

Then, almost suddenly, with the opening of the Lever House on

New York's Park Avenue in 1952, the International Style seemed firmly established on these shores. Rectangular steel frames clad in glass seemed the logical, indeed the only way to build America's skyscrapers, corporation palaces, huge tenement houses – such as those at Lake Meadows in Chicago – and shopping centers and motels, the new and specifically American building types that now came into being. Had you asked any European about it, he would surely have called the glass box the American style. Along with Coca-Cola, jazz, and automobile traffic jams we now began to export the architecture we had imported only recently and reluctantly.

"The twentieth century revolution in architecture has been accomplished," announced Henry R. Luce of *Time, Life,* and *Fortune,* "and it has been accomplished mainly in America – no matter how great our debt to European genius." He said it to the 1957 convention of the American Institute of Architects and in a tone of triumph and confidence, a mood widely shared in the Eisenhower years. America seemed on top of the world. We had our foes, to be sure. But there was as little room for tradition in the new structures as there was room for neutral nations in John Foster Dulles' foreign policy. The self-righteousness of the Functionalists suited the mood. Were we not as dynamic as the new skyscrapers? Was our modern faith not as universally valid as the universal spaces they contained? Could we not rise above the petty problems of the earth as their stilts rise above the ground? If the buildings seemed slick and often unsatisfying in their oversimplifications, why, so did that brief, complacent epoch that produced them. Air conditioning, after all, could make up for the discomfort caused by the sun blazing at all that glass. Acoustical tiles would subdue the din of the open work halls. There wasn't a problem in the world that couldn't, somehow, be licked if you only half tried. On these smooth glass skins, the reflection of reality, however grim or complex, seemed, somehow, always beautiful.

One of the most featured "form-givers," to use the word the Luce writers were most fond of, was Gordon Bunshaft, chief designer of Skidmore, Owings, and Merrill, a large, efficient, competent architectural firm that is in itself a symbol of the new, corporate architecture. Lever House was the *chef d'oeuvre* that instantly caused his name to be dropped, like so many olives, into the nation's cocktail glasses. With that on New York's Park Avenue, the International Style had surely arrived.

Though all glass, the Lever House – the office and advertisement of the Lever Brothers Company, a leading manufacturer of household

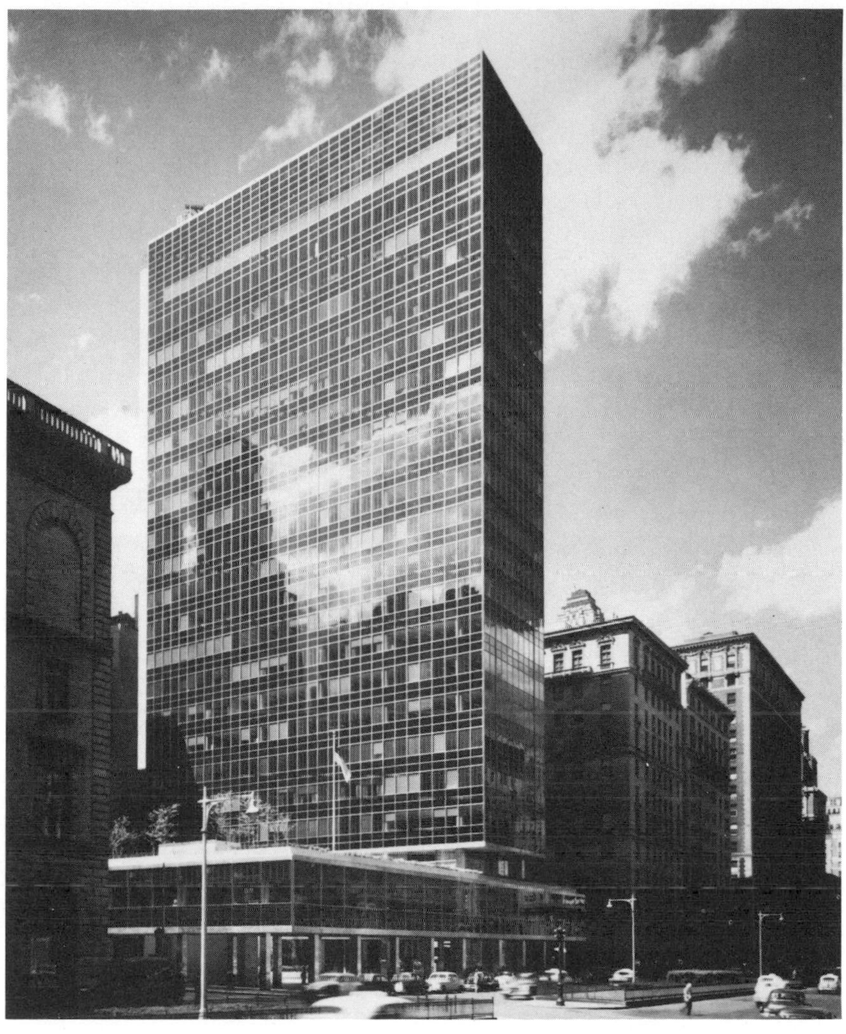

Lever House: The International Style has arrived

products—nevertheless resists polemic stones. I think it is a noble building. The nobility rests mainly in the composition of its two intersecting masses, balanced in their proportion but contrasting in their shapes. A two-story horizontal box, which contains an open court, occupies an entire block. Resting lightly on this box to one side is the twenty-one-story tower or slab that occupies only a quarter of the site. More noble yet, the whole building is lifted above the ground on columns. This opens the attractively paved and landscaped court to the people who walk on the street. This concept marked the beginning to a whole new approach to skyscraper design. For Bunshaft and his clients here discovered that concentrating the needed office space in one slim tower, leaving open space for air, sunshine, and the enjoyment of people, was, in the long run, more efficient and economical than covering the ground with setbacks and costly, as well as ugly, ziggurats. Among other projects, Bunshaft later repeated the feat, if anything even more impressively, with the Chase Manhattan Bank near Wall Street.

Lever House, however, is notable for another important reason. It amalgamates much of the best that the Functionalist crusade had to offer: Here was Gropius' dramatic, yet rational, interlocking of masses, Mies' dream of an utterly simple glass shaft, and Corbu's pilotis, as well as, on Lever's two-story box, the roof garden that returns the open space to people which the building covers.

Thus, competently and dramatically forged into one to meet American needs, the main tenets of the new architecture seemed to emerge as a home-made American style. It *looked* as technological as a jet plane.

In reality, however, it wasn't. Not really.

10. Wooed but Not Wed

Buckminster Fuller, the true technocrat and Functionalist, charged harshly, but not without justification, that "the 'International Style' brought to America by the Bauhaus innovators, demonstrated fashion-inoculation without necessity of knowledge of the scientific fundamentals of structural mechanics and chemistry."

"The International Style 'simplification' then," Fuller went on, "was but superficial. It peeled off yesterday's exterior embellishment and put on instead formalized novelties of quasi-simplicity, permitted by the same hidden structural elements of modern alloys that had permitted the discarded Beaux Arts garmentation. It was still a European garmentation. The new International Stylist hung 'stark motif walls' of vast super-meticulous brick assemblage, which had no tensile cohesiveness within its own bonds, but was, in fact, locked within hidden steel frames supported by steel *without visible means of support*. In many such illusory ways did the International Style gain dramatic sensory impingement on society as does a trick man gain the attention of children. . . .

". . . the Bauhaus and International Style used standard plumbing fixtures and only ventured so far as to persuade manufacturers to modify the surface of the valve handles and spigots, and the color, size, and arrangements of the tiles. The International Bauhaus never went back of the wall-surface to look at the plumbing . . . they never inquired into the overall problem of sanitary fittings themselves. . . . In short they only looked at problems of modifications of the surface of end-products, which end-products were inherently sub-functions of a technically obsolete world."

What Fuller seemed to be saying was in essence what the Functionalists said first. It is still true. We must harness science and technology not only for "weaponry," but also for "livingry," as he puts it, not only to escape to the moon but also to build ourselves a decent place to live down here. Modern architecture, however, fell in love with science in a most unscientific manner. In the courtship of art and technology the maiden, technology, is still rather elusive. Artists all, the early Moderns kept wooing and wooing. But they never really got to bed with the lass. They found themselves forced to indulge in self-gratification.

Nor did Lever House meet the lofty social goals the Functionalists had set themselves. And simple Seagram turned out one of the most expensive buildings in the world, topped in square-foot expense only by the overadorned Sam Rayburn Building.

Both, of course, are custom-built. The claim that each new commission forces the architect to reinvent the wheel overstates the case a little, but it is not much of an exaggeration. Much as the designers of the Rayburn Building had every stone—seven million pounds of marble!—cut to measure like the ancient Egyptians, so does Mies order a new type of steel I-beam for practically every one of his buildings.

Lesser architects order theirs from Sweet's Catalogue, a wondrous document of ten volumes, weighing a total of at least a hundred pounds. It is issued every year and contains the manufacturers' catalogues of thousands upon thousands of building products from steel beams to door knobs and what have you. So rather than invent the wheel, the architect assembles it spoke for spoke from Sweet's. But only architects doing over a quarter-million-dollar business a year receive it. The small fry, presumably, go to the lumberyard.

An architect I know was recently in need of a rather special door for remodeling a house. After three days of studying Sweet's, he found twenty-seven manufacturers, nine of whom offered door assemblies that promised to fit. He managed to get four of them sufficiently interested in his problem to send detailed literature so he could see if the door could be adapted to his design. In the end only one was suitable, but the manufacturer wouldn't bother to supply it because it was too small a job. My man ended up with a carpenter. And the Department of

Housing and Urban Development, understandably, finds rehabilitation of deteriorated buildings a very expensive proposition.

Some components are, of course, standardized. But they are standardized by the manufacturers' association in a given line, such as plumbing fixtures, and there are 120 such associations. The bathroom-tile people don't even talk to the bathroom-fixture people and the design of standard items are, on the whole, far less attractive and practical than what European firms now offer. Architects who desire an outstanding job often design even their own lavatories. Since the manufacturer must make them in quantity to recover his cost of such special designs, he puts them on the market and Sweet's gets still bigger. Nor is there as yet a satisfactory system to test new building components such as doors, windows, building stones, and so on. Tests are conducted, of course, but there is as yet no uniform system for the recording, filing, and dissemination of data and specifications. Specifications are issued by a multitude of large clients and agencies, including the Commerce Department, the Army Engineers, the Government Services Administration, the Air Force and others, but they are all somewhat different. There is an industry-sponsored Building Research Institute but, dependent on voluntary support, it has scant funds and no teeth. Whenever anything new is proposed, manufacturers and building trade unions team up to resist it. In Pittsburgh, for instance, double the needed amount of vent stacks are required in apartment buildings. There are too many politically vocal cast-iron foundries around to repeal this building code requirement.

We've made some technical advances, of course. But if you inquire about fundamental ones, architects are apt to cite curtain-wall construction, for instance. It dates back to 1883 and William Le Baron Jenny—thirty years before the Model-T Ford rolled off the assembly line. Or they'll tell you about new prefabricated concrete slabs which now replace many glass or metal curtain wall panels. They are, however, specially designed for every building, while some panels were not.

Each new president of the American Institute of Architects keeps stressing the need of architects to team up with building component manufacturers to improve their products so they could be more generally used. But it hasn't happened yet.

The fact is that Modern or not, machine age or not, architecture has long ago lapsed back to what it has always been. And that was never a social art for Gropius, Mies, and Le Corbusier "to return to." The Bauhaus and CIAM only changed our *expectations* of architecture and, for a while, its intent. But they did not change the concept of architectural practice.

It therefore sounded curiously hollow when the leaders of AIA only recently echoed the brave, half-forgotten Bauhaus and CIAM manifestoes. "The architectural profession should assume responsibility for nothing less than the total man-made environment including the use of land, water, and air, an environment in harmony with the aspirations of man," announced Philip Will, Jr., then AIA's president. His constituents applauded and voted to increase their dues, mainly to combat what architects call "package dealers," that is, firms which will not only design but also construct and furnish buildings—not all of them bad. But AIA, though it tries rather feebly, has accomplished little in the areas of setting up modular standards for building components, in building research, cooperation with building product manufacturers,

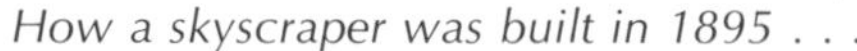

How a skyscraper was built in 1895 . . .

contractors, and homebuilders, let alone in providing low-income housing. Nor did Philip Will's statement serve to increase his profession's social awareness. "Responsibility for the total man-made environment" or not, the practice of architecture continues as usual.

This practice has historically never concerned itself much with the place to live, certainly not the places of common people. It has built temples and palaces of all kinds, and some of them are rightly called "frozen music." They are what culture is built on. As to shelter, people before the machine age did quite nicely on their own. The house of ancient Greece, with its atrium, was surely a lovely and livable place. Although many Romans lived in miserable hovels that Nero could all too easily burn in a fit of urban renewal, the houses of Pompeii, as do those of all past ages, compare rather favorably with ours. We'd miss only the indoor plumbing. But plumbing or not, we admire and often

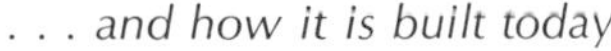

. . . and how it is built today

Architects still dream of temples and palaces

copy the folk architecture of the past with increasingly nostalgic enthusiasm.

Now things *have* gone wrong. Though it has brought us undreamed-of blessings and comforts, the machine is disrupting and polluting our environment. The alternative, as Corbu stated it, is indeed architecture or revolution, order or chaos. In Richard Neutra's phrase, the issue is indeed "survival through design." But when Functionalism was replaced by Expressionism and Kitsch, even the crusaders gave up the struggle, or, to put it more kindly, fought the battle only on the false premise of style.

Le Corbusier was the first. Always a painter and sculptor as well as an architect, he suddenly contented himself with creating architectural art. His Unité at Marseilles was his last search for social solutions. Impressed into the concrete at the foot of the building is his Modulor, the silhouette of a man with outstretched arms. It serves as a symbol of Corbu's belief, echoed by most architects, that all architecture must be built to the human scale, proportionate to the dimensions of the human body. The Modulor, though it is rather a mystical symbol, also represents a complex system of measurements on which Corbu proposed that all architectural dimensions and industrial, modular standards should be based. In his own work he would often cheat a little on these "absolutely precise" measurements if they did not yield him the proportions his artistic eye demanded.

Then, while Lever House was still being built, Corbu designed his chapel at Ronchamp, a search only for a new sculptural form. He rightly called it "completely uninhibited architecture . . . unexpected, amazing." The siren song instantly lured most architects of our time away from social concerns into the abstract realms of art.

About 1950 Gropius, too, quit worrrying about a rational building process and followed Le Corbusier. His Baghdad University has much of the exuberant sculpture, the "magnificent and correct play of shadows under the light" that Le Corbusier said his architecture stands for.

Only Mies has remained consistent. He kept himself chained to the mast of his youthful beliefs. He, who has been imitated most, now stands practically alone. He had never concerned himself much with the specific and petty problems or needs of man, but always with an almost spiritual quest for universal validity, for the key to the mystery of space, for the perfect proportion, for ultimate simplicity. It was ever less to achieve ever more. His Gallery of the Twentieth Century in Berlin is the perfecting of the Barcelona Pavilion.

An assistant once asked Mies what might be done to get less sun, heat, and glare behind one of his glass walls. "*You* find the solution," replied Mies, the purest of all artists of architecture. "I am only stating a principle."

III. CONTEST OF FORMS

1. Expressionism

Paul Rudolph's Art and Architecture Building at Yale, in all its monumental complexity and complex monumentality, did not, of course, spring full-blown from its designer's head, like Minerva from the brow of Jupiter. Expressionism in manifold ways—forbidding or appealing, lithe or massive, cubic or curvacious, exciting or dull—has co-existed with Modern architecture all along. It grew up with the Functionalists, somewhat like the pretty girl next door. They first played and then flirted with her—even Mies did, very early, with his Liebknecht-Luxemburg monument. She seduced a good many of them, and these affairs proved mostly inspiring and wholesome. In the end, however, it seems she moved in and took over, and, in the name of unrestrained passion in the quest of beauty, all but wrecked the house of morality and reason the Functionalist movement had tried to build. The offsprings of the movement—Rudolph, for instance, was a student of Gropius—are hers, although, as is so often the case in these delicate situations, neither they nor their fathers like to acknowledge it.

Not that Expressionism necessarily lacks respectability. The Functionalists talked as though it did, simply because whatever Expressionism is, it seemed to them in opposition to their social and aesthetic ideals of what a building ought to be and to do for people.

The fact is, of course, as Rudolf Arnheim stated in his brilliant article in the fall 1964 *Journal of Aesthetics and Art Criticism,* that Functionalism must also be *expressed.* The form-follows-function advocates point to nature and say: "Look, the shape and all the attributes and characteristics of a leaf or a turtle or a zebra have a definite reason for being the way they are. They have a function, and yet they are always beautiful. Ergo, if you make a building or a piece of furniture completely functional it is also automatically beautiful." By beauty they mean order, harmony, balance, proportion, unity, and parsimony. The analogy breaks down, says Arnheim, because, in the first place, nature is always in the state of growth and change, it is dynamic, while man-made objects are static. In the second place, natural shape is not wholly or even essentially accounted for by function. A maple leaf functions very much like an oak leaf and yet it is quite different looking. It may be true that once one is cut out to be a turtle, a turtle's shape and color reflect the most convenient way of leading a turtle's life. But the character or style of a turtle is not essentially accounted for by its functional shell. No one has quite explained just why a zebra's stripes are shaped and colored the way they are.

One answer is that the functional building or chair is meant to meet not just the comfort of the body but also that of the mind. Richard Neutra, in fact, does say that painting Lincoln's portrait on a billiard ball is entirely functional if the player believes that this will help him win the game. At this point the semantic discussion obviously becomes ridiculous. Taken literally, Functionalism, as a clear and logical definition of a style, cannot even cling to the assertion that it always clearly expresses how the thing works. We'd be unhappy with the looks of a television set if all its complex maze of wires and tubes were exposed. The designer hides these ugly, untidy innards. He "styles" the thing, as the current jargon has it, and somehow tries to make it fit man's visual sensibilities.

Louis Kahn, in his quest for new architectural form, emphasized, rather then hid, the ducts and exhausts of his Richards Medical Research Building at the University of Pennsylvania. He emphasized them so strongly and dramatically that they do far more than serve their technical function. No one would call the building Functionalist. In fact, some scientists working in it complain that it doesn't function very well at all. The dominant urge on Kahn's part was the expression, the dramatization of these towers that contain the ducts and other

Medieval defense inspires . . .

. . . 20th century novelty

mechanical services – "service spaces," Kahn calls them. The mechanical function of the stacks, which recall the strange beauty of the clustered medieval towers at San Giminiano in Italy, serves only as a rationalization for this expressionist urge. He also sees beauty as order, harmony, balance, proportion, unity, and parsimony – as something that can do without ornamental icing. The difference is that Functionalists, like Mies, conceive of o., h., b., p., u., and p. as subordinated to classic clarity and simplicity. What makes the Expressionists expressionistic is that they want to present o., h., b., p., u., and p. in terms of baroque, dynamic opposition and energy.

Both concepts claim superior morality. The neoclassicists believe they have found Truth. Mies likes to quote Thomas Aquinas and his definition of truth as *adequatio intellectus et rei,* "truth is the equation of thought and thing." (Aquinas, a philosopher friend tells me, goes on to say "for a house is said to be true that expresses the likeness of the form in the architect's mind." This means, of course, that no one else is really qualified to evaluate the "truth" of the house, because how can we share the architect's intellectual perception except insofar as he reveals it?)

The Expressionists are moved by sentiment, by human feeling, and seek to evoke this emotion, this experience in the beholder.

Art and architecture historians are forever struggling to sort all this out. Some of the leading ones in this country met in May 1962 at Columbia University to exchange learned views on the matter in a long day's symposium. It proved a most helpful discussion, but, as in many other such explorations, it seemed obvious that we are still much too close to the architectural creation of our time, much too involved in the currents and cross-currents of the creative process and the polemics they spark, to be able to classify what goes on as neatly as we can classify the architecture of past styles. "Perhaps," said Professor Henry-Russel Hitchcock of Smith College at the end of the lengthy transcript, "we can conclude by saying there is no formal conclusion."

A look at the sources helps, however, if for no other reason than to reinforce the definition of architectural Expressionism as non-Functionalist. Is Expressionism, asked Adolf K. Paczek of Columbia at the same conference, taking us back quite a way from Kahn and Rudolph, "simply the son or daughter of German Romanticism in music and art? If so, who was the father? The philosophy of Hegel, Schelling, et al.? Indeed, what are its literary sources? They patently go back a long way – not only to Romantics like [the German poet] Novalis, but also to the *Sturm und Drang*, the expressionistic genius of a Georg Büchner [the dramatist] and it is not mere coincidence that Alban Berg chose Büchner's *Woyzeck* as a libretto, just at the time of the beginning of the new Expressionism with which we are concerned today. What then is Expressionism? Can it be defined as the expression of inner experience as different from outer, visual experience? Or the expression of form (i.e., the visual) as different from structure? And can inner experience be equated with emotion—which would bring us right back to Romanticism where emotion prevails over the structure or imposes its own structure, not rooted in function? That in turn leads us to music, particularly to Wagner, and from there to Schumann and possibly to the Beethoven of the late quartets. Admittedly, this is a far cry from [the early modern architect] Bruno Taut, but after all, architecture has its roots in culture as a whole—whether consciously or unconsciously."

"Could one," asked Hitchcock a little later in the discussion, "subsume such things as Fauvism under Expressionism?"

Robert Rosenblum of Princeton thought this would lead to confusion. "It is better to narrow the definition. It is a very national problem, particularly German."

A broader definition, it was more or less agreed, would include a great many words such as romanticism, fantastic, visionary, and utopian architecture, symbolism, sensualism—in short, a whole collection of highly individual responses. In broad, general terms, Expressionist architecture also evolved out of the Art Nouveau style—the style of Van Gogh and Edvard Munch, of Tiffany, of limpid, sensuous, twining, and twisting plant ornaments which, in Art Nouveau architecture, were not merely applied to the surface, but took over the entire structure so that structure and ornament became one.

A summit of this strange "new art," though a highly individualistic one, is Antoni Gaudí's Sagrada Familia church in Barcelona. Begun in 1883 and still unfinished, it seems pure architectural fantasy, a sculpture of whim and emotion. Although somewhat Gothic in feeling, it is a new, a sensuous, flowing, swelling, and contracting Gothic, all seemingly formed of soft clay. The curved spires of this church recall stalagmites building upward towards heaven, covered with polychrome mosaics and crowned with bizarre shapes. The portals are overflowing with a gooey, intricate brew of plants and animals. The gables are covered with what looks like melting snow but is carved of stone. It might all have been built on some surrealist beach and of giant driftwood, held together by dripping wet sand and encrusted with bits of sparkling, polychrome crockery. It took an incredible persistence of

Art Nouveau—
limpid and sensuous

fantasy and genius of engineering to build this unique monument. Gaudí's persistence and genius was too far removed from the reality of building to have much influence on the course of architecture.

But there are strong bridges from the mystic spirit of yesterday's Art Nouveau forward to today's architecture of Kahn and Rudolph. These bridges were Frank Lloyd Wright and Eric Mendelsohn and, after Ronchamp, Le Corbusier.

Wright's late work—his vision of a Mile High Skyscraper, his sketches for a Grand Opera and Civic Auditorium in Baghdad, and his posthumously completed Civic Center for Marin County, California, for instance—come close to Gaudí's fantasies. Most of his long life, however, he kept down to earth. He had no use for classic intellectualism, whether of Hellenic Greeks or of Thomas Aquinas, but sought what he called "organic architecture" which either by form, or by use of nature's materials, or both, was somehow to unite man with his land. As Sybil Moholy-Nagy has pointed out, he was the first architect in history who was required to take on a whole continent alone. Indeed, I would say, this is what he conceived as his mission. Sullivan, whom Wright liked to call half mockingly his *lieber Meister,* or dear master, had dreamed of an indigenous American architecture. Wright believed he could bring it off. His Prairie and Usonian houses, in particular, were to be an architecture growing out of the American soil that would turn all of us European immigrants into true Americans. "We have

A Gaudi-esque fantasy kept down to earth

Frank Lloyd Wright in 1904 and . . .

. . . Paul Rudolph in 1963

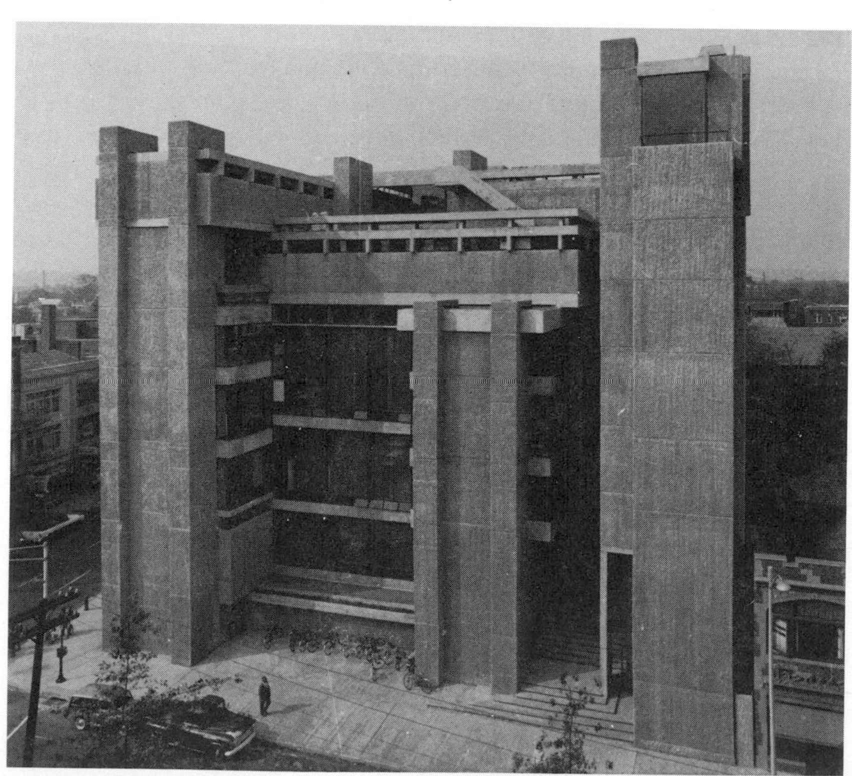

neglected our ground as the basis for our culture and tried to get culture from the pavements and factories of the world," he declared. Since native Indian tepees and pueblos had little to offer him, he sought his inspiration far from the sources of Western civilization, in Bronze Age Crete, in Japan, and in Pre-Columbian America.

Wright's early work, as we saw, had a profound influence on the Moderns in Europe. It had this influence because Europeans were, at the time, romantically searching for new expressions, while Americans, in their pragmatic ways, were quite satisfied with what they had. The Europeans taught us to recognize and, lately, even idolize this prophet in America's midst, though when you come right down to it, America has never followed him much further than a few dozen romantic houses and that at once barbarous and sophisticated sculpture on Fifth Avenue—the Guggenheim Museum. Wright failed to establish an American architecture, let alone an American visual culture, because, for once, he was even more didactic about architecture than the Moderns. You may not dare leave a broom in a Miesian living room. In a Wright house you can't even put flowers anywhere but in the very vase he has inflexibly built in. The master builder has determined your every step in a totally planned environment. He has provided all your personal expression for you and more. None of your personal pictures on the wall or roses by the door. The result is almost invariably an impressive and harmonious work of art. In a house for Americans, of all people, it is also a fantastic misjudgment of their character. We like our freedom to be spontaneously messy.

Nor are we, as a people, prepared to abandon the Western humanistic traditions that, beginning with Jefferson, are firmly implanted in the American mind. Wright was chagrined no end that his own government never invited him to design a public building in Washington. Much as he fumed against John Russell Pope's Jefferson Memorial—indeed a rather sugary confection—as "a fashionable effigy of reaction," a "betrayal of our substance," and a "confession of impotence" while "indigenous creative art has gone begging for its life," Americans love it. It is a symbol of the American identity, Japanese cherry blossoms and all, affirmed and reaffirmed by millions of pilgrims and the enthusiastic picture postcards they send home. Nor is it any less American because it was inspired by an ancient pavilion in Rome than anything that might have been inspired by a Pre-Columbian temple in equally distant Mexico. Our officials, by sticking to Washington's classic tradition, showed a better grasp of America's popular sentiment than did Wright by denouncing it. Official Washington, the

Rayburn Building to the contrary notwithstanding, is a trifle less reactionary in its architecture today. But it will still not tolerate indigenous, creative, Expressionist art in its classic environs.

In 1962 a national competition for a memorial to Franklin D. Roosevelt, judged by some of the country's most distinguished designers, was won by Norman Hoberman, David Beer, and Joseph Wasserman, a team of young sculptors and architects gathered in the firm of Pederson and Tilney. It was an abstract composition of simple, yet infinitely varied sculptural shapes—eight soaring tablets that were to be inscribed with FDR's most memorable words. It might have become, I believe, one of the great monuments of our time. Official conniving killed it and with it the confidence that official competitions might help us seek out fresh, young talent. The commission was later given to Marcel Breuer who came up with a similar concept which the Fine Arts Commission again rejected.

Wright, however, floundered not only on the country's classic tradition, but also because in the course of his life America became urban. Frank Lloyd Wright hated the city. He preached against it and sought to destroy it. The Guggenheim pillbox, visually busting an entire eye-span of Fifth Avenue, is one symbol of this. His Broadacre City, his city of the future, which would spread everyone out over the countryside on one-acre lots, was to be "everywhere and nowhere," the very antithesis to a sense of place.

When, in the thirties, Europe's Functionalist crusaders brought their architecture to this country, they were fully willing to acknowledge their debt to Frank Lloyd Wright. Yet he felt himself threatened as if by a foreign invasion. In what amounts to spite, he abandoned his earthy principles. His late projects, as Hitchcock put it, "are often megalomaniac, sort of his answer, just to show off what *he* could do!" It was sadly ironic. Lately, however, Wright's romantic Expressionism is again gaining the upper hand. Both Rudolph's Art and Architecture Building and Kahn's Richardson laboratory echo Wright's Larkin Soap Company Building in Buffalo of 1904.

But the smile of the alluring girl next door beckoned even more seductively in the form of tiny sketches of grand visions. They were drawn by Eric Mendelsohn, for the most part while he was on guard duty in the trenches of World War I.

Born in 1887 in East Prussia, the son of a businessman and a very musical mother, Mendelsohn received much of his architectural training in Munich before the First World War. Munich in those days was a center of German Expressionism. Mendelsohn spent much time in the artist cafés and studios. He saw a good deal of Kandinsky, Franz Marc, August Macke, and Alexei von Jawlensky—a group which called itself the *Blaue Reiter*, or Blue Rider. This group was devoted, as Marc put it, to perceiving the "inner mystical construction" of the world or, in Macke's definition, the "expression of mysterious forces." These erupted in Mendelsohn's sketches.

After the war, Mendelsohn joined the Novembergruppe and remained loosely connected with the Modern pioneers in Berlin, though he never thought that he quite belonged in the Functionalist camp. Yet he also denied to the last that he was an Expressionist. This term was until about the time he died in San Francisco in 1953 as dirty a word as "International Style" is now.

Mendelsohn's sketches show a variety of imaginary buildings of a kind that no one had ever seen before. He first presented them to the world in 1919 in Paul Cassirer's art gallery in Berlin as "Architecture in Steel and Concrete." Some were entitled "factories," "railway terminals," or "film studios." Once or twice they were labeled "residence." Most of them were just "imaginary" buildings. A few depicted what architecture has often been called—"frozen music." One soaring structure of swirling circles, for example, was entitled "Toccata in D Major." Another, a broken, angular composition, "Bach, Violin Concerto"; a third, a round tower consisting of pleats, was called "Brahms, Cello Sonata."

There was only one other architect who had conceived something remotely like it, the Italian Antonio Sant'Elia. He was born in Como in 1888 and killed in the First World War, twenty-seven years later. As so many young intellectuals in Europe at the time, Sant'Elia was gripped by his idealized notions about America's skyscrapers, by dreams of unlimited technological opportunity. He envisioned the *Cittá Nuova,* the new city of the future, freed of tradition and convention, built only by the enthusiastic spirit of a new generation. It was, as we behold it in his legacy of hundreds of drawings, a city of soaring skyscrapers of complex shapes, their elevators a prominent exterior fixture, pierced by roads and ramps at various levels, a city of enormous railway stations, outlandish factories, and gigantic monuments of sheer fantasy.

Sant'Elia figures prominently in the annals of visionary architecture which, somehow, always foreshadowed the changing shape of our place to live before the functional need for the shape was felt or the technique was at hand to realize it. It fell to Eric Mendelsohn to offer his visions in the architectural market, as it were, though Mendelsohn

No longer a dream

himself realized only one of his fantasies — the Einstein Tower in Potsdam. That was in 1919. It, too, is a monument, really, serving as a laboratory and topped with an observatory. The tower was built by private funds to prove that the sun's spectral lines deviate from those of a terrestrial source of light, a part of Einstein's Theory of Relativity. It is still standing today, a work of flowing, sinuous sculpture, and it stands as the first, prophetic antithesis to the bare and square Functionalist architecture that was just then emerging. The tower, to be sure, shows some semblance to similarly plastic forms in Gaudí's work, but it is Modern in feeling. Mendelsohn saw it as a monument of "the mystique around Einstein's universe," and no such manifestation of architectural mystique was to be repeated until Ronchamp, thirty-four years later.

After this one youthful, sculptural fling, Mendelsohn accommodated himself to the prevailing rationalism. Mendelsohn's own luxurious house of 1929, Am Rupenhorn, in Wannsee, a Berlin suburb, for instance, was bare and square Functionalism through and through. Here, too, was the much touted technology: A glass wall to the terrace disappeared into the ground at the touch of a button! That was about as far as architectural technology had come.

With this house and, more significantly for a skeptical public, with his Columbus office building on Berlin's busy Potsdamer Platz, Mendelsohn managed, somehow, to take the harsh, self-consciously avant-garde edge off Functionalism. His marvelous department stores for the

Schocken chain in various German cities, furthermore, are an agreeable synthesis between straightforward Functionalist simplicity and evocative Expressionist drama. He accomplished this by adding a new dimension to early Modern architecture—an interplay of contrast between swirling curves and cubic forms. These department stores are architectural showmanship at its best, not because they are stunts, but because they are dynamic structures of appealing vitality. Mendelsohn was popular and successful and had one of the largest architectural offices in Europe.

When Hitler came to power, Mendelsohn went to Israel where the flamboyance of his buildings was restrained by the mandatory use of stone, the harsh, somber landscape and the harsh, bright sun. He arrived in the United States in 1941, a year of war, not of building. Not the most affable of men, Mendelsohn found it almost easier to make enemies than to make friends. Though he loved this country, particularly the colorful San Francisco Bay area where he ultimately settled, he bitterly suffered the fate of the immigrant. But in the end he got his

The first, prophetic antithesis to Functionalism

Mendelsohn vision . . .

. . . realized by Eero Saarinen at Dulles Airport

chance. Commissions to build four synagogues and Jewish community centers in this country proved outlets for his creative élan. These temples in Grand Rapids, St. Paul, Cleveland, and St. Louis, designed between 1946 and 1950, are rich and inventive in form. Though always restrained by good taste as well as tight budgets, they have the emotive power that Nikolaus Pevsner said a religious building ought to have: to "convert visitors into worshippers." Yet they no longer startle and excite as a visit to, say, Frank Lloyd Wright's almost bizarre Beth Sholom Synagogue at Elkins Park, Pennsylvania, does. Mendelsohn's name simply did not have the aura of the prima donna in this country which Wright had laboriously cultivated, so that by 1959, the time of the Elkins synagogue, an eccentric performance was positively expected of him. Mendelsohn, nevertheless, ventured free and relatively uninhibited architectural forms at a time when Christian congregations still saw the only gateway to heaven in a pseudo-Gothic arch and Jews clung timidly to "syna-gothic" adaptations of Romanesque and Byzantine domes. What persuaded Mendelsohn's clients to his new forms and often lavish use of Modern art was the way he ingeniously solved their practical problems. He knew how to use movable walls to expand an

Another Mendelsohn vision . . .

. . . realized by Walter Netsch at the Air Force Academy

intimate sanctuary for the large High Holiday crowd. And he knew how to integrate social halls and school rooms in a building complex that is, overall, always proudly and devoutly religious in character. His most promising synagogue designs, however—for Beth-El in Baltimore and Emanu-El in Dallas—were never built.

But Mendelsohn's wartime visions did rise in steel and concrete—though not built by him. He was still alive when Frank Lloyd Wright's Johnson Wax Buildings at Racine of 1940 and 1950, Luigi Nervi's Turin Exhibition Hall of 1948, and Eduardo Torroja's Madrid Hippodrome of 1949 appeared. The resemblance of Walter Netsch's Air Academy Chapel at Denver of 1959 and Eero Saarinen's Dulles Air Terminal near Washington, D.C., completed in 1962, to Mendelsohn sketches of 1917 is almost eerie. By then the new engineering of tension had made his "elastic" structures possible. At the time he sketched them, he had no idea how they might stand up.

2. Shells

Take a piece of paper and set it on edge. It will fall down, of course, and support nothing, not even itself. Curve this same piece of paper and hold it, somehow, along its edges, and it will not only stand up but will also easily support a pencil. A piece of flimsy notepaper, folded into creases, will carry the fairly heavy scissors on my desk. If you conceive of the bent or folded paper as a building, you find that enclosure and support are one. Nature is full of such self-supporting, protective enclosures, some of incredible strength, considering the actual frailty of their material: Consider eggs, sea-shells, and snails. Try crushing an egg with just the pressure of your hand! Its rigidity does not depend on the firmness or thickness of the shell but on its ingeniously curved shape.

It seems that two German engineers, Walter Bauersfeld and Franz Dischinger, were the first to apply shell construction to architecture. I doubt that they responded to some Hegelian historic necessity to span large spaces for an emerging mass society, as some writers theorize. Nor were all the resulting forms the product of this technological development. The forms, as we have seen, were dreamed of before, and some free forms are even now constructed—or you might say faked—by different means. Mendelsohn, for instance, had intended to cast his plastic Einstein Tower in concrete. But materials for formwork were hard to come by right after the First World War, and he was forced to make it a conventional masonry structure heavily and sculpturally plastered over. Le Corbusier didn't even consider the new technique for Ronchamp's flowing curves and swerving nun's coif roof. The chapel is laboriously built of old-fashioned masonry. (At the Philips Pavilion for the international fair at Brussels in 1959, to be sure, he tried his hand at a thin shell structure. But the structural concept was that of engineer J. Xenaxis. Corbu never considered it an important part of his *oeuvre*.)

About 1922, in contravention of local building codes, Bauersfeld and Dischinger constructed a planetarium for the Zeiss optical works in Jena, Germany. The dome, with a diameter of 131 feet, is a reinforced concrete shell that is only just over two inches thick. The principle soon assumed a variety of shapes. The French engineer Eugène Freyssinet, three or four years later, built market halls at Rheims in the shape of a barrel vault. The Italian G. Baroni, in 1934, built an iron factory at Milan in the shape of a hyperbolic paraboloid, a sort of saddleback shape. In 1938 Baroni built a warehouse at Ferrara that resembles an upturned umbrella. Luigi Nervi's great assembly hall at the UNESCO building at Paris stands up on very thin concrete walls on the same principle as folded paper.

All of this was largely inspired by the superb reinforced concrete bridges which Robert Maillart, a Swiss architect who died in 1940 at the age of sixty-eight, poured, as it were, across some forty deep valleys and ravines in his country. As early as 1901, he discarded the old

U. S. highway engineers still haven't caught up

concept of separating post and beam and integrated the bridge itself and its supporting vault into one graceful, delicately balanced span. I wish the highway engineers in this country, with their mostly clumsy, ponderous bridges and elevated freeways, would try to catch up with Maillart's great art.

Johann August Roebling's invention of spinning cables of large diameter and fastening them to resist high tensile forces, dramatically demonstrated by his Brooklyn Bridge of 1857–1883, also had decisive influence on the architecture of tension. Eero Saarinen's Kresge Auditorium at Cambridge, Massachusetts, his hockey rink at Yale, and that marvelous, slung roof of the Dulles Airport Terminal are descendants of Roebling's engineering genius. So is Kenzo Tauge's Olympic Swimming Pool in Tokyo of 1964.

Buckminster Fuller's Dymaxion dome derives from a structural system Alexander Graham Bell developed to build large kites. He made tetrahedra of metal rods or tubes which, he discovered, would also serve ideally for prefabricated, mass-produced buildings. Fuller's dome skeletons remain monotonously shaped domes, a form which has so far proven of limited practical and aesthetic utility in architecture. As yet, at any rate, the most impressive advances in the new architecture of tension have been made in concrete and by the great masters of this material, Luigi Nervi, Eduardo Torroja, and Felix Candela. Concrete—a mixture of cement, water, and either sand or gravel aggregate—reinforced with steel bars or wire, on the other hand, is incredibly adaptable to just about any shape you want to give it. Concrete endures enormous compressive stresses, and the steel inside absorbs those of tension. Reinforced concrete pieces can either be precast in a factory or poured, more or less all in one piece, on the building site. Nervi perfected a method he calls "ferro-concrete." He sprays cement mortar on wire mesh which gives him amazingly thin shells of nearly indestructible strength.

"It was simple. . . the obvious solution. . . the logical thing to do," Nervi told architecture critic Ada Louise Huxtable when she interviewed him about his feats of spanning huge spaces with little more than mortared sand and structural logic. Simple or not, shell construction is also an important technological innovation, the only one, really, since the Gothic cathedrals, that applies science not just to the method but to the concept of building.

"Well building," said Sir Henry Wotton about 1600, paraphrasing the Roman Vitruvius, "hath three conditions: commodity, firmness, and delight." Before the Jena planetarium "firmness" in building was based on piling horizontal upon vertical elements so that they best supported each other. Throughout history the structural arrangement was also an integral part of the "delight" of the building—the architectural style of each period. Thus the basic element of Egyptian architecture was the post and lintel, or beam, applied in almost oppressive massiveness on a superhuman scale. The Greeks' unsurpassed refinement of balance and proportion achieved a serene elegance by placing pitched roofs of wood framing over the columns. The Romans created a new architecture of monumental interiors out of the arch and concrete vaults. The arch not only gave architecture its name, but revolutionized it. A circular arrangement of arches resulted in the dome and the inspiring piety of such early medieval structures as Hagia Sophia at Constantinople. As the arch became pointed—an ingenious accomplishment of stone engineering—it was used in an intricate skeleton frame which made the Gothic cathedrals possible. Here were the real forerunners of modern construction. The Gothic builders eliminated the heavy masses of masonry used by the Romans and replaced them with the equilibrium of forces created by the interplay of thrust and counterthrust of slender ribs. This interplay is most clearly visible, perhaps, as you look up the magnificent central nave of Notre Dame in Paris.

The Renaissance combined and perfected all these structural systems and all the unending capabilities and varieties of brick, stone, and marble, in an often sublime, wholly artistic architecture. When iron and steel became available as building materials, and almost concurrently, concrete was rediscovered and reinforced, the architects of the nineteenth century hastened to hide them within structures which now only pretended to the style of earlier structural methods. Only the engineers with their bridges and train sheds and occasional architectural exhibition pieces like Paxton's Crystal Palace or Eiffel's famous tower dared expose the new materials and new construction methods to public view. It took a number of decades until unabashed steel and glass construction was accepted, even by architects, as a new aesthetic leading to a new style.

During the incubation of their architecture, Modern architects took no notice of the new development. Before the Second World War the engineer Nervi had built his Municipal Stadium of Florence with its daring cantilever roof over the grandstand and with elegant staircases that coil, unsupported, into the air. He had built a hangar in Rome, a huge, lacy, vaulted structure which not only enclosed more space with less material than anyone ever did before, but also, by so doing, created entirely new sculptural shapes that gracefully contracted and expanded and flowed into each other. Torroja, a Spanish engineer who worked mainly in Latin America, accomplished at the Zarauela race track near Madrid an even more incredible grandstand roof, an enormous, fluted cantilever, counterbalanced by vertical tie-rods behind the stanchions. You just don't believe it can jut out like that—"Look, Ma, no hands!"

Soon these auspicious buds broke out all over as strange, new flowers. Architects, however, plucked them only some time later, in the fifties, when Functionalism began to give way to Expressionism. Even then, they rarely made the new technique truly their own. Outstanding thin-shell construction remains the prerogative of engineers.

Though you can give these structures just about any shape you want to, their form, to be truly efficient, follows its own intricate laws that must be discovered and mastered with complex mathematic calculations. This kind of engineering is the product of merciless logic—a logic that may follow inspired intuition or laborious structural analysis, but logic just the same. The object of the game is always to achieve whatever it is you are after—the enclosure of space, a span across a river, a sheltering cantilever roof, a ramp, or a staircase—with the greatest possible economy of means. Economy of visible weight, effort,

Capricious forms built on merciless logic

and material will invariably reward you with grace and surprising beauty. "To build correctly," says Nervi, "is the essence of architecture."

Significantly, in order to build "correctly" all the way, from the concept to the last finished detail, he, Torroja, and other outstanding masters of concrete shell structures, are not just designers, engineers, and architects, but also find it necessary to be their own contractors and constructors as well. The all too often conflicting demands of design and actual construction are thus brought together in one mind. There are always different ways of doing things, and only the work's creator can really choose the right one. This is the only way, as Nervi put it, "to keep the mastery of his work," a mastery whose structural correctness can be checked by computers, but whose visual correctness, as Nervi admits, remains a matter of intuition and poetry.

It is not surprising that his new architecture is most highly developed in the Mediterranean countries and in Latin America rather than in Central Europe and North America. Mediterraneans seem to have a less formalistic, less inhibited, and more spontaneous, exuberant attitude towards art and architecture. Perhaps, in contrast to Protestant, iconoclastic puritanism, there is in the Catholic religion a greater appreciation of pomp and incense, of Mardi Gras and art in all its emotional and evocative manifestations as an expression of the joy of living. Such Baroque art is in a constant state of flamboyant evolution. Change is tradition. For the Latins, established tradition in the manner of building or other creative endeavors is therefore not piously insulted by the new as it is, or used to be, in our less fortunate clime.

More importantly, wood, steel, and glass are rare and expensive in the sunny countries while concrete, like masonry, is plentiful. North America's architecture has always been determined in large measure by the fact that the materials of post-and-beam construction are relatively cheap, while labor is expensive. In the southern countries these materials are expensive, while labor is readily available. Concrete with its often elaborate formwork requires much labor.

This accounts for Italy's quick interest in Nervi's large hangars, warehouses, and factory buildings which are so handsome that he was soon asked to build such representational structures as the Central Station in Naples (with architects Giuseppe Vaccaro and Mario Campanella), the UNESCO assembly hall in Paris (with Marcel Breuer and Bernard Zehrfuss), the Pirelli skyscraper in Milan (with Gio Ponti and a number of other architects), two handsome sports palaces for the 1960 Olympics in Rome (with Antonio Vitellozzi) and—his only

"To build correctly is the essence of architecture"

building in this country—the Port of New York Authority bus terminal at the end of the George Washington Bridge. Unlike the airy shells of Nervi's European work, the bus terminal is a vigorous, trussed structure which seems an extension of the bridge. The open concrete trusses visually complement the steel cross-bracing in the bridge towers. The huge building, opened in 1963, consists of three levels two blocks long and straddles a depressed twelve-lane expressway. It was built to provide for almost two thousand buses and fifty thousand passengers daily. The structure was entirely cast in place and its exposed concrete mixture determined by intensive research.

The impetus for free-form architecture in the United States, however, had come, not from the engineers directly, but via Latin America. In 1942, New York's Museum of Modern Art, America's great maker of taste and fashion, mounted an exciting show: "Brazil Builds." A decade before, MOMA had approvingly stamped Functionalism as "The International Style" and declared it in vogue. In 1938 it invited Gropius and Herbert Bayer to exhibit a retrospective of Bauhaus work up to the time when Gropius left it in 1928. Now it discovered and introduced another startling aspect of Modern architecture. Here, parading down MOMA's influential runway, were the early models of Oscar Niemeyer's first Modern Baroque creations, notably that unabashedly lyric Church of St. Francis of Assisi at Pampulha near Belo

Baroque in a modern language

Horizonte. At Pampulha thin concrete vaults were no longer the stuff of a poor man's steel-starved Quonset hut, but of a highly emotional architectural expression, recalling Mendelsohn's sketches. The shell roof undulated as two small arches to gain momentum in the tall nave which is echoed once more in yet another small arch. The curvaceous sweep framed a bold, polychrome mosaic and was dramatically balanced by a square, strongly tapered tower. There were similar works by Lucio Costa, Roberto Burle-Marx, Henrique E. Mindlin, and Alfonso Reidy. Though the show was Brazilian, all these new buildings had a strong French accent, the unmistakable accent of Le Corbusier. Corbu, in collaboration with Costa and others, had just completed the Ministry of Education Building in Rio, and with this one visit proved the greatest influence on Latin American architecture since the Baroque of the conquistadores. In a way, Le Corbusier was sneaked into the U.S. from south of the border. MOMA subsequently followed up with more extensive Latin American shows, displaying the ever more voluptuous shapes.

In 1953 the first two free-form structures appeared in the United States: Yamasaki's airport in St. Louis (with George Francis Hellmuth and Joseph William Leinweber) and Matthew Nowicki's Arena in Raleigh, North Carolina (with engineers William H. Deitrick and Fred Severud). Both use the new technique in a restrained, functional way to span great spaces. The airport, though poorly planned and in its concrete far less impressive than in arty publicity photographs, is nevertheless a handsome work of architecture. Another instance is the bowl-shaped Stadium for the University of Illinois by Harrison and Abramovitz. Jorn Utzon's National Opera House, in Sydney, Australia, is probably the most fantastic structure of them all. It was the result of an international competition and occupies a promontory in Sydney's harbor. It consists of a composition of bellowing, interlocking concrete shell vaults and, together with the stepped masonry podium that leads clear down into the water, creates a weird, abstract landscape. Little more than a freehand sketch, when first conceived by the Danish architect, it proved far more difficult, more costly, and time-consuming to build than had been anticipated. The original cost estimate was for $7\frac{1}{2}$ million dollars. To date it has cost 35 million dollars and Utzon resigned in the course of bitter quarrels with the authorities.

Eero Saarinen was probably the first North American to fully and deliberately exploit the great emotional drama of these structures. At M.I.T. he was still somewhat restrained. His Kresge Auditorium is a straightforward, smooth dome, supported at three points, the shape of one-eighth of an orange. The straight edges are plain glass wall. Since the building is relatively low and plain, it is also a bit insipid. There is nothing much that happens, or develops, or grows on you as the eye takes it in.

The Yale Hockey Rink, Saarinen said, "is a building in which we have not hesitated to dramatize and emphasize." Structurally it is one big central arch spanning the length of the rink and a hanging roof coming down from this arch in a slight curve. From above, the building looks somewhat like a big boat upside down. This impression is dramatically heightened by a sweeping jigamaree that juts out in front. Actually it holds a light fixture. It also focuses your attention and adds to the whole puzzling, but enchanting, interest of the building.

From there Saarinen went on to his swirling, restless Trans World Airlines Terminal at Kennedy Airport—the closest anyone has yet come to the fantasy architecture of Gaudí. It's pure sculpture, Expressionist sculpture. The exterior shape is somewhat reminiscent of a Mendelsohnian bird poised to fly off, though such symbolism, Saarinen said, was the last thing he ever thought about. The interior, somehow, sucks you in as into a huge conch—everything is fluid, circling, and curving. It is as playful a building as any outrageous toy of a Marie Antoinette. It is sheer architectural exhibitionism. And, to me—it's delightful.

Swirling restlessness

It is all the more delightful if you look at the TWA Terminal as the youthful fling of the man who designed the Dulles Air Terminal. Saarinen had to get really drunk on his Expressionism, taste it to the full in all its dangerous potentials before he could make the best of the innermost truth this heady wine can bring out in an artist. At Dulles he was man and architect enough to know where to stop.

Dulles Airport is twenty-seven miles west of Washington, D.C., superbly sited in Virginia's lovely rolling hills. The terminal building itself seems almost dainty when you see it first, a teasing, fleeting vision of a white Viking boat floating in the haze, guarded by expressively carved bollards.

After a turn in the road it appears again. Now the profile is crisp and bold. You discern the two rows of columns straining outward like slanted tent poles to tauten the canvaslike roof slung between them. That bollard has turned into an aloof, very matter-of-fact control tower.

As you come up to the building what seemed lithe becomes immensely powerful. The grace is still all there, but there is also something modern architecture has not given us often: a strong facade, articulating a forceful mass. This mass is formed by the colonnade of sixteen huge piers which break through the upswept roof and grip it from above. The terminal rests majestically on a stepped platform.

Each step contains a ramp and has canopied entrances to the building's two lower levels. This is one aspect of the terminal's superbly functional organization, the first to do considerably more for air travelers than impress them and give them sore feet and confusion. Another is the "mobile lounges." They are comfortable waiting rooms on wheels that take the passengers a mile out where the lounges' snouts connect directly with the airplane entrance. They save you the miles of walking on hard terrazzo floors you have to do in other airports. Besides, it's cheaper and more efficient to service the planes out there rather than let them taxi to the terminal.

The great structure was just taking shape when Saarinen, who died in 1961 at only fifty-one, last visited the site. He kept looking up, relates one of his associates. Then, after a long pause, he spoke for all of us when he exclaimed:

"Boy, this time we've really got something!"

It happens seldom enough. I can think of only two other tension-built structures, other than the works of Nervi, Candela, and Torroja, that appeal to me. One is Hugh Stubbins' "pregnant oyster," as they call it in Berlin, the festival hall America donated to that city. It is a handsome, rational, pleasantly accommodating building. Stubbins has given it a thoughtful refinement of detail that makes this a gift that does us proud. The other is, much like the TWA Terminal, sheer Expres-

Stubbins' "pregnant oyster"

Inside a "whale" . . .

. . . a glorious hallelujah

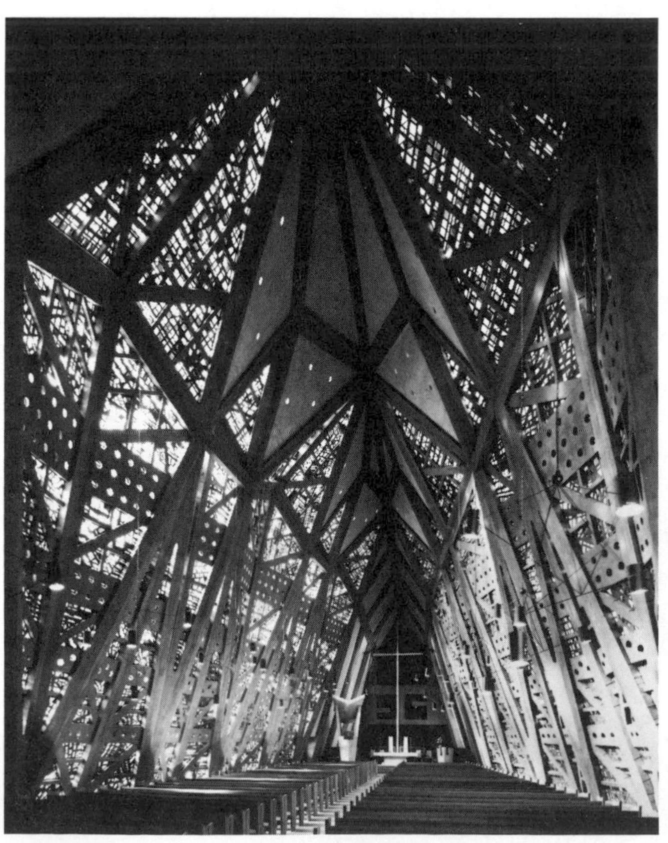

sionism, but of a somber, deeply religious kind that reminds me of Georges Rouault's paintings. It is Wallace Harrison's First Presbyterian Church in Stamford, Connecticut, the one that has been so often compared to a whale. Harrison here used reinforced concrete shell construction for a specific artistic effect. While his mind was occupied with this commission, he visited Sainte Chapelle in Paris, the exquisite Gothic chapel whose nave consists almost entirely of stained-glass windows. Resolved to do likewise in modern terms, he embedded chunks of colored glass, imported from Chartres, into the folded concrete shell. The colored light fills the sanctuary from floor to the very top of the arched ceiling, and you enter it as into a jewel. The entrance is emphasized through a low and dimly lit narthex that makes the nave seem all the brighter—a trick the Egyptians liked to use. The effect was impressive enough on the rainy day of our first visit to want us to come back to attend a service. That Sunday the sun was bright. The sounds of the choir became one with light and space. Harrison's nave, focused on the cross, became one glorious hallelujah. It was truly a religious experience.

That's about it. A few splendid utilitarian halls, and, besides Dulles, a few Expressionist statements. Perhaps that is all we can expect from the new engineering, though I wonder why it hasn't aroused the engineers themselves to the more daring, more exciting, more beautiful structures they are surely capable of. Fully sixty years after Maillart's first tension span across the Inn River at Zuoz, Switzerland, our engineers still built, in the nation's capital, a Theodore Roosevelt Bridge that not only fails to be graceful but is, in fact, disgracefully massive and ugly. You can defend a traditional Beaux Arts design so close to the Lincoln Memorial. But when all that Roman massiveness, like the tendrils of an octopus, branches and curves every which way to accommodate twentieth-century automobile traffic, you have no design at all but an aesthetic disaster.

I know of only one serious attempt in this country at this time to probe the potential of tension-supported thin-shell concrete for a place to live. That is Bertrand Goldberg's famous Marina City in Chicago. The round twin towers with their dramatic, curved balconies contain apartments on top and parking ramps below. They contrast well with the strong, horizontal line of an adjacent office building, also in raw concrete. The combination of apartments, business and a marina, ice skating rink, swimming pool, gym, theater and restaurants—Goldberg calls it "living over the store"—makes good use of expensive downtown land and creates a truly urban environment. Goldberg might have made it a little more inviting, however, by separating automobile and human access to his towers. As it is, you enter as through a garage. Marina City is, nevertheless, evidence that exciting architecture can also serve people and be popular.

Despite the frowns of federal public housing officials, Goldberg, with the passionate if somewhat mystic faith of an apostle, went on from there to build round, plastic concrete structures for a public housing project for the elderly on Chicago's State Street. Again it is a bravely handsome project. This time he paid more creative attention to the immediate surroundings. The round towers are part of a pleasing setting that includes a little park and a community center.

As yet the new building method has not resulted in substantially greater economies. But here is at least a promise, as exciting as Mendelsohn's visions, that the new forms might also have new social meaning.

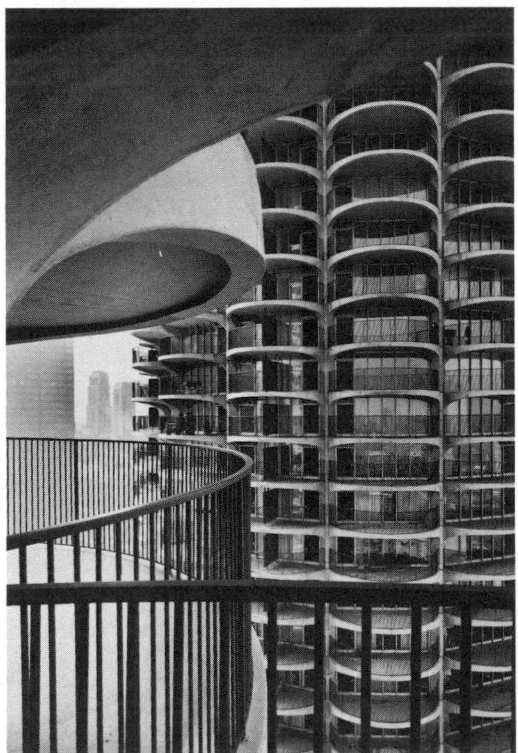

Thin shells to live in

3. Revolt from Reason

In Ronchamp an elderly villager put down his beer with finality. "*Ce n'est pas une église, c'est un monument,*" he declared. (It is not a church but a monument.) In Paris over Dubonnets and in New York over Martinis, where the concern was not so much with architecture of worship as with worship of architecture, the new chapel was instantly pronounced the greatest building of our time. Whether or not it is, it is certainly the most influential. It will probably remain a conversation piece as long as it stands.

Ronchamp is a village of some three thousand people in the Vosges Mountains that separate France from Germany, thirteen miles from Belfort. Its chapel, Notre Dame du Haut, crowns a hilltop that rewards the pilgrimage up a steep, winding path with a panoramic view over the valley of the Saône River. Pagans are said to have worshipped here long before the first Christian shrine was built, and no one knows quite when that was. There was a long series of chapels. A recent one was destroyed in the First World War and rebuilt only to be destroyed again by artillery in the Second World War. This time the Bishop of Besançon wanted to build something more than an ordinary chapel. He wanted an act of faith, of faith in our time, and sent to Paris for Le Corbusier.

That was in 1950. In the summer of 1955 the building was dedicated. It is quite small. There are pews inside for only about fifty people, with standing room for about two hundred. But its east facade, with a pulpit and altar sheltered by the cantilevered roof, is a backdrop for outdoor services for as many as twelve thousand pilgrims, now augmented all through the year by thousands of sightseers.

The visitor is treated to a capriccietto of shapes and all kinds of sculpture as unfamiliar as objects from another world. Before this such a thing had only been seen in modern art galleries, never in architecture. It leaves even Gaudí's vaguely Gothic eccentrics way behind. Mendelsohn's sketches always show rhythmic consonance; Le Corbusier's chapel relies on deliberate dissonance for its effect. If architecture is "frozen music," Mendelsohn's sketches were Wagner. Corbu's chapel is Hindemith.

The three major themes, as you approach up the path, are a white silolike tower, the convex white wall punched by arbitrarily placed and shaped window openings, and the massive toroid projection of the brown roof.

As you take in the building, these three elements dissolve into startling surprises. The silo tower turns into a half-shell, hiding two others. The brown roof disappears within the punctured facade. The walls swerve and slant backwards, curving in and out of what Le Corbusier calls the "ineffable space" within.

Ineffable it is. The building, with its frozen restlessness, adds up to an experience that cannot be quickly grasped, let alone explained. The play of soft and hard shadows on the whitewashed walls recall, to me at least, the lovable folk architecture on Mediterranean islands in their all-encompassing whiteness. But why attempt to associate or intrepret? "Abstract art which, rightly, nourishes so many passions in these days, is the *raison d'être* of Ronchamp," wrote Le Corbusier. He goes on to speak of "plastic equations, symphony, music, or numbers (but devoid of metaphysics)." No one can presume to argue with him about his abstract art work on behalf of anyone else. It is, like all modern art, an intensely personal statement that can evoke no other than intensely personal reactions. That, alone, if we look for its meaning to society, may be quite salutary at a time when our confused aesthetic sentiments, gauged by Gallup polls, are so often merely fed back to us everywhere in the form of collectivized, ingratiating mediocrity—on film, on television, in furniture stores, and in architecture.

If, like the elderly villager over his beer, you conceive of Ronchamp as a monument, architecture critic G. E. Kidder Smith may well be right to call it "the greatest building of our time." The line between architecture and monumental sculpture is hard to draw, particularly when a monumental sculpture serves as a shrine. The Parthenon was not meant as a shelter either. It was built to mark a sacred place.

Ronchamp, however, also marked an abrupt and radical departure in Modern architecture that has so far left us even more confused than we were before. Nor was it just the beginning of a new phase in Le Corbusier's work, like Picasso's change from his Blue Period to Cubism, say. It was, in the life work of one man, the very antithesis of what he had done before. Impatient and impassionate, Le Corbusier had felt misunderstood and rejected. His "machine for living" idea was ridiculed around the world. His winning design for the League of Nations was deviously tossed aside. He had inspired the United Nations headquarters building, but was driven from the U.N.'s architectural concilium under a cloud of scandal. So now he turned from what he had said was a new concept of what architecture is, namely a responsible social art for a new age, to what architecture had always been—the art of the individual monument.

"Voilà . . ." he wrote impetuously over the preface to his little book on Ronchamp. *Voilà*! Here it is! I have shown you.

Voilà!—an act of faith in our time

Much of Le Corbusier reminds you of Picasso

Ronchamp remains unique in Le Corbusier's *oeuvre* – though some architect, so help me, copied it almost literally for a drive-in bank in Miami. But its premise that architecture is abstract expressionism determined all of Le Corbusier's subsequent work and, indeed, much of all the architecture that followed it.

The little white shrine surely threw all notions that form follows function or structure into a cocked hat. Nervi's structural revolution has also created undreamed-of new forms. They were motivated, however, by the age-old desire of the master builder to span the largest possible space with the least possible means. Although artistic intuition is inevitably involved in their creations, that intuition is in a constant dialogue with technical and functional reason. Corbu's flamboyant new forms, on the other hand, were motivated by the probably equally age-old desire to exercise emotional power. In this respect it is somewhat akin to Picasso's *Guernica*. "A modern tool able to open up fresh roads in a mechanistic society!" he scribbled on the margin of one of his sketches for Ronchamp. He designed this tool not long after his friend, the architect José Luis Sert, the painter Fernand Léger, and the critic Sigfried Giedion had jointly issued a manifesto stating that "the people want the buildings that represent their social and community life to give more than functional fulfillment. They want their aspiration for monumentality, joy, pride, and excitement to be satisfied."

At the time he worked on Ronchamp Le Corbusier received the commission to design the plan and public buildings for Chandigarh, the new capital of Punjab on an empty plain at the foot of the Himalayas in India. A little later he designed the monastery Sainte Marie de la Tourette, near Lyons, for Benedictine monks. In 1961 he was at last invited to design a building in the United States, the Arts Center at Harvard.

All these buildings, to be sure, can be and are endlessly rationalized in terms of their function and service to the people who use them. A few practical innovations do, indeed, remain once you have peeled layer after onionskin layer of abstract, mystical gobbledegook from the explanations of Corbu's disciples. These innovations boil down to the original five points of a new architecture Corbu had proclaimed in the twenties: the stilts, the roof gardens, and all the rest. To these he added another, his *brise-soleil*, or sunbreaks, giant Venetian blinds, usually of concrete, on the outside of buildings.

In a rational way he had realized most of these ideas, back in 1936, in collaboration with Oscar Niemeyer, Lucio Costa, and a number of other young Brazilian architects in the Ministry of Education Building in Rio de Janeiro. It is a marvelous building, superbly right for its location in congested, downtown Rio, for Rio's climate, and for its specific purpose. It is still being copied, often for different locations and purposes which, even when it works, is somewhat like playing "Silent Night" for an Easter celebration.

Corbu's sculptural forms, so reminiscent of his painting, also had their antecedents in some of his previous work, mainly the delightful fantasy land of his roof garden at the Unité d'Habitation at Marseilles.

At Chandigarh, La Tourette, and Harvard he dramatized, and overdramatized all this, however. He really let go with uninhibited, primitive, savage power. Gone are the sensuous curves, the sunny, Mediter-

Corbu's roof garden fantasy

Uninhibited, savage power

ranean whitewash of Ronchamp. At La Tourette everything is at hard, right angles, rigid, and ruthlessly direct. You pass through the well-kept grounds of the old monastery, an undistinguished but not unpleasant building, to get to the new—and find an ancient ruin on a magnificent hillside all overgrown with weeds. The weeds even sprout on the roof and in the crevices of the brute concrete structure. They are not monastic neglect but Le Corbusier's intent.

At the entrance, when I visited this seemingly unfinished building recently, stood a young Negro monk. His handsome, intelligent features, his immaculate white robe, his exquisite, soft-spoken politeness seemed to me a personification of human culture. Everything about him seemed the distillation of thousands of years of man's accumulated knowledge, devotion, and art. We had, he informed me, arrived outside visiting hours. *"Je regrette profondement, monsieur,"* said this young monk, his ever so slight gesture of profound regret strangely at odds with the aggressive structure he guarded.

The chapel, however, was open. It is a long, narrow, tall, rectangular box appended to the side of the building. No light enters it. Only side altars in a low annex are illuminated by large, round holes in the ceiling. These project as conic and cylindrical shafts above the roof. Their insides are painted in brilliant primary colors which the light reflects.

You enter by a small side door. The knob slipped from my hand, and the door banged shut. This naked, concrete cave heeds no laws of acoustics. The reverberating thunder was fearful.

I am still wondering whether the civilized, white figure back in the shadow of the savage entrance did not shudder a little in this punishing noise.

4. "Less Is a Bore"

"Woe to him," wrote Nikolaus Pevsner a few years ago in his discussion of Ronchamp in *An Outline of European Architecture,* "woe to him who succumbs to the temptation of reproducing the same effect in another building, a building less isolated, less remote, less unexpectedly placed, and less exceptional in function."

Woe to us, our architects have succumbed everywhere.

It was inevitable. We are still searching, desperately and uncertainly, for a way to translate the will of this epoch into a visual culture. Somewhat nostalgically we admire the days when bishops and crowned heads told their subjects what was beautiful and fitting, when there was no question who was the tastemaker. Nor was the style of a Louis XIV, say, entirely an arbitrary imposition on his subjects and the lesser princes of Europe who adapted it so eagerly. The plan and architecture of Versailles was in tune with and expressed the prevailing philosophy of state and life. In America today Philip Johnson would sigh, as he did in an interview, that he'd like to be *l'architecte du roi,* the king's architect. Who, alas, is king? As the country's official architect for our public buildings, Philip Johnson could unquestionably give us better architecture than the camels the paltry committees of the federal government's General Services Administration produce when they think they design a horse. But an American President would never really back him. He wouldn't think it right to impose his taste on the nation.

We are on our own. No sooner had the International Style arrived than we decided it didn't suit us. Everyone greatly admired Lever House, and the Seagram Building got even more ecstatic rave notices. But one Park Avenue, we felt, was enough. Until the Pan Am Building ruined the street, it was the only modern one in America with some architectural consistency. We were afraid, however, that more of such glass-box canyons would get monotonous. One trouble was and is that single glass boxes elsewhere almost inevitably destroyed the harmony of the cityscape. The change from the old to the new was too abrupt.

Modernity was also by now somewhat anachronistic. "Modern" is the antonym of "old-fashioned." You are Modern only in rebellion against what was accepted before. We in America never really felt rebelliously outraged about the architecture that preceded the Lever Houses in our cities. Nor was there really a reason in the world to get upset about Rockefeller Center, say, or the Chrysler Building, or the Empire State Building, or even the humdrum office and apartment buildings that made up our cities. These often created problems, but

Ronchamp turned into a drive-in bank: "Woe to him . . ."

they weren't problems of style. They are problems of crowding, of circulation, of urban design and general efficiency and livability. If Lever House brilliantly solved a good many of them, its countless imitators surely did not. They only wrapped the same old problems into a shiny glass facade that, more often than not, only made matters worse. Walk into most any new glass box in New York or Cleveland or Los Angeles and you find the lobby, if anything, more confusing and cluttered than in a thirty-year-old building. The corridors are lower and apt to be even more oppressive. Space is poorly utilized, work space more cramped and noisy. Whether the glass curtain-wall is up or down hasn't made any difference, except, perhaps, on a higher air-conditioning bill.

The Austrian painter Fritz Hundertwasser protested that "a man in an apartment building should be able to lean out of the window, as far as his hands can reach, and scratch off the plaster. He should be permitted to paint everything pink, as far as he can reach with a long brush, so that from afar, from the street, one can see: Here lives a man who is different from his neighbors, from the cooped-in flock! He should also be able to cut up the walls and make all kinds of changes, even if he thereby destroys the architectonic-harmonic image of a so-called masterpiece of architecture. And he should be allowed to fill his room with mud or plastecine."

The Austrian's suggestion shows that the disenchantment against Functionalism is by no means confined to America. Nor is it, as Functionalism itself was, confined to artists and intellectuals—though only Bohemian intellectuals go so far as to advocate that we exchange the sanitary unlivability of Functionalist housing projects with the unsanitary unlivability of slums. On the subject of glass boxes, per se, there is, for once, common cause between intellectuals and public opinion, between Jane Jacobs and Joe Doe.

Leger, Sert, and Giedion were right when they proclaimed, a bit condescendingly, that "the people" want monumentality. Mumford fumed against Functionalism's "distorted picture of modern civilization." Eero Saarinen, having completed his Miesian General Motors Technical Center near Detroit, stated in 1956 that "our architecture is too humble. It should be prouder, more aggressive, much richer, and larger than we see it today." Two years later he added: "I feel strongly that modern architecture is in danger of falling into a mold too quickly—too rigid a mold. What once was a great hope for a great new period of architecture has somehow become an automatic application of the same formula over and over again everywhere." This feeling was general in the fifties.

So here over his drawing board broods the poor architect, staring at a blank sheet of paper. He has a commission, and he must make a name for himself. Success in our time means fame. Nervously he leafs through the latest copy of his favorite magazine. There, striking his eye with the force of an inner inspiration, is a picture of the miracle on the hilltop of Ronchamp. *"Voilà!"* Le Corbusier had said. "Oh, boy!" says our architect as he picks up his pencil.

We shouldn't blame him. Nor can we accuse him of plagiarism. The spirit of Ronchamp was in the air. Expressionism had always been with us and was ready to come to the fore. It had happened in painting and sculpture, what with the prices people suddenly paid for Jackson Pollocks, and it was bound to happen in architecture as well. Every sensitive architect felt it in his knuckles as he picked up his pencil. His hand was moved by the spirit of the times as much as by the expression Le Corbusier had given that spirit up on that hill in the Vosges.

Zeitgeist, as the Germans call it, the spirit of the times, is a wondrous thing. "One of the real enigmas of history," says the art historian Paul Zucker, "is the ubiquitous power, nameless yet clearly recognizable, which underlies every human act and created object in a given age. All forms, from handwriting to greeting, from dancing to costume, from table manners to courtship, have one quality in common: style."

Styles would change slowly, almost imperceptibly, in the past. Today new modes of expression flash around the world at the fearful speed of electronic impulses. Before the canvas is dry or the cast has hardened a work of art created in Paris is already known to magazine readers in Salina, Kansas. Literally millions of people are often familiar with the drawings and models of a new building even before the ground for it is broken. This constitutes a commitment. Utzon's opera house in Sydney, for instance, has proven almost impossibly difficult and expensive to construct. But the model of the thing had received so much publicity around the world that the Australians would not dare abandon it although they fired Utzon from the job. They grit their teeth and, by Jove, they're going to build it. Traffic congestion or Potomac flood, we are going to build that Kennedy Center in Washington for the sole reason that a hasty fund-raising sketch has committed us.

New art and architecture are written about, analyzed, explained, attacked, and defended long before they are really experienced, let alone understood. While the incredible velocity of change is undoubtedly an indication of great vitality, it also makes it difficult for anything to settle. It is impossible to distinguish style from fashion, the real thing from the fad.

Yet the major shifts and currents in art do have great influence on all of us. The enigma of the *Zeitgeist* has us all in its grip. In 1952 the ship that took my family home from Europe anchored for a few hours in Barcelona. My wife and I took an aimless stroll about town. Around one turn, in the distance, I suddenly saw the towers of Gaudí's Sagrada Familia. I gripped my wife's arm and turned her around. I didn't even want to go near such a horrible manifestation of decadent Art Nouveau Expressionism!

A few years later my outlook changed, and I could have kicked myself for having missed this opportunity to see a work of architecture which I now consider at least important and highly interesting. Just what accounts for this change of mind I couldn't say if you buried me under five hundred copies of Giedion's *Space, Time, and Architecture*, the bible of all true believers in Modern Functionalism. It just happened somehow. I also began to like the once generally despised Beaux Arts architecture of Washington's Federal Triangle. Why, I find as impossible to explain as the fact that you and I now laugh at the funny dresses women used to wear even ten years ago. They seemed perfectly natural then.

When we finally did travel to Barcelona again two years ago we immediately took a taxi to Sagrada Familia. I found it not merely interesting but positively delightful. What incredibly creative whim and daring! I loved the soaring curves and twisting forms. I was enchanted by the glistening color.

That year—1962—Philip Johnson and other staunch trail blazers of Functionalism walked a picket line to save that great, phony reconstruction of the Baths of Caracalla on New York's Thirty-fourth Street—McKim, Mead, and White's Pennsylvania Station.

Along with the resurgence of Expressionism, history was joyfully rediscovered. Before it had ever been really "in," the International Style was "out." Less was considered not more, but a bore. For most architects it was, as John Burchard and Albert Bush-Brown described it in their *The Architecture of America,* much like the annoying moment mountaineers might experience. "After hours of toil on an unknown terrain, they triumphantly reach the top—of the false summit. . . . The men who stood on the false summit seemed to have won an architectural victory. Far below lay the crevasses they had crossed. But the true summit seemed perhaps farther away then the false summit had thirty years ago."

A new assault began with a new battle of the styles—deep down in the valley, I fear.

5. Rectangular Plasticity

As we turned to Expressionism, Mies was suddenly reduced to the position of a revered, bright moon in the architectural firmament. The sun was Le Corbusier, that Picasso of architecture. We began to see everything in the light of this sun. His bright inventiveness warmed all modern buildings in some manner—even Mies placed his on stilts.

A few who ventured too close to his new forms—they called themselves "brutalists"—were burned. The enormous influence of Ronchamp and Chandigarh in this country is mainly a reflection of lesser stars in Le Corbusier's immediate orbit—Kenzo Tange, José Luis Sert, and Oscar Niemeyer.

Tange is a Japanese architect, born in 1913, who made his debut at thirty-six with his Peace Memorial Museum in Hiroshima. It is a simple, moving pavilion of a design which seems to distill Corbu's style before Ronchamp. He continued to follow and, as it were, to interpret Corbu's work. His city hall at Imbari renders the brute forms of the Chandigarh Palace of Justice a little more gently. His city hall in Kurashiki presents the cubic turmoil of La Tourette a little more smoothly. Like Corbu, Tange dramatizes not the facade or the overall envelope of the building but its various functional and structural components. He composes each post, beam, room, hall, staircase, window, and whatnot as a child would put building blocks together. His blocks are raw, naked concrete that are projected and recessed, raised and lowered at random.

Tange calls his forceful abstractions "vitalism." He avers that they are not abstract at all, but, to the contrary, constitute a "typification" of all the things that go on inside the building. Thus, if he needs a large room on the second floor, he simply places it precariously on a much smaller room below. If he needs light in a given spot, he punches a hole in the wall. If he needs a post and a beam, you'll know it is there. Everything is expressed with merciless directness. He is different from Corbu in that he is less exuberantly arbitrary and more polite, more considerate of our aesthetic sensibilities.

From Tange's interpretation of Corbu derives, I should think, the forthright design of Boston's new City Hall, the result of a competition won by three hitherto unknowns, Gerhard M. Kallman, Noel M. McKinnell, and Edward F. Knowles. Its bold directness makes you wonder how they got away with it in conservative Boston. Since it is superbly sited and set off on the new Government Center Plaza, this rugged, concrete sculpture might fit quite well with the strong, plain Yankee tradition of Boston's downtown buildings. Besides, the arrangement of the building, with its open court, entered through a columned void, makes much good sense. From this court the various departments of City Hall are clearly defined and easily accessible. It is, in fact, a superb building, perhaps the most attractively sensible built in its decade in America.

Cubic turmoil a little more smoothly

Airplanes and space rockets on Washington's Mall

In the small residential scale of Boston's Washington Park this style of building, as Gropius' TAC (The Architect's Collaborative) ventured it for a YMCA Recreation Center, is badly out of place. Next to pseudo-Colonial town houses in Washington's Southwest Urban Renewal Area, Charles M. Goodman's imitation of the Tange style for the Hawthorne School is an aesthetic disaster.

Gyo Obata's National Air and Space Museum on Washington's Mall, across from the National Gallery, seems to me to promise a more sensitive interpretation of Tange's "vitalism." It was a tough problem. How do you house a display of airplanes and moon rockets in these Beaux Arts classic surroundings without utterly disrupting them? And you can't decently stuff them into still another Roman temple, whether it's the adorned Roman of the National Gallery or the stripped and decolumnized Roman of the Smithsonian's Museum of History and Technology. Obata approached the problem from the inside out. He decided the place should not be a mere hangar in which people view the planes and rockets only on the ground or admire their bellies as they dangle in the air. He wanted us to see the displays from different levels and angles. This led him to a great space surrounded by galleries on different levels with stairs leading to them. He gave life to this space with massive free-standing shafts that support the roof and house the mechanical equipment and elevators. These shafts do not divide the space into small rooms but merely define different areas. Visitors will thus not be confronted with an immense hall, the very sight of which could cause aching feet. They will, furthermore, always have a wide open view of the green Mall and the sky because there will be large windows. An air museum needs air.

Obata covered his hall with a skylight to give it an open feeling. The windows bulge out as large bays—a happy idea since conventional window walls would make the exterior look like a factory, an appearance that would scarcely harmonize with the other buildings on the Mall. He further shaped the structure by topping it with a massive, overhanging roof that contains the research and administrative offices. This roof is enhanced by a decorative ribbon of windows to give them light and a view. The restaurant, a further, distinct element, is wedged like a box beneath the roof into the east wall. At this writing construction of the building has not yet begun. The design is most promising. It seemed to evolve logically or, if you will, organically. It is most assuredly not a conscious adaptation of another man's style. Just why, at a time when the work of Tange made such a profound impression on his peers, it should have so much of the "vitalist" feeling about it, is again part of the mystery of *Zeitgeist* that surrounds all art.

If Tange smoothed the overall forms of Le Corbusier, José Luis Sert uses Corbu's vocabulary only to build disciplined, inventive, rational buildings wholly his own. He might, presumably, use some other style of expression, but he happens to like that of Corbu, who was his good friend. He finds that for him it does the job best.

If you visit Cambridge, see Le Corbusier's Art Center first. Then walk a few blocks to the Harvard Yard and see what, at the Holyoke Center, Sert has done in the same style. Here the concrete is also partly unpolished. But it is poured in attractively patterned wood forms. The sun screens give the building a unique but no longer wild facade. Plane contrasts with plane, masses are piled on voids and voids on masses. There are those bold, random window openings, the stilts, light shafts, and the sudden accents of bright color. Here it all makes sense. You can read the meaning and purpose of the building as you contemplate it. Under the stilts are shops, animating the building but not dominating it on the street as store fronts usually do. The punched-in openings turn out to be delightful loggias for outdoor dining and lounging adjacent to the faculty dining rooms. The colors don't startle but add a note of gaiety to what is not a monolith but an inviting environment.

As at the Palace of Justice in Chandigarh there is also an enormously tall, arrogant portal. However, this one isn't an awesome gash but the entrance to a pleasant arcade, a gallery of urban sophistication, much like the Gallerie at Milan or the Burlington Arcade in London. You can walk through, or stroll through, and from here you can enter the

A fresh design with important innovations

various parts of the building. The arcade helps make it not one colossus but sort of a town that you can take in at your own pace. It is fun, even, to walk about in the offices. Their halls, corridors, and rooms each have a distinct and lively identity; they are full of surprises, which is quite an innovation in office buildings.

Sert and his associates have repeated the feat of taming Le Corbusier's cacophonous fury into a most civilized yet expressive building complex at Boston University. Sert's married students' dormitory on the Cambridge side of the Charles River, however, is not only appealing because of its fresh, light quality of design, but also because of an important breakthrough in the grouping of high and low buildings.

One trouble with urban design in our cities is that we have either very high or very low buildings. The reason there have been no buildings of intermediate height is that it doesn't pay to install expensive elevators for merely five or six stories, yet no one wants to climb that far. Sert's innovation is as simple as the legendary egg of Columbus. (To prove that he could make an egg stand on end, the wily explorer is said to have banged it on the table and flattened it on one end.) Sert simply built the twenty-two story buildings with their elevators and then linked them with bridges to terraced buildings of seven, five, and three stories. The first three stories of both the towers and the low buildings are walk-ups. Beginning at the fourth floor and above, the apartments are serviced by elevators that stop at every third floor. From there you walk up, down, or across the bridge corridors.

There are other inventive features. One nice touch, for example, is that Sert has placed the laundry rooms at the top of the building rather than in the usually dreary basement. They are adjacent to wonderful roof terraces. The girls can enjoy the view and take a sun bath while they wait for the diapers to run through the washing machine. The most heartening aspect of this delightful complex is that, with its handsome, paved plaza that is ideal for outdoor meetings and performances, the lovely playground, the out-of-the-way parking, it has a real sense of place. It has atmosphere and character.

One of the most exciting works of modern architecture I have come across is Sert's small museum at Saint Paul de Vence on the French Riviera. Here a sense of place was almost unavoidable. For one, a more breathtaking natural setting can hardly be imagined. For another, the environment was designed for a specific and enchanting collection of paintings and sculpture by Braque, Chagall, Bonnard, Kandinsky, Miró, and Giacometti of the Fondation Maeght. Always stimulating, yet never overwhelming, the museum achieves the integration of art and architecture which, as has been so much lamented, seemed lost in our time. The architecture appears prominent only in the form of the two, inverted barrel vaults over the roof of the main gallery that give

An enchanting setting to enjoy art

the building a simple, photogenic trademark. They are, to be sure, a bit of a *tour de force*. But the place needed something to declare itself. For the rest, spaces, light, art works, small pools, and restful inner courts, the sculpture court with the Giacomettis, and the outdoor labyrinth with Miró's fantastic sculptures, all form one marvelous, enchanting symphony. There are often hundreds of visitors. Unlike most other museums, you feel that the place is built for you alone, for your intimate experience of the art on display. Sert never tries to impress you. He wants the paintings and sculptures to do that.

Again, Sert used some of Le Corbusier's vocabulary, though the Fondation Maeght has a distinct personal note. Others, too, tamed Corbu's random and rectangular plasticity to good advantage. Breuer certainly brought it off superbly with his Whitney Museum of American Art, a work of architecture all the more successful because, for all his Corbuesque sculpture, Breuer stuck to the Functionalist restraint of his Bauhaus days. Walter Netsch's University of Illinois campus in Chicago is another example. Keyes, Lethbridge, and Condon's Tiber Island apartment and town house complex in Washington, the most attractive architecture of this kind I have seen, is another. Whittlesey and Conklin's town houses at Reston, the New Town in Virginia, are in this style. In all these buildings, Expressionism has been turned into a sensible, expressive architecture.

It may be that what counts is not the vocabulary, but what you say with it.

6. Le Corbusier Streamlined?

If Tange and Sert rationalized Le Corbusier's forms, Oscar Niemeyer streamlined them. Niemeyer, born in 1907, is the extraordinarily talented Brazilian who worked with Corbu on the Ministry of Education Building in Rio de Janeiro. He played a leading part in the collective design of the United Nations headquarters building in New York. And he was one of the first architects to venture, at Pampulha, a swinging thin-shell construction.

Like most Latin American architects, he is much concerned with the social aspect of housing. In Brasília, his country's new capital, however, where he designed all the prominent government buildings, he displayed only his brilliant showmanship.

The surrealist creations at Brasília are all of thin concrete, as though they were paper sculptures. They are veneered with white marble, as polished as his forms, and the word for these ingratiating apparitions is "lyrical." Hollywood loves him though its set designers probably never heard his name. When there is need for a romantically luxurious scene in an ultramodern setting—stars twinkling, soft music, tinkling fountain, Audrey Hepburn in long gown standing prim and a little shy, Cary Grant, in tuxedo, nonchalantly leaning against the balustrade—

the balustrade is likely to be Niemeyeresque. It's Modern played with feeling.

Much as one might swoon over the photographs, out on the high, naked construction site of Brasília, some six hundred miles inland from the coast, I found Niemeyer's widely dispersed architecture disappointing. The first of his buildings I came to was the Palace Hotel. It is a long, nine-hundred-foot slab on stilts, whose uninviting front facade consists only of pegboardlike cement blocks. In fact, you aren't invited at all. The entrance is somewhere under the stilts amidst a lot of parked cars. It consists of a narrow, darkish flight of stairs leading down into a basement reception room. Once you have checked in—and, in my case, discovered that the laboriously made reservation was never received—you climb right up another flight of stairs into a somewhat confusing lobby.

This business of crawling down into Niemeyer's structures, or, at any rate, never being informed just where he wants you to enter them, frustrated me all over his city. True, there is a break in the inverted arches which surround the Alvorada Palace to denote the entrance to the glass box behind them. (We are told the President is deliberately housed in a goldfish bowl so the people can see how he lives. But in the first place there are no people anywhere near, only tourists who

A glass box in lyrical wrapping . . .

. . . and a stage set in marble

come a long way in cars to gape and take pictures. When the President is at home, furthermore, the guards keep these tourists well beyond shooting range, including, to my regret, that of my long-lens camera.)

The Executive Palace has a wide, perilously unrailed ramp leading to the second floor porch. Fortunately, only soldiers are exposed to its danger when they march up to stand guard. Everyone else gets into the building, as into well-nigh all others in Brasília, at some inconspicuous place deep down somewhere under the inevitable stilts. The ramp on the Parliament Building splits. One part also leads to a second floor porch, the other to the roof. These ramps, too, are strictly for the guards, one of whom politely pointed his tommy gun at me when I started to walk up. I didn't miss anything by being chased down, though: The flat roof of this building, from which the famous dome and bowl rise—an upside down and a right-side up tea cup on a flat trap, denoting Senate and House of Representatives, respectively—is level with the mall and its speedway, and there is no view anyway. You enter and leave the building by being driven down into a tunnel at the end of a sunken road. If you have no chauffeur and are forced to walk, you face a danger almost equal to a tommy gun. The one narrow sidewalk, squeezed against the wall, barely accommodates a timid cat. I never did find the entrance to the twin-towered legislative office. It, too, must be underground somewhere.

So is the entrance to the Cathedral which is buried altogether. Only the spire, unfolding like a lotus blossom, rises above the ground, a poetic piece of sculpture. The rest is not architecture either, but a concrete dugout.

Here I go, looking for architecture. We must, architects tell us, experience the forms and enchantment and visual poetry. I do, indeed, relish Niemeyer's exquisite styling, his flowing trapezoids swinging in and out of sumptuous arches. I found them pleasing as well as original, though, as I said, the smooth, surrealist imagery comes off better through the camera lens. In actual concrete, the lonely plains of Minas Gerais overwhelm them. Le Corbusier's original, savage forms at Chandigarh, it seems to me, stand up far better in the similarly wild plains of Punjab.

From Niemeyer, I'm afraid, derives much of the whirling and swirling Miami architecture that we see far too much about. Churches seem particularly susceptible to Brasilianized versions of Ronchamp in the midst of staid suburbs. Harold E. Wagoner's confections, complete with electronically controlled mood lighting, come to mind. His *chef d'oeuvre* promises to be the new National Presbyterian Church in the suburbs of Washington for which this stout congregation has sold to the wreckers a lovely Victorian-Romanesque structure with a ninety-nine-year-old tradition downtown. Or consider, just to indicate that even remote Wyoming is warmed by the sun of Brasília, Charles Deaton's Wyoming National Bank at Casper. Its huge, concrete "flower petals" sprout out of the corner of a flat box. On one side that box is adorned with a clumsier version of Brasília's Alvorada Palace. On the other . . . Enough. I am sure you get the idea.

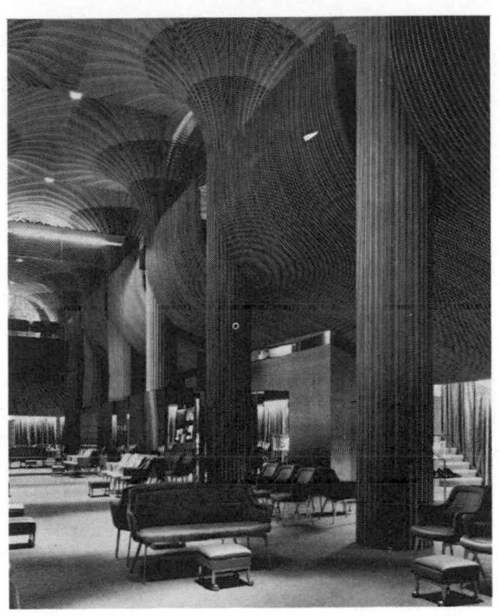

7. Enigmas of Art

I was recently invited to attend the deliberations of a committee of scientists at the National Institutes of Health. We sat, crowded around a small, gray, steel table, in a dingy and delightfully cluttered office—a latter-day den of St. Jerome—to await enlightenment from an architect. The scientists at NIH wanted to build a sort of faculty club on Cedar Lane in Bethesda, Maryland. It was to be a place, across the street from their forbidding, government-issued campus, where men of different disciplines could informally run into each other and exchange views over lunch or a drink, and where they could also have congenial space for lectures and their extracurricular teaching of younger scientists in the community.

They wanted a friendly, simple, relaxing building. The classrooms and lecture halls were important. More important in their minds was an urbane atmosphere, removed from the institutional jejunity of their fluorescent-lighted laboratories and offices. They envisioned a lounge and dining room for good conversation, an inviting bookstore, a view upon the trees of the attractive site they had already purchased. Whatever form this vision would take, it was not to disturb its pleasantly innocuous setting of set-back suburban homes nor the all too easily aroused sensibilities of their residents.

A relief from visual Muzak

It was a special problem, but not, it would seem, an outlandish one. Between the visual Muzak of roadside motels and the artless insipidity of the usual school or electronic research plant, there was, however, no precedent on which they could focus their vision. Wurster, Bernardi, and Emmons' Center for Advanced Study of Behavioral Sciences in Palo Alto, California, came closest to their dream, perhaps. This modest, monastic cluster of simple redwood buildings has unpretentious charm. Much of this charm relies on the unusual natural beauty of the ground, an old estate, into which it is fitted. That, as well as the Californian architects, were far away from Bethesda, Maryland. The NIH scientists also admired the Cedar Lane Unitarian Church, designed by Pietro Belluschi and Keyes, Lethbridge, and Condon, farther down on their street. It has much of the imaginative flair of the beautiful wood churches Belluschi built in Oregon and other Northwest states. But that was a church and not a faculty club.

It is, perhaps, symptomatic of the state of architecture today that well-versed men found themselves quite at a loss where and how to find an architect who might provide what they were looking for. One could only think of the stars, the big names sparkling as on a marquee and on the color pages of the mass circulation magazines. They couldn't quite see a little Seagram Building, or a Richardson Laboratory, an Arts and Architecture Building, or a New Delhi Embassy—not on Cedar Lane. If such edifices are not *eo ipso* "elegant monuments to nothingness," as Mumford has asserted in an angry moment, they were surely not very close to anything the group had in mind. The committee tried a star or two, anyway. The reply was politely routine. The stars are busy men, flying hither and yon to their far-flung commissions. The whole burden of devising the great world architecture of our time rests somewhere between their briefcases and their press interviews, immeasurably aggravated by the insane demands America makes on its popular heroes. At any rate, the chairman felt a little guilty after having made these inquiries. It was like having asked Marlene Dietrich to perform at a college class reunion.

The committee decided to interview a young architect who is billed, rightly, I believe, as a member of "the now maturing younger generation" of architectural talent. There is a captivating intensity about the flaring churches of Victor Lundy. And there was a captivating intensity about the handsome young man who now entered the scientists' den. Like Louis Kahn, of whom a very famous young lady has said she would love to take him on her lap and hug him, Victor Lundy could not possibly be more likeable. Like Kahn, he is shy. Kahn, however, simply will not let an interviewer interrupt his self-absorbed, messianic stream of consciousness about his art. It pours out as relentlessly in a private talk as in a lecture room. Lundy would pause politely when one of the NIH committee interjected a question. His response would take every question right back again to the lofty heights of his enthusiastic devotion to artistic abstractions. He talked about the play of spaces, the challenge of arches, the emotion of light, the purposeful beauty of concrete. It was the gallery talk, and a rather poetic one, of an esoteric curator of abstract art. There was not a straw in this bubbling stream on which the committee, for all its good will, could fasten their hopes for a faculty club.

Poor Lundy must have sensed their frustration as he packed up the photos of his architecture he had shown them—close-ups of subtle curvatures and undulations, soaring hyperbolic arches, playful fantasies of space and light. "I suppose I am really an artist at heart," he sighed as he left. He left us feeling that if he were to design the club for the scientists it would have to be built on his charisma.

I feel the same way about Louis Kahn. It is easy to see why he has so many true believers. Child of immigrants from the island of Osel in Estonia, at the time of his birth and again today a province of Russia, Kahn came to architecture via a strict Beaux Arts education at the University of Pennsylvania. He brought with him the wonder-wise world of East European Judaism, a world so beautifully depicted by Sholem Aleichem and Marc Chagall. Everything in this world is mysterious, and there is deep wisdom in the mystery, even the mystery of very little things. One can share the wisdom by attuning oneself to the mystery, by listening to the moon, as it were, by dreaming one's way through the cruelties of earthly existence. The outsider can never enter this world on rational terms. It is at once too simple and too lofty. Like Chagall's paintings, it is always the same. It doesn't change with the times.

Until he designed the Yale University Art Gallery at the age of fifty, Kahn had built almost nothing. He was hardly known beyond the group of fierce admirers and students at Yale who saw in him something of a saintly Gandhi who led the counterrevolution against Functionalism. It wasn't—and perhaps even today isn't—what he did or said that established his charisma. Kahn says, for instance:

> Art is a form making life in order—psychic
> Order is intangible
> It is a level of creative consciousness
> forever becoming higher in level
> The higher the order the more diversity in design.

The mystique of such poetry works best in the presence of this slight, small man with the thick glasses and a face seared by hot coal in a childhood accident. He says it with such humble simplicity. One understands why the high-placed lady would hug him.

You needn't know any of this to be impressed by the Yale Gallery, though. The interior of the building was designed as an open loft, much like Mies might have done it, because initially it had to serve a variety of purposes. The exterior, too, has much of Mies' severity, but is superbly fitted with the older buildings. It is proud yet unobtrusive. The excitement was caused by the unusual construction of his concrete frame, make up of tetrahedronal elements in the Buckminster Fuller manner which he left exposed in the ceiling. This, and a deliberate, unfinished roughness throughout the building, was at the time a matter of philosophy. In a more aggressive manner the full exposure of the guts of a building, pipes and all, was the credo of the Brutalists in England led by Alison and Peter Smithson.

You must either be very susceptible to the guile of the tastemakers or know Louis Kahn, I believe, to be impressed by the Richards Medical Research Building. The building doesn't work the mystique, its creator does. And I wonder if that much mystic Expressionism isn't an anachronism today. A laboratory, of course, has as much right

A monastery for science

to express its laboratoriness as any other "institution of man," as Kahn is so fond of saying. Then shouldn't this expression be directly meaningful to the people who work there and visit? Is it?

At the Salk Institute at La Jolla, California, however, Kahn has suppressed the mystic expressionism which made the Richards laboratories so famous. I suspect Dr. Jonas Salk, of polio vaccine fame, had a great deal to do with that. He wanted a scientific monastery, an environment where scientists, unraveling the secrets of life, work side by side with humanists, who would relate these scientific discoveries to human values. Only Kahn, he felt, could give form to his idea. But only Salk's idea, in turn, gives life and meaning to Kahn's somewhat brooding, monastic structure. Their joint planning must have been often torturous, but, miraculously, the two are still friends. And the building has a compelling simplicity and calm—quite aside from the ingenious flexibility of its laboratories—that makes it quite convincing when Salk says: "Only excellence should come out of this." It may well be the great monument Kahn deserves to have created.

The most extreme reaction to Functionalism to date, however, comes not from the Beaux Arts-trained Kahn, but from a formerly prominent Modernist, Hans Scharoun. The history of midcentury architecture can hardly ignore his Philharmonic Hall in Berlin, which has received little attention in this country. Perhaps that is lucky, for an epidemic of Scharounism on our shores would be a disaster, I believe, for America's already feverish architecture. Scharoun, born in 1893, designed many creditable buildings in Berlin before the Second World War, notably some very livable moderate income housing. Since the war he has contributed some original and valid ideas to the city's reconstruction.

If anyone were to ask what happened to the influence of Frank Lloyd Wright since his death in 1959, Scharoun's Philharmonic is probably an even better answer than Paul Rudolph's Art and Architecture Building. There is much of Wright's Beth Sholem Synagogue at Elkins Park in the shape and concept of the building. There is also much more, and it is incredibly complex, mystifying, and ugly. Scharoun's basic idea, if I understand his anthroposophic explanations correctly, is not unlike Kahn's. He, too, is concerned with institutions of man. He would have one building express community, and be a medieval town all in one, with corridors like winding streets, interior town squares, and all the rest. He even throws in the landscape. The conductor stands in the middle of a deep valley surrounded by the audience which is placed on a multitude of oddly angled and overlapping terraces, or "vineyards," as he calls them. All done in light wood, the frozen restlessness of the space is not without beauty. The acoustics, I am told, are good.

The trouble with the building is not that Scharoun let his complex interior determine the shape of his exterior, but that he deliberately and defiantly confounds this complexity into an architectural "happening." It is impossible to "read" the meaning or structure of all these protrusions, corners, angles, balconies, portholes, and turrets tucked under an undulating roof. What's more, he uses all kinds of materials whether they harmonize or not. His colors, beginning with the dirty yellow paint of the raw concrete, are atrocious. The details, though I am told this is not deliberate, are raw to the point of "brutalist" abandon. The worst of it is that all this is offered with an aura of pretentiousness. The building "radiates fantasy in aesthetics," says the architect. "The harmony of man: space and music . . . through the spiritual radiance of architecture," proclaims a guidebook.

The Philharmonic stands but a stone's throw from the Berlin Wall, on a weed-grown desert of flattened debris that was once the throbbing heart of the city. To one side is a small church that miraculously survived the bombing with relatively little damage. Across the way, Mies van der Rohe's Gallery of the Twentieth Century, an art museum, is rising. It will be his purest structure yet: eight columns, a thick slab of a roof, and a square glass enclosure within. It will be the most Miesian of them all.

Across the road from Scharoun's complexity . . .

Never before in history has such a weird setting juxtaposed such utter opposites in architecture. Both represent an extreme of divergent concepts of art. Neither is of much help to our committee at NIH which merely wants a pleasant building that should, of course, also have "delight" as well as "commodity" and "firmness."

The NIH scientists, to finish my story, picked Harry Weese to design their faculty club but ran into trouble raising the money to build it. Victor Lundy meanwhile came up with a most forthright and disciplined design for a new U.S. Tax Court building in Washington.

. . . is the ultimate of Miesian simplicity

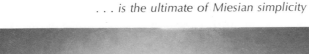

8. Restraint

"If you are a sculptor and you carve a block of granite," designer Charles Eames has written, "it will be impossible for you to produce anything *really* bad. This is because the material will impose some pretty severe restraints on what you can or cannot do. But if, instead of granite, you use Plasticine it will be almost impossible to produce anything really good. And this is because Plasticine is so free of restraints that there will be nothing to guide you, nothing to show you what you cannot do, or tell you when you have gone wrong.

"Today we live in a Plasticine world. The restraints of the past are being broken down. We are free to do what we like and the result is the sort of disorganized, amorphous horror of a city like Los Angeles. The greatest task facing designers today is to try to rediscover the restraints of earlier culture; though to do so, not in a spirit of revivalism, but in an effort to create new restraints appropriate to our time."

The broken restraints of the new Expressionism are not only those of structure—the building which could now be shaped any which way. They are also largely the old restraints of "commodity," as Sir Henry Wotton called it. The new architectural stars pronounced all architecture worthy of the name to be pure art and nothing but art. "Architecture is the play of forms under the light, the play of forms correct, wise, magnificent," said Le Corbusier. "And, my friends, that's all it is . . ." proclaimed Philip Johnson, and almost everybody believed it.

In a lecture in 1955 Johnson proceeded to explain that anything else was a mere crutch. He counted six in addition to the crutch of structure: the crutch of history which was no longer valid; the crutch of the pretty drawing which was too easy; the crutch of utility ("I would rather sleep in the nave of Chartres Cathedral with the nearest john two blocks down the street than I would in a Harvard house with back-to-back bathrooms!"); the crutch of comfort; the crutch of cheapness; and the crutch of pleasing the client.

It was heady talk, an elixir for the architecture students at Yale who thought "less a bore" and now watched their heroes walk, free as never before, into the wonderful new world of Plasticine. All you had to do now was shape it.

In a way it was the old Bauhaus antiacademism all over again, except that the Bauhaus also took the john and people without two-block bladders into account.

The trouble is that architecture can't have its own elixir and cure the world, too. It is wonderful to hear Philip Johnson liberate young souls at Yale from all those silly crutches. The boys cheer lustily in these revival meetings when they are told: "It's got to be clear, back in your own mind, that serving the client is one thing and the art of architecture another." Or when Louis Kahn tells them at length: "I am scared stiff of people who look at things from the money angle," and then proceeds to tell them that his art center for Fort Wayne will cost twenty million dollars when his clients thought they could spend no more than ten. He had, he said, conceived of a magnificent complex of buildings; he had created an entity that was a wonderful thing, it was art, and that entity was now impossible to destroy.

The students also cheer when Philip Will, Jr., tells them that they "should assume responsibility for nothing less than the total man-made environment." That's going to be a little difficult without those crutches. Without restraints, as Eames said, it is almost impossible to produce anything really good. The art of architecture is one thing and an environment for people is another. "This is still a period of disintegration in all the arts," Johnson acknowledged ten years after he had advocated throwing the crutches away. "There is no particular advantage to chaos, but that's where we are." He might have told them at Yale, for in his heart he had always known it. Again, he had had his tongue in his cheek. In contrast to Yale's Rudolph and Kahn, he—and a few others—did not seek to overthrow the short-lived tradition Gropius,

Mies, and Le Corbusier had established, but to build on it, to make it richer, and to soften it a little. In that sense his work, after he broke with Mies, is not entirely unlike Niemeyer's. While Niemeyer reflects the hot sun of Corbu, Johnson stays much closer to the Miesian moon. His flowing sculpture is always disciplined by his rational, classicist mind which believes in order and harmony.

This is true even where Johnson plays with Expressionism for sheer delight of it—his "Roofless Church" at New Harmony, Indiana, a shrine for the Rappite sect, and his precious little pavilion at Dunbarton Oaks in Washington, D.C., for the display of Pre-Columbian jewelry and artifacts. His Kline Science Center at Yale shows that the game has its dangers. It is slick and unappealing. His New York State Exhibit for the New York World's Fair shows that the game can also be just fun.

Johnson, however, is really a better architect than Niemeyer. His swinging, stylish, sculptural facades—on his museums at Fort Worth, Texas, and Lincoln, Nebraska, for instance—are less melodramatic than Niemeyer's, which is good. His way of moving us to and through his buildings is far more dramatic, which is even better. He knows how to give his architecture a festive, enjoyable atmosphere. His addition to New York's Museum of Modern Art is an elegant joy, particularly the sculpture court.

When it came time to build the Lincoln Center, this new, romanticized Miesian classicism had become an idiom that could be harmoniously shared by several architects.

There is much to be said against such centers: The whole city ought to be a cultural center, and operas, theaters, and music halls should be distributed around, so each can add some monumental architecture to the cityscape and each can become a magnet for the cafés, restaurants, special stores, artist studios, and other pleasant things. Look what Carnegie Hall has done for its end of New York's Fifty-seventh Street.

There is also much to be said in favor of a center in addition to the obvious practical consideration of shared parking and public transportation stops. We need attractive public spaces in our cities—public parlors, as it were, that are representative, a little ceremonial, and out of the humdrum. Obviously there shouldn't be any cars. A pedestrian shopping-mall is something else again, too. Ideally, the good public space has both shops and temples to the Muses. There should be a variety of things to see and do. It should be a place you dress up for—even if you don't have theater tickets.

We have rarely accomplished this kind of place in American cities,

Johnson: No crutches but still close to Mies

because it requires that individual buildings cooperate with each other and that someone pays for furnishing attractive spaces between them. Private builders, however, rarely cooperate, and public officials rarely spend money on fountains, attractive pavements, and planting, let alone sculpture or benches. A well-endowed cultural institution is therefore our only opportunity. Lincoln Center seized this civic design opportunity extremely well, though it should be much gayer, less pompous. There should be more flowers and benches.

The design is the work of a committee of outstanding architects under the chairmanship of Wallace K. Harrison, who also headed the committee of architects of the United Nations buildings and is, in a

A romanticized classicism that is easily shared

way, John D. Rockefeller's *architecte du roi*. The location was forced on the group by Robert Moses, at the time – 1955 – New York's housing, urban renewal, highway, parks, fine arts, and planning czar all rolled into one. There was, at first, some unhappiness about building an opera house on rundown, somewhat out-of-the-way Lincoln Square. But under its impact the area began to improve even before the Center was completed and turned out to be perfectly accessible. This success certainly proved Ed Stone all wrong when he justified the inaccessible location of his Kennedy Center in Washington with the argument that "an opera should not be used as an urban renewal project." An opera house should be where the action is, and that is downtown. Lincoln Center is.

Harrison undertook the design of the opera house which dominates the Center's great plaza with Johnson's wonderful and "witty" fountain, as someone called it. Johnson also designed the State Theater for ballet and musical comedy. Max Abramovitz, Harrison's partner, designed the Philharmonic Hall. Eero Saarinen took on the Beaumont Theater with a library by Skidmore, Owings, and Merrill tacked on. Pietro Belluschi designed the Julliard School of Music which is also part of the complex. The architecture is varied, though all of the same travertine, and the three main buildings on the plaza have formal colonnades. The arrangement of the big temples on relatively small space, at once formal and intimate, dignified and engaging, could not be better. Strolling along the procession of open spaces between the buildings is an enjoyable and festive event.

The architecture of the Center's opera, ballet, and concert halls—an instant product of the clash between Functionalism and Expressionism—is less successful. It is a compromise and tries too hard to be Classic. Some critics have gone so far as to say it is a disaster. This seems to me silly snobbery. "The Merry Widow" is not a disaster simply because it is not a Verdi grand opera. I, for one, like operetta and even a bit of schmaltz, and I was quite enchanted when Max Abramovitz' Philharmonic was completed. Here, it seemed to me, was a style of building that is of our time but has continuity as well, a style that is monumental yet human and that we can live with. I was even more enchanted when Johnson's ballet theater opened. Though the exterior is a bit bland, particularly on the sides, the front colonnade has dignity, and the interior is grand. It is a thrill to walk up the well-scaled stairs and then find yourself in this marvelous Mississippi riverboat foyer, no doubt the most elegant promenade in America. I even forgive Johnson the Elie Nadelman sculptures. True, they look like giant soap carvings, but their scale is superbly right.

As the center piece, as it were, Harrison's new Metropolitan Opera House is a little more daring in form. In fact, it incorporates some Expressionist features: The barrel vaults on the facade which is reminiscent of Mendelsohn's design for Beth El Synagogue in Baltimore (which was never built) and the swirling, sculptured staircase which is reminiscent of Eero Saarinen's TWA Terminal. But Harrison's great skill and discipline has sublimated these features into a building that is, as it were, quite stately, though no one could call it great. What is more, it functions superbly and for all its somewhat cumbrous lavishness succeeds in what it set out to do—to recapture the spirit of grand opera.

These three main Lincoln Center buildings are conventional, if you will. But wasn't it time we found a generally acceptable convention? I grant it is "middlebrow architecture for middlebrow art," as Mrs. Huxtable put it. If, indeed, they will, as she says, "represent twentieth-century America with fidelity, if not with brilliance," it is an image that need not make us blush. Others promptly and quite properly adapted it.

Welton Becket's Music Center in Los Angeles unfortunately spoils the effect of its colonnade of elegantly tapered pylons all around with its obtrusive and badly designed silver aluminum framing of the dark glass. It looks cheap and incongruous, like nailing a chromium strip around a mahogany dining table. William Pereira and James Langenheim's Los Angeles County Museum makes a handsome urban design out of one museum by breaking it up into three buildings. They are set lightly on a raised plaza which, like an island in Venice, seems to float in a shimmering pool. There could be no more decorous way to set the museum apart from the audible and visible noise of Wilshire Boulevard. Here, too, classically simple, geometric frame structures are softened by subtly sculptured concrete columns. The walls are faced with beautifully textured marble tiles. The concrete columns, however, are painted, which is less disastrous parsimony than Becket's silver mullions, but regrettable, nevertheless. While the Music Hall interior, though it works well, is rather Hollywood chi-chi, Pereira's interior atrium is a simple and delightful space. There are few museums in the world where art is as effectively displayed as in these well-arranged galleries with their good mixture of artificial light and daylight. The thick carpeting is a blessing; no museum feet.

I had, however, second thoughts on the somewhat contrived neo-neo-Classic delight the big houses at Lincoln Center had wrought, when the Center's Vivian Beaumont Theater was completed in the fall of 1965. Eero Saarinen's design is surely the most outstanding solo performance in the ensemble. It was completed four years after Eero's

Designed with rational passion

untimely death at fifty-one, and he would have been proud of it. He had been trying more intensely, more earnestly, perhaps, than any of his peers to find an approach to our architecture that would "knock the pins out from under our smugness," as he put it. His efforts led him to a disconcerting variety of approaches—the Miesian General Motors Tech Center, the MIT Chapel and Auditorium, the Yale Hockey Rink, the super-Gothic Yale Colleges, the Scandinavian village for theologians at Concordia, Fort Wayne, the flamboyant TWA Terminal, the brawny Dulles Air Terminal. "Such versatility, as a rule, indicates lack of character," wrote Nikolaus Pevsner in the Washington *Post*, "but not so in his case. It must rather be seen as a highly imaginative architect's passion for experimenting."

The passion of this sober Finn was always rational, always with the aim not to show what *he* could do but what good architecture could do to solve a problem. "I align myself humbly with Le Corbusier and against Mies van der Rohe, although I admire his achievements immensely," he told German colleagues in 1958. With the Beaumont, it seems to me, he returned. Here he aligned himself again not with esoteric abstraction of glass reflections, but from Corbu's rhyme to Mies' reason.

Now that I saw them together with Saarinen's work, I suddenly found Johnson's, Harrison's, and Abramovitz's columns and arches too ingratiatingly decorative. They lack conviction. The Beaumont is also classic, but without sweat or striving. The building does not rely on our mental associations with classicism but in a powerful way conveys its spirit. It recalls not Schinkel's Biedermeyer but the Parthenon. The Beaumont, too, has columns, but they carry a heavy load. Lined up only on the flanks of the building, they support eighteen-foot deep trusses that span an uninterrupted theater space of 150-foot width. The trusses form a block in which the bulk of the Library and Museum of the Performing Arts is contained. The block is pierced by a stagehouse so placed that, if you see it at all, it fits in handsomely with the rest of the building, which is quite a feat for a theater stagehouse.

The interior is also uncompromisingly simple. The glazed, sunken lobby manages to convey all the festive elegance of its larger neighbors but without any gilt and trimmings. It is just as marvelous a space as is the auditorium, which is all in red and not black, but "bittersweet chocolate brown," as the man from Saarinen's office who showed me around explained. Saarinen, he said, designed it so that even from the farthest seat a spectator could "see the expression in Julie Harris' eyes, which are pretty small."

For glamour, if that is the word, the Beaumont is reflected in a square pool with a rocklike, sensuous Henry Moore sculpture which at once balances and contrasts the severe reflection of the building.

This image is beautiful but not startling. The single, organic, and self-contained sculpture, lonely in a vast expanse, is set against the pure geometry of a structure. It is given mood by the mystery of still water and has something of the Zen mystique of the temple garden of Kyoto about it, much as the Renaissance interpreted classic antiquity. This Kyoto image has become almost a cliché. But we must be careful with that word. For when is the repetition of formal expression a stereotype, and when is it the assertion of a style that gives us the conformity without which order is impossible? We cannot yearn for the visual harmony that was the glory of past periods, as I do, and at the

Eero Saarinen's final mastery of restraint

same time denounce repetition. The great advantage of conformity, as any child senses when it wants to dress exactly as the other kids do, is that it gives us the security of being part of the brotherhood of man, of a community. In art, it furthermore liberates the artist from the compulsion to be original. Once his vocabulary conforms to a language everyone understands, he's got a chance to say something meaningful. Saarinen's Beaumont Theater, I believe, does.

It does because Eero Saarinen leaned quite heavily on the crutches Philip Johnson would have his students throw away. Saarinen worked within confining restraints. There were, first of all, the limits imposed by the requirements of the common effort to make Lincoln Center a unit. This dictated the scale, the setting, and the use of travertine. He meticulously heeded, in collaboration with Jo Mielziner, the formidable restraints of a well-functioning theater. And he stayed within the always confining limits of economy and "pleasing the client" as well. At the end of his life Eero Saarinen acknowledged restraint and mastered it. As I stand before New York's proudly assertive CBS tower, before Dulles and Beaumont, I find myself saying: "This is it!" These buildings, in this moment in history, could not be designed in any other way.

9. Kitsch

Along with *weltschmerz, blitzkrieg,* and *sauerkraut,* the German word *kitsch* has recently crept into the American language. It is a most useful word. *Kitsch* has also swept over much of our architecture. We could do without.

Webster III says *kitsch* derives from the German dialect word *kitschen* which originally meant scraping mud from the street and has come to mean slapping a work of art together. Gilbert Highet, however, says it is derived from the Russian "keetcheetsya," which means "to be haughty and puffed up." That sounds more like it, for kitsch is usually not carelessly slapped together but, on the contrary, obtains its horrible authority as a result of meticulous labors. Salvador Dali's mawkish, religious paintings (to wit, his "Sacrament of the Last Supper" at the National Gallery), are meticulous and savvy. Kitsch caters to popular taste, it plays on heartstrings that tickle soft glands to produce tears, sighs, erotic, or otherwise pleasantly emotional sensations. It employs sentimentalism, sensationalism, and slickness and, to various degrees, it is ubiquitous.

In judicious doses kitsch may even be necessary. It somehow sweetens life. I for one like to cry in movies, and am often fascinated by some hideous garden sculpture of an unclad Lolita or startled doe. I adored the oh-so-touching poems in praise of motherhood, adorned with crayoned flora, which our Irish elevator man in New York used to tape on the walls of his shaky lift. People who find life otherwise bland should not be reproved for adoring Dali's Last Supper or, for that matter, hanging a reproduction of it over the davenport that displays a black velvet pillow with the Lincoln Memorial embroidered in gold and deep blue. Often, of course, the house that greets you with a colored cast-iron jockey on the lawn is dour to strangers and unfamiliar ideas. The home with the "home-sweet-home" signs may well lack genuine home life. And the man who fancies salt and pepper shakers that spice his food out of the oversized breasts of naked little ladies obviously needs this kind of aphrodisiac. We all try to make up for our shortcomings, and the stuff in the roadside garden ornament stands and souvenir shops needn't really bother us. The horrible greeting card from your neighborhood dry cleaner can make you feel superior for hours.

It is sad, of course, when kitsch seeps into an otherwise good performance and no art, "fine" or "applied," visual, musical, or dramatic, is immune to it. Keen critics point up these afflictions, as Stanley Kauffmann did in his *New Republic* review of Truman Capote's *In*

"Styled" to the latest architectural fashion

Cold Blood. Of one overwritten passage Kauffmann wrote: "This is Reddiwip writing—goo that gushes out under the force of compressed air and that, unless one puts it to the test of taste, looks like the real thing." This, in many ways, is the essence of kitsch. There is always a real thing, a substantive form or emotion or idea, a real Lincoln Memorial that was embroidered on a velvet cushion, or genuine whipped cream that is somehow made gooey and perverted. In architecture and industrial design the difference is often a difference between designing and "styling."

There is no compelling need to put our liturgical art to the test of taste. The kitsch within our churches of all denominations probably heightens religious experience for more people than it repels. If you don't want to worship in the saccharine tastelessness of Washington's National Shrine of the Immaculate Conception (whose Pastiche-Byzantine is, in fact, far more endurable than much "modernistic" religious kitsch), you can visit some other church. Political kitsch, too, is really dangerous only if it serves totalitarian purposes and its manipulators can force the exclusion of all else, as Hitler and Stalin did. It is really just a nuisance one can even find amusing, when, as the monument to Vittorio Emanuele II on Rome's Piazza Venezia, it spoils the

Headquarters of the artistic counter-revolution

It dazzled the disenchanted and made sense

cityscape. It hurts one's patriotic pride only a little when, in the form of an heroically oversized bronze cast of a photograph, it is passed as a national memorial to the battle of Iwo Jima in the national capital. Out there in Arlington and enmeshed as it is in a maze of super highways, it's pretty well out of the way.

It is more offensive when a big hunk of marble kitsch is plunked squarely on New York's Columbus Circle where it is to launch Huntington Hartford's counter-revolution against Modern Art. That could and should be a beautiful plaza. You may choose not to go inside and pay your admission to see the Dalis and the more time-honored mawkishness of Bouguereau or the more erotic pre-Raphaelites which Huntington Hartford has put on display. But you can't avoid the awkwardly shaped and clumsily ornate mausoleum in which Edward Durell Stone has embalmed these paintings. One feels a pang of collective guilt about it as one passes by in a taxi.

When Stone, the greatest architectural kitsch-monger of them all, decided "to go to bat for beauty," he had us all dazzled for a moment. His United States Embassy in New Delhi seemed to make sense, even if you discounted some of the more effusive touting of the "form-giver" image builders in the Luce magazines. There was much dignity and grandeur in that squared-off temple. There seemed almost something of the enchanting simplicity of the Barcelona Pavilion about it, the way the sparse, thin columns supported the flat, cantilevered roof. But it seemed more classic in its symmetry and far more monumental with its huge, floor-to-cornice entrance opening, half filled with the great gilded seal of the United States. Yes, it seemed lyrical to see the delicate structure raised on temple stairs and reflected in the pool. It was 1955 when the pictures of the model appeared. We were disenchanted with pure Functionalism and ready for the romantic touch. It made sense, in India, to wrap a glass box in shading grilles so our ambassador wouldn't bake to a crisp. It also made sense, in India, to borrow the form of this grille from the motifs of India's Muslim architecture. Why not gild the columns and stud the white grilles with gold knobs? Placing the offices around an enclosed court with a fountain, atrium fashion, was also a rational thing to do. Besides, we trusted Edward Durell Stone, who, with Philip L. Goodwin, had designed one of the country's first International Style buildings, the Museum of Modern Art.

It also seemed fair enough that, for the Brussels World's Fair, Stone produced a repeated New Delhi Embassy in the round. The United States Pavilion he designed was really a big umbrellalike canopy of plastic, enclosed by a drum that consisted of a lattice system of steel straps. It was quite the right idea for a fair, ingeniously engineered.

There is nothing wrong with holding on to a good thing when you've got one, nor with repeating an architectural idiom. Idioms become styles and we suffer more from a lack of style in our contemporary

A gift-wrapped memorial to culture and Kennedy

environment than from the monotony a consistent style is alleged to produce but doesn't. One important ingredient of a valid style, however, is appropriateness in its application. While Stone's gilded lily at New Delhi seemed appropriate for its purpose, its application to most of Stone's commissions, from gas stations to school buildings and pharmaceutical plants to the John F. Kennedy Center for the Performing Arts, surely wasn't. Indiscriminate use of a good thing is another element of kitsch and it works retroactively. Marshmallows with Reddiwip may be a diverting dinner dessert. For breakfast they are nauseating. At this point I am more than a little disenchanted with the New Delhi Embassy.

This is not say that Stone has exclusively indulged in self-plagiarism. The Huntington Hartford Gallery has no grilles or toothpick columns. Neither does his Perpetual Savings and Loan Association building in Los Angeles, a vertical agglomeration of arcades with greenery oozing out all over, and Washington's National Geographic Society headquarters with its marble fins and lid roof. He promptly repeated this one a few miles away in a suburban shopping center. Yet it is probably his best building since 1938, though, with the rather noble shaft woefully unrelated to the busy base, it is far from good architecture. I welcome it because it is still better than most contemporary efforts in downtown Washington.

I am, however, upset by the Cultural Center which Congress has ordained to be the only memorial to John F. Kennedy in the capital. To place this huge structure along the Potomac just north of the Lincoln Memorial is arrogant and impractical. The waterfront should have been kept open and culture should be easily accessible to everybody. Why, how, and by whom, during the Eisenhower administration, Stone was selected for this important commission is hidden from democratic scrutiny. Kennedy himself tenaciously stuck to the site and the dubious concept of wrapping opera, theater, and concert hall all in one architectural package even after it became clear that the combination would produce tremendous parking problems and leave no room for rehearsals, storage of scenery, and other facilities that make the difference between a working cultural center and a mere festival hall. Stone first proposed a 70-million-dollar version of his Brussels Pavilion. When this was deemed too expensive, he switched to New Delhi on a giant scale—six hundred feet long, two hundred feet wide, and a hundred feet high. There are no grilles, however. It is enclosed with bland marble with two Babylonian entrance openings and adorned by the

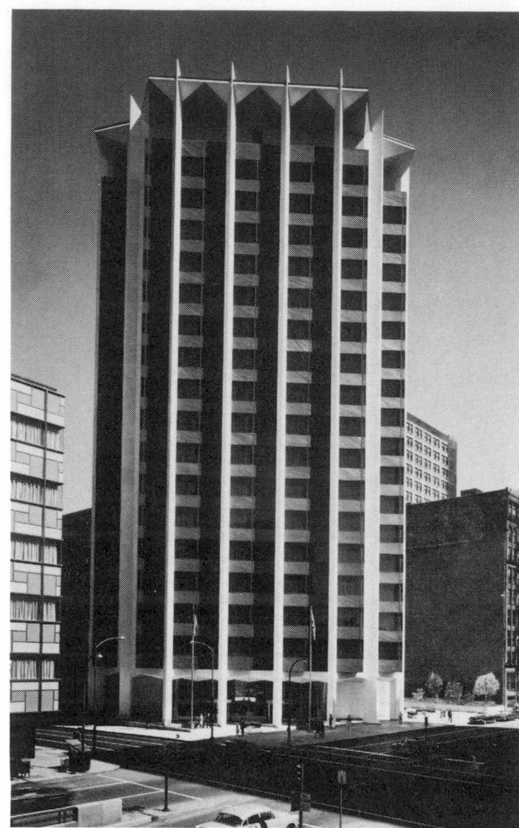

Not modern but modernistic

ephemeral columns supporting the flat lid, baskets with greenery dangling between them. Without this gift wrapping we would have nothing but a colossal white box. With it we have overscaled kitsch. One could weep.

Kitsch will, of course, always be with us. In the past, however, it was mostly cheap and years behind in style. It is only lately that with affluence and progress it has become expensive and modernistic. It now meets the need of an affluent society. This, I presume, is why it has proved so infectious in our architecture. No sooner had Stone thrown his gilded grilles into the battle for beauty than men like the gifted Minoru Yamasaki also felt "the Bauhaus blinders falling from his eyes." He wrapped gold-anodized aluminum grilles all over his Reynolds Metals Company Branch Office outside Detroit. From the grille he went on, much as Stone did, to all manner of lacy Venetian Gothic of which he fashioned a conference center for Wayne University into what Vincent Scully has called "a twittering aviary." Busy arabesques of all kinds have since adorned all his commissions. To sugarcoat the shock of the awesome giganticism of New York's twin-towered World Trade Center, which is to dwarf the Empire State Building, Yamasaki styled its base in a streamlined version of the pointed arches of the Doge's Palace in Venice. Like Stone, Yamasaki is a most popular architect.

From New Delhi and the Wayne University campus, architectural kitsch has spread like a virus all over America. The roadside stands, motels, storefronts, and bank branch offices that escaped Howard Johnson Modern Colonial now blossomed forth with Stone grilles and Yamasaki folds, laces, and Venetian Gothic. Expense alone restrains the office and apartment builders, though when they are out to convey an air of luxury, they, too, often employ architectural kitsch. Luigi Moretti of Rome, with Milton Fischer of Washington, plastered his own modernistic brand of concrete icing on the curvacious design of the Watergate apartment buildings in Washington, D.C. It will crowd Stone's *Kulturpalast* and turn this part of the Potomac waterfront into a kind of Miami Beach.

The New York World's Fair of 1964-1965 probably sprouted more of

"A twittering aviary"

this kind of cheaply ingratiating architecture in one place than we have ever seen in this century. It dazzled the eye with a chaotic accumulation of architectural stunts and colossal banalities, much as it dumbfounded the ear with a relentless din of sweet Muzak and electronic hawking of all kinds. Sure, there was fun. There were even bright flashes of beauty. But the fun was the fun of thrill, souped up by the constant Benzedrine charges of artificial stimulation. It was not the fun of an elation that you only get when your senses respond because you are in happy empathy with a happy environment. The beauty was in the flowers and some beautiful girls which no planner could plan and no designer design. Only a few of the man-made things, the undulating rows of telephone booths, for instance, were really handsome.

There is no use bemoaning this missed opportunity—missed, if you consider what great impetus Paxton's Crystal Palace at the first world's fair in 1851 and so many fairs since have given to the art and techniques of architecture. The monumental razzle-dazzle of the corporate pavilions and stunt shows of organized religion have been mercifully dismantled. Michelangelo's *Pietà* is safely home in St. Peter's. The one really good building in the whole sorry show, the gracefully disciplined Spanish Pavilion, has been shipped to St. Louis. Instead, we are left with Charles M. Luckman's banal U.S. Pavilion, a square doughnut on stilts. It is too early to know if we will heed the lesson of it all: Robert Moses, the fair's irascible director, had dismissed all attempts at planning and design controls. "Greek and Barbarian, traditionalist and modernist, conservative and iconoclast, right wing and left, all look alike to us." If they strained for anything with their wild, pop art structures, the designers strained for originality and one-upmanship. And Moses was right. They all seemed alike.

Though this American surreality, circa 1964, characteristically slashed by a monstrous freeway and full of messy alleys, showed us a frightening image of ourselves, we can also do better. That year I traveled to Lausanne and saw the Swiss National Exposition. It is held only once every twenty-five years and is not really a fair, but a means by which the Swiss take stock of their country and their aspirations. There was no advertising of individual products, no one had to outscream the other fellow. There weren't even any pavilions in the traditional sense.

Instead, the "Expo's" chief architect, Alberto Camenzind, hitherto little known, organized the whole thing into major thematic sectors. Each dealt with a general topic—agriculture, industry, commerce, national defense, the art of living, and the "Swiss Way," the most fetching exercise of dignified yet critical introspection I have ever seen in an official display. A team, consisting of an architect, a graphic artist, and a script or program writer, was in charge of each sector. Camenzind told each team to design multicellular clusters of strictly temporary structures (some of the New York structures seemed laboriously and expensively built for eternity), open spaces, and displays in its own distinct style. Each cluster was so arranged that you could gain a quick, overall impression of its displays by ambling along its main artery. Or you could get an overall impression by riding a little monorail right through the exhibition buildings. Once you knew what you wanted to see, you could delve into all the rich details.

It was a pleasure to stroll about. At the New York fair you were constantly pushed hither and yon by bullying buses or electric carts. At the Expo the walkways were only for people. The layout was expansive, affording impressive vistas of the structures—some of wood stained in color, some of a taut plastic material—all in surprising, simple, functional, and pleasing shapes. Their rich variety was enhanced by the landscaping with its grass-covered mounds, trees, pools, fountains, and sculptures. Yet you didn't tire as there was always a place to sit down and have your feet massaged on ingenious little automats.

In New York the amusements were relegated to a neglected corner of the playground. Here a marvelous, old-fashioned circus, a few tasteful sideshows, and games for children were dispersed throughout the grounds. Everything, inside and out, had amazingly high quality of modern design, and never had I seen good, and often abstract art so effectively employed as a means of communication. The entrance to the national defense exhibit, for instance, consisted of a dramatic labyrinth of battered, torn, beautifully rusting steel plates. At the end, quite suddenly, was a large photo of an atomic mushroom cloud. What more needed to be said?

I couldn't help recalling all the meaningless gimmickry in the home design and furnishing department of the Moses fair as I entered Switzerland's displays on the "art of living." New York was dismal with its "traditional" electrically lit kerosene lamps and plastic brick, Edward Durell Stone's unlivable "modern" atrium house with its empty gestures, translucent plastic pedestal chairs, and gaudily styled pastel-colored kitchen gadgets. The Expo presented the full range of community living from new playground equipment and adult recreation to the culture of good eating and table decorations. In between were fascinating displays on urban planning, demonstrations of the use of art in home and community, and a number of model apartments.

Furnished only with outstanding, though mainly inexpensive designs, these emphasized the efficient use of limited space with such things as ingenious cupboards, wash basins, and work areas. If this was a lesson in home economics and good taste, it was also sheer delight to see so much useful beauty in one place.

The highlight of the Expo was its gay, colorful canvas and cable structures, clustered around a little harbor on Lake Geneva. They housed a variety of restaurants, specializing in regional food and wines, and looked like giant sails bulging in the wind. We sat, unhurried over our *fondue,* watching people, boats, and gulls. In the haze beyond the lake, we were told, you can sometimes see Mont Blanc.

It was a long way from Flushing, not only in distance, nor even in the difference between an exposition and a fair. The main difference, it seemed to me, was that in New York they were only trying to sell, sell, sell us more of what we already have. The talent of our designers and architects served only the hucksters. And it is they, not we, who build our environment. In Lausanne design served to show us what we need; it was exploring values we might seek.

And that was also the theme of Expo 67, the international exposition in Montreal, whose designers were largely inspired by Lausanne. Searching for a leitmotif, the exhibition's planners (they all seem anonymous team players in contrast to Robert Moses's overexposed one-man show in New York) came across a quotation by Antoine de Saint-Exupéry. "To be a man," Saint-Exupéry wrote, "is to feel that through one's own contribution one helps to build the world." Montreal's resulting theme, "Man and His World" was not just a catch phrase. Both the national and international exhibits endeavor to show how man struggles to cope with his bewildering environment, natural and man-made, in various ways.

I have already mentioned Moshe Safdie's Habitat which alone was worth the Montreal effort and may rank with the Crystal Palace at the London exhibition of 1851 and the Eiffel Tower of the Paris exhibition of 1889 among the important architectural contributions only a large fair can make.

The rest of Expo's architecture, though far more restrained than that at Flushing Meadows, will hardly make the architectural history books. Buckminster Fuller's U.S. Pavilion, his largest dymaxion bubble yet, is a magnificent structure, and its interior displays are a delight. But will it prove to have a direct application to the problems of "Man and His World"?

I am quite certain, however, that Expo's exemplary planning will.

To be sure, there is nothing spectacularly original about it. Artificial islands have been created before. We have seen subways and monorails, good arrangements for the circulation of large numbers of people, well-designed rest areas and tasteful centers for amusements and festivities, noise control and countless other amenities. But it has seldom been applied with such success to make our cacophonous architecture as harmonious and not only interesting (New York was that!) but also enjoyable and considerate of people.

The lesson appears to be that good planning and urban design is far more important than good architecture. In many of its pavilions and, of course, its amusement area, Montreal, too, had its share of kitsch. It belongs to a fair with its easy appeal and it draws the crowds, as any good huckster knows. But it was kept in its place and not allowed to usurp the real thing. And that made Montreal, indeed, a contribution to building the world.

10. The Right Angle

There are some, though not many, American architects who left the steel and glass of the International Style but not the irrefutable logic of the right angle to which Saarinen returned with his Beaumont Theater.

Gordon Bunshaft and the New York office of Skidmore, Owings and Merrill followed up the Lever House with a number of other masterly glass-box corporation palaces, notably the Connecticut General Life Insurance Company Building in Bloomfield, Connecticut, and the superb Chase Manhattan Bank in New York's financial district. Bunshaft also began to use sculptured concrete about 1955 with his design for the Banque Lambert, an imposing office *palais* opposite the Place du Trone in the heart of Brussels. He sculptured what amounts to a cage made of cross-shaped concrete elements which both supports and encloses a box on stilts.

At Yale, for the Beinicke Rare Book and Manuscript Library, the form of these cross-shaped elements is even more plastic but also a little less graceful. The box at Yale appears squatty and quite massive in its surroundings of Classical and pseudo-Gothic buildings. At Brussels there is clear glass behind the sculptured framework. The Yale trusses frame thin, translucent marble panes. These appear opaque on the outside but are translucent enough to give the interior—essentially one enormous hall which contains the book stacks – a dim, eerie light to protect the often brittle old volumes. The trouble is that you expect clear glass in these frames, that you think they ought to be windows. The marble in them, however, gives them, to me at least, the depressing aspect of blind eyes. The paved plaza with a sunken sculpture court adorned with Isamu Noguchi's geometric sculptures heightens this stern, surrealist effect. The idea of placing offices under the plaza and providing them light, air, and charm with the sunken court – first used at the Chase Manhattan – is, however, ingenious.

My point is not to berate the Yale Library, but to praise SOM's use of subtly sculptured facades with their play of light and shadow on essentially International Style buildings. This enables them to get along with their neighbors much better than the polished harshness of glass does, particulary since the scale and shape of the sculptured elements can be varied to adjust to their essential features. Though I think he missed at Yale, at Brussels Bunshaft had come up with an innovation that others could and did adapt to good effect. He used his richly patterned facade as an essential part of his structure which somehow always seems to make an architectural innovation more convincing, even to people who don't particularly think about why a building stands up.

Marcel Breuer carried the idea a little further. He also used what amounts to deeply sculptured window frames of precast concrete to build the walls of his IBM headquarters at La Gaude, France, and, later, in his design for the similar Department of Housing and Urban Development in Washington. Like so many building blocks, these frames form load-bearing walls rather than curtains. Within the sculptured frames Breuer placed a host of mechanical devices such as air-mixing boxes, pipes and cables. This was an added stroke of genius since it gives these buildings that much more interior space and flexibility.

Before Bunshaft's Banque Lambert was actually built, his colleagues in the San Francisco office of SOM put a sculptured base – half arches, half stilts – under the bare and square fourteen-story shaft of San Francisco's John Hancock Insurance Building. It was much applauded because it introduced a bit of Expressionism at the bottom but didn't go all the way. The combination, however, is not a success. Mixing different spirits seldom works, except in a Martini.

A consistent combination of the sculptured window-frame facade rising on a sculptured arcade, however, became a fairly widespread style in office buildings. It promises to dominate the effort to complete

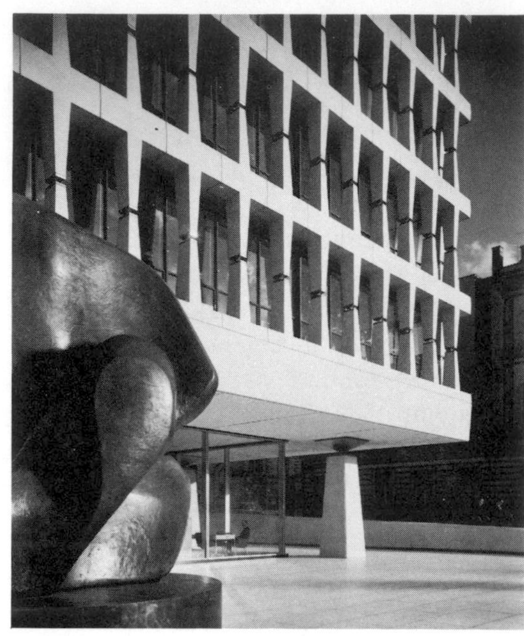

A sculptured cage

A dim, eerie light inside

A load-bearing wall containing ducts and pipes

Pennsylvania Avenue in Washington, D.C. in the Beaux Arts manner that Daniel Burnham and his friends introduced to the capital early in the century. As a match for the massive orderliness of the Federal Triangle, with its ornate and lively facade, it seems to me quite appropriate. I only hope our restless architects and planners stick to it because, as Mies has so often said, "it is better to be good than to be original."

If SOM's designers stuck to the right angle as a matter of essentially conservative sophistication, it seems to be rather a matter of conviction for Harry Weese and Ieoh Ming Pei. Weese told *Fortune*'s Walter McQuade that he rejects "the *ruins* school, or hair-shirt style, [which] calls for great piles of strong concrete forms—fine for druidic worship with the windows and furniture removed. The *nuts and berries* school prefers much bare unpainted wood in roofs and walls, with quintets of recorders playing and beards growing. The *bump* school wants to be utterly frank and honest; the rooms are hung outside the walls, to be seen in their full shapes. It's a little like turning the human body inside out and showing the gall bladder. The *temple* school goes in for placid buildings sitting on top of podiums, symmetrical, perfect,

"We are rational animals and . . .

pristine, separated from the asphalt world by bosky groves of trees. But all is not lost. We are rational animals and this thing is soon going to settle out and take a general direction. There will soon be more discipline by logic and need, and less by priests and chants."

Weese says he hates a building that brags, the instant styles that "spring up like orchids and look like the morning after." He even came right out and said it: "Architecture is a social art, not a free art."

Weese matches his verbal eloquence with equal architectural eloquence. In Chicago's Hyde Park-Kenwood area he has built clusters

. . . architecture is a social art."

of simple, relatively inexpensive town houses of brick and concrete that are at once urban and urbane. His small Arena Theater in Washington's Southwest, also a straightforward concrete and brick structure that frankly declares itself, has much individuality and character without being pretentious or arty. Weese has followed this up with a number of schools and theaters across the country whose touch of emotion is simply part of their good common sense. He was trained in the craft shops of Eliel Saarinen's Cranbrook.

Ieoh Ming Pei, born in China, is a graduate of the Massachusetts Institute of Technology. He, too, believes that architecture serves purposes nobler even than the composition of "frozen music." His interest is focused on new technological advances in building as a means to meet new human needs. He is, perhaps, the foremost urbanist among the celebrated architects of the day, not only because he often works as a city planner—he drew the masterplan for Boston's Government Center, for instance, though others have designed its buildings. He is an urbanist, also, because for him the individual building counts only in the context of the cityscape. He sees it as a room in the great house that the city ought to be.

Pei finds Mies still relevant, though he also finds the tremendous possibilities of plasticity which Le Corbusier has opened up hard to resist. "We're like children walking into a candy store," he says.

"The big commissions of the monumental sort—they usually don't come my way," Pei told Mrs. John F. Kennedy before, much to everyone's surprise, she chose him to design the Kennedy Library at Harvard. The popular magazines had never proclaimed him a "formgiver." Before he had built anything, William Zeckendorf picked him as the house architect of Webb and Knapp, the enterprising real estate development firm. During his years with Zeckendorf, Pei managed to raise the design quality of speculative developments to a height it had never before attained in America, an accomplishment for which Zeckendorf must also be given much credit. Pei's Kips Bay apartments in New York, the Mile High Center in Denver, and the Place Ville Marie in Montreal are perhaps not original, but just plain good architecture. His concept for Society Hill in Philadelphia, three superbly proportioned towers marking the exceptionally thoughtful modernization of this historic neighborhood, is, furthermore, a truly outstanding achievement of urban design. In all his many urban renewal projects Pei has managed to assimilate the aesthetic innovations of midtwentieth-century architecture without ostentatious gimmickry, and that is more than most others have done.

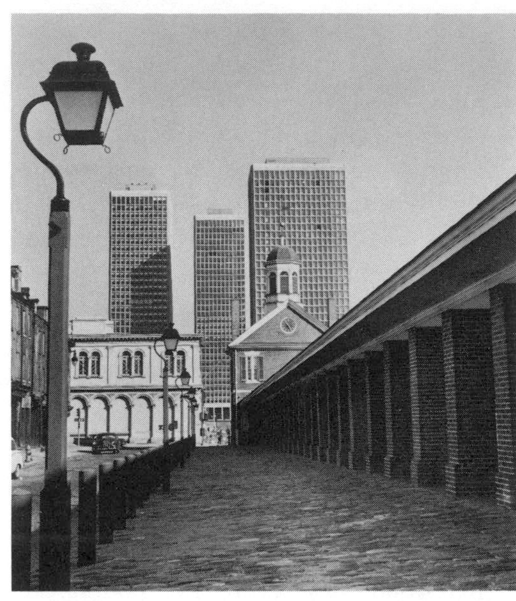

Pei's superbly proportioned towers

I have seen Pei's National Center for Atmospheric Research in Boulder, Colorado, and his Everson Museum at Syracuse only in drawings and photographs. With their craggy Corbu look, I suspect on both that Pei couldn't quite resist the candy store. He's young, and these were his first commissions since he left Zeckendorf's crumbling empire and ventured out on his own. Yet, Mrs. Kennedy and her international jury of eighteen of the world's most outstanding designers, guided by William Walton, chairman of the Federal Fine Arts Commission and a long-time friend of the Kennedys, searched long and conscientiously for the right man to design the library. Jacqueline Kennedy visited all the architects her distinguished advisers had put on the top of the list. In the end she felt "that Pei's best work, as John Kennedy's in 1960, was yet to come."

Noting that there is a "new breed of architects . . . interested not so much in the expression of personal taste and favorite forms as in people," Rice University recently honored I. M. Pei as a "people's architect." The term might have been dreamed up on Madison Avenue if not in the Kremlin. But Rice, I feel, had a point. Its architecture faculty, quite naturally, had to limit the honor and named only eight. In addition to Pei, the "people's architects" are Pietro Belluschi, Vernon de Mars, O'Neil Ford, Charles M. Goodman, Victor Gruen, John Lyon Reid, and Marshall Shaffer. One could easily add another dozen or so from among those whose work is frequently published in the architectural magazines. And space in their pages is almost as limited as the chairs at the head table of Rice's honor awards banquet. There are obviously, among the 24,000 registered architects in this country, some as yet unknowns whose work is not merely fallout from the stars but earnest and conscientious. The very young, in particular, are beginning to ask not what architecture can do for them but what they can do for architecture as a means to build us a good place to live.

Leading among the dozen or so that, had I been asked, I would have submitted to the Rice faculty, are Whittlesey and Conklin; Chloethiel Smith; Keyes, Lethbridge and Condon; Robert Geddes; Vincent Kling; and that great pioneer of socially conscious architecture in America, Oscar Stonorov.

I would also include Wurster, Bernardi and Emmons to join their San Francisco colleagues, John Lyon Reid and Vernon de Mars, on that list. San Francisco has lately produced a remarkably sensible and sensitive crop of architects and the Bay Area, consequently, has, on the whole, better architecture than any other American area. San Francisco architects tend to explain this phenomenon to themselves by citing the common hold of the Bay Area tradition, much as Chicago architects like to talk about continuing the tradition of the Chicago School. Neither actually do, in any but the most tenuous manner. San Francisco is rightly proud of its greatest historic architect, Bernard Maybeck, whose buildings have somewhat of a local flavor because he hardly built anywhere else. Chicago has a school because Jenney, Holabird and Roche, and Sullivan built the first unabashed skyscrapers there. Despite the rah-rah, I can't find much of the old school tie in the new buildings of either city. San Francisco still has an occasional bay window simply because it is the best way to enjoy the sun without the wind. Chicago still builds skyscrapers, but that's about it. What makes so many San Francisco architects so good is that theirs is one city in America which is truly beloved by its inhabitants and they force their architects to respect it—at least some of the time. There are few Chicago architects who put their city above their own or their client's ego. The builders of the ugly hundred-story John Hancock glass obelisk are not among them.

It is no accident that in spirit, more than in form, the work of the people I have so unjudiciously singled out in this chapter is so often akin to the more recent architecture of Northern Europe. Architecture has, of course, become as international as the civilization it serves. Flying an airplane, driving a car, operating a typewriter, drawing water, or the way of cooking a meal is the same in Nairobi, Stockholm, or Kansas City. Only the climate and, to some extent, the most easily available materials retain any influence on the kind of shelter needed for these activities. Air conditioning and reinforced concrete are diminishing even these last regional restraints.

Under these circumstances it is difficult to maintain regional differences in architecture or even city planning. But I am sure a rebellion against global monotony is not far away. People will demand an indigenous architecture for sentimental reasons. And the technicians will provide it when the art of architecture will truly get married to technology and science. For true technology will acknowledge differences in climate, geography, and the economics of available building materials. And science will acknowledge psychological and anthropological differences in space perception, living and working habits, and other cultural patterns.

Even now the rest of the world, and Northern Europe in particular, though it has been influenced by the seesaw of architectural preoccupation, has avoided America's extremes. There are, I believe, two reasons. For one, the Europeans love their cities and wouldn't risk disrupting them. For another, they have traditionally directed their architects' energies toward housing, while we leave it mostly to private enterprise. Scandinavia, England, West Germany, France, and Holland have thus managed to get rid of their slums and, on the whole, keep their old and make their new places to live remarkably livable.

The most outstanding architect across the seas today is no doubt Finland's Alvar Aalto. A prolific artist who advanced very early from the Functionalists, Aalto has a very personal style. His *oeuvre* reflects many of the currents and cross-currents of contemporary architecture, and he has come up with as wide a variety of different forms and approaches as any of the famous form-givers. He has by no means always stuck to angular geometry. On the contrary, Aalto is the master of the undulating curve, the flowing space and, often, of considerable intricacy in his design. His M.I.T. dormitory astounded the Moderns in 1947 with its serpentine shape. He chose it so that from all its windows the students would look diagonally, rather than straight, on the automobile traffic along the Charles River. This, he found, provides a more tranquil view. Nor is it quite correct to label Aalto's work particularly Finnish just because his buildings in Finland, as elsewhere, fit so well into the landscape. His community centers in numerous Finnish towns, notably the famous one at Saynatsalo, appear rustic, to be sure. They look as though they'd been there since the Middle Ages. To a large extent this appearance is due to their coarse brick—which is not a traditional Finnish material at all. As Jurgen Joedicke

As though it had been there all along

put it, "Aalto's architecture is always adjusted to the psychology of the people for whom he builds and to the needs of their particular situation. For him the yardstick is the individual person with his own special requirements, not the vision of a new society for which a new architecture would be appropriate."

I consider this a great tribute. For we do greater service to the society of tomorrow, it seems to me, if we try to straighten out our own than if we strain to get ahead of ourselves. This is not to say that I would repress great prophets in our midst. But the songs in a musical comedy, for example, that are written with an eye on the hit parade seldom make it. Those that are written to meet a specific situation in the show often do. The Taj Mahal was built as a monument to the Shah of Jehan's wife, not as a monument to eternity or even to delight. For delight is a fickle lady who soon spurns those who chase her too hard.

When Ieoh Ming Pei got his certificate as a "people's architect," he characteristically replied not with woolly pronouncements on social goals, which, he said, have basically always remained the same. He delivered a brilliant little essay on Baroque plazas. "We, too," he said, "need order and discipline in our cities."

11. Change

"It is not necessary," Mies van der Rohe once said, "to invent a new architecture every Monday morning."

That, however, seems just about what America's architects are currently doing. But it only seems that way. Actually no one, except the thin-shell engineers, has invented a new architecture, unfortunately, since the Bauhaus and Ronchamp. Everyone is camouflaging the same old architecture in ever new forms. There is rarely new content. It's forms, forms, forms. Pristine, transparent, Functionalist forms. Complex, massive, Expressionist forms. Sculptures in the sky. Sculptures hugging the earth. Classic forms. Streamlined marble. Kitsch.

Form, architects used to say, follows function. Now rationalization follows form. Sometimes it is clever. But there is little the "form-givers" have contributed to build us a better place to live.

"Vive le change!" replied Philip Johnson to a (mild) foreign critic of the current architectural scene in America. The implication seems to be that the kaleidoscope is in itself a virtue. Change, we are told, is the only constant in our time. Our environment is constantly changing. Why not architecture?

It makes some sense, if the restless change means that we are experimenting our way out of visual confusion. But even that, it seems to me, cannot be accomplished with a preoccupation with form per se, a mere chasing after new "delight." Without new "commodity" and "firmness," it's *plus ça change, plus c'est la même chose,* Philip! The more things change, the more they remain the same. The anarchy of forms surely does not add up to more attractive and livable cities.

Recognizing this, architects, a few years ago, gave much currency to the notion that there should be foreground and background architecture. The idea was that the exciting forms would be reserved for the important public buildings to accent a sober, serviceable architecture for all the rest. A leading proponent of this concept was Paul Rudolph. No sooner had he uttered it, however, than he proceeded to build his masterpiece in sinuous and vigorous architectural sculpture—a building that overwhelms its neighbors. Yet it is nothing but a parking garage located in downtown New Haven, a brooding Druid temple to the automobile.

The background-foreground notion is still valid, but it doesn't work unless architectural emphasis shifts from self-expression and frantic "form-giving" to disciplined environmental design. The shift has to be made at the top, by the leading talents because in our society—and to a lesser degree in all others as well—we all play "follow the leader." If chiefs make a fad out of nonconformity, the Indians will go on a veritable binge. Every architect looks upon every commission as his great opportunity to create a masterpiece and rightly so. But as long as the masterpiece is judged primarily on the basis of its originality, we rarely have quality or meaning. We can't divide the profession into background and foreground architects. Nor can we leave the background to the hacks. "If Le Corbusier can design Ronchamp, so can I," the hacks say—and turn their fakery into a drive-in bank.

It boils down to a question of morality. Although today's office towers dwarf church steeples, I am not prepared to believe that our society really deems the care and feeding of automobiles worthy of the most prominent structure in the cityscape. With a new architectural morality reluctantly returning, the new battle cry is now "Urban design!" Here, too, some critics detect a preoccupation with form, with a superficial battling for beauty, a fiddling and fussing with great plazas and grand vistas. This is fine, but only part of the answer.

Consider the American house, circa 1965.

A century earlier, a man liked his place to live, unless he was poor and lived in a shack. His house had the personal distinction our species craves. Within the same region and town, it was not fundamentally different from that of the next fellow. He saw no need to differ his housing any more than his dress. Within the same style he could express his personality with subtle variations of shape, color, and ornament.

The house was well built and usually so oriented to the sun that he could keep it reasonably cool in the summer and make it reasonably warm in the winter. He was, in fact, remarkably ingenious about that. The interior arrangement suited the way the family wanted to live. There were rooms where everyone would do things together. There were rooms for individual retreat. The spaces for work, for services and storage were conveniently placed but didn't get into the way of leisurely activities. Odds and ends were in the attic and potatoes and apples in the basement. The children didn't have to crash into the parlor if there was company. And father never had to smell the garbage or the kitchen.

In an effort to be fair to the contemporary house I once more, before writing this, scanned all the architectural magazines that litter my study. I found mostly rather bizarre sculptures, concrete clam shells on a cliff, scaled down pastiches of Louis Kahn's laboratories or Paul Rudolph's Art and Architecture Building, misunderstood Mies in wood, and tortured Tange in brick. The interiors show rhapsodies in spacecraft, living-room barns that soar and open every which way. They photograph beautifully, though the master of these houses probably starts beating not only the children but also his wife before the architect's fee is paid. Everybody must constantly get into everyone else's way. There are preciously few recent, architect-designed houses whose interior arrangements approximate the good sense of the old house on Elm Street in such a way that it can be run without servants. Richard Neutra's did. Lately I have seen a few—by Hugh Newell Jacobsen, Winthrop Faulkner, and Anshen and Allen among others—but not enough to make a trend. The trouble is that architects no longer address themselves to the problem. They design either for rich and eccentric clients with very special demands and tastes, or for themselves. A lovely house built for an elderly couple and their collection of African masks may turn out very photogenic. It will hardly contribute much to the cause. A house built by a young architect for himself is usually the big, expensive shingle he hangs out to the world. He must make it exotic to get attention.

Very few houses, however, are custom-designed by architects because it doesn't pay—for architect or builder. The vast bulk is built by speculative builders who give the public what it wants. The builders, however, read the architectural magazines and architectural innova-

Hugh Newell Jacobsen . . .

. . . and Winthrop Faulkner: Not enough to make a trend

tions, though often disguised by currently popular icing, are somehow worked into their product. Frank Lloyd Wright, for instance, pioneered the carport, the casement window, the utility core and the cathedral ceiling. Le Corbusier contributed the split level. I doubt that the builders would have thought of the picture window without the Bauhaus. From glass walls to patios and terraces, Modern architecture has introduced a pleasant relation between indoor and outdoor living. But that was about forty years ago.

Lately, however, there have been no fundamental architectural design innovations to inspire the builders. With the trend towards town houses and cluster development, we are beginning to see advances in planning. Technological improvements, however, are mainly restricted to housekeeping machinery. There have been none on the house itself. In part this is due to building codes. They do not permit such apparently helpful innovations as plastic plumbing. In part it is due to the stuffy regulations of the Federal Housing Administration. If the Harvard student dormitories had been dependent on FHA, which they weren't, Sert would never have gotten away with his ingenious, though Spartan, space arrangements, his unplastered interior concrete walls, or his economic use of elevators.

The essential cause of this conservatism is economic. The banker,

Modern houses to feel at home in

the builder, and the owner himself are afraid that a house that differs from the true and tried in more than its superficial veneer would impair its resale value. What's more, any attempt to better organize the house for the kind of rewarding family living people enjoyed a century ago would at once become more expensive. This, in turn, is the penalty for our lack of technical progress in housing.

A few large and enlightened builders do work with accomplished architects, and the results are gratifying. Edward P. Eichler's houses by Anshen and Allen and other outstanding architects in Northern California are an example. Edmund G. Bennett's houses by Keyes, Lethbridge, and Condon in the Washington, D.C. area are another. So are the houses in the New Towns, such as Reston, and in urban renewal areas which are architect designed. They are aesthetically more pleasing and often more livable than the eclectic suburban ranch and rambler models. Again, it is mainly a matter of form. They haven't gotten us out of the doldrums because here, too, government, bankers, and builders dictate to the architect "what the public wants," and that is to allow the patient to dictate to the doctor what medicine to prescribe. The architects gripe, to be sure. But most of them, like a recent jury of the important *Progressive Architecture* design contest, consider the individual house no longer an architectural problem. "No social significance," one juror commented. Much creative, scientific, and technical ingenuity has gone into the design of the space capsule. But no one has lately taken a good look where the children play in a house when there is company in the parlor, how we dispose of garbage, how we can read the Sunday papers in the bathtub in comfort and peace, or even how to fit a television set in with the rest of our furniture. We don't really quite know how a family lives, and how its house might be arranged so it lives well.

Perhaps the *Progressive Architecture* jury felt that only what the bureaucrats call "multi-family dwellings" have "social significance," despite the undiminished dream of most Americans for a house of their own. Here, too, we are just beginning to pick up again where the Modern movement deserted its revolution. Lately we've had only facades and forms to admire. Functional glass box or Expressionist sculpture, the depressing, long corridors are, if anything, worse than in Victorian tenement houses. The interior layout is mostly thoughtless and heartless and less efficient than a filing cabinet. Beams, columns, and awkward recesses and protrusions mess up the living space. Only larger dimensions, fancy trimmings, larger lobbies, and a swimming pool on the roof distinguish the much deplored projects for the poor from the luxury apartment houses for the rich. Nor am I convinced that the fluorescent lighted, air-conditioned work halls in our office skyscrapers provide fundamentally better working conditions than the counting houses in Charles Dickens' time.

Architects talk a great deal about space these days. The word has become a cult, the sublime and forever undefinable objective in art and architecture. We hear it ad nauseam: the dynamics of space, the interpenetration of space, the new concept of space, spatialism, spatial experience. As Leonardo Borghese said, science is much concerned with space these days, so the architects will not be left behind. After the athletes come the clowns.

Whatever space means to the architects, it does have a tangible and as yet too little explored meaning for architecture. Literally translated, the Sanskrit word for space, I am told, means "opportunity for things to happen." To create such space is the job of architecture. It must provide this opportunity in two ways. First, in the practical sense of inviting the activity the space is meant to serve—to sleep, to eat, to perform certain work, to make and listen to music, to meet spontaneously, and so forth. And second, in the psychological sense of giving us "a sense of space." Erik Erikson defines a "sense of" as something that pervades surface and depth, consciousness and the unconscious. It is, he says, "at the same time, ways of *experiencing* accessible to introspection, ways of behaving, observable by others [the children I mentioned, who stormed into Saarinen's chapel], and unconscious *inner states* determinable by tests and analysis."

Good architects arrive at spaces that are thus satisfying by intuition. Some artists and critics, such as Bruno Zevi, Kevin Lynch, Gyorgy Kepes, Bruno Goldfinger, Philip Thiel, and others, have recently probed beyond the fashionable space cult. *Structure in Art and in Science,* edited by Kepes, is rewarding reading on the subject. Only a few, however, have as yet put architectural space to test and analysis. Notable among those who have is Edward T. Hall of the Illinois Institute of Technology. Hall discovered some interesting differences in the way people of different cultures perceive and react to space. Japan's traditional house would be quite unbearable to an Arab. A Latin American business man doesn't feel he's getting through to his partner unless he practically sits on his desk and fumbles into his face. Within each culture you can almost mathematically determine what size and shape of space is sociofugal and keeps people apart and what space is sociopetal and brings them together. If you drive through the Holland Tunnel, says Hall, you feel that you are risking your neck at twenty-five miles an hour. On the New Jersey Turnpike the sixty-mile-an-hour speed limit is frustrating because at that speed you barely have the sense of moving at all.

As A. E. Parr wrote, "the devotion of modern architects to the study of the physical properties of materials, and of structural features, is well known and universally acknowledged. But it is difficult to find any evidence of equally vigorous encouragement, promotion or sponsorship of investigations into the stresses of the mind that their own designs might create or alleviate. Such matters have been left to artistic conviction without benefit of research, perhaps in a subconscious and mistaken fear that knowledge of the dynamic principles of harmony and pitch might hobble a composer's creative genius."

Beethoven got along without that knowledge, at least in terms of modern musicology. I surely would not want to see his symphonies entirely replaced by electronic music. I also like "frozen music" and would not want to live in a world built only by technology and science, surely not in Bucky Fuller's dymaxion world of bubble domes, megastructures, and super-cities.

It is precisely because I hope to avert this fate and hope to escape the slide-rule mentality of the engineers that I believe architecture can no longer get by with a few geniuses who are blessed with creative intuition. Even Le Corbusier did not achieve a truly human scale in all its dimensions, though he stamped many of his buildings with his Modulor. There aren't enough Le Corbusiers to make our environment human—a setting where the individual can find himself in creative activity and in nature. This calls for design, sensible, creative design of everything from the coffee cup to city planning, from useful ways of preserving old buildings to the invention of as yet undreamed of structures for as yet undreamed of purposes.

Since it is not within our power to endow the vast army of competent architects we shall need for this job with creative genius, we should at least endow them with humility, purpose, and knowledge. This much is entirely within the power of the architectural profession itself. It would seem, in fact, essential for its survival.

If this comes to pass the contest of form—Functionalism versus Expressionism, Mies versus Corbu, rationalism versus romanticism, or what have you—will seem utterly irrelevant. Neither will win out over the other. The contest has already become meaningless, much as the crusade of Christianity versus Mohammedanism petered out unresolved when the whole thing suddenly seemed no longer an issue worth crusading for. This is not to say that either Mies or Corbu have lost, or will lose their importance or our respect any more than Christ and Mohammed have lost theirs. It is to say that valid form still follows function. And, as Arnheim says, "The endeavor of an architect and his clients must indeed start with a commitment to the purpose of the building—but not just as a useful object, not just as an object whose usefulness deserves to be shown, but as an object whose function translated into a corresponding pattern of visible behavior will enhance the spirit of our existence and conduct as human beings.

"Whether we can hope to reintroduce this commitment without first reestablishing meaning in our practical life remains an open question."

IV. MAGNIFICENT VISTAS

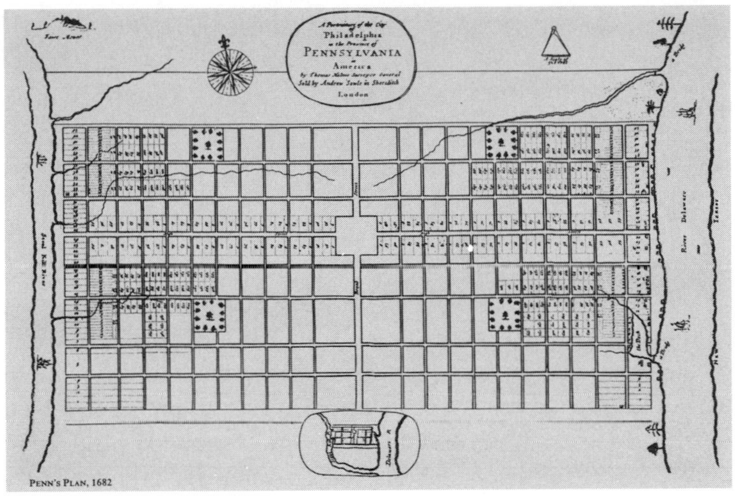
PENN'S PLAN, 1682

1. "Publick Concerns"

There is no account of the exact circumstances. I suppose on April 28 or 29, 1704, a messenger from Governor Francis Nicholson's office rode up to John Page's house at Middle Plantation, Virginia, and delivered a sealed letter.

It is, however, a matter of historic fact that John Page, a wealthy and prominent colonist, of all people, member of Virginia's General Assembly and donor of the land for Bruton Parish, was ordered to move his home because it interfered with the plan for the new town of Williamsburg.

The Journal of the House of Burgesses of Virginia contains this message from the governor, dated Thursday, April 27, 1704: "I recommend to you to give Directions that the old House belonging to Mr. John Page standing in the Middle of Gloucester Street be pulled downe that the Prospect of the Street between the Capitol and Colledge may be cleer and that you take Care to pay what shall judge those Houses to be worth."

Action was prompt. A week later, on May 5, it was "Ordered That the Sume of three Pounds be paid to Mr. John Page out of the Money in Mr. Treasurers Hands from the Late Impositions on Liquors Servants and Slaves—

"Ordered That Mr. Henry Cary forthwith sett the Labourers imployed about the Building the Capitol to pull down the four old Houses and Oven belonging to Mr. John Page which stand in Gloucester Street and have been appraised and that they lay the Bricks out of the Street on the Lott of the said John Page."

Said John Page was, of course, not unaware of his relocation. After the destruction of Jamestown, Virginia's General Assembly had decided to establish a new capital at Middle Plantation, to be called Williamsburg. Governor Nicholson, who had also himself planned Annapolis, when he was governor of Maryland, took a hand in drawing up both the plan and the legislation to implement it. It was, according to John W. Reps, "beyond doubt the most detailed piece of town planning law yet adopted in the English colonies. It specified the exact amount of land to be set aside for the town proper, the capitol building site, the public landing areas on the two rivers, and the roads leading from the town proper to these outlying river port areas. In great detail the law also defined the form and principal dimensions of the capitol building, including the pitch of the roof, the size of the windows, and many elevation specifications.

"The principal street, the Duke of Gloucester Street, was named in the act. All houses built on this street were to be set back six feet and to 'front alike.' For other streets the directors of the town, Nicholson among them, were authorized to adopt rules and orders governing dwelling size and setbacks. The town was to be divided into half-acre lots to be sold after public notice. Each purchaser was required to construct a dwelling within two years. Minimum house sizes were specified, with the larger houses required along Duke of Gloucester Street. All lots on the main street had to be enclosed with 'a wall, pails, or post and rails' within six months after the dwelling was completed."

Indeed little was omitted in this statute that the General Assembly could provide to guarantee a Capitol Building and a town which would, in the words of the act, result in a ". . . convenient sitting . . . at a healthy, proper and commodious place, suitable for the reception of considerable number and concourse of people, that of necessity must resort to the place where the general assemblies will be convened, and where the council and supreme court of justice for his majesty's colony and dominion will be held and kept."

John Page's house and that of some others, however, were in the way of the proposed Duke of Gloucester Street, the main axis, three-quarters of a mile long, that runs along the divide between the two

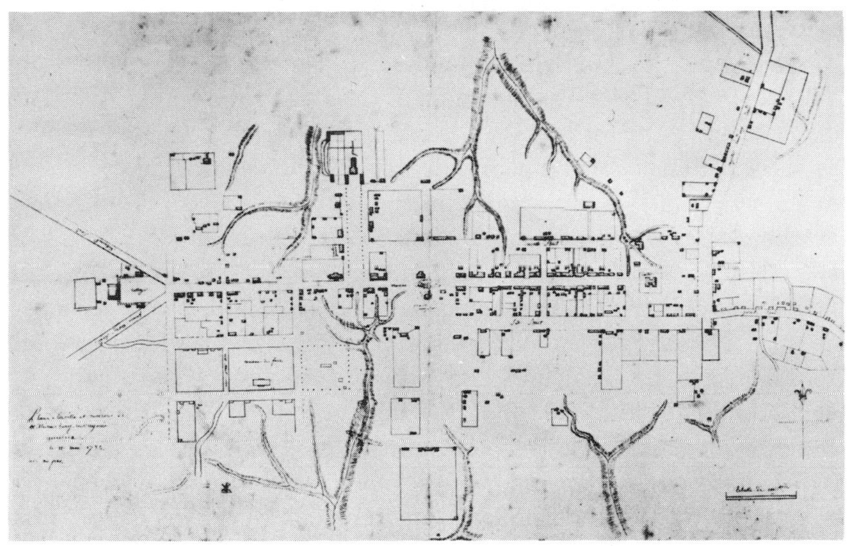

City planning was accepted as a public necessity

rivers and connects the Capitol with the College of William and Mary.

As far as anyone knows, Mr. Page consented to the dismantling of his home willingly and in good spirit. As a result—and thanks to John D. Rockefeller, Jr.'s restoration of Colonial Williamsburg in 1927—we now have one of the loveliest urban vistas in the country.

The forced relocation of the Page house is a telling footnote to history—the neglected history of city planning in America. It is a good little story to remember when people in zoning and planning hearings across the country carry on about the rugged, unregulated individualism of their forefathers and how no red-blooded American should ever submit to picayune restrictions.

Williamsburg was neither the only nor the first planned city in America. Our history of urban design begins four hundred years ago with the plan for St. Augustine, Florida, ordered by Don Pedro Menendez de Aviles in 1565. In fact, from Plymouth, Maine, to Los Angeles, California—with such particular gems as Savannah, Georgia, New Orleans, Louisiana, in between—all Colonial towns were meticulously planned, some, to be sure, for the common defense, but all for common convenience and amenity as well. The most imposing of them all, perhaps, was the "green country town" William Penn planned in 1682 between the Delaware and Schuylkill rivers. In the center of Philadelphia, as Captain Thomas Holme, who worked with Penn, described it, "is a Square of ten Acres; at each Angle are to be Houses for Public Affairs, as a Meeting-House, Assembly or State-House,

Market-House, School-House, and several other Buildings for Publick Concerns. There are also in each Quarter of the City a Square of eight Acres, to be for the like Uses."

Though Philadelphia's plan was, for a Colonial town, exceptional in its scope, the careful provision for "Publick Concerns" in every neighborhood was general. The formal objective of all planned towns was—and remains—to give visible form and symbolic order to civic life. In New England the religious and public buildings were grouped around the common green. In the South, as in Charleston, South Carolina, Mobile, Alabama, and New Orleans, community buildings and community life focused on a waterfront plaza. "The Laws of the Indies," proclaimed by Philip II of Spain, governed all Spanish settlements in this hemisphere and were America's first planning legislation. They prescribed a central plaza large enough "for festivals in which horses are used." It was to be surrounded by the church, the town hall, the customs house, arsenal, and other public buildings. The remaining sites on the plaza were to be used for shops and dwellings for merchants.

In addition, said the Law of the Indies, there was to be a common of adequate size so that even if the town should grow "there would always be sufficient space for its inhabitants to find recreation and for cattle to pasture without encroaching upon private property."

An admirably brief regulation ordained appearance: "Settlers are to endeavor, as far as possible, to make all structures uniform, for the sake of the beauty of the town."

The charm of the past did not just happen

A final admonition cautioned the settlers not to admit Indians to the community until construction was complete ". . . so that when the Indians see them they will be filled with wonder and will realize that the Spanish are settling there permanently and not temporarily. They will consequently fear the Spaniards so much that they will not dare offend them and will respect them and desire their friendship."

The Spaniards, like the French, the English, Dutch, and Swedish brought their ideas of city planning, along with their language, dress, social and religious beliefs, with them from their homelands. The predominant influence on all of them—though perhaps indirectly and subconsciously—were the early Renaissance towns, notably the ideal utopian town as conceived by Antonio Filarete in his *Treatise on Architecture* written between 1461 and 1464. This town was laid out on a gridiron plan, had its market square, a wall perimeter, and restricted size. Houses and townfolk huddled rather closely together for warmth and protection, but the size and openness of the community space contrasted strongly with the narrow streets and crowded compactness of the built-up surroundings, a thrilling surprise every time you came upon it.

Williamsburg is in concept a baroque city, much influenced by Christopher Wren's scheme for the reconstruction of London after the fire of 1666. Its intimate scale (it was designed for a population of about two thousand) nicely balances residential intimacy with abstract grandiosity. But the *bastide* and other early American towns were planned along essentially medieval concepts.

Most of us have been taught to look upon the Middle Ages as dark and ignorant. I am in no position to prove otherwise, and have, to my regret, never gotten around to follow G. K. Chesterton's advice to read "not historians, but history." I do try, however, to read the meaning of cities as I walk through them. Baroque cities with their grand vistas, I find—the grandeur of Pope Sixtus V's view from the Piazza del Popolo in Rome down the Via Corso, of Versailles, or of Haussmann's boulevards in Paris, or of Major Pierre Charles L'Enfant's and Daniel Burnham's great Mall in Washington—seek to *impress* man. The medieval town *expresses* man and the variety of his needs. The baroque city puts God into distant, abstract perspective. The medieval town seeks God in the human soul. The baroque city is built as a monument. The medieval town is built as a place to live.

This doesn't make the intimate, human town any less reverent—just think of Chartres. There is nothing impious about a bakery on the marketplace adjacent to the cathedral so people can buy a loaf of bread on their way home from vespers. Nor is there anything plebeian about a tavern next to the museum or opera house, where you can discuss your feelings about art in convivial surroundings. There is nothing anarchistic about shops around a government palace—nothing, that is, unless religion, art, or.government seek absolute power.

There is, I find as I attempt to read cities, much to confirm Chesterton's suspicion that "if the eighteenth century was the Age of Reason, the thirteenth was the Age of Common Sense."

This in no way diminishes the beauty and overwhelming impact of Bernini's columns, of Burnham's civic centers, or of his Washington Mall. But, as Lewis Mumford says, "Let us not obscure the essential nature of the change from medieval universality to baroque uniformity, from medieval localism to baroque centralism, from the absolutism of God and the Holy Catholic Church to the absolutism of the temporal sovereign and the national state, as both a source of authority and an objectivity of collective worship."

Dazzled, and rightly so, by the grandeur of baroque cities, we tend to think of the period that built them only in terms of its aesthetic accompaniments. "The unearthing," says Mumford, "and the measurement of classical monuments, the discovery of Plato and Vitruvius, the reverence for the Five Orders in Architecture, the sensuous delight in antique ornaments and in the new unburied statues—all this threw a garment of aesthetic decency over the tyrannies and debaucheries of the ruling powers."

While we should never confuse Renaissance accomplishment with baroque excess, we are now, I believe, reluctantly turning away from the absolutist urban design concepts of the Age of Reason, groping for a new renascence of the Age of Common Sense, or, at least, I think we should. The baroque concept, beginning with L'Enfant's design of our national capital, Burnham's adaptation of it, and his City Beautiful movement, has dominated what city planning there was in America right into our time. Baroque absolutism is also the premise of the city planning of the Modern movement—conceived at the Bauhaus and by Le Corbusier with his Radiant City and most completely realized at Brasília.

The danger today is that in our current rebellion against this formality, we reject all planning. But if common sense doesn't govern our environment, nonsense will. It does in fact. If we don't build our cities in the public interest they will continue to be ruined by private exploitation.

Planners are fond of asserting that they "can't play God," and it is their current fashion to cloak defeatist nonplanning in some mystical nimbus called "the continuing planning process."

Common sense as well as American tradition demand that the building and rebuilding of our communities make careful and comprehensive provisions for "Publick Concerns" to assure a "convenient sitting at a healthy, proper and commodious place."

2. "Reciprocity of Sight"

The largest of the comprehensively planned cities in North America is Washington. And it is, perhaps, ironic that the first new capital founded by an idealistic democracy in the wake of the downfall of Renaissance absolutism, was also one of the first major cities to adopt a baroque plan as a whole.

The very first, the prototype of an entirely baroque city, is, of course, Versailles. It was designed about 1690 by André Le Nôtre for the greater glory of the Sun King, Louis XIV of France. No sooner was Versailles completed in 1710, when Czar Peter the Great followed the example at St. Petersburg (now Leningrad), the new capital of his Russian Empire. So did Karl Wilhelm, Margrave of Baden, at Karlsruhe, Germany. And fully a hundred years later the clear, geometric grandeur, devised by a servant of despotism, was still so compelling that L'Enfant, a man of firm democratic conviction, could conceive of a great city in no other way.

Jefferson, to be sure, had different ideas for the Federal City at first. He proposed to build it along a gridiron plan, an adaptation of William Penn's plan for Philadelphia, "the old Babylon revived . . . & exemplified." His only complaint about Penn's city was that "the obligation to build the houses at a given distance from the street . . . produces a disgusting monotony." The contrary practice, he wrote, "varies the appearance & is much more convenient to the inhabitants." Jefferson considered the prohibition to build beyond a given height, however, "to be a good restriction."

Jefferson's idea to start settling the new city in a fairly limited area around the essential government buildings would have avoided, as John W. Reps points out in his *The Making of Urban America,* the scattered, piecemeal growth that L'Enfant's Washington was to encounter. But in the end he joined George Washington in giving L'Enfant complete freedom to develop his own idea. And if the two dismissed the impetuous Frenchman just about a year after he began his great work, it was due only to his eccentric and insubordinate behavior, not to any doubts about "the grand plan."

Such doubts about L'Enfant's "city of magnificent intentions" and "city of magnificent distances" have, however, persisted to our day. Morris Birbeck, who had come to America from England to establish a colony in Illinois, complained already in 1817 that the Italian marble columns of the new Capitol showed "how *un*-American is the whole plan." And Lewis Mumford writes in his *The City in History* in 1961 that L'Enfant carried over "into the new age the static image that had been dictated by centralized coercion and control."

Mumford, nevertheless, credits L'Enfant with a "true planner's insight" and pays "due tribute to the quality of L'Enfant's imagination." Most Americans, furthermore, are proud of their capital and impressed by it, and few will deny that its monumental heart, marked by that magnificent shaft, the Washington Monument, is one of the most beautiful urban sights in the country. Mumford's criticism is, nevertheless, of more than historic interest because it strikes at the root of still persisting baroque city-planning ideals. Only a critical examination of old concepts can constructively lead to new ones.

There is, to begin with, an important difference between the old cities, such as Rome, Paris, or London and others, where baroque urban design enhances important monumental aspects, and cities such as Washington or Brasília which are baroque in their entirety. A somewhat ostentatious living room with high ceilings and large dimensions contributes to the beauty and livability of a house. If all rooms in a house are ballrooms, it may be a grand palace, but it won't be very livable, certainly not without a great many servants and lavish furnishings.

Baroque planners learned from the great and vital rediscovery of the Renaissance that architecture and urban design must be treated as a

Leonardo da Vinci proposed tunneling traffic 500 years ago

single theme. It was a rediscovery because the famous *Ten Books on Architecture* the Roman architect Vitruvius had dedicated to Emperor Augustus had just been found collecting medieval dust in the monastery of St. Gall. Vitruvius emphasizes the relation of the building to its site, its surroundings, and the divine elements. The ancient Greeks, whether or not they planned their temples on the basis of an elaborate mathematical system, as Constantinos Doxiadis asserts, were surely fully cognizant of the interaction of buildings and landscape. They created their temple cities, says Vincent Scully, as "an unmatched dialogue between oneness and separateness, men and nature, men and the facts of life, men and the gods." There can be no better definition of what a good city as a good place to live is all about.

The first Renaissance theoretician of urban design was Leon Battista Alberti. Like a good many other Renaissance men, such as Vasari, Filarete, Fra Giacondo, Leonardo da Vinci and Albrecht Dürer, Alberti devised numerous designs for ideal cities and these had a profound influence on the urban renewal of Italian cities that began at about the time Columbus set sail for America.

These urban renewal efforts were motivated by the desire to improve circulation, sanitation and defense. They still are today. Defense is still on our minds, if you consider the continuing talk about air raid shelters and the fact that the Federal Highway Act of 1956, the most powerful force in contemporary city building, was sold to us by the Eisenhower Administration as a national defense measure.

The most imaginative of the Renaissance urban renewal schemes were the concepts developed by Leonardo da Vinci. Inspired by his revulsion of the crowding and squalor he found in Milan which had led to an outbreak of pestilence that decimated its population in 1485, he sketched a new city straddling the river. Its waters would be diverted into six or seven parallel canals that would stream through the settlement to supply water and carry away the waste. The city was to be built on three levels: the lower for water and sewage (hydraulically controlled so swift streams could clean them), the middle for vehicular movement, and the upper for the pedestrian enjoyment of the "gentlemen" of the city.

Leonardo also proposed movable wooden houses so city workers could live in the fields to plant and harvest crops and, at the same time, improve their health. Leonardo anticipated the green belt as an open space around the city, the modern idea of satellite or New Towns, and the tenet that urban growth is not necessarily an advantage but should and can be deliberately limited. More than four hundred years later this concept was again advanced by Ebenezer Howard. It was eventually adopted by the British Government in the New Town Act of 1946.

The most brilliant and influential Renaissance city planning was Domenico Fontana's design for the renewal of Rome, commissioned by Pope Sixtus V. The Renaissance formulated scientific principles of perspective which led to a new perception of space. This, in turn, led to

Leonardo's concept for a clean city

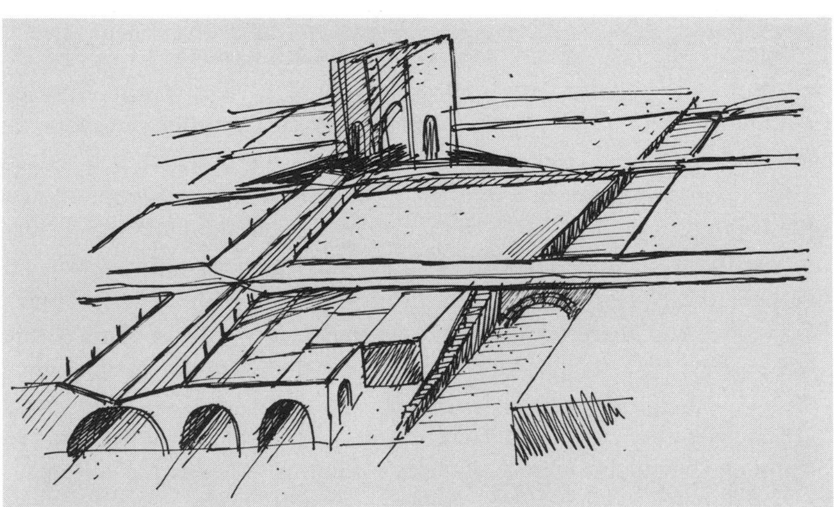

a new manifestation of urban form that followed a newly felt functional need.

Sixtus' renewal, like that of all the other Italian cities, was also, of course, prompted by a need for slum clearance, improved sewage and water supply, tax reform, better administrative organization, and a comprehensive transportation system. But Rome, as the capital of Christendom, had a special problem. Pilgrims swarmed into the city in ever greater numbers to see and partake in religious ceremonies at the sacred spots of the city. They found only confusion.

Sixtus' great achievement was to restructure the city with a system of highways which, as Edmund N. Bacon points out, provided more than the backbone for the modern transportation system of Rome. Sixtus marked out the key points of this system with tall obelisks left over from the days of the Roman Empire to accentuate their importance, focus perspectives and heighten the perception of space. The movement of people, now experienced as a procession, became part of the vistas, part of the scene. People no longer merely looked at urban design, they were immersed in it.

"Perhaps the most important single thing that Sixtus did," says Bacon, "was to re-think the street; to see it as a functional device for getting people about efficiently on foot, on horseback or in a cart, and at the same time see it as a place for the drama of life. But his street merged into the square, a rich and ceremonial place, dominated by an architectural form, giving the quality of life to all of the area touched by it."

Thanks to Sixtus, says Bacon, "we see Rome as a great human experience, richly modulated by the diversity of visual symbols dispersed throughout the city, giving special flavor and character to each part, and providing nodal points for the rallying of loyalties, a quality that could be given to it only by the architect, but by the architect related to the city through the medium of total design structure."

What was important in Rome, as it was in the Renaissance renewal of cities like Florence and Turin, was a piecemeal modification. It was not, as Mumford noted, a wholesale rebuilding of the entire town. "If one uses the term precisely," Mumford explains, "there is no renascence city. But there are patches of renascence order, openings and clarifications, that beautifully modify the structure of the medieval city."

In the baroque era, Mumford continues, some of this spirit lingered on—in the Spanish Steps or Bernini's squares, for example. But "as soon as the Baroque order became widespread, uniform and absolute,

"Nodal points for the rallying of loyalties."

when neither contrast nor evasion was possible, its weaknesses lay revealed. Clarification gave place to regimentation, openness to emptiness, greatness to grandiosity."

Not even Versailles is as grandiose a concept as L'Enfant's Washington. L'Enfant had a fairly discouraging site to begin with—a triangular swamp bounded by the Potomac and Anacostia rivers and a half-circle of gentle hills between them. In the center was a mere mound, Jenkins Hill. To this site L'Enfant adroitly applied Fontana's urban design structure as Le Nôtre abstracted and formalized it for the Sun King.

The abstraction and formalization of Renaissance concepts at Versailles was due not only to the underlying absolutist philosophy, but also to the fact that Le Nôtre—like L'Enfant in Washington and later Lucio Costa at Brasília—planned from scratch. It was not, as in Rome, a matter of connecting and relating existing points of significance. These points had to be created, somewhat like the abstract painters of today, who having forsaken "representational objects," create their own objects of interest.

At Versailles the central, dominating point is the Palace, of course. From there, eastward beyond its forecourt, the Place d'Armes, the town is composed along three radial avenues. They are much like the three vistas that branch out in a *patte d'oie,* or "goose foot," as the French call it, from Fontana's Piazza del Popolo, originally the main entrance to Rome.

Westward, beyond the rear terraces and the *Parterres d'Eau*, the water gardens, and along one long center axis, the *Tapis Vert*, is the park of Versailles. It is, as Paul Spreiregen says, crisscrossed by "a veritable encyclopedia of vista axes—some long, some short, some single, some multiple." In the distance shimmers a large reflecting pool and even the sky is tied into the composition.

The punctuation in this network are the *rond points*, the dramatized intersections of these various axes. They are an invention, originally, of the French nobility which was fond of hunting. If you cut long straight clearings in the forest, the nobles found, you could spot game running from one wood to another. From such an intersection you could scan two or more pathways simultaneously. The *rond points* soon became places of social meeting and from parks the idea soon spread to urban design.

With a generosity surpassed only at Brasília, L'Enfant adopted all this to his plan for Washington. He started with the Capitol which he placed on Jenkins Hill, "a pedestal waiting for a monument," as he called it. From there he rolled a *Tapis Vert* right down to the river and this is crossed by another wide swath, at one end of which he placed the President's House, now called the White House. (Paul Rudolph is quite right, of course, when he advocated that this formal symbolism should logically have been completed by placing the Supreme Court at the other end of this cross axis instead of stashing it unceremoniously somewhere into the shadows of the Capitol.)

From the Capitol, also, radiate L'Enfant's major avenues, imposed upon a gridiron street pattern and dotted with *rond points*, "to preserve through the whole a reciprocity of sight." The Grand Avenue, as he called this *Tapis Vert*, now the Mall, is 400 feet wide and a mile long. The principal avenues were to be 160 feet wide so that each of them was equal to the Champs Elysées. All in all—a modern highway engineer's dream—more than half of the six-thousand-odd acres included in his plan were given over to highways.

Here was indeed the framework of the baroque city *par excellence* and if George Washington, Jefferson and the other founders of our republic accepted so monarchial a scheme, it was because they saw its ostentatious generosity as an expression of the Age of Enlightenment. Jefferson, in particular, was repelled by "a depravity of morals, a dependence and corruption" which he found in the cities of Europe and was, at the time, altogether convinced that America had best do without cities altogether. If a city was needed to accommodate the national government, it might as well, he seems to have felt, be spread out and verdant to minimize the dangers of crowding, fire, and yellow fever, which were very much on everyone's mind at the time.

L'Enfant, nevertheless, conceived the Federal City as far more urban and mundane than it turned out to be—at least for a long time. He provided "for the market with the town house, the barge landing with the government building," as Spreiregen has written. "The poise and assurance in the gentlemen of his era was not shaken by marketing in proximity to a palace. After all, where does one best enjoy a good drink or the purchase of a fish but out in the open—simultaneously viewing the splendor of great architecture and a grand vista?"

The barge landings, however, didn't last long because Washington never became the great commercial port its founders had reason to hope it would become. Baltimore was too far ahead. And if the good drink and fish are hard to come by in L'Enfant's monumental Washington, it was because his avenues were too wide, his *rond points* too vast for true urban life and bustle to develop. There never was, and still isn't, much reason for people to congregate on the Mall along the monumental avenues. And although Washington is the first American city to open a fair number of sidewalk cafés, it is interesting to note that there are none on any of L'Enfant's *rond point* circles. Only now, in a new age of affluence and leisure are we at least thinking to artificially stimulate popular enjoyments with cafés and all kinds of diversions

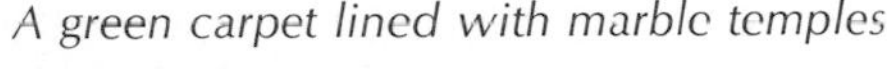

A green carpet lined with marble temples

on that desert. For that is what Nathaniel Owings' new plan for the Mall, prepared in 1966, is all about. But to date, the action is in Georgetown with its narrow streets and more compact layout. And here, in modest nineteenth-century dwellings, as I noted earlier, and not along the grand avenues, is also the most favored and expensive residential area in the capital.

If Washington falls short of L'Enfant's ardent dream, as it surely must, it is, Mumford noted, because "the framework was there, but the contents were absent. For one thing was lacking: the power to execute the plan by building. The order existed on paper, but not in fact."

Sixtus V rebuilt much of the Rome of his time in five years, and Baron Haussmann changed the face of Paris in not much more time. The virgin forests of Versailles were transformed into a great work of art and humming with life, festivities and intrigue within forty years. Washington is still incomplete. Although this nation surely doesn't lack the resources to build a great capital, democracy lacks the absolute power—and, for that matter, the will—to carry out an absolute plan. "L'Enfant forgot," says Mumford, "that time is a fatal handicap to the Baroque conception of the world; its mechanical order makes no allowances for growth, change, adaptation, and creative renewal. Such a command performance must be executed, once and for all, in its own day."

The capital city has grown, of course. The inner city, the District of Columbia, is now the ninth largest in the country and its metropolitan area includes two million people and is one of the fastest growing in the country. But although this growth is primarily dependent on the federal government, the symbolic and monumental seat of that government, the Washington its top officials and the tourists see, and the actual living city are in reality two separate entities.

Not only is the national capital with its marble palaces, its diplomatic receptions, pomp and circumstance, a thing apart. It also, due to a silly political arrangement and simple political arithmetic, neglects the Other Washington.

The silly arrangement, of course, is the fact that under the management of three Presidentially appointed Commissioners, the District of Columbia is run directly but absentmindedly by a busy Congress like some territorial possession. The fact that the majority of the District population is Negro and the majority on the House District Committee is white-supremacy Southern, accounts for the political arithmetic which adds up to chaotic frustration, much of it deliberate. The majority of the Negro population, furthermore, is poor, confined in a ghetto with limited access to transportation to jobs and recreation, and thus on a sidetrack of the American way of life.

The authorities—not only Congress and the President but also the National Capital Planning Commission, the Fine Arts Commission and other multitudinous agencies—are primarily concerned with the Official Washington and its image. The officials hardly notice the Other Washington as they speed through it to offices in the monumental core or back to homes, recreation, and a life that is usually set apart in lovely suburbs and special places like Georgetown. This is where most new playgrounds and libraries are built and most civic improvements are made. And this explains why the new Kennedy cultural center is built, not in the center of the city, but, as its manager Roger L. Stevens put it, "in the geographic center of Washington's cultural elite," the carriage trade in the suburbs.

The dichotomy, however, prevents Washington from becoming the great capital the nation deserves. In Paris, London, and most other seats of government, capital and city are one. Each benefits from the combination. The pomp and ceremony of government is enhanced by the intense cosmopolitan life around it. And vice versa. Paris and London, of course, are not only governments but also economic centers. Washington is not.

In Washington the isolation of officialdom from a stimulating urban life—the opportunity to encounter people of different vocations and interests, of sparking ideas and exposing ideas to many minds—is sadly apparent. One result is, for instance, officialdom's sad innocence in matters of taste and art, which has caused us more than one embarrassment abroad. Snobbish foreigners, who still hold that the United States is gauche, really mean that Washington is gauche. But how are they to distinguish when elsewhere a capital represents its country? I know of more than one talented young expert who idealistically went to work for the federal government but left within a year or two because he found it spinning creaky wheels in a cultural and (despite five mediocre universities) academic desert.

L'Enfant's "reciprocity of sight," it seems, turned out to be mainly scenic.

And even the intended scenic aspects were saved from total obliteration by two circumstances alone. The first was Alexander Robey Shepherd, who, assuming dictatorial powers as District Commissioner, carried out a series of major civic improvements after the Civil War. "Boss" Shepherd constructed many miles of sewers, paved many of the dust-choked streets and avenues, provided water facilities and spacious parks, and, most importantly, hid both Washington's many architectural misdemeanors and the few of its glories alike behind an abundance of trees.

The tree planting, in particular, was naturally greeted with outcries of "waste of public funds." Even today Americans have not yet quite understood that public commodity and amenity require public expenditures as urgently, if not perhaps as obviously, as expenditures for the common defense. Nor has Congress yet understood that the realization of a single-minded baroque plan requires the exercise of baroque power and lavishness. It hasn't shrunk from such exercise when it comes to its own edifices, such as its Sam Rayburn Building, or its reckless tampering with the Capitol itself. But it is traditionally parsimonious and jealous when it comes to the general setting of the Capitol. Boss Shepherd, at any event, though found innocent of the personal corruption with which he was charged, was dismissed after only four years in office.

If Shepherd's administration of first aid was essentially pragmatic, the second rescue effort was entirely idealistic—Daniel Burnham's City Beautiful movement. It was, if you will, a baroque revival, and as such, of course, uniquely suited to lift Washington out of its quagmire.

3. The City Beautiful

In the century between L'Enfant and Burnham, a century of muscle flexing and empire building, the art of city planning was all but forgotten in America. With unlimited space, opportunity, and natural resources seemingly boundless, the country saw no need for it.

Our cities expanded as enormous work camps of the Industrial Revolution. They were laid out along a rigid gridiron pattern, the simplest way to put the sewers down. As a rule they simply skipped natural obstacles, except in a few places like San Francisco, where the gridiron climbed clear up Nob Hill.

Industry, the *raison d'être* of the work camp, was located in the center, sliced up by railroads. The residences surrounded it. As industry grew, it leapfrogged this residential ring and formed an outer belt. Meanwhile small industries and commerce infiltrated these trapped residential belts and made them less desirable. Those who could afford it thereupon did some leapfrogging of their own, forming new residential areas beyond this "gray belt," leaving slums behind. Business followed these middle class fugitives and established new "uptown" centers.

Thus, as developer Robert A. Futterman has said, "every American city shows these alternating bands of glory and garbage." To keep up with the Joneses meant moving from one place to another, and this became something of an American tradition that still continues. Today, as Futterman put it, "wherever the frog leaps he is powered by an internal combustion engine." Yet there are still many city planners who will tell you that this is the inevitable law of organic growth.

Daniel H. Burnham, considered the country's leading architect around the turn of the century, held much the opposite view. "Make no little plans," he said, "they have no power to stir men's blood." And what glory there is in the garbage Futterman spoke of, is largely the doing of Burnham's City Beautiful movement.

It began with the World's Columbian Exposition, the Chicago fair of 1893 that came to be known as the White City. Burnham and his partner John Root were the architects in charge. Frederick Law Olmsted as consulting landscape architect recommended the site at Jackson Park near which the University of Chicago is now located, and was responsible for the general plan. Richard Hunt, McKim, Mead, and White and other notables of the day designed the buildings. The sculptor Augustus Saint-Gaudens was put in charge of sculptural decorations and fountains. He told Burnham at the end of one of the

What did it matter that it was mostly plaster?

group's long, feverish meetings: "Look here, old fellow, do you realize that this is the greatest meeting of artists since the fifteenth century!"

If it wasn't quite that—what with Louis Sullivan only reluctantly and belatedly invited to participate with one building—"it most certainly was the nearest thing to it that nineteenth-century America could furnish," says Reps in his *The Making of Urban America*. The result of the team's labors was a sensational novelty, in contrast to the dingy industrial cities of the time, a vision of some earthly paradise that might yet be created in the new century.

Somewhat in the manner of the Paris Exposition four years earlier that had made the Eiffel Tower famous, the gleaming white buildings were, in the baroque manner, disposed symmetrically around a formal court of honor. Their domes and columns echoed Roman temples. "A city of palaces set in spaces of emerald, reflected in shining lengths of water which stretch in undulating lines under flat arches of marble bridges and along banks planted with consummate skill," reported an ecstatic writer in *Harper's Magazine*. I don't know about the bridges, but the buildings certainly were not marble but plaster. It didn't matter.

The "violent outbreak of the Classic and the Renaissance," as the unhappy Louis Sullivan fumed, had, indeed, "penetrated deep into the constitution of the American mind," though his charge that they there effected "lesions significant of dementia" overstated the case. The achievement of the new Washington and the new civic centers the Chicago fair inspired was not so much the Classic and Renaissance temples that were built in often remote parks, but the parks themselves. The "frosted pastries on a tray," as Jane Jacobs has called these Beaux Arts buildings, were rarely a success, except, perhaps, as a new source of civic pride. Not a few are surrounded by dead areas, strewn with empty whiskey bottles and other litter, and instead of uplifting their surroundings, depress them. People stayed away, all the more so because many of these culture palaces never managed to generate enough culture to remain more than pompous shells. But many of the "trays" are still a blessing. They furnish much needed open space in the city and the parks serve it as vital lungs.

Most of the parks—ultimately for some seventy cities—were designed by Frederick Law Olmsted, perhaps America's greatest prophet of livable cities. He owed much to Thoreau. But he was the first to create Thoreauvian settings of lakes, meadows, rocks, and wooded heights right in the center of urban surroundings—a radical departure from the formal palace gardens of the Old World aristocracy we had imitated before him.

His first great triumph, long before the City Beautiful movement, was his design of New York's Central Park which won a national competition in 1851. Among its innovations is the strict separation of a system of walkways separate from the driveways. People on foot, thanks to Olmsted's under- and overpasses, don't get mixed up with vehicles. Even today, though combustion engines mix hardly better with humans than the horses and their carts of Burnham's day, this almost ludicrously simple idea is still only tenuously accepted.

Neither is Olmsted's simple tenet that both parks and urban design ought to relate to the climate and natural surroundings. At Stanford University, under California's bright sun, for instance, his clients insisted on their visions of an Ivy League campus with generous expanses of turf. In the end Olmsted's far more suitable scheme of compact building arrangements, paved areas, and cooling fountains was at least partially accepted. Thanks to him Stanford also still has a mile wide, permanent greenbelt to separate the campus from Palo Alto.

Olmsted was not only a great landscape architect but also a compassionate humanist. He was deeply involved in the great social issues of his time: urbanization, immigration and, most of all, slavery. He travelled extensively in the antebellum South and his book, *The Cotton Kingdom,* proved, according to Mumford, "far more damning than the violent melodramatics of Harriet Beecher Stowe." He ran a successful model farm on Staten Island. He organized the Civil War Sanitary Commission, which later became the Red Cross. At Yosemite he headed the commission that gave us our first national park. And to build his great parks, he was forever fighting greed, official stupidity, and corruption.

Such spirit was nowhere more needed than in Washington. The capital was in a sorry state when the Burnham group met there for the thirty-fourth annual convention of the American Institute of Architects in 1900 to celebrate the centennial of the capital's founding. The L'Enfant plan was all but obliterated. In many ways the jungle had come back.

Right from the start the landowners and commercial speculators, not the government, asserted control over the development of the city. That had led to L'Enfant's dismissal, for even George Washington respected Daniel Carroll, the greatest landlord in the District, more than the integrity of the grand plan. Washington also pleaded in vain with his friends to settle in the residential district L'Enfant had laid out around the Capitol. But the pull and lure had right fron the start been westward. The city ran away from the imposing structure that was to be its center. It still does. The plan, it turned out, was too vast and ambitious to compel orderly development, even in a century which everywhere else in America saw spectacular growth. The Capitol, the seat of the legislative power of that continent, still dominated a landscape which, as Mumford put it, was filled "with a spreading mass of urban flotsam and jetsam, cast overboard in the storm of capitalist enterprise."

The Mall, in particular, was a disgrace. It had become the city's principal sewage collector. At one time there had even been talk of building a summer White House to spare the President and his lady the stench of the place. Along its northern edge were lumber and coal yards. Along the Potomac, where John Quincy Adams had taken his early morning swims, was a malarial swamp the Army Engineers had just begun to fill in. The Baltimore & Ohio had laid its tracks across the head of the Mall. Beyond this the Pennsylvania Railroad crossed it, with its station on the Pennsylvania Avenue side. The Baltimore & Potomac had its station where the National Gallery now stands. And much of the space in between the tracks was cluttered with storage yards and parked railroad cars.

When Andrew Jackson designated the site for the Treasury Building, he stabbed his cane right in the path of Pennsylvania Avenue, the intended ceremonial axis from the Capitol to the White House. And although there was much congressional debate in 1846 about the relative merits of James Renwick's "toothpick Gothic" or Romanesque design for the Smithsonian Institution, there was no question about its intrusion on the Mall.

The first attempts to get congressional action on a monument to George Washington were made in 1819. When neither President John Quincy Adams nor Henry Clay could get anywhere with Congress on the matter, a society was founded which, in 1836, called for a competition. It was won by Robert Mills.

L'Enfant had envisioned an equestrian statue of George Washington at the point where his north-south and east-west axes intersect. The engineers missed the spot by 370 feet, due to foundation problems, when they erected Mills' magnificent obelisk, luckily without the wedding cake embellishments he had intended around its base. The cornerstone was laid in 1848. It took thirty-seven years to complete, what with obstruction by the Know-Nothings, fund raising difficulties, the Civil War and an indifferent Congress.

The celebration of the capital's centennial, however, put Congress in a somewhat friendlier mood. The architects' beautification conference, as we would call it today, did not go unheard. Senator James McMillan of Michigan, chairman of the Senate's Committee on the District of Columbia, invited Burnham, Charles F. McKim, and Frederick Law Olmsted to submit specific plans for a more beautiful inner city, provided, of course, they would furnish it without cost to the government.

The committee promptly embarked for a summer in Europe. "How else," Burnham had written McKim, "can we refresh our minds except by seeing . . . all those large things done by others in the same line?" How else, indeed?

The McMillan Plan, as it came to be known, transformed, as it were, L'Enfant's baroque urban design into a baroque park design. It concerned itself, not with the living city but with building sites and open spaces. The Mall was to be extended three-quarters of a mile westward to the Potomac banks. There was to be a new Memorial Bridge. And along with its trees the McMillan Commission planted such white marble temples as the Lincoln Memorial, which at last gave L'Enfant's layout the lacking third dimension.

The plan was produced within a year. There was a gala viewing of the models and sketches at the Corcoran Gallery and, according to Charles Moore, Senator McMillan's assistant, "there came President Roosevelt [Teddy, of course], interested, curious, at first critical and then, as the consistent scheme dawned on him, highly appreciative."

But gala model viewings and even appreciative Presidents make scant impression on Washington's jungle. Congress' first response was to propose an enlargement of the railroad holdings on the Mall by fourteen acres so that a huge new station and train shed could be built. Even Senator McMillan defended the appalling scheme.

It so happened, however, that in London Burnham, McKim, and Olmsted chanced upon Alexander Cassatt, none other than the president of the Pennsylvania Railroad, which also owned the Baltimore & Potomac and had just acquired the B. & O. The architects proved eager and persuasive guides. Presumably avoiding all railroad stations, they showed Cassatt the beauties of Hyde Park, the Bois de Boulogne in Paris, and the glory of Versailles. In the end he gave in.

Cassatt volunteered to withdraw his railroad from the Mall and to collaborate in building the present Union Station, to be designed by Burnham, provided Congress would compensate him for the expense. This much Congress agreed to. But the House of Representatives had not been asked to concur in the appointment of the McMillan Commission. "Uncle Joe" Cannon, the Speaker of the House, vented its collective ire and approved no other part of the plan.

Far from discouraged, Burnham maintained, however, that "a noble and logical diagram once recorded will never die, but long after we are gone . . . assert itself with ever growing insistency." What kept it alive through World War I was mainly the American Civic Association which has recently become Urban America, Inc., and has, thanks to a generous injection of philanthropy on the part of Stephen R. Currier, gathered new momentum in recent years.

It was not until 1922 that the Lincoln Memorial was dedicated. It took another ten years to complete the Memorial Bridge with its imposing landscape schemes on either side. The Federal Triangle, a monstrous bureaucratic ghetto with its three-quarter mile runs of wall-like facades, was built, due mainly to the prodding of Andrew Mellon, between 1928 and 1938. Mellon's National Gallery followed three years after that. And although it seems that it has been there forever, the Jefferson Memorial completed the picture-postcard Washington as we know it today only in 1943.

Frank Lloyd Wright called this Beaux Arts Roman pavilion "an arrogant insult to the memory of Thomas Jefferson," and "a confession of impotence." It was that, in a sense, considering the vitality of his own and other mid-twentieth-century architecture. But, although this is still heresy among modernists, this and all the other mediocre pomposities the City Beautiful movement has wrought form a backdrop for an emotional experience we can no more imagine otherwise than we could physically remove the buildings. They are certainly far better than the more recent marble monstrosities on the Mall, notably the Smithsonian's Museum of History and Technology, which seems to me not bad, but horrible.

Yet even today, fully sixty-six years after it was conceived, the Federal City Beautiful is by no means completed. Though President Kennedy had the most offensive of the World War II "temporary buildings" removed from the Mall, the "tempos" of World War I are still standing. At the urging of his then Secretary of Labor, Arthur Goldberg, Kennedy also instigated the ambitious plan to rebuild Pennsylvania Avenue as the magnificent thoroughfare from the Capitol to the White House that L'Enfant had intended it to be.

Not since Jefferson, in fact, had a President harbored such great ambitions for the city of Washington as John F. Kennedy. He wanted it to become "to a degree, a showcase of our culture."

A renaissance seemed, indeed, to be dawning in those brief, bittersweet thousand days of his regime. His lovely First Lady hosted sparkling soirées at the White House which at once gave a new and heartening glow to our national culture. As the President's cultural advisor, August Heckscher, though he lacked the personal rapport with Mr. Kennedy one might have wished for, established at least a token concern on the part of the executive branch of the federal government for the arts and architecture. Other men of taste and understanding such as Arthur Goldberg, Arthur Schlesinger, Jr., and, most of all the artist William Walton, were ever close to the Presidential ear.

Goldberg drafted the executive order which ordained that federal buildings, "particularly those located in the nation's capital" must "provide visual testimony to the dignity, enterprise, vigor, and stability of the American government" and should "embody the finest contemporary American architectural thought."

Together with Jacqueline Kennedy, Walton persuaded the President to drop a disastrous scheme to destroy the lovely historic houses on Lafayette Park, across from the White House, in favor of huge, pompous federal offices. A new architect, John Carl Warnecke, placed the offices behind the newly restored residential rows. Though his choice of dark red brick and mortar was unfortunate, Warnecke's scheme prevented the White House from being dwarfed and gave the nation an outstanding example of how to harmonize large modern structures with worthy old ones.

Here, then, was indeed a beginning of "the finest contemporary American architectural thought," which Walton as chairman of a Fine Arts Commission that is as fully in tune with our times as that of Daniel Burnham was with his, continues to insist on with wit and admirable persistence.

The Pennsylvania Avenue Commission, headed by Nathaniel Owings of Skidmore, Owings, and Merrill, had its plan ready to await President Kennedy's return from Dallas. Though bold and ambitious, it shows altogether proper respect for the baroque Beaux Arts character of monumental Washington. Its sunken automobile expressway at E Street, designed to channel heavy through-traffic away from the avenue, as well as ingenious provisions for underground parking, promise to meet modern needs. The plan would furthermore at last link Washington's downtown business district to the city's monumental core.

Only with its first proposal for an oversized National Square, meant as a grandiose terminus at the White House end of the avenue, did

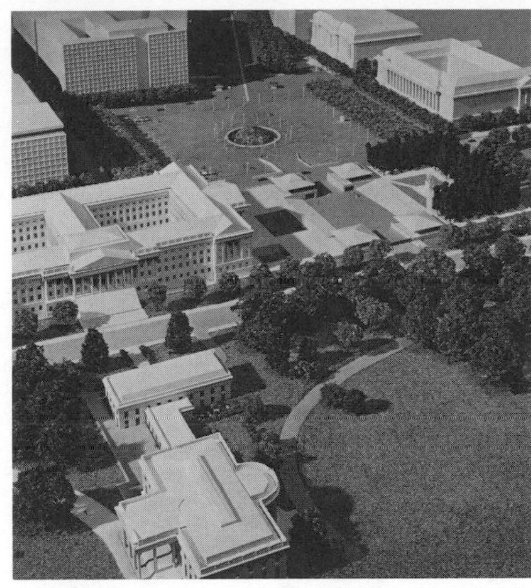

A new National Square to end the grand axis

the Owings Commission go a bit overboard in its enthusiasm for baroque pomposity. On second thought, however, it shrunk the huge parade ground by almost half so that it now has at least a chance to become the lively urban and urbane center that Washington so sorely needs.

No less possessed of magnificent intentions for the capital than their immediate predecessors, Mr. and Mrs. Lyndon B. Johnson are lending wholehearted support to this promising work of civic design. As a logical and intelligent completion of Burnham's City Beautiful, it deserves "to assert itself with ever growing insistency."

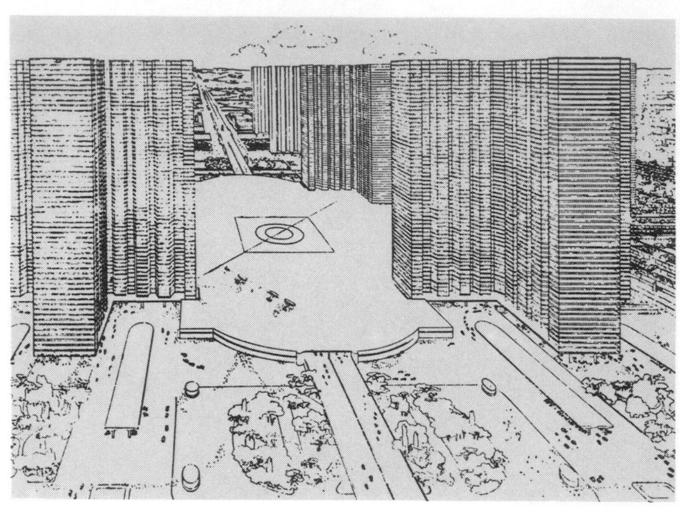

4. The Radiant City

Le Corbusier, on his first visit to the United States in 1935, caused quite a sensation when he proclaimed that New York's skyscrapers were too small.

They are only negative, he amplified in a famous letter to Kenneth Stowell, then editor of the *American Architect.* The New York skyscraper, as Le Corbusier saw it, has, he wrote, "brought traffic to a standstill. It consumes the very life of the population and eats up whole districts around itself, emptying them and bringing ruin. Build the skyscraper bigger and more really useful, [place it in a park] and it will reclaim a vast amount of land, will compensate for depreciated properties, will provide a perfect system of circulation, and will bring trees and open spaces into the city. The pedestrian will have the freedom of parks over the whole ground area and the cars will travel from skyscraper to skyscraper at a hundred miles an hour on one-way elevated roads placed wide distances apart. . . .

"Notice how the great hotels and apartment houses [around Central Park] have naturally come to be built here so as to have the advantage of looking out on space. But Central Park is too big; it is an island in a sea of buildings. Crossing it is like traversing no-man's-land. The trees, grass and . . . space of Central Park ought to be multiplied and spread over the whole of Manhattan. . . .

"Millions of city dwellers have moved out to the country. They arrive and settle down and in so doing they cause the destruction of the country. The result is a vast, sprawling built-up area encircling the city—the suburbs. All that remains is the dream. . . .

"This suburban development makes necessary the hours spent daily on subways, buses and commuter trains; it causes the destruction of that communal life which is the very marrow of the nation."

Today this sounds quite familiar, as Peter Blake, who reprinted this letter in his splendid book *The Masterbuilders,* has noted. American planners have taken Corbu's concept very much to heart. They are trying to make our cities "radiant" and open, punctuated with glistening skyscrapers, spaced far apart, and linked by ribbons of expressways. Beginning, I suppose, in 1947 when Stuyvesant Town, a middle income housing project, was built on New York's East River, they have dotted our cities with huge slabs rhythmically planted in huge open spaces. The trouble is that there is usually nothing in that open space but mangy grass along with desultory shrubbery for the rich and KEEP OFF signs for the poor.

Worse, as Jane Jacobs has explained at length, the Corbuzation of

It all came to pass

a city destroys the street, which, it turns out, gives it structure and cohesion and is really the vessel of urban life.

Life, by definition, means animation, and animation means movement. If the city is to be human, the movement must be human, not a movement of machines that whiz by at a hundred, or fifty or thirty miles an hour, but the movement of people on foot. The point of this human movement – ebbing and flowing, surging and halting, vacillating and determined – is not merely to get from one point to another, but to perceive what is in between. One of the great things about a good city is that there are always things to see. The beauty and unique comfort of it is that you can see these things without yourself being seen. Nothing like a good city gives you a sense of community and at the same time preserves your privacy.

At one point in his journey, Milo, the little boy in Norton Juster's wonderful children's book *The Phantom Tollbooth*, arrives right in the middle of Main Street. But he saw nothing at all.

"'It's really a very pleasant city,' said his friend Alec as he strolled down the street, pointing out several of the sights, which didn't seem to be there, and tipping his cap to the passers-by. There were great crowds of people rushing along with their heads down, and they all appeared to know exactly where they were going as they darted down and around the nonexistent streets and in and out of the missing buildings.

"'I don't see any city,' said Milo very softly.

"'Neither do they,' Alec remarked sadly, 'but it hardly matters, for they don't miss it at all.'

"'It must be very difficult to live in a city you can't see,' Milo insisted, jumping aside as a line of cars and trucks went by.

"'Not at all once you get used to it,' said Alec. 'But let me tell you how it happened.' And as they strolled along the bustling and busy avenue, he began.

"'Many years ago, on this very spot, there was a beautiful city of fine houses and inviting spaces, and no one who lived here was ever in a hurry. The streets were full of wonderful things to see and the people would often stop to look at them.'

"'Didn't they have any place to go?' asked Milo.

"'To be sure,' continued Alec; 'but, as you know, the most important reason for going from one place to another is to see what's in between, and they take great pleasure in doing that. Then one day someone discovered that if you walked as fast as possible and looked at nothing but your shoes you would arrive at your destination much more quickly.

Soon everyone was doing it. They all rushed down the avenues and hurried along the boulevards seeing nothing of the wonders and beauties of their city as they went.'

"Milo remembered the many times he'd done the very same thing; and, as hard as he tried, there were even things on his own street he couldn't remember.

" 'No one paid any attention to how things looked, and as they moved faster and faster everything grew uglier and dirtier, and as everything grew uglier and dirtier they moved faster and faster, and at last a very strange thing began to happen. Because nobody cared, the city slowly began to disappear. Day by day the buildings grew fainter and fainter, and the streets faded away, until at last it was entirely invisible. There was nothing to see at all.' "

We can't blame it all on Le Corbusier. For one thing, our planners have adapted only the superficial, pretty-picture aspect and that only in small part without consideration of the reasoning behind Corbu's concepts and their essential mechanics. What they did with these concepts was about like trying to improve an old-fashioned buggy by putting a shiny airplane cockpit on it. It looks terrible and it won't fly.

But the fault lies not with the inevitable modernization of existing cities. Nor can we avoid high buildings if we want to accommodate all the people who want to and should live and work in the city. The skyscraper was not, in the end, the invention of an architect, but, as Jean Gottmann, the distinguished professor of human and economic geography, points out, the product of an economic revolution.

The main reason for the development of the skyscraper, Gottmann writes, "is not the intensive use of real estate, though the real-estate market has done very well with the high towers, nor is it the efficiency

Designed for speed

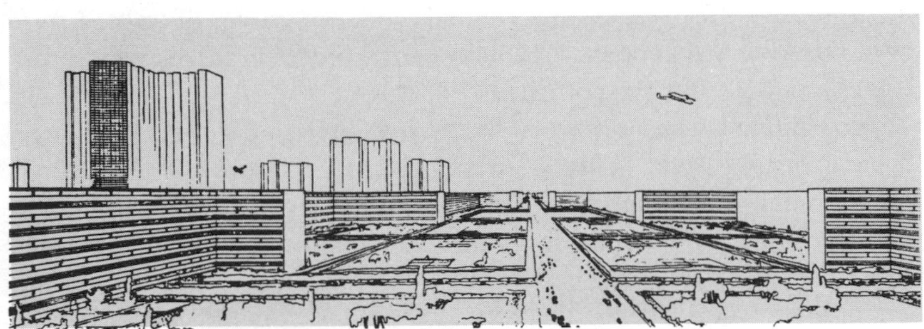

of office organization. The skyscraper is an expression of the social evolution of employment, of the labor force today. . . .

"To run our plants and factories, what we depend on most is not the supervision of the machines or the transfer of the goods, but the effectiveness of communication. . . . In skyscrapers grouped in the city a million white-collar workers can be close to one another. They can meet easily to exchange opinions, transact business, acquire information, and obtain whatever expert interpretation, legal counsel, or technological advice they may need. . . . This is what makes the skyscraper and creates the skyline: the need for agglomeration. Now we begin to see in the skyline an expression of the intricate web and huge volume of communication generated by, and indispensable to, the modern transactional way of life."

Nor is it the fault of the open spaces which we must and should have to let air and sun into apartments and give them a pleasant view. The fault lies with the fact that until recently the planners lacked the inclination, and now that they discovered the need they lack money, zoning, or whatever, to put on these spaces the facilities for the communal life which Le Corbusier said is "the very marrow of the nation."

Le Corbusier first presented his vision of the Radiant City to amazed Parisians at the Salon d'Automne in 1922—thirteen years before he first actually saw a skyscraper and twelve years before he wrote his critique of New York. This first version was called "City of Three Million Inhabitants."

It was, much like Ebenezer Howard's Garden City, a reaction to the sordid industrial metropolis of the time and designed to (1) decongest the center of cities, (2) increase the density to reduce travel distances, (3) improve traffic circulation, and (4) enlarge the landscaped areas to the point where Le Corbusier would build on only 12 per cent of the land area. In the center was to be a landing platform for flying taxis surrounded by skyscrapers for commercial enterprises for ten to fifty thousand employees each. You would hardly see them from the ground as they would be screened by dense groves of trees. From there large sunken expressways with pedestrian overpasses would run to the four points of the compass.

Surrounding the center were to be zigzagging apartment buildings forming open garden courts. Surrounding *them* were what Le Corbusier called "superimposed villas," duplex apartments with large terraces. Then came the garden cities. The point was that the expanses at the foot of the skyscrapers were to be one huge park filled with restaurants, cafés, shops, theaters, and other community buildings,

buildings with two or three terraces arranged for seating, and open or covered garages.

If this vision amazed Parisians, they became downright angry when Corbu proposed three years later that a section of central Paris be torn down to make room for such a skyscraper-dotted park. His answer, anticipating urban renewal, was: "The modern doctrine of city-planning proclaims that to urbanize is to raise values. The center of Paris must be reconstructed upon itself—as a biological and geographical phenomenon."

A later plan, of 1937, imposed the skyscrapers a little more gently on Paris, relating them, as he put it, with "delicious grace" to the city's historic heart with the Louvre and the Ile de la Cité. He now actually coined the magic word: The time, he wrote, had come for *"la refonde générale des villes,"* the "general renewal of cities." But "all detailed construction within the city," he warned, "should be undertaken within the provisions of total necessary and sufficient plan. But this urban plan can only be correct if it is dictated by regional conditions, which, in turn, are functions of national conditions. It is recognized today that city planning cannot remain strictly a municipal affair. By means of land, rail, water, and aerial routes, city planning is even the manifestation of national life."

Even thirty years later this is at best recognized only in theory. On paper Le Corbusier applied the basic tenets of the Radiant City—separation of motor vehicles and people, segregation of local and through traffic, dense and if necessary high-rise housing in parks to keep everyone close to nature—sun, space, vegetation, steel, and concrete, in that order—in various forms to numerous cities. None of all

Prophetic but not very radiant

this was entirely his own invention. Sant'Elia and particularly Tony Garnier, who designed a fascinating futuristic city back in 1901, contributed a great deal. So did Walter Gropius, Marcel Breuer, and Ludwig Hilberseimer at the Bauhaus as well as the Dutch Modernists under the influence of de Stijl.

The planning concepts of these Moderns, as bare and square as their buildings of the time, were realized mainly in housing projects across the world, relatively isolated and formal arrangements of building blocks that generally bore as little relation to their urban and natural surroundings as their International Style glass boxes do to the older buildings around them. A good example of such planning, and seen in isolation a most impressive one, is Mies van der Rohe's Lafayette Park in downtown Detroit.

I know of only one new and complete community actually built on such planning—the little town of Nagele in Holland, designed by Jacob Bakema. I found it a precious little place, not without visual appeal but surely without life and charm. You enter from the main road, across a quadrangular square and past the quadrangular city hall into a three-dimensional Mondrian painting—its long white bars of row houses precisely and squarely composed beyond a huge, green expanse of lawn. And, although all the buildings, strung out on the endless Dutch flatland under that enormous sky, seem almost diminu-

No money for a three-dimensional Mondrian

tive in scale, you feel a bit like an ant crawling on a canvas. To comprehend Nagele as a human you need the distance the full appreciation of a Mondrian painting requires. You should be up in an airplane.

Due to financial difficulties—and, perhaps, also lack of appeal—Nagele has not yet been completed and economies frustrated some of Bakema's ideas. As a Dutch architect friend wrote me in his expressive school English: "So the 'village of brightness' got no money for extra brightness, what for an experiment should have been sure in the right place."

But if Bauhaus and de Stijl planning in its pure form fortuitously failed to catch on, Le Corbusier's Radiant City, spread around the globe by CIAM, had an abiding influence.

When Corbu himself, however, at last got the opportunity to design an entire city, Chandigarh in India at the head of the Himalayas, he departed from his Radiant City. He essentially followed a plan worked out by Matthew Nowicki and Albert Mayer before the Indian authorities hired him. Corbu's monumental government buildings are placed at the head of Chandigarh. Across an avenue the city is stretched out along a grid pattern. Each square contains a neighborhood with its own essential shops and school. The grid of streets both defines and connects these. Through it all winds a continuous park.

I haven't seen Chandigarh but am told that it is all still pretty raw and devoid of life. Corbu made the original Nowicki-Mayer plan more rigid and geometric and changed its cluster of neighborhood bazaars into continuous shopping streets. This may have something to do with the sterility of the place that so many visitors complain of.

For as Mumford has observed, Corbu's planning lamentably lacked a sense of the intimate texture of daily life. His oversimplified handling of the entire city in terms of abstract spatial elements, conceived on a grandiose scale, had a dehydrating effect upon housing and planning throughout the Western world.

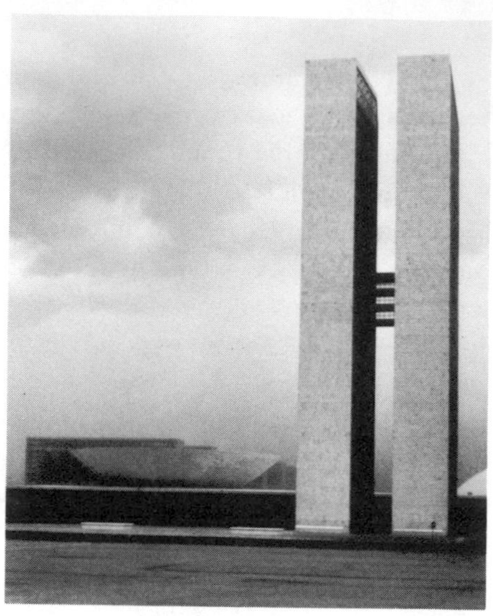

5. Symbol in the Mud

Like a flag, Brasília was posted out in the wilderness, five hundred miles inland from Rio de Janeiro—a symbol of Brazil's determination to turn from the soft, seductive beaches of her colonial past to a new, pioneering future in her promising interior. Someone has hailed the new city as more than a modern frontier town, an "authentic manifestation of the new civilization which is Western in its essence, technical and scientific in its basis, and universal in its range." It was planned by Lucio Costa. But Le Corbusier's influence is as ubiquitous as the whirling sand.

I visited this authentic manifestation shortly after its official dedication in 1961. For the two-hour flight from Rio there was nothing but an angry horizon and green and purple gloom below. When, at last, the plane made its bouncy descent, I longed for solid ground, for civilization, for people huddled together for warmth and comfort—for a city as we know and love it.

The gay bustle of Brasília's temporary air terminal quickened this anticipation. Here people *did* huddle together and, undoubtedly, lovers do meet amidst the noisy, very hectic, very Latin crowd. It seems in Brasília people hang around the airport as islanders gather on the dock, or, more aptly perhaps, our own pioneers of earlier days loitered with greedy, suspicious curiosity around arriving and departing stage coaches. Too busy, too poor, or both, to dress like travelers, the airline employees, guides, porters, and others who belong, blend indistinguishably with the loiterers in shirt sleeves who don't belong.

Twenty-four hours later I was glad to join this bustle again. I felt let down. It seemed to me I hadn't seen people for a long time. They seem lost in this Kafka city, this brave, new world which Costa and Niemeyer have engineered and styled in the image of Le Corbusier's *machine à habiter*. Its scale and aseptic serenity supersede humans. Only at the airport does humanity burst out of the sleek glass building, which although temporary, is nevertheless designed in the high modern style of Brasília's architecture.

As prescribed for the Radiant City, there is the "monumental artery" with the thinly spaced slabs of the government buildings standing like huge filing cabinets on either side; the side lanes, sunken into the ground, obstructing neither the traffic nor the grand vista; and Corbu's invention, the high-rise apartment blocks that hover on stilts over flat lawns lined in the distance by walls of row houses.

Costa's plan for Brasília emerged from a national competition judged by an international jury that was headed by the distinguished British city planner Sir William Holford. Designed for a population of a million and a half, covering 167 square miles, the plan resembles the shape of an airplane. The residential areas are in the wings, as it were, and the monumental government and other public buildings are strung along the body—an enormous central mall, some ten miles long. At the intersection of the two is the commercial "downtown" area and the underground bus terminal. The whole is embraced by a large artificial lake.

"We have to finish in five years or the forest will come back," Costa stated in 1957, his mind, undoubtedly, on the political thickets as well. For once committed, Brasília's founder, the then President of Brazil, Juscelino Kubitschek, had to raise his flag fast, lest the heroism it was to inspire vacillate under the impact of second-thought reasoning. Having been halfheartedly and intermittently projected ever since 1789, the "instant city" was ordered and actually delivered within his five-year term of office. More than a hundred thousand people now live in this audacious complex. And although, like Washington, it functions as yet only as the country's administrative capital, it already seems more representative of Brazil's aspirations than our federal city.

On newsstands and in tourist shops everywhere in Brazil you find the trapezium shape of Niemeyer's Alvorado Palace columns on books, pamphlets, tourist trinkets and lapel pins. The planes and advertising of the Brazilian airlines display the pineapple crown of Niemeyer's cathedral. "You will visit Brasília, of course?" the hotel clerk in Rio asked me the moment I checked in. And the taxi driver who took me sightseeing in the old capital spoke enthusiastically of the new, which he considered a modern-day miracle far more important to him than moon rockets. The new architecture has given a whole country a new identity.

Only for a moment, however, could I see how this architecture adds up to a new place to live. That was from a distance of almost ten miles, as my taxi turned from the airport across one arm of the artificial lake that embraces the plateau on which Brasília is spread. There, beyond the sea of stunted trees, ran a somewhat broken string of diminutive white shapes along the horizon. It seemed a mirage—distant and unreal under the enormous sky. The lake was but a thin gleam of light.

Then the road turned to follow the lake shore. The panorama was lost in the muddy detail of bulldozed lots which bear crude signs reading "France," "Italy," and so forth, to denote the embassies to come. We were still on embassy row when the storm broke and shrouded the utopian vision, wild shrubbery, mud and all, in a curtain of red sand. By the time the rain turned into more mud, I was too close to see the city for the buildings.

Costa has proclaimed that Brasília should have "the virtues and attributes appropriate to a true capital city." He set out, in other words, to create deliberately monumental spaces. To meet this ambition a perceptible relationship between the various buildings is as essential as wings and proscenium are to a stage or as the proximity of trees is to a forest. True, an effulgent actor may be able to hold an audience on an empty set. But I dare him to command attention under Brasília's expansive sky. A widely dispersed group of trees, like so many lighthouses beyond the sea, offers little promise of shelter. Each attracts only to itself, diffuses the promise, and confuses the emotional response a closer and more related group would evoke. It is the same, or seems so to me, with Niemeyer's effulgent architectural statues in Costa's vast gallery. His central mall with the all-important, triangular Three Power Plaza on one end, a not-yet-designed City Hall on the other, and a projected Television Tower as a focal point about two-thirds along, is no less than four miles long (a mile and a half longer than Washington's Mall or the Champs Elysées) and, I would judge, almost a half-mile wide.

The Plaza derives its name from the fact that Parliament, the Executive Palace, and Supreme Court stand at the three vertices of its paved expanse. Although located at the very end of the ceremonial speedway, it is, I suppose, the real center of Brasília, which its geographic center, the crossing point of the two arteries, is not. There Costa placed a more or less invisible underground bus terminal.

There is a grove of palms, but it is not on the Plaza or where people walk. The lake below the flat plateau cannot be seen from the mall. Only the skyscraping "H" of the Legislative Offices stands out, two thin, parallel twenty-five story slabs bridged in the middle. The Senate dome and the Chamber of Deputies bowl (a washtub for laundering the nation's dirty linen, people quip) timidly hug its base. The other buildings are also relatively low and diminish in the long perspective. The Cathedral spire pushes insignificantly out of the ground, like asparagus in spring, arbitrarily placed on the side of the mall on which the speeding cars assume the size of ants somewhere far along the perspective line before one is aware of them.

When the sparse greenery matures on the red soil of the wide center strip—which it is struggling to do—it will change only the color of this Daliesque desert. There are, to be sure, no melting watches. But neither are there people. There is nothing to induce them to walk these forbidding distances. They will have to drive even to the Cathedral, which is miles from the residential areas. And unless Niemeyer can persuade the worshipers to take a healthy Sunday morning walk, he will, like most architects of our time, see his noble structure rise on a parking lot.

A perhaps more serious and already clearly discernible flaw in the plan is the location of the air terminal. It is off to one side of the town across one arm of the lake, very close to the projected villa area and quite far from one of the two residential districts. Its road will soon create the usual traffic pressures in the closer residential area. What is more, the present jet-plane approach covers a good half of the city, which is hazardous and uncomfortably noisy for the inhabitants. While Brasília's planners have prepared themselves for the onslaught of the motor car, they have no defense against the airplane which is already very much upon them. Brasília was largely built by airlift.

Niemeyer's apartment superblocks in which people live consist of clusters of four-story buildings of identical size and shape arranged in a pleasing Cubist composition. Each cluster houses three thousand people and includes a school, a community center, and a chapel. The sun screens and color of the apartment slabs vary and they have more gaiety and vitality, I thought, than Brasília's rather self-conscious public monuments. What is wrong here, it seems, is only that a sophisticated treatment is squandered on the same trite, forty-year-old solution to housing a lot of people in a limited space. Yet space is the one thing abundantly available in Brasília.

According to Costa's plan the superblocks are designated by a letter-number combination; the buildings in each by a letter; and the apartments in the usual manner. You may find Big Brother at Q3-L-201. What an Orwellian nightmare! I am glad the planners apparently forgot to specify the lettering on the shops, rows of small, uniform boxes which line the streets between superblocks. Their inscriptions offer the only variety and interest in these pits of boredom. Their monotony is surpassed only by the straight lines of row houses which form square after identical square of second-class—or is it third-class?—housing. For residential Brasília is strictly segregated by income groups. No chance for the chap at Q3-L-201 to escape to one of those postage-stamp-sized garden plots (where nothing grows as yet) unless he makes the next rung on the civil-service ladder.

What chance the construction workers will have to escape their "free town" ghetto remains to be seen. It is, like most man-made social evils, the product of utopian idealism which denies today's human needs for the sake of tomorrow's fancied perfection. Brasília's planners wanted to be sure that the accommodations for the workmen are strictly temporary so as not to spoil their vision of the new capital which Kubitschek said will bring with it "a time of plenty and of true brotherhood" for all Brazilians. The labor camp was placed some ten miles out of sight and, to attract workers, levies no taxes and is virtually unpoliced and uncontrolled—makeshift shanties, rats and all. Almost needless to say, as a tourist attraction it rivals the Three Power Plaza, although, as in Rio's infamous *favelas*, its equally dismal slums, it is not safe to venture far from the car. Since my visit—the day after a jealous lover burned down a number of huts—the authorities are paving some of its streets. With such improvements, I'm afraid, the "free town" will remain in all its squalor to remind future generations that brotherhood scarcely begins with marble monuments.

It is easy, of course, to ridicule this brave effort. Washington's early visitors also sneered, as did one John Cotton Smith in 1800, about "the deep morass covered with elder bushes which were cut through the width of [our capital's] intended avenues."

It took Washington about a hundred years to come to the point where Brasília was five years after Kubitschek decided to build it. It was built, as André Malraux has said, "by the will of one man and the hope of a nation." And that, without the absolute powers of Sun King or Napoleon III, is one of the most remarkable achievements of our time.

I recently called on Kubitschek, who was exiled by the regime of President Castelo Branco, and now lives in New York. "I didn't originate the idea of moving the capital from Rio; I only realized it," he said with unexpected modesty. For modesty was probably the only virtue he did not bring to the feat. On the contrary, he so totally and deliberately identified himself with the relentless propaganda that turned the construction of Brasília into something of a national obsession which dangerously bankrupted the country, that he has often been charged with fostering a cult of personality. He is, I believe, the only democratic statesman who, during his elected term of office, had a monument erected to himself.

Happily, however, Kubitschek does not look like the blandly heroic marble head sticking out of a huge marble slab that I disadmired on my visit to Brasília some years ago. An athletic sixty-four, olive smooth and with olive complexion, he looked very lively and relaxed. Though immaculately dressed, he took his shoes off as we chatted. Even so, he seemed so charged with energy that I fully expected him to catapult out of his easy chair at any moment right through the ceiling and, for all I knew, straight back to his Presidential "Palace of Dawn."

Brasília, he told me in precise but halting English, "is the most recent of only fifteen cities in five thousand years of human civilization that have been intentionally built as new capitals. One of the earliest of them was Akhetaton in ancient Egypt, which was built about 1360 B.C. by the will of Pharaoh Ikhnaton. That's why some people called me Mr. Pharaoh," he said with a laugh. "But they were wrong."

"In the first place, it took seventeen years to build Akhetaton. I built Brasília in five—well, nine years, to be exact. Second, the Pharaoh built a monument for the dead. Brasília is a monument for the living. Third, Akhetaton was deserted sixteen years after Ikhnaton died and has been a ruin ever since. My opponents, though some undoubtedly had it on their minds, could not dare desert Brasília. It is fast growing and fast fulfilling its intended role of radiating civilization out into our untapped jungles."

"I seized the last possible moment to build Brasília," he added. "Today it would be impossible. For one thing, costs would be far too high." He is probably right. At any event, although his opponents now rule his country, Juscelino Kubitschek's monument is—"by a miracle," he smiles—still standing. It ought to be.

But while history should honor the incredible drive and energy of this modern Pharaoh, I would hope that design of his city will soon be considered old-fashioned. It seems to me not "the authentic manifestation of the new civilization" but an updated edition of the old, baroque one.

We need, I should hope, more than magnificent vistas and deserve better than automobile distances. In the New Towns and a few, scattered efforts to make old, existing neighborhoods pleasant and livable again—to rehabilitate them—I discern a new, humanistic approach to city planning. The British, in particular, have rediscovered the human and aesthetic values of what the editors of *Architectural Review* call "the townscape."

But as we in the United States began our "urban renewal," we designed most of it, insofar as we designed it at all, much like Brasília. Modernized baroque rationalized with pretentious science fiction is still widely considered the highest state of the art.

V. URBAN RENEWAL

1. "Beautiful as Well as Clean"

In 1956, the year the Brazilian parliament authorized the construction of a new capital in the wilderness of Brazil, the Redevelopment Land Agency, authorized by Congress of the United States to clear and rebuild the slums in the national capital, was already ten years old.

All this agency had managed to accomplish in that decade was to reduce the worst 560 acres of these slums, southwest of the Capitol, to much the same desolate desert as that on which Brasília was built.

In 1961, the year Brasília had a permanent resident population of seventy-five thousand and was officially dedicated, some four hundred well-to-do families had at last moved into Washington's new Southwest Urban Renewal Area. Their lonely apartment building was still a desert. And although some of the slum children they replaced were by now grown men fighting in Korea, there was still no specific, agreed-upon, overall development plan for the area. It was covered by bureaucratic bickering thicker than its weeds.

The excuse is that southwest Washington was the nation's first urban renewal program, a laboratory as it were. Now operating in some eight hundred communities of all kinds across the land, it began with high hopes and a low sense of urgency that seems to persist despite periodic official pep talk.

Urban renewal has made many mistakes. But most of its critics—a strange alliance of liberals, sociology professors and ultraconservatives—tend to blame the rash for the measles. For urban renewal has forced a reluctant nation to come to terms with the problems of its cities. It opened a Pandora's box of unexpected evils and everyone is shocked to find that the urban disease is worse and its cure more complex than we had so naively expected.

Like it or not, the federal urban renewal program is nevertheless the only cure we've got. It is, as architect Roger Montgomery put it, "the only adequate system for planning and replanning our metropolitan areas. Out of the slum clearance program cities have forged their first effective tool for governing the urban environment, for building it according to plan within a market economy." The box had to be opened some time, though real hope, as the Pandora of the legend also found, is only deep at its bottom.

The first federal skirmish against the slums began in the hot enthusiasm of the New Deal days. The housing movement, led by such practical idealists as Katherine Bauer-Wurster, managed to persuade Congress in 1934 and again in 1937 to assist municipal slum clearance efforts with the aim of replacing blight with "decent, safe and sanitary" public housing. It seemed easy.

But after the war the stench and shame of the slums were worse than ever—and right under the noses of Congress. The public housing approach had been proven utterly insufficient for blighted areas as large as Washington's Southwest. Landscape architect Elbert Peets first suggested that the area be merely cleaned up and rehabilitated by replacing the most decrepit structures with public projects. But on second thought there seemed to be little gain in patching up a huge poorhouse. It seemed more profitable instead to turn the old slum to entirely new uses.

This, however, could not be accomplished by replacing small parcels, piece by piece. It is often essential to replace several small buildings with one large one, to convert an entire block into a park—in short, to rebuild an entire area. What's more, not only public buildings, but structures of various kinds are needed to provide homes, work, and services not just for the poor, but for all kinds of people. These were obviously best provided by private builders willing to abide by a new overall plan. Washington's Southwest, like similar slums elsewhere, was both so rundown and underdeveloped that it required even new sewers, water mains, and streets to make it livable.

In 1949 Congress voted federal assistance for such an approach and proclaimed it a national goal to provide "a decent home and a suitable living environment for every American family." Known officially as Title I of the 1949 U.S. Housing Act, the new program was called "urban renewal"—and with equal justification—"urban devastation," "Negro removal," and "dehousing." It mustered the ancient, sovereign right of the state to appropriate, with just compensation, private property for public use. Until that time this power was exercised mainly for military installations, public works, and public housing. Now the exercise of eminent domain for public *use* was extended to encompass the public *benefit*. The confiscated land is cleared and resold to private developers for private profit at varying discount rates. This interpretation of public benefit is shared by few European countries, not even the "welfare states." European governments usually only lease their land to private developers. But the Supreme Court, in its 1954 decision *Berman* v. *Parker*, upheld the broad American concept of eminent domain. "It is within the power of the legislature," the Court said, "to determine that the community shall be beautiful as well as clean, well-balanced as well as carefully patrolled."

The power rests with the states which, in turn, delegate it to local governments. The condition of federal assistance is a local program deemed "workable" by federal standards. They require a long-range program of slum prevention, housing and building code enforcement, relocation of displaced people, and the participation and approval of a representative citizens' advisory committee of the planning and rebuilding.

Urban renewal, as its federal administrators keep emphasizing, is thus entirely initiated, planned, and executed by the local community. The rub is that local self-determination is circumscribed by the fact that federal assistance is available only for some things and not for others, although the range is amazing. There are federal grants for planning of all kinds, new approaches to public transportation, the preservation of historic buildings, the "beautification" of streets and parks, land purchase for open space and recreation, cultural and educational buildings, and a host of other things. Nevertheless, a community gets federal help to build new housing, for instance, but not to build new public schools or to raise teachers' salaries. In the federal highway program the almost irresistible lure of large sums of federal money has more often than not proven disastrous. It is cheaper for cities to pave themselves over with monstrous six- or eight-lane interstate freeways with nine federal dollars for every one of their own than it is to bring their existing road system up to date for which they get no help at all.

In the urban renewal program, however, precise federal prescriptions seem to me necessary. The federal government happens to be more liberal than many of our local communities. Even as it is, local political pressures have far too often used federal funds to make the rich richer and keep the poor out of sight and dump Negroes back into the ghetto.

Under William Slayton's direction, furthermore, the federal Urban Renewal Administration has made a valiant attempt to cajole, pressure, bribe, and regulate local communities into good planning and good architecture. The results have been impressive. And I hope that his successors in the new Department of Housing and Urban Development who would give the local governments more flexibility under their Model Cities program, will not relent on this vital issue. The advice and approval of a board of competent, independent architects seems to me just as vital as the often perfunctory rubber-stamping by a citizens' committee.

For, despite all the talk and agony about it, city planning and urban design are still in a deplorable state in this country. Practically every city in the country now has a planning commission or agency, and some have two or three. It is a very busy organization, which in 1965 spent anywhere from 12½ cents (in Houston) to $1.31 (in Pittsburgh) per inhabitant per year.

The commission, as I wrote in the *New Republic* some time ago, tells the sanitation department where the sewers should go as the city grows. It also tells the real estate boards where the big deals are, which is mainly determined by how closely people will live together in the various parts of the city. It puts down on a chart what happened ten years ago and what happens today. Then it draws a line between the two points and projects that line to the next ten years. This is called city planning.

Official city planning also watches what thousands of individuals and their firms and organizations do, and tries to understand this by statistical analysis, probability mathematics and conversions into averages. This is projected into guesses about the natural, "organic" growth of the city.

The result is a zoning map which has lots of colors. The zoning board implements the zoning map—but not very often. The map has no votes and doesn't pressure anyone. The planning department also worries about traffic. It figures out which street should be noisy with trucks because lots of people live on it and which should be quiet, because only a few people live on it. Then the highway department comes along and builds its highways where it damn well pleases, because there is lots of pressure for highways. Finally, the planning department rearranges its projected sewers and population densities. This is called coordination.

Sometimes the highway department doesn't make up its mind where the highway should go. This frustrates the planning department and makes some people very angry because they don't know whether they'll have to get out of the way or not. This is called poor coordination; it depresses real estate values and slows progress.

The planning department also (sometimes) has ideas for a new park or for keeping the buildings low where high buildings would spoil a view. This is called upsetting the apple cart. "Apple cart" is a folksy name for what sociologists call the "power structure." The apple cart is pushed by the mayor, the city council, or both, who employ the planning department staff. What upsets their cart, of course, is not the park or the low buildings but the protests. People always protest that parks are only for loafers and that low buildings don't make as much money as tall ones.

Sometimes a city needs a new public housing project or a new concert hall. That is called a planning problem. When a planning problem occurs the city planning department calls in a planning consultant from out of town. The consultant doesn't know the city or where the project or concert hall would look pretty or where it would be convenient for the people who will use it. But he makes a survey and a big study, which tells all about tax revenues and real estate values and the attitudes of people who don't want a project or concert hall to get into their accustomed ways. Then it recommends the least offensive site. The concert hall is put into a park because it doesn't earn any revenues and the value of the park no longer matters anyhow. The project is put into the Negro district because Negroes have the best attitude.

The sites are then put on the map and the map is made into a model. The project and the concert hall are put into the model in the form of white boxes which everybody admires. Then an architect is called in, shown the white boxes and told to make a housing project or a concert hall out of them. It must be so high and so wide and so deep. The architect has been trained to create architecture. But now he has kids who want to eat. So he designs a big white box just so high and so wide and so deep. If he tries to use beautiful stone on the box or put a mosaic on it, there's a scandal. No one wants frills for the taxpayers' money.

If a newspaper, as happens rarely, criticizes not the expense but the unsightliness of the ill-proportioned and barren box, the chief city planner writes a letter to the editor. The one Robert B. Jones wrote to the *St. Louis Post-Dispatch* some time ago reads in part: "The stature of a community's image must be based upon a program of action commensurate with a balanced dispersal of available resources," which is, I suppose, as good a reason as any for the balanced dispersal of ugliness.

Some planning commissions are joined with the city housing department or authorities as a hangover from the days when urban renewal was to provide housing. The up-to-date ones are all by themselves. None is ever joined with the city planning department because then either or both might do some city planning which would upset the apple cart. The urban renewal department and the city planning department don't talk to each other. They coordinate. This means that they look at each other's maps and models and smile. Then they go back to their respective jobs and coordinate some more.

A few years ago the people in the federal Urban Renewal Administration, who don't worry too much about the local apple carts, decided that urban renewal should follow some sensible plan. The cities, they thought, shouldn't go on using money and energy just fixing the stairway when the kitchen was perhaps in much worse shape and repairing either would do no good so long as the roof kept leaking. Since the cities, despite their city planning departments and colored maps, didn't have such a plan, the national renewers promised the local renewers federal money—two-thirds of the expense—if they'd only prepare one.

They are called Community Renewal Programs. The CRP's are scientific. They don't stop with the stairwell the mayor wanted fixed; they take a look at what thousands of individual people and firms and organizations do, and try to understand it by statistical analysis, probability mathematics, and conversions into averages. This is projected into guesses about not only the growth but—and here's the new twist—also the probable rate of deterioration of the city and the cost to fix it up.

But CRP is not a master plan or overall design for the city. To create one, as Boston's renewer, Ed Logue, has said, would be trying to play God. This seems more fitting for Sixtus V or Baron Haussmann than for those who must labor for a community's image with a program of action commensurate . . . etc. Planning such a program of action makes

The "Chinese Wall" in Philadelphia . . .

. . . was replaced by Penn Center

CRP tremendously complex because nobody knows—or at least no two people agree—*what* the city is after. Looking at the stairwell and the kitchen, and even at the roof, still doesn't tell us what the remodeled house should look like or how it should work.

So CRP is really a priority fix-up schedule for needed repairs. It will also tell us that if we tear down a one-hundred housing unit, one hundred families will be out in the cold unless we build one hundred new ones. But it tells us nothing about *how* these new units are to be built. That is called implementation and not a proper planning function. Implementation is up to—I suppose, Sixtus V, or whoever pushes the apple cart.

There are some exceptions to this. I've mentioned Ed Bacon in Philadelphia. But there is also Charles Blessing, the chief planner in Detroit, who has a clear and realistic vision of what his city ought to be. There is Ed Logue, who started the program in New Haven and is renewing Boston. There is Justin Herman in San Francisco. These men are members of a growing new breed of talented urbanists who manage to combine a sense of design with a skill in management.

But Washington is so far not one of the cities blessed by such leadership. The federal city is ruled by Congress which means that it has not one apple cart but several dozen. Every municipal detail—even the acquisition of trash containers—involves the whole, majestic, cumbersome, checked and balanced machinery of our national government.

And if I return to that city once more, it is not only because I live there and know it most intimately, but also because I feel that its Southwest urban renewal contains a good many important lessons. It was not only the first of the cataclysmic urban renewal efforts but also, sad to say, probably the best.

2. ". . . for Every American Family"

Before the bulldozers began to move, there lived southwest of the Capitol some five thousand families, mainly poor Negroes. They were crowded, amidst a messy array of small industrial plants and warehouses, into dilapidated, rat-infested row houses and, worse, wooden alley shacks. Half had no toilets and nearly a third no plumbing at all. Although, with its view over the Anacostia river and proximity to the Capitol, this area had been planned by L'Enfant as an elegant residential district, it had barely been surveyed until the Civil War. Then it became a dumping ground for small industries and their workers. Later a railroad cut it off from the rest of the city as the new freeway does now.

Some of the people who lived in this mess still flock to the Southwest on a nice Sunday, just to stand silently about and take another look at the area from which they were uprooted. It is a pathetic sight. For obviously, relocation assistance or not, "decent, safe and sanitary" or not, the places to which they were moved do not give them a new sense of belonging. Wherever they now live, it isn't a real community.

Neither, as yet, is the new Southwest.

It is, to be sure, one of the most desirable and attractive districts for well-to-do people in town, in fact, in any American city. It has marvelous views across the channel, much greenery, and its many elegant apartment buildings, towering above clusters of town houses, landscaped grounds, plazas and swimming pools, new schools, churches, an enchanting small theater, and a shopping center, make up a fascinating museum of midcentury American architecture. The display includes some of the best architecture in the country along with some of the worst ostentations of architectural mediocrity north of Miami. Like most contemporary architecture, its plan also shows a remarkable absence of social concern.

The first plan for the new area was advanced by architects Louis Justement and Chloethiel Smith in 1952—five years after the Redevelopment Land Agency was launched. It proposed to save the inner city by building an attractive residential neighborhood that would lure the well-to-do and their tax money back from the suburbs. Along with the convenience of walking to work, they would be offered the amenities of a true metropolitan capital.

The Justement-Smith plan would have linked the new neighborhood with the rest of the city with a strong, elegant esplanade along Tenth Street, leading from the Mall and the Old Smithsonian on the Mall to the channel waterfront. The Southwest Freeway was to follow the existing railroad tracks to reduce its damage to the area.

This concept deteriorated in long hassles. One initial bureaucratic objection was commendable. The authorities felt that the total displacement of the area's poor Negroes seemed bad politics. They advanced the splendid idea that private developers provide a certain amount of housing in each project at a rental of no more than seventeen dollars per room per month. Private developers, however, proved unable to do this, and this rent ceiling was removed in 1959.

The highway engineers, for their own unfathomable reasons, objected to placing the new freeway along the railroad. They insisted on creating an awkward island between the railroad and their concrete ribbons. The island can contain nothing better than random and poorly designed commercial establishments that could be anywhere and are of no use to either the government offices to the north or the residences to the south. They are nothing but an unnecessary traffic generator and a nuisance.

But most of all, the downtown business men objected to the whole Justement-Smith scheme, particularly the proposed Tenth Street Esplanade, because they feared competition for the traditional downtown area. In the face of these obstacles the official planners did what they always do. They vacillated and prepared ever new studies.

Then, *deus ex machina*, William Zeckendorf appeared on the scene in March 1953 and brought a new plan. It was drawn up by I. M. Pei and Harry Weese and was a refined version of the Justement-Smith proposal. At the height of his ambition at the time, Zeckendorf offered to rebuild the entire Southwest all by himself.

It was a dramatic and dazzling proposal and would have created an entire new town within the city—its low rows of houses squarely enclosing inner courts, its tall apartment slabs, its town center with shopping and community buildings, schools, churches, library and waterfront shopping area and its imposing Tenth Street Mall and an adjacent L'Enfant Plaza—all cast in the same architectural mold. And the mold, the rigid linear layout with its building blocks and landscaped squares, reorganizing the old street pattern, was in the Prussian neo-Classic tradition of town planning, the tradition that leads from Schinkel's early nineteenth-century schemes straight to Hilberseimer's city planning lessons at the Bauhaus. It promised for once what U. S. cities have so sorely lacked this past century—the discipline of visual order and harmony. That still seems worth a try.

Pei's L'Enfant Plaza and Tenth Street Esplanade were, furthermore, to be places of splendor in scale with the grand vision of the McMillan Commission. There was to be an opera house, exposition halls, a nearby hotel, and restaurants. In the end, however, William Zeckendorf lost the financial capacity to deliver even on those portions of the plan he was finally allowed to execute. But the Zeckendorf Plan raised the sights of both the community and the bureaucracy. And although the bureaucrats tore Pei's concept all apart again, concern for architectural design remained for a while. Though the land was divvied up among different developers, the Redevelopment Land Agency fixed its price for the major parcels in accordance with objective assessments of its value and let the buyers compete on the basis of architectural excellence judged by juries of outstanding architects and planners. This is what accounts for the architectural museum.

Meanwhile, the bulldozers began their much criticized wholesale Negro removal. Washington's Southwest was, of course, not the only place where this was done.

In terms of national averages the urban renewal program has replaced far fewer people than freeway construction and other public, not to speak of private, rebuilding. And only the urban renewal program has made a sincere and elaborate effort to help its victims to reasonably adequate new quarters. There is much argument about this relocation effort and the bureaucrats and their critics keep throwing statistics into each other's eyes like kids playing in the sand.

The renewers say that, again, on the national average, 87 per cent of their victims have been officially relocated. The others just somehow disappear before the relocation workers drop around a second time. For reasons of their own they don't want to have anything to do with officialdom.

Some of these people now live in public housing which, on the whole, is considerably more attractive since, appointed by President Kennedy, Marie C. McGuire took over this federal program. But the older projects are still so dismal that in Boston, for instance, a majority of the people driven out of the West End area refused to move into them.

The vast majority is being moved into buildings that are, if not deteriorated, certainly deteriorating. And if they are Negro they stay in the ghetto. In some places, notably Chicago, much of urban renewal, in fact, moved precisely into those areas that had begun to integrate. The low-income Negroes were uprooted and dumped right back into the all black areas, many of them into that national disgrace, the two-mile long row of high-rise public housing casernes along State Street. But in all our major cities there was less residential integration in 1960, according to reliable studies, than in 1950.

The statistical sand-throwing game is therefore rather meaningless. It blinds us to the real issues, which are:

One, that cataclysmic slum clearance doesn't make any sense at all unless new and better housing is physically ready and waiting for the people who are cleared out. In most European countries this is a legal requirement for all government rebuilding efforts.

Two, that a combined slum clearance and rehousing effort serve to disperse the ghetto.

And three, that in both renewal and new construction we stop merely producing new buildings and individual projects and start to create communities. It is not enough to update our urban architecture. To make it a good place to live our efforts should be directed toward turning the city into an orderly aggregation of livable neighborhoods.

This is not only a matter of social justice or moral decency, but, I believe, of white middle-class self-interest and urgent necessity. There was and is nothing wrong with converting a low-income neighborhood into a middle-income neighborhood. "Cities inhabited by the poor are poor cities," says Charles Abrams. And poor cities are poor for the poor as well as the rich. It is and should be an aim of urban renewal to lure the fugitive white middle class back downtown. But that is only half the job. We have hardly begun the essential other half—but more about this later.

In the end the Southwest *did* succeed in attracting some twenty thousand well-to-do people and most of them *did* return from the suburbs. After nearly twenty years and a public expenditure of $65 million and at least four times that much in private investment, these people moved into some remarkably handsome new housing projects. Some of them have significantly advanced the cause of urban architecture.

Chloethiel Woodard Smith's Capitol Park includes five large apartment buildings and numerous charmingly clustered and varied town houses set in landscape architect Dan Kiley's generous planting. The project is by no means avant garde; you would scarcely even call it Modern in style. The brick apartment buildings with their rich, balconied facades and particularly the design of the town-house clusters in colorful pastel hues with their arched passageways are, however, even more titillating and important architecturally than any avant-garde effort would have been. In a manner so pleasing it becomes positively exciting, they manage to combine an appeal to familiar associations of prettiness with our intellectual demands on honest modern

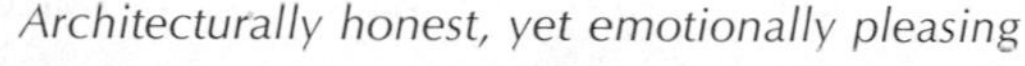
Architecturally honest, yet emotionally pleasing

Privacy and charm in a dense settlement

architecture. They seem "traditional," whatever that means, and yet they are entirely of our time. Their natural, smiling friendliness is, in addition to the landscaping, handsome light fixtures, and other lovingly designed details, a matter of scale that is perfectly attuned to people.

Charles M. Goodman's River Park, in contrast, deliberately strives for novel effect. The project is a cooperative, consisting of a big apartment building that looks down on barrel-roofed town houses that are packed as tightly as a medieval town. To me it achieves its effect with drama and flair, though to many others its jazz notes with some strong Le Corbusier strains are a bit too jarring. Indeed, the financial sponsorship of the Reynolds Metal Company shows a bit too obviously in the lavish use of all manner of unnecessary silver aluminum tinsel. Yet I find the overall effect as forceful as it is gay and buoyant. It is much fun to walk through Goodman's alleys and to let yourself be surprised by his little plaza. I have rarely seen the intimacy and delight of a medieval town so well recaptured with honestly modern means.

As a work of modern architecture, the Tiber Island project by Keyes, Lethbridge and Condon is probably the most eloquent of the three. Working in brick and reinforced concrete the architects have chosen an idiom derived from the boldly interlocking cubes and emphasized the building-block structuralism of Kenzo Tange. But the architects have taken all the brutality out of it without diminishing the strong vigor of their statement. With its wonderful integration of assertive town houses and boldly sculptured apartment buildings, grouped around a grand plaza that is built over a parking garage, Tiber Island achieves a unity that the other two projects lack. The same architects have successfully repeated this theme in an adjacent, somewhat less expensive project called Carrollsburg Square.

Any one of these three design concepts is strong enough to have given the entire area some unity with sufficient variety in detail to avoid monotony. But not only are these three totally different from each other. There are also a number of humdrum buildings in between. The Babel of all these different architectural languages makes the Southwest woefully incoherent.

True, most people want variety. It seems part of the restlessness and uncertainty of our times. But then each of the thirty or so different buildings of Berlin's new Hansaviertel is quite different from the others, yet the area as a whole appears delightfully harmonious. It seems that if we want variety, we must design for that, too, as for everything else.

High and low buildings eloquently combined

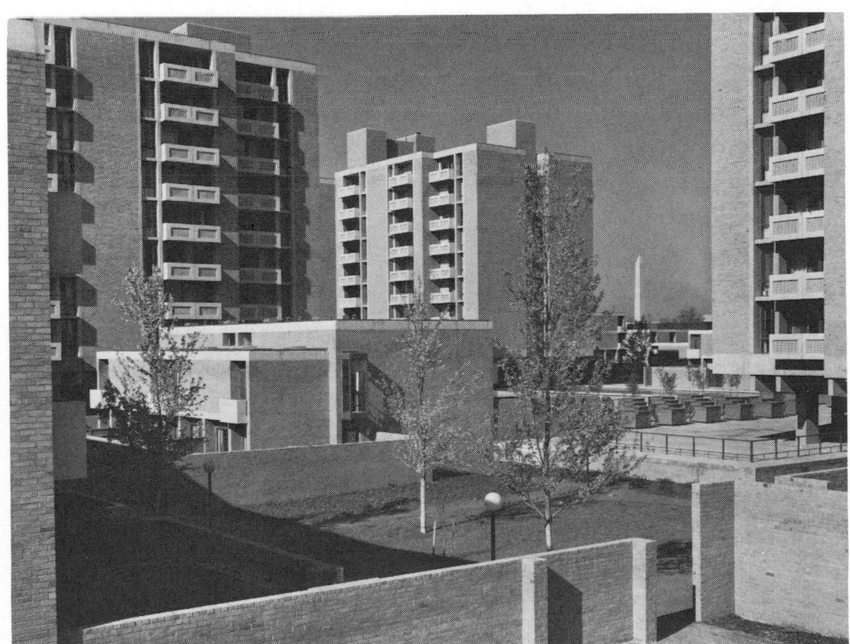

One of the architectural advances of the Southwest is that its good buildings are honestly modern without touting their modernity to the detriment of popular appeal. The reason may be that they didn't try to show off and managed to get along without resorting to either the excessive use of the glass of the International Style or the bizarre whimsies of modern Expressionism. Only I. M. Pei's Town Center apartments are, I fear, a bit self-consciously glassy, bare, and square. Chloethiel Smith's Harbor Square project, in contrast, seems self-consciously overloaded and busy.

Another important advance is the happy mixture of low town houses and tall apartment buildings. Until they were built, conventional planning wisdom, under the influence of Le Corbusier, demanded that the ground space between high-rise slabs be vast, useless, and dull. The Southwest was first to fill that space with town houses and their patio gardens. Without taking air and sun away from the slabs, they restore the street and add interest and a sense of neighborhood, both visually and factually. Factually, since the town houses attract families with small children for whom elevator apartments are not an ideal habitat.

The planning fault of the Southwest is that it has neither the structure nor all the facilities to make up a community, a place. It is neither part of the city nor is it a self-contained neighborhood where people feel fully at home and can stay put if they want to. The ill-placed freeway, reinforced by industrial junk and a massive phalanx of government offices, walls off the residences. The originally proposed gateway and link, the Tenth Street Esplanade, is sealed off on one end and leads nowhere on the other. It was sealed off when the authorities insisted, rather than flanking it with two federal offices, they would bridge it with one. Along the Esplanade is to be a plaza formed by offices and a hotel. Past this L'Enfant Plaza the Esplanade will lead to an insipid dead end, to be known as an Overlook, with a parking garage under it. It is hard to imagine anyone going there to look at anything, except young couples who will drive to the secluded place to look at each other in the darkness of their automobiles and neck. There is nothing wrong with that, though I am sure they'd be just as happy at some other less valuable and strategically located piece of real estate.

What's more, the new buildings and projects just seem strewn haphazardly across the land. The area has no heart, no anatomy, at all.

In lieu of a heart Zeckendorf and I. M. Pei have endowed it with a typically suburban, low-slung shopping center, all but submerged in the mass of parked cars surrounding it. There are now plans to rip it up and

A city sub-urbanized

build a new center, designed by Chloethiel Smith. It is to be flanked by large apartments and sorely needed offices to provide the people of the area with the dentists, doctors, and other professional services they need and that they must now drive suburban distances to get to. There is to be a shopping arcade, underground parking, restaurants, a skating rink, and all the rest to create the kind of modern *agora* that has proven so successful at Rotterdam's Lijnbaan and Stockholm's new satellite towns, Vallingby and Farsta. It is promising. It is also ironic that after only a few years this urban renewal area has to be renewed again.

I doubt, however, that the new town center will manage to fully overcome the lackluster exurban character of the area. It derives from the many small buildings that seem heedlessly scattered about. The trouble with these churches and schools is not only that their architecture ranges from the merely undistinguished to the outright bad. Even Charles Goodman, who did so well at River Park, let us down with his Hawthorne School which seems to me a poor and pretentious attempt at brutalism. The sight of this imitation of Tange next to insipid imitations of eighteenth-century town houses facing each other across the street is a shameful architectural joke. It makes it pretty difficult for our generation to ridicule the eclecticism of the Victorians. The only really distinguished new structure is Harry Weese's delightful and much praised Arena Stage.

The trouble is also that these structures behave as though they were out in the suburbs. They hog large and often unkempt areas of land which the large residential complexes in between crowd rather densely.

"Colonial" and concrete in a chaotic concoction

They thus try to make up for the lack of urban scale by shouting for attention.

It is, as I said, sad. For the Southwest, with a little more insight and political daring, might so easily have become a sophisticated new district to help make Washington the cosmopolitan world capital it deserves to be.

Despite these shortcomings, an encouraging community spirit is nevertheless beginning to develop. The return of the white middle class to the city, this seems to prove, brings with it more than tax money. It also brings a new social concern and leadership.

There is a public housing project, Greenleaf, next to the area that had been built before urban renewal came. The urban renewers studiously turned the backs of their new luxury apartments to Greenleaf. At one of them there is even a physical wall. Some contact evolved nevertheless, in part through the Parent Teacher Association of the school, in part through the ministers of the new churches that moved in.

At first the Negro children from Greenleaf would walk across the street in the summer and rub their noses against the fences of the luxury-apartment swimming pools. Then someone arranged for buses to take them to a distant municipal pool. Now they are to have one of their own, along with other improvements of their dreary project. What's more, no protest has been heard about the new moderate-income, subsidized apartments that are to be built on the last remaining parcel of the renewed area.

Nor is it an accident that Mrs. Lyndon B. Johnson chose Greenleaf to plant one of the first azalea bushes in her "beautification" campaign. Greenleaf, in fact, is at this writing about to be "rejuvenated" with new playgrounds and a pleasant new mall. The benefits of urban renewal, it seems, are beginning to trickle down.

3. A Whimper of Confusion

Urban renewal got a new boost when President Johnson told Congress in January 1965: "I propose we launch a national effort to make the American city a better and more stimulating place to live." Yet that year, as in years past, Congress appropriated eight times more money for space exploration to get us to the moon than for urban renewal—$5,190,396,200 as against $675,000,000.

Congress, and for that matter the vast majority of its constituents, were clearly not yet in the mood to launch the national effort in earnest. We still aren't. Perhaps it is just as well.

For so far we are only dimly aware of the dimensions of the urban crisis, let alone what constitutes "a better and more stimulating place to live." To some, actually very minor, extent, our legislatures have made use for some fifteen years of the power to determine that the community shall be beautiful as well as clean and well patrolled. But the federal bulldozers have pushed about rather aimlessly. With very few exceptions they have failed to clear a path through our urban confusion to give us a view of the kind of city we want.

It is only very recently, and not because of any federal program but because of such new communities as Reston, that we are gaining some insights into what both our new and our old communities might become.

We are only now beginning to discover that, whatever beauty means, we do indeed have the power and the obligation to determine a meaningful physical framework for creative living—though it is part of such creative living that the individual has a multitude of choices within the inherent requirements and necessities of modern life.

We are now, I hopefully believe, beginning to see that the power and obligation to shape and reshape our urban environment is not merely the power to improve the better functioning of traffic, investment returns, and sewers, but the better functioning of people. It is not a matter of patching up our cities along computer formulas of a cost-benefit ratio. We are beginning to become aware that the costs are the immeasurable penalties of continued social injustice and of what has been expressed by such slogans as "the isolation of man," "alienation," "the meaninglessness and absurdity of life." It can all be summed up in the single word "Watts." And the real benefits are what we half smile about and half hope for when we talk about "the quality of life" and "the Great Society."

It may be an elusive goal, perhaps more elusive than the race to the moon. It is nevertheless obvious that, as President Johnson put it, "our society will never be great until our cities are great."

If Washington's Southwest was, despite all shortcomings, the best of the cataclysmic urban renewal efforts, St. Louis' Mill Creek is probably the worst, although that sad, early mistake at Boston's West End received far more adverse publicity.

St. Louis had done a lot for itself at about the gaslit time of the "Meet Me in St. Louis, Louis," Louisiana Purchase Exposition of 1904. Along with big industrial plants, proud commercial palaces, a great railroad station, and some of the finest and gaudiest Victorian residences in the country, it built the wonderful Forest Park, with its splendid zoo, museum, outdoor opera, and lately its very handsome planetarium. The spirit lasted through the Calvin Coolidge days, when a typical City Beautiful civic center was constructed in the heart of town, crowned by the Civil Courts Building, an ill-shaped tower that is quite lovable in its assertive ugliness.

Came the Depression, war, the flood of automobiles, and the lure of affluent suburbia. Like other cities, St. Louis lost population and self-confidence. Downtown began to decay.

To cure its ills, the city applied an excessive dose of the standard patent medicine: a network of monstrous freeways that invited even more cars and congestion, a number of standard public housing projects that caused more troubles than the slums they replaced, and cataclysmic clearance of a huge downtown area.

For years, the 465-acre Mill Creek Valley, bulldozed in 1959, remained a wasteland overgrown with the weeds of indecision. Slowly a disorganized array of a variety of unsurpassably mediocre buildings appeared—a printing plant here, an apartment house there, a few suburban industrial plants along the edge. The planners say it was all "on schedule" and "according to plan." Again, the schedule was but the expedience of nonplanning. And this for the city's key area that commands a magnificient view over the city clear to the Mississippi where Eero Saarinen's marvelous steel Gateway Arch was beginning to rise.

The weeds flourished because here, as in Washington's Southwest, New Haven's downtown, and other renewal areas, the land was cleared before there were firm commitments about who was going to do what with it. St. Louis' city fathers compounded this difficulty by insisting that only local interests be allowed to share the spoils of urban renewal. They rejected the Zeckendorfs and other bigtime out-of-towners. Their suspicion is, perhaps, understandable. Since John Jacob Astor made his fortunes on the pastures of Manhattan, our giant real estate speculators have not always been overly concerned with the public interest.

Yet only a Zeckendorf or some other powerful Maecenas could have forced a bold concept. By now not only a few daring developers but a good many large investors as well had discovered, as one of them put it, that "there's a lot of romance in urban renewal. No killing, mind you. Just a nice, fair profit at little risk. It takes some expenditures to get your fishing license, such as a good architectural design that will dazzle the renewal authorities. But the way the government has set up the financing terms, no one has ever foreclosed."

Good architectural design would have seen at once that there is a straight visual axis from the Saarinen Arch by the river, past the civic center and the railroad station with its whimsical, sensual fountain by Carl Milles, up to the slopes of Mill Creek. Here is the spine of St. Louis, which, strengthened with civic beauty and cultural and commercial enterprises, could give new vitality to the whole city.

Saarinen saw this axis and proposed to carry it from his Arch which frames the charming old Courthouse up to the Civil Courts Building.

But Saarinen's concept has been badly compromised. The new buildings along the Mississippi lack taste and a disciplined basic form. Worse, St. Louis decided to build a huge stadium, designed by Edward Durrell Stone, in the shadows of the Arch. This ill-advised project will undoubtedly accomplish the opposite of what was intended: Instead of attracting people to live and work in the city, the inevitable, congested confusion of the stadium visitors and their cars will scare people away from downtown to spend their money somewhere out on the highways. No one will want to remain longer than necessary amidst an agglomeration of smelly automobile stables that inevitably cut up the sidewalks. Highways lead not only into but also out of the city.

Beyond the Union Station the axis—Market Street—now veers off southward just as it should climb the hill up into the Mill Creek area. It is, furthermore, cut off from downtown by the huge Distributor Expressway. What begins with a bang, as Edmund Bacon observed, now peters out in a whimper of confusion. What's more, six years after the bulldozers came, I found Mill Creek a disgraceful monument not to urban renewal but to urban devastation. Only a fraction of the destroyed area had been haphazardly rebuilt. Again, here was wholesale Negro removal. Again, there was no aim or purpose.

Almost despite the urban renewers, I also found a strong ray of hope. Finally St. Louis had admitted an out-of-town developer after all: James H. Scheuer, now a Democratic Congressman from New York. On 11 of 465 acres, he and Chloethiel Smith had built La Clede Town for people of moderate income. It was built under the so-called 221-d-3 limited profit provisions of the Federal Housing Act.

Some people have criticized Mrs. Smith's architecture for its cuteness and the occasional shutters that don't shut and the silly gaslights on the street which she didn't choose. It is true that as pure, well-designed modern architecture, Mayer & Whittlesey's nearby and slightly more expensive project is more classy, perhaps. It is almost Miesian in its severity. Its appeal is intellectual. La Clede Town appeals to the heart. With its "coach and four" pub, outdoor café, "Ma and Pa" grocery store, and coin laundromat that invites the women to meet and gossip, the town is lively and exciting and, better still, proves that the Jane Jacobs kind of thing works. It proves that the old-town conviviality can be recreated in modern terms and modern times, automobiles, picture windows, air conditioners, and all. And that it can be done with a low budget for low rents.

The bureaucrats in the Federal Housing Administration, of course, were skeptical to the point of obstructionism. They didn't like wood siding, stores in a residential area, and a lot of other things. Finally Mrs. Smith and Scheuer won out with most of what they wanted. The victory was complete. La Clede was immediately fully rented.

Now Mrs. Smith and Scheuer are going on to extend the La Clede project with more town houses and large apartment buildings. With it, there is hope that the whimper of confusion at the crest of Mill Creek might still be turned into some sort of urban design.

One day Mrs. Smith walked that crest and looked at the rising Arch in the distance. She thoughtfully returned to her hotel and emerged the next morning with a sketch that was none of her business to draw. There might still be some order, the sketch showed, if some of the buildings the planners had proposed were moved back somewhat and the Expressway canyon were bridged with strong buildings. Thus could be created not an avenue but at least an elongated, mall-like park with big trees. It would culminate in a great plaza with big fountains and terraces that Scheuer would build and thus form a visual counterpoint to the Arch down on the other end of the axis.

The St. Louis Plan Commission, apparently happy with the way it had botched a great opportunity, did not like this saving proposal. Luckily, however, Mill Creek is the responsibility of the Land Clearance Authority. Land clearer Charles F. Farris seems confident that the Smith plan will prevail.

I have dwelled on Washington's Southwest and St. Louis' Mill Creek at some length because both—the first with its predominantly good, and the second with its predominantly bad, architecture—seem to me to demonstrate that cataclysmic urban renewal programs of this kind are not the answer to our urban dilemma—certainly not without a bold, comprehensive plan in which coherent urban design follows strong social concern.

I have said as much about architecture. In planning—architecture on a larger scale—the dilemma is the same. Form follows function. Nor can we evade the imperative of historic continuity if the result is to be human. Our humanity is not a sudden event, no matter how abruptly we invent new gadgets that seemingly change man's way of life. Though not immutable, our humanity seems a matter of slow, natural evolution.

I know of only one large-scale urban renewal effort to date which has recognized this in an effort to make an entire city more livable. It is a relatively small city that is still easy to comprehend and to really know—New Haven. It has a population of 152,000 living on six square miles, and a dozen years ago it was dying.

The secret of New Haven's amazing convalescence, however, is not so much the injection of some $500 million of public and private investment—with federal grants averaging $458 for each resident. Nor is it the multitude of complex urban programs, both physical and social, that were applied here. It is, ultimately, the result of determined leadership of a strong mayor, Richard C. Lee, who had the good luck to attract very savvy redevelopment administrators, first Edward J. Logue and then Thomas Appleby.

Logue went on to renew Boston, which promises to become another heartening accomplishment. Tom Appleby is now heading the Redevelopment Land Agency in Washington, where his great talents are sorely needed.

New Haven, too, began with rather indiscriminate bulldozing. It leveled its deteriorated downtown district and got badly burned when its chosen developer, Roger Stevens, an investor in theatrical enterprises as well as real estate, failed to come through with the money. But Lee and Logue soon moved on all fronts at once to revitalize commerce, improve transportation, refurbish old houses, build new housing of all kinds as well as new schools, fire stations, and industrial parks. It was all done under a comprehensive, clear plan and soon combined with an extensive effort to improve the school system and public welfare services and to combat poverty.

At Court Street, which was so badly deteriorated that, I was told, even tough sailors were scared to follow the streetwalkers into it, Lee and Logue pioneered the planned rehabilitation of a whole city block of charming nineteenth-century row houses. The effort proved expensive and the street now demands high rents. But Court Street called national attention to an important new approach to federally sponsored urban renewal that has since been effectively used elsewhere in low income neighborhoods, notably at Harlem Park in Baltimore and Washington Park in Boston.

Around Wooster Square, New Haven's renewers pioneered the careful and comprehensive rehabilitation of an entire neighborhood, much as you would restore a rundown garden to health and beauty. They weeded out only what was decayed, salvaged what was salvageable, and judiciously planted new attractions, notably a new school that also serves as a community center, attractively designed by Skid-

A New Haven street pioneered slum rehabilitation

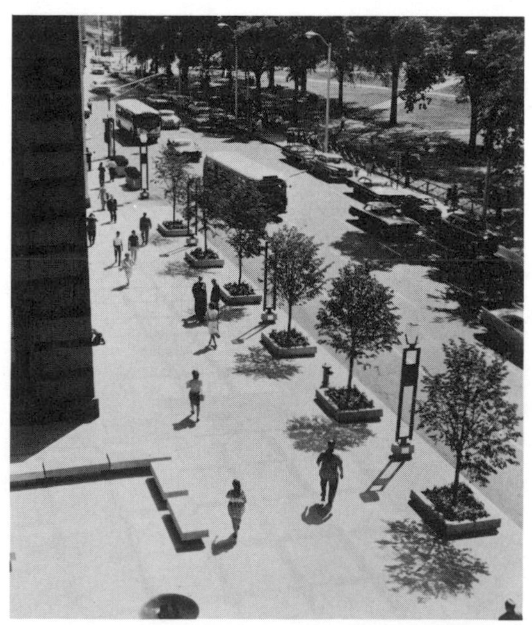

Handsome new street furnishings across the Green

more, Owings and Merrill. The Wooster Square approach is now being repeated in the Dixwell neighborhood.

New Haven's urban innovations also include the use of existing, rehabilitated houses for the indigent under the public housing program. It is, to my knowledge, the first city to attack the horrible clutter of public signs on the street. In front of City Hall, facing its famous Green, landscape architect Hideo Sasaki, along with handsomely repaving the sidewalk and making it attractive with potted plants, ingeniously combined new light fixtures with simple and legible new traffic signs. The light standards are shaped like large hairpins and the NO PARKING, BUS STOP, and other messages in modern letters are placed between the two poles. Where no signs were needed, Sasaki placed wastebaskets or plants in his hairpins. It is unfortunate that no other city has yet imitated, if not his design, at least his creatively intelligent approach. That, too, I suppose, takes a strong, energetic mayor who really cares enough about such only seemingly trifling things to go argue it out with the traffic engineers, a pretty obstinate bunch to argue with.

Richard Lee's understanding of the importance of good design is manifest in his selection of architects for his many projects. The list, along with lesser known but daring talents, includes such illustrious names as the Saarinen firm, Philip Johnson, I. M. Pei, and Mies van der Rohe, who is currently designing a housing project. These talents have produced much unusually interesting architecture and have given the mayor's effort great flair and style. I quarrel with some of the new buildings which seem to suffer a bit from Yale esoterics. But I enthusiastically salute the fact that, perhaps because of Yale's interest and backing, New Haven sought and on the whole succeeded in obtaining outstanding architecture not only for its new municipal buildings but also for its public and subsidized housing. Of the many new, what the Europeans call "social," housing projects, I especially admired Karl Koch's Liberty Square and John M. Johansen's Florence Virtue Townhouses. Both show that simple design need not be inane and that economical design need not look institutional.

One of the few even more attractive moderately priced new neighborhoods resulting from urban renewal I have seen is St. Francis Square in San Francisco. The design, by Marquis and Stoller, was judged best of six proposals submitted to Justin Herman's energetic Redevelopment Agency. It is sponsored by ILWU, the longshoremen's union, and its delight rests in the fact that it appears not as a "project" at all, but as a gay environment. What I remember best of Marquis and Stoller's creation is not their architecture so much but two little three-year-old girls chasing each other across one of the lovely interior courts. One was as blonde as could be. The other was pitch black. When the little blonde finally caught up with her friend, she nearly smothered her in a long, exuberant hug.

Such scenes and places are rare, however. And it is a measure of the admirable spirit of Mayor Lee's effort that more than half of the new housing produced is for people of below average income, and that figure will still go higher as currently planned social housing projects are built. Too many of the urban renewal apartments benefit only their developers.

Lacking good schools, parks, order, safety, and amenity, few families with children venture to move back where father works—in the downtown center. And that, apart from the attempt to build new residential neighborhoods like the Southwest or Mill Creek, is where the big cities shifted the emphasis of urban renewal.

A good place to play

4. Enhanceable Romance

When footsore tourists from Salina, Kansas, say, send a picture postcard home on their visit to New York, it is more likely to depict Rockefeller Center than the Statue of Liberty. Rockefeller Center attests to the fact that they have experienced the big city.

The huge gray limestone slabs are surely no great architecture. The ground plan, providing conventional, symmetrical Renaissance vistas, "reveals nothing," as Sigfried Giedion observed. The gridiron street pattern runs through as everywhere in the city. And yet Giedion was right when he prophesied back in 1941 that Rockefeller Center would point the way to the new civic center—"a public place which, like the agora of Athens, the Roman forum, and the medieval cathedral square, will be the community focus and popular concourse."

Rockefeller Center was built during the Depression instead of the opera house that John D. Rockefeller had originally intended there. It was designed by a long list of architects—Reinhard and Hofmeister, Corbett, Harrison and MacMurray, Hood and Fouilhoux—and neither they, nor anyone else but Giedion, quite saw the significance of its essential and simple idea until, in the late 1950's, it was reimported from Europe. Nobody, that is, but the tourists from Salina and a great many people who live and work in New York City.

They sit alongside the flower displays and quiet pools of the magnificent mall. They admire the rather silly Prometheus, floating awkwardly above his fountain. They watch people eat or ice skate in the sunken court over which the brightly gilded statue presides. They rush through the underground concourses. They shop or hurry to work or back home. They stand patiently in line at Radio City Music Hall. They come to see and be seen, or for no particular reason but to feel part of humanity.

All this was incidental. Rockefeller Center was designed, as Raymond Hood, one of its architects, put it, on pure calculation of cost and return. Yet he and his colleagues threw more than flowers, flagpoles, benches, fountains, sculptures, and a festive setting into the bargain. For the first time in the history of the modern city, they rescued the hapless biped from the automobile. And they thereby returned to us another very good reason for going downtown besides earning or spending money.

Whether he knew it or not, Hood and company discovered, as the astute architecture critic Douglas Haskell has observed, that modern urban life was "an enhanceable romance."

The romance, of course, has sadly faded in the motor age. Automobile congestion has made downtown hard to get to and around in and an unpleasant place to walk and shop. With business investments consequently dispersed to less expensive and more accessible locations, downtown declined. Idiotically, downtown merchants who suffer financially from this decline still keep egging on the highway engineers to bring more cars into the central business district, as though, as Victor Gruen has pointed out, even an expensive Cadillac had ever bought a nickel's worth of merchandise. Most of them still don't see that they would be much better off if we kept cars out and brought *people* in.

This, of course, is more difficult than paving downtown with parking lots crisscrossed by federally financed freeways. It requires creative, comprehensive planning. It is expensive. But what some people find even more annoying to part with than money are their conventional prejudices. Professor E. A. Gutkind's recent assertion in a letter to the New York *Times* that the "city centers of today are the cancer of urban existence" is still widely shared by other Cassandras who, in the face of America's apparent relish for suburban scatteration, feel that saving downtown is not worth the effort. As Gutkind, a University of Pennsylvania urban studies professor, says, "electronics and computers work against the ever-worsening concentration in the central areas of cities.

Closed-circuit television can easily replace face-to-face meetings and contacts and the herding together of people in business compounds."

There are always moralistic undertones in these attacks on Babylon. Nor are they new. St. Bernard of Clairvaux in the twelfth century was probably not the first to deplore the evil city.

As an unprofessorial student of the contemporary urban scene, I find that people enjoy being herded together in pleasant surroundings where there are things to do and see. Electronics, computers, and closed-circuit television or not, the large corporations which in the fifties made their contribution to downtown decongestion by moving to rambling new headquarters out in the sticks have regretted it. They discovered that they must periodically send their junior executives to refresher courses and academic conferences so they can make the human contacts and gain the professional inspiration which, downtown, comes about spontaneously. They also find it difficult, among other things, to recruit secretaries to places where these girls can't get their hair or some window shopping done in their lunch hour. Besides, it's awfully frustrating for a girl to try and strike sparks with a boy she meets only on a television screen, closed-circuit or otherwise.

Charles Abrams contends that American women fresh out of college now shun New York because the city keeps destroying places where they could meet young men and be courted. They avoid such parks as there are, because they are unsafe. Few of our cities have enough places where young people—people of any age, in fact—can meet easily and spontaneously. Spots such as New York's Greenwich Village are terribly overrun and their taverns usually turn quickly into traps for affluent and concupiscent sales executives. The good people of Georgetown keep complaining that their taverns attract hordes of boisterous teen-agers from all over the Washington suburbs who then spill noisily into their sedate residential streets. The only sensible answer is not to have one Greenwich Village, cluster of Georgetown taverns, or St. Louis Gaslight District in town, but to create many such attractions and have a lively downtown.

In Europe, where people have traditionally loved their cities, it has always been understood that downtown is "where the action is." On the continent, in contrast to rural serfdom, the city was in the past and is still considered a citadel of bourgeois freedom where even princes were proud to build their palaces. Only in England, with its puritanism and aristocratic relish of the country estate, was the garden party considered more virtuous than the opera and downtown bustle considered vulgar and shocking.

The "action," however, is more than the concentration of offices, markets, cultural offerings, specialties, and variety. It is even more than the essential center, the heart and the brain, without which the urban body cannot properly function, electronics, computers or not. It is—and this is, I believe, more important today than ever—the essential counterpoint to the sameness and ennui of our homogeneous residential surroundings. No one, rich or poor, commuter or child-leashed "homemaker," likes to spend a lifetime vegetating in the crabgrass ghettos of suburbia. "When you are alone / and life is making you lonely / you can always go—Downtown," says the popular song. Downtown makes urbanization urbane, it turns civility into civilization. It is, or should be, as planner Edgardo Contini has said, "an expression of our collective wealth and imagination." Main Street had always been just that before it deteriorated.

This deterioration is not only sad for the downtown merchants who Professor Gutkind, I presume, would have give up and take jobs in a nice, big anonymous chain store or else go into the computer-controlled mail-order business. It is sad and quite unhealthy for all of us.

Gutkind's solution is "that cities must be decongested internally and decentralized externally. Both are interdependent and both lead to the only way out of the present chaos—that is, to regional planning on a large scale, creating a new pattern of settlement and industry over vast areas."

Where have you been these past thirty years, professor?

Except for the planning, regional, large-scale, or otherwise, this is precisely what happened and caused the present chaos. All our inner cities, as reported by the 1950 to 1960 census, lost population and thus "decongested internally" and the new suburban pattern of settlement and industry decentralized all over the countryside. And since there were no centers out there, no downtowns, the suburbanites and their merchants who had fled the wicked "cancers of urban existence," discovered that they had to invent them all over again.

Thus we began after World War II to build the new trading posts in the exurban wilderness—the regional shopping center. It is one of the few uniquely American building types.

The exurbanites found that the roadside supermarket or even a branch of a downtown department store was not enough. They needed medical and other professional services, offices for the real estate brokers, employment offices, post offices, auditoria, theaters, eating places, spaces for exhibits and some fun and excitement. But none of this, they discovered, would help very much if, as downtown, people would have to fight their way through heavy automobile traffic to get to it. Thus, instead of placing their buildings along the highway in the conventional fashion, the new shopping centers clustered them around spaces where people could walk without being pulped by combustion engines. The cars were parked on the periphery.

Victor Gruen's Northland regional shopping center near Detroit, built in 1952, was one of the first spectacular ones. Like Rotterdam's Lijnbaan, which had been designed a few years earlier, Gruen handsomely endowed it with art and amenities. His clients protested at first that the flowers would be stolen, that children would drown in the fountains, that the trees would mess up the pavement which would, at any rate, be too expensive to keep clean, and that they would go bankrupt if the customers couldn't drive right to the threshold of their stores. But in the end they gave in and now make good money. What's more, as Gruen reported, the quiet protected pedestrian areas of his center "proved the fulfillment of pent-up demands and desires for which no opportunity had previously existed in the suburban environment."

Northland, Gruen says, "became the place where friends met, where new friendships were started, where gatherings of all sorts were held, where ladies met for luncheons and families met for dinner. Inactive civic, cultural, and art organizations became active, and many new ones were started because they finally had a place in which to meet. The theater in Northland, at least during the summer months, is the only one in all of Detroit which shows legitimate plays, and the vast public areas are the ideal setting for popular concerts, Fourth of July celebrations, and political gatherings around election time."

The new competition aroused the downtown businessmen. In most American cities they formed new associations to plot, plan, and promote the sorely needed revitalization of the central business district. And, although most of them reject federal doles for the poor as un-American, they see it as the federal government's sacred duty to subsidize them. The government, as I noted, obligingly shifted the emphasis of its urban renewal program from the slums to the downtown business districts.

Philadelphia's Penn Center, Pittsburgh's Golden Triangle, Boston's Government Square, Denver's Mile High Center, Baltimore's Charles Center, Detroit's new waterfront development, New Haven's new downtown, Hartford's Constitution Plaza, Fresno's wonderful mall, and even New York's Lincoln Center, are some of the more spectacular results. Most of them, with the exception perhaps of Philadelphia and Fresno, are conceived of, and function as, gleaming new islands that stand apart from the rest of the city. They are not fully and carefully woven into the city's texture as part of the city's ecology.

As with modern architecture, much of the inspiration for modern urban design came from Europe. Yet much as Europe's new architectural concepts were strongly influenced by the Chicago School and Frank Lloyd Wright, so were her urban design concepts influenced by Clarence Stein's Radburn Plan and Rockefeller Center.

These new concepts began to take shape with the reconstruction of Rotterdam and Coventry.

5. Dancing on the Street

Rotterdam had always been known as a fine harbor in front of a terrible town until the Nazis destroyed both. The Luftwaffe raid of May 14, 1940, left the embers of eleven thousand buildings in the inner city burning for forty nights and days. Yet even before they had died out, the city's chief architect, W. G. Witteveern, was already poring over maps and plans in one of the rooms of the miraculously spared Municipal Library to plot Rotterdam's reconstruction. His architect friends did not have to be told where they would find him. In secret—since the country was occupied and Hitler's Gestapo would surely have arrested them for such subversion—an underground planning group evolved a splendid new master plan for a truly modern new city.

The Dutch government-in-exile in London was aware of this work and boldly removed what proved the greatest impediment to the modernization of other European cities that had been destroyed in the war: the multitude of individual owners of small properties who asserted their rights and thus made large-scale, comprehensive development difficult, if not impossible. The Dutch, in the interest of orderly and controlled redevelopment, appropriated all land in the destroyed inner city of Rotterdam immediately after the bombing and turned it over to the municipality.

Before the Nazis destroyed it, the Lijnbaan, in the heart of downtown, was a congested, dirty old street. Today, designed by J. H. van den Brock and Jacob B. Bakema, it is an enchanting pedestrian shopping district laid out in the form of a cross and entirely reserved for people on foot. It is gay and resplendent with lush flower displays, sculpture, sidewalk cafés, benches and, in the summer, even colorful and noisy parrots which, perching on poles, delight the children and add to the bustle. Behind both sides of the simply and uniformly designed three-fifths of a mile long row of small shops are tall, massive apartment buildings that give the long and narrow axis a sense of enclosure. At regular intervals—and this was an important design innovation—it is also bridged by canopies adorned by hanging plants, so you never feel its length. There are also canopies along the shops to keep you out of the rain. The broader cross axis widens imperceptibly towards Coolsingle, a wide boulevard, and City Hall, to form a fine plaza.

The pedestrian preserve quickly worked wonders. Specialty shops and new amenities and, with them, people returned to the inner city. And those sixty-six stores in an attractive setting soon did as much, economically, for the rest of downtown Rotterdam as Rockefeller Center has done for midtown Manhattan. But Rotterdam did even more, as I discovered when, on my first visit, I backed into "Meneer Jacques" trying to get the full perspective of Coolsingle into my viewfinder.

"Pardon me," I said. When I looked around, I thought I saw just a flicker of a smile on his haughty mien. It seemed due not so much to my photomaniac clumsiness as to my startled amazement to find this portly, imperturbable citizen cast in bronze. The lovable statue of no one in particular stands, holding his hat behind his back, to watch the rebirth of Rotterdam with obvious pride.

Rotterdammers like him didn't much believe in art and ostentation before the World War II catastrophe. Now not only the city fathers but grateful individual citizens and business firms—who, in this country, endow our cityscape with billboards—have lavished sculpture, fountains, mosaics, reliefs, and flower displays of all kinds on the rebuilt central business district.

The most outstanding of the new public sculptures is Ossip Zadkine's memorial to the bombing. It is magnificently sited overlooking the harbor. Pigeons swarm all over this contorted symbol of a city with its heart torn out. It reminds me a little of Picasso's *Guernica*.

"The Thing," as Rotterdammers call Naum Gabo's giant abstraction on the sidewalk in front of Marcel Breuer's Bijenkorf department store, is less well placed, the way it obstructs the sidewalk. The pigeons seem to be afraid of the wire strung eighty-five feet up and it says little to me in all its hugeness, except "how lucky for Breuer." It casts a nice shadow on his forbidding facade.

Another famous work is Henry Moore's wonderful brick relief on the Bouwcentrum, an institute for the study and advancement of building techniques such as we in the United States sorely need. But Rotterdam's new delight stems not only from these prominent art works but from the many, almost casual pieces amidst the city's hustle and bustle. We lock such sculpture and adornments into museums. The Dutch put them out on the street, on their buildings, and into little parks. Encouragingly, it is all modern, though not necessarily abstract. Most of them are contributed by business firms which consider them better public relations than gaudy billboards.

The Lijnbaan idea of car-free shopping has been applied in a growing number of existing streets, notably on Copenhagen's Strøget and Amsterdam's Kalverstraat and, more recently, in American cities as

Not just to shop and to work

well. It works handsomely in Kalamazoo. But in Toledo, Ohio, it was a flop when that city, with more enthusiasm than good planning, merely closed off a street to automobiles but failed to provide adequate parking and a well-functioning new traffic pattern. The flower boxes and statuary alone didn't do it.

Coventry went further than a pedestrian mall. Like Rotterdam, it too was almost completely destroyed and, as the lucky outcome of a six-year-long hassle between planners and skeptical city fathers, was rebuilt with the world's first wholly pedestrian precinct in the center. This is made possible by a fairly tight expressway loop, half a mile in diameter, around the downtown area. Directly off this expressway are parking spaces for ten thousand cars, a good many of them on the roofs of stores. This allows 20 per cent of the commuters to use private automobiles. For the rest there is an excellent public transportation system.

The pedestrian precinct is on two levels reached by squares and ramps. It is handsomely linked with the central civic square where, not unexpectedly, a bronze Lady Godiva relishes her well-known ride. On the other side, on a slight elevation, stands the Cathedral. Only the tower has remained of the grand Gothic structure after that fearful moonlit night of the Nazi bombing raid. The old spire still dominates the scene and the designers were careful to honor it with manifold dramatic views. The new, courageously modern cathedral by Sir Basil Spence is proud yet unobtrusive.

The rest of Coventry's new architecture, however, is considerably less impressive. In fact, the banality of the new buildings rather detracts from the superb urban design of the reconstruction. So, despite much good effort, does the lackluster drabness of the central area. Coventry just isn't Rotterdam. It is a relatively small town that, bypassed by industry and the main arteries of commerce, never gained much importance. It isn't even the office center for the motor, aircraft, and machine-tool plants that have made it an industrial city, since their offices are out where the factories are. On the other hand, there are some sixteenth-century buildings left and the city's architects, notably Donald Gibson—with the help, to be sure, of the Luftwaffe—have done a superb job of integrating modern efficiency and amenity with Coventry's medieval texture. All this is unfairly overlooked by those who complain that Coventry's pioneer city planning effort lacks excitement.

But no one can say this of Kassel, the German city just a bit smaller than Coventry, with its 250,000 population, which also rose from al-

An urban stairway lined with shops

most complete wartime destruction and which followed Coventry's planning concept almost identically. If Kassel is more lively and exciting, it is probably due to its natural setting along the hilly slopes of the Fulda river as well as to Germany's much touted "economic miracle." Kassel, furthermore, *is* a regional center and was dominated for centuries by the ambitious landgraves of Hesse—an early one was known as Philip the Magnanimous—who were much inclined towards civic ostentation. This, though built by a Social Democratic city administration, is reflected in Kassel's new *pièce de résistance*—its Treppen Strasse. It is a wide stair leading uphill to where the railroad station is, lined with stores, a beautiful green strip in the center, and outdoor cafés on its landings. It was designed, as the result of a competition, by Werner Hasper.

Victor Gruen, with his plan for Fort Worth, Texas, published in 1956, introduced the idea of a pedestrian city center in America. At Fort Worth he attempted to turn an entire existing downtown business district into a pedestrian oasis. The plan was thoroughly convincing and much like Coventry's, except that at Fort Worth most existing buildings would have been left standing. Goods and services would have been brought into the car-free district by underground tunnel at basement level. Pedestrian circulation would have been helped along

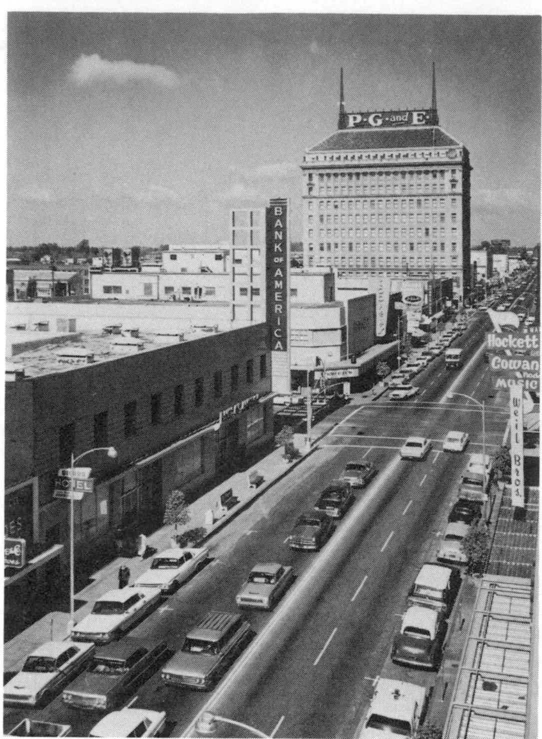

Fresno: A new city . . .

with slow-moving electric carts. The plan was defeated mainly by the local parking-lot operators, a powerful enemy of pedestrians in any city. But, as someone observed, the Fort Worth plan is the only unborn baby who had hundreds of grandchildren.

The most exciting of them I have seen on this side of the Atlantic is Fresno, population 154,000. The best thing about it is that neither bombs nor cataclysmic bulldozers had to clear the way for the transformation. Few serviceable buildings were destroyed and most remaining ones are just that—serviceable. Only a few stores have spruced up their storefronts. The signs are unfortunately still ugly and chaotic. But they appear in an entirely new, delightful, and efficient environment that consists not only of the pedestrian mall but a new courthouse, convention hall and civic center—a new downtown that is both functionally and aesthetically related to the rest of the city.

The feat took five years of planning, rerouting of a contemplated highway, a rearrangement of traffic patterns and, of course, the creation of ample parking spaces. Then six long blocks of the main shopping street and a block each of three cross streets could be closed to cars and trucks and be civilized. The sophisticated design of the patterned

. . . without destroying the old

pavement, the fountains, sculptured waterways, light fixtures, trash bins, planter boxes and islands of trees, flowers, and shrubs is by landscape architects Eckbo, Dean, Austin & Williams. It is just a bit overdone, more ostentatious than Lijnbaan. But the idea was new and the architects felt they had to make their point. They did extremely well.

The pavement is easy to walk on and softly ebbing and flowing so rainwater won't collect. The fountains, cascades, pools, and jets, all of different and fascinating designs, are automatically geared to the wind velocity so people won't get wet. In some, the water gushes along stylized brooks that splash over richly colored and patterned adobe sculptures. Some you can cross on little bridges, others tempt you to run along them, dragging your hand in the water. All of them help cool the mall in the hot Fresno sun.

For the grown-ups there are places to sit in the sun amidst greenery, in the shade under arbors, or, protected from the wind, behind handsome mosaic walls. For the children there are marvelous little playgrounds, some donated by merchants, that keep the kids occupied while mother is shopping. There are, of course, sidewalk cafés and a number of excellent sculptures. And between all these wonders wind noiseless little electric trains, driven by attractive girls who will collect a dime from you and let you on or off wherever you wish. Business along the mall, needless to say, has increased considerably.

The new sense of belonging and cohesion the new downtown center has given Fresno and its more than sixty ethnic groups joyfully bursts out during the city's Art Festival. It started with the mall's opening festivities but has become an annual affair. There is, of course, nothing unusual about the local cultural offerings reinforced by professional out-of-town performers. What makes the festival Fresnian and unique is the spirit of it all. This is William Saroyan's city and here on the mall is where Saroyan's America comes to life with Japanese and Armenian folk dancing, a Buddhist choir, and the multicolored array of little faces in front of the storyteller's booth that listen enraptured while a young Fresno actress tells them about Cinderella.

Here surely the urban romance has been enhanced as never before in modern America. But for a new downtown center to quicken the pulse of the city, as we are now beginning to see, requires planning and building in the total context of the entire area it serves—in terms of where people live, where they work, how they move about, where they can get air and sunshine, and what they require of downtown that they can't get in their neighborhoods.

At the agora, the forum, the medieval cathedral square, and the downtown centers that grew out of them, this didn't have to be planned. These hearts quite naturally grew with the rest of the urban body and adjusted themselves to the body's changing functions, needs, and tastes.

The helter-skelter development of the industrial and motor age diseased this organic anatomy with its tumorous growth. The surgical operation of downtown renewal, to be effective, must restore this heart function and quality. That means that the downtown center must be equally accessible to all parts and all the people of the city—you can't have a viable center for the rich and another for the poor, one for businessmen and one for housewives. It must be all encompassing—not one for culture and another for business, one for lowbrows and one for highbrows. It must be singular—two centers, like the Prudential Center and the Government Center in Boston, will stop both from being *the* center, and the more recent "midtowns," as in New York, have inevitably, if slowly, killed off the old downtowns. And it must have identity—so people can identify with it, know when they are there, and send a postcard home about it.

A viable downtown requires the greatest possible extent of variety, not only of goods, services, culture, and recreation, but also, as our planners usually forget, of people actually living there. The excuse is that downtown land is too expensive for downtown apartments. The cost of dead, deserted streets, empty buses, subway trains, and parking lots, not to speak of urban scatteration is surely much greater. In a recent snowstorm in Washington, snow removal downtown was badly delayed because all the workmen lived out in the suburbs and were stuck there.

As the regional shopping centers have shown, it is vital to keep cars out of the way of people who must be allowed to walk, stroll, stop, criss-cross, and meander at will. Since people need sunshine and fresh air more than cars, it is best to put the people on top. And to put everything within easy walking distance large centers are best built on two or more levels.

Last but by no means least, a viable downtown center must be inviting, attractive, stimulating, and lively from the start. This is not only a matter of architecture, but, as the best of them have shown, also, or perhaps foremost, of the furnishings. Hartford's Constitution Plaza—a platform over a big parking garage lined with big office buildings—for instance, has little to offer but one hotel and some very dull bank and brokerage establishments. Yet people flock to it and climb up those stairs—although the view of the river is obscured by elevated freeways—simply because it is such a pleasant environment to be in. Landscape architect Hideo Sasaki has garnished it with a forest of potted trees and other greenery, a fountain, a clock tower, a variety of different pavements, benches, and vistas.

Philadelphia's Penn Center is also endowed with much of this and it is, furthermore, despite some planning compromises, a splendid accomplishment of urban design that, for a change, relates well to the rest of the inner city. When Edmund Bacon's bold and imaginative multilevel Market East project is completed—without too many timid compromises, I hope—Center City Philadelphia will undoubtedly be a beacon to guide the rebirth of the cities of the future, much as the Rome of Pope Sixtus V, whom Bacon admires so much, paved the way for the Renaissance city.

As yet, however, Penn Center is populated only by very purposeful people who rush to their desks or the subway. At night it is empty for, as in most of our expensive new downtown centers, there are only airline ticket office windows and curtained banks to look at, and that isn't much. The action is all on adjoining Market Street with its gaudy movie awnings and somewhat seamy shops displaying girlie magazines and such. The trouble is that only big and dull stores can afford to move

A new downtown . . .

into the new centers. Besides, it takes time for liveliness to develop. Yet there is, I believe, a way to seed it judiciously. I discovered it in Berlin.

What impressed me most about Berlin's new Europa Center was not so much that the ice-skating rink was frozen and full of swirling motion in the heat of August. It was that, next to a very gay flower stand, a hurdy-gurdy man was grinding out music far sweeter than our dreadful ubiquitous Muzak. That evening I complimented one of the gifted architects of the place, Werner Duettmann, on having created an environment that so instantly attracted such delight.

"Shush," he whispered, "we are paying that organ grinder!"

I thought it a marvelous idea. I wish our new city centers would indulge in such life seeding. In the long run the hurdy-gurdy men, flower vendors, and popcorn stands would surely pay for themselves. They would undoubtedly attract more people than far more expensive advertising.

The most exciting and endearing downtown center I have seen is Stockholm's Sergelgatan which Warsaw is now almost literally duplicating.

. . . where there is more to do . . .

Stockholm, with a metropolitan population of over one million and the highest car ownership ratio in Europe, met its phenomenal post-war expansion with a comprehensive and clear masterplan. Swedish planners had understood as early as 1941 that the bulk of commuter traffic would have to be carried by public transportation if the inner city was to survive. The new subway began operation in 1950 and its expanding system determines and controls both metropolitan growth and downtown concentration at the same time. The growth takes place in a constellation of satellite communities at the end of the radiating subway lines. The downtown concentration is achieved by gradually and judiciously rebuilding the inner city on several levels. The subway,

. . . than work and shop

which is a joy to ride and carries about a quarter of Stockholm's total traffic, is supplemented and coordinated with a freeway program which forms a loop and a cross, two arms of which form tangents to the central business district. Within it will be forty-five thousand off-street parking spaces.

Sergelgatan, the hub of the new downtown redevelopment, was built between the two subway stations where old buildings had to come down and the ground dug up anyway. It consists of five eighteen-story office buildings, evenly spaced and identical in proportion, though different in their facade treatment. They stand on a podium which contains two levels of stores and has delightfully designed roof gardens. Below are three stories of parking garages and the subway entrances with their concourses. Cut through this podium, flowing like a broad, leisurely river, is a handsomely paved and furnished pedestrian shopping boulevard that spills into the colorful old flower and produce market in front of the old Concert Hall.

Even on Sundays when the stores are closed, the place is throbbing with humanity. People come out of the earth, emerging from the subway, from Kungsgatan, which is Stockholm's Broadway, from the quiet parks and museums, from all parts of town. They come not only to shop and to work but also to eat or just sit in the cafés, to see a movie or just people. They sit secluded up on the roof gardens or on the benches right in the mainstream. The boys up on the bridges watch the girls passing below. Old people sun themselves. Children chase each other between the planter boxes. Artists display their paintings or chalk them on the pavement and people smile admiringly and toss pennies. There is some of the elegance and festiveness of the Champs Elysées and the tasteful architecture reflects this. There is also some of the folksy scrubbiness of Times Square and the often jazzy storefront advertising reflects *that*. There is nothing precious about the place.

I was taking it all in one fine summer day when a crowd gathered. I pushed my way through and was surprised to find old acquaintances. Three bearded young minstrels were lustily singing American folk tunes to their guitars. They were the same English students, singing their way through Europe, I had encountered the week before on Copenhagen's Strøget. Only this time their girl friends who passed the hat for them, though equally pretty, were Swedish, not Danish.

I enjoyed their serenade the second time even more than the first. On narrow, meandering Strøget, some of whose lovely houses date back to the sixteenth century, the wandering minstrels seemed to belong.

One all but expected such bygone enchantment along with the old pewter and antique spinning wheels that are sold there.

But to find such spontaneous, unselfconscious folk art in the shadows of modern glass and steel office skyscrapers, I thought, was a compliment to the place. On Professor Gutkind's television screen I would scarcely have given these boys another look. Here in a bustling city they seemed to spell much new hope for urban man.

6. Freeways to Urbicide

"Traffic is not important. What is important is how people live," says the English architect Theo Crosby in his splendid little book *City Sense*. "There is no sense in planning for traffic without planning even more intensively for people's other needs."

Yet in America we are totally and insanely obsessed with traffic, automobile traffic. We plan for little else. What real *city* planning, as opposed to traffic planning, is done, what little urban renewal has accomplished, is but a minnow in the flood tide of automobiles we keep inviting into the city with more and more freeways. Never before has there been as much movement, remorseless, repetitive movement often for its own sake, as in this country today. Since we consider the city primarily as a traffic problem, rather than a place to live, we have engaged the highway engineers to fix it. They wield the only real power in shaping the city, which is about as sensible as handing the power to reform the municipal police to Lucky Luciano and his pals.

The big gun that the highway builders—reinforced by the powerful automobile, concrete, oil, rubber, trucking, and construction interests—keep pointing at city officials is the $46 billion federal highway program. It pays them ninety dollars for every ten the city must spend to build interstate freeways wherever the highway engineers want them. At this writing only one city, San Francisco, has had the guts to refuse this lovely federal money—all of $250 million—in order to preserve its parks, homes, communities, appearance, and livability. The rest have, with growing reluctance, accepted the bribe to commit urbicide and are beginning to regret it.

Wittingly or not, the highway builders are playing a cynical game. The best that can be said for them is that they act on the belief that, as Henry Ford put it forty years ago, "the city is doomed." They speed this doom by Los Angelizing our cities, a process which automatically keeps increasing pressure for more freeways.

They first run a freeway or two smack downtown "to make it more accessible to commuters." The businessmen, of course, are delighted. Downtown, however, is already congested with cars. So when the first freeways are completed and more cars flood into the city, two things happen. One, still more are dumped on the streets, which makes them still more congested. And more parking lots and garages are built, which displace still more people and businesses who now must move out of the city.

It has been generally established that fewer people travel downtown after freeways are built than before. Bulldozing homes and businesses for freeways and parking also removes reasons for people to go downtown. There are, of course, more cars, but the net gain in private auto travel is all too frequently offset by a greater loss in public transit travel.

Downtown thus loses more customers and more businesses. The merchants thereupon clamor for more freeways to "relieve street traffic" and bring the customers back.

A better solution might be to use public subsidies for public transportation rather than to promote ever increasing use of private cars for the journey downtown. But the freeways have so scattered people around that this is deemed "unfeasible" by the highway builders, if not downright un-American. Public transportation, which, in contrast to freeways, is supposed to pay for itself, requires concentrations of people in walking distance of the fare box. Since people have no other means of getting about the car population is currently growing one-and-a-half times faster than the human population, which makes still more freeways inevitable.

In Los Angeles this vicious circle has already turned over 66 per cent of the inner city to the motor car, moving or standing. The freeways have totally cut off those who don't have cars from jobs. And an adequate social life, let alone recreation, now often requires two cars in the family. This, as I noted before, accounts to some extent for the explosion at Watts where only 14 per cent of the people were found to own automobiles. Most other cities are well on the road to Los Angeles. Just look down upon them from the air and observe how much valuable downtown land is given over to highways and parking lots. Someone claims the national average is 25 per cent, but that seems low even for Manhattan which has hardly any open parking lots.

Mumford has said that when the American people, through their Congress, voted for the highway act in 1956, "the most charitable thing to assume about this action is that they hadn't the faintest notion of what they were doing." I wonder. As has often been said by Mumford and others, the automobile has become the Sacred Cow of the American Way of Life. "Why not?" asks Leland Hazard, a Pittsburgh community leader with a special interest in transportation problems. "It has become the best instrument of aggression since the cave man's knobbed club. While we Americans were getting civilized the auto was probably as harmless a device for working off aggression as any." We enjoy the automobile and, as Mumford has said, act much like the man who, demented with passion, wrecks his home in order to lavish his income on a capricious mistress.

We were thus, in the hysterical days of the McCarthy years, perfectly willing to believe General Lucius D. Clay, who recommended it, that the highway program was a necessary defense measure, although no one has bothered to expose the fact that our extravagant *Autobahnen* were built with underpasses too low to let even a small Atlas missile get through. We are also, much as we might ridicule the statement, perfectly willing to believe that what's good for General Motors is good for the country. There isn't a highway discussion in which we are not told that anything short of total surrender to the private automobile would irretrievably wreck the national economy.

Serious economists will tell you that this is nonsense. We have had many a year in the past two decades when the automobile industry was slack yet the overall economy did quite well. The highway cost-benefit rationalization, furthermore, is patently phony. The highway plans are made by the State Highway Departments. Between cities they have done an efficient job. In the fifteen years ending in 1972, this crash program will have built forty times more highways than the Roman Empire built in five hundred years. And, although most of today's *Autobahnen*, invented by Hitler (also as a defense measure), are a terrible bore, they are very convenient when you are in a hurry. They have also undoubtedly saved a number of hamlets, villages, and small towns from annihilation by truck and car because they usually route through-traffic around them.

The trouble is that conventional highway planning refuses to do the same in the big cities. The State Highway Departments cannot or do not wish to see any difference between open country and dense urban areas. Their aim is to bulldoze their interstate roads into the center of our largest cities, because if they don't, they lose all that lush federal money. In Atlanta, for instance, two highways intersect right downtown, requiring an interchange cloverleaf that consumes no less than 140 acres. They are cheered on by some suburbanites and most suburban developers who peddle the illusion that the freeways can get the commuters downtown at sixty miles per hour. The actual national average automobile speed in the city, freeways or not, is six to eleven miles per hour, depending on the city. This is about the same commuting speed attained by our fathers and grandfathers in 1910 at considerable less expense in public money or values.

The location of the urban freeways is inevitably determined when the State Highway Department engineers doodle some lines on the city map. The preferred locations are the low-income Negro areas because they offer the least political resistance. They can also be justified as "slum clearance" which indeed they are in a ruthless sort of way. The doodles are then rationalized by elaborate studies that miraculously always prove these "proposed traffic corridors" faultless. As Arthur D. Little, Inc., the only management consultant firm which has so far dared to incur the wrath of the highway lobby with an objective systems analysis study, has recently found in a review of Washington's freeway system, these "current studies cannot be considered basic research; they are one-shot efforts producing plans and projections under constraints of time, funds, skill and politics." The federal Bureau of Public Roads' cost-benefit formula, the Little report found, "is inconsistent and incompatible with urban transportation needs. . . . By limiting alternatives it places undue restraints on the community's choice of options."

That is putting it mildly indeed when you consider that, as against a federal interstate freeway program of $46 billion, the federal government did not come around to offer aid for urban mass transit until 1964 when a piddling $375 million program covering three years was approved. This subsidy, furthermore, is not for 90 per cent but only for two-thirds of the cost. Chicago alone would need this amount to make its rapid transit system efficient—as efficient, say, as that of Stockholm. Yet one rapid transit line can carry thirty thousand people an hour as against twelve lanes of superhighways needed to do the same job by private automobile. What's more, at least in Washington, which everyone says should serve as a national example, the highway lobby's spokesmen in Congress threaten to cut off rapid transit funds as soon as anyone suggests curtailing the freeway program.

The freeway ribbons are not only fiercely expensive (a mile in Chicago, for instance, costs about $15.6 million) but totally unproductive and destructive. They permanently remove hundreds of acres of land from the tax rolls. One cloverleaf interchange alone consumes about eight acres. Elevated freeways blight everything under and around them. They chew up public parks. They divide communities. They displace thousands of people and either destroy or maim fine old buildings, neighborhoods, and vistas. The Embarcadero freeway, which slashes across San Francisco's Ferry Building at the foot of Market Street and cuts off the city from the Bay, is one example. Washington's Whitehurst Freeway between Georgetown and the Potomac is another. Now the highway builders, despite President Johnson's appeals on behalf of national beauty, historic preservation, and urban qualities, are planning to build a monstrous elevated freeway that will ruin the Mississippi riverfront of the charming French Quarter of New Orleans.

If traffic were at least well served by these monsters, one might consider them an expensive sacrifice. But traffic inevitably becomes worse. After much of old Boston was covered with a spaghetti of concrete ribbons, it experienced the nightmare of a total traffic standstill.

At about 3:45 P.M. on December 30, 1963, a clear and sunny day, thousands of suburban housewives who were shopping downtown decided simultaneously to start home "to avoid the rush hour." At 4 P.M. the usual rush hour began and for five solid hours all downtown traffic was suddenly frozen. Drivers fumed, fretted, and sat. Nothing moved.

The simple reason is that while these freeways take you into the city, they don't take you around within it. They are limited access highways, designed for sixty-miles-per-hour speeds, which means just that. Access to them is limited to widely interspersed ramps with such wide curves that most of them take up a whole city block. Since all those housewives plus the regular commuters tried to get up on those ramps at the same time, they were obviously jammed. If you build more access ramps you defeat the whole idea of a limited access highway and leave nothing of the city, except perhaps a few lonely skyscraper offices amidst parking lots, gas stations, and concrete ribbons.

What has happened in Boston has occurred in most major cities at one time or another. But so far, despite mounting opposition, the highway builders ruthlessly keep on Los Angelizing them. The danger in that is not only that we murder the city, but also that we murder people by poisoning the urban air with ever more lethal carbon monoxide.

The answer is planning—not for traffic but for people. People everywhere—not just in America—will, I fear, continue their love affair with the automobile. Mumford says the temple of the Sacred Cow is crumbling. I don't see it. I don't see the Golden Calf that might replace it, not just as a status symbol but as the means of unprecedented individual freedom to move almost anywhere at will.

Flying about in private helicopters is a lovely idea, but an impractical one. Even if the things could be made inexpensive and simple enough for everyone, someone would still have to invent some sort of radar-beam air roads to prevent utter chaos in the sky. That seems unlikely.

We may, at best, in the distant future, be lucky enough to substitute the noisy and poisonous gasoline engine with an electric or some other kind of motor. We might even replace wheels by riding on air cushions. But we shall still need roads.

Although we cannot, even in the city, abolish the automobile altogether, we can curb the absolute freedom of this Sacred Cow just enough to give people on foot at least equal rights. We can, in fact, so organize our urban areas that for the people who live in them, the car becomes a luxury rather than a necessity. That must be the aim.

This means, first of all, that the federal government stop subsidizing freeways in the city and start to subsidize *transportation*. Most planners know that the freeways lead only to urbicide. They don't really believe the highway engineer's complex after-the-fact rationalization. But they accept freeways because the 90 percent federal freeway aid and the 50 per cent federal aid for other highways is the only money they can get to improve transportation. And transportation, of course, costs money.

Rather than being forced to build freeways, the cities should be given federal assistance for whatever means of transportation is most suitable and efficient under its specific circumstances. Several mayors, notably John Lindsay of New York, have advocated this. The highway lobby's retort is that federal highway funds derive from highway gasoline and truck taxes and should therefore be spent for the benefit of combustion engines and truck drivers. This makes as much sense as pledging cigarette and liquor taxes to the advancement of smoking and drinking.

Secondly, federal, state, and local planning, taxation, and assistance efforts should not, as at present, encourage but discourage urban sprawl. We must stop scattering our housing, our work and employment, our commerce, education, culture, and recreation indiscriminately all over the place and start pulling all these essentials of life together into viable communities—the new ones in the country and the existing ones in the city and suburbs. In such communities people are more apt to stay put, they would have a reasonable range of their daily activities reasonably close by, and they wouldn't have to waste their time cluttering up the roads.

We like the automobile mostly for its ability to provide door-to-door service. But, as planner Sam B. Zisman observed, we have to take a somewhat less literal view of the "door" in this door-to-door service. Since cars are fouling up the very threshold of our bedrooms and stores we should, and are beginning to, think of the door as the entrance to a human sphere reserved for human enjoyment. It is absolutely ridiculous that not even graveyards in America are protected from the intrusion of automobiles.

I shall discuss current efforts to plan and build communities in later chapters. One of the most important things about them is that we make the essential distinction between a road and a street. "A road," as James Marston Fitch has noted, "is for moving people and goods from where they are to where they want to get to, while a street is for people who are already where they want to be."

The road serves mechanized transportation. But a good street serves commerce in ideas and goods. It is therefore primarily a pedestrian facility. It serves man. Note the word "primarily"—not all streets need to be blocked to vehicles. A judicious number of them serving only immediate local needs and moving slowly can add life and convenience to the street.

It is a disastrous mistake, as you can see on many of our main streets, to try to use the street for both fast traffic and human commerce. It is an equally disastrous mistake, as a look at any of our freeways demonstrates, to treat a road within the city like a superhighway out in the open. Superhighways are needed to help motorists who have no business in the city to circumvent it. If they want to come in, they'll have to behave in a civilized way. There is no reason for them to go sixty miles an hour, nonstop, to save three or four minutes' time which they then lose in the effort to find parking space.

In a livable city, social, economic, and aesthetic values are more important than roads. That means that roads run between communities and neighborhoods and help to structure them, not through them. It means that in parks, waterfronts, and densely settled areas the roads are placed underground, as Leonardo da Vinci suggested five hundred years ago. And it means that rather than constantly building new freeways, we make carefully selected existing roads in the city more efficient for automobiles and trucks. This can be done, as Toronto has shown, with traffic signals that are computer controlled to expedite traffic on the basis of demand and rush-hour priorities. It can be done, as in Berlin, where simply blocking off side streets with bollards and flowerpots has created limited access express streets. It can be done with underpasses on road crossings, pedestrian over- and underpasses, and many other ways.

Most importantly, we should relieve the private automobile of the two functions for which it is very ill suited—commuting and taking us quickly about town. Rapid transit in various forms can do this much faster and more efficiently, economically and conveniently. "Preoccupied with the auto," says Hazard, "we have neglected rapid transit research while our basic transit industries, beset with government nagging and truck competition, fell into a research-obviating neuroticism." They are at last beginning to come out of it.

Following the lead of Stockholm, Rotterdam, Milan, Helsinki, and other European cities, San Francisco and Washington are now building the first new subways in America in over fifty years. Cities that have rapid transit are beginning to improve and extend it.

The very immediate future holds lightweight electric rapid-transit trains that are already being tested and that will be as different from New York's grim, old IRT as the Dc-3 is from a modern jet plane. They can be built relatively inexpensively, which will leave us more money for more rapid-transit mileage throughout the urban area. They will be attractive, comfortable, and practically noiseless. They won't keep anyone waiting or even standing, since computers, working on the same principle as pushbutton elevators, will dispatch as many cars as are needed to seat everyone who has entered the station. Like elevators we will undoubtedly soon ride the new rapid-transit trains free because cities will realize that it is much cheaper for them to provide public transportation as a public service than to ruin themselves with ever more motor roads and parking places. Berlin is already seriously considering this.

Meanwhile, it would not surprise me at all if in the face of the havoc the freeways are raising, some of our cities were to discover that to do nothing about mounting automobile traffic is also an alternative. The planning officials of Amsterdam discovered this some time ago. "We are certainly disturbed about the increase in cars," one of them told me. "But our city is not only packed with cars, it is also packed with beautiful buildings and history and we are not going to sacrifice them for freeways. Nor can we build a subway because of the high water level and sandy soil. So we decided the best thing to do is to do nothing at all. We figured if driving and parking downtown becomes too annoying, people will give up after a while, leave their cars at home, and take the streetcar or their bicycles. And that is precisely what is happening."

Amsterdam is crowded with cars, but not more and probably less so than cities where the automobile is pampered. It is one of the most beautiful and livable cities in the world, though perhaps not for drivers. If a driver forgets to put on the brake as he parks his car by a canal and it plunks into the water, he must not only pay for having it fished out but is also heavily fined. Amsterdam's officials refuse to put up guard rails. Even this slight concession to the automobile, they feel, would spoil the charm of their city.

In San Francisco, where the citizens also rejected more freeways, they are reinstating the old ferries again. Last I heard, despite all dire predictions by state highway engineers, San Francisco was still standing and doing fine.

All this does not mean that we should outlaw the automobile. It has given people new freedom to move about that not even a Stalin could take away if he tried. But the city and its people must come first. In such planning and building the fun and excitement and mobility that comes with the car will also have its rightful place. For as Crosby said, "Traffic is not important. What is important is how people live."

VI. THE NEW COMMUNITY

1. The Sight of It

Tapiola in Finland is the happiest place to live I have seen built in recent years. It is not a housing project or suburb, but what has come to be called a New Town, a comprehensively planned, socially and economically balanced community for some seventeen thousand people.

Tapiola's office and apartment towers, like the steeples of a medieval town, beckon you across the cold, blue haze of the gulf all the way from Helsinki, six or seven miles away. The bus takes you through enchanting archipelago scenery across bridges and forested islands to the edge of the town center, a masterpiece of urban design.

The heart of the town center is a relatively small, paved plaza you step up to almost ceremoniously. It is built under a natural grouping of tall, old trees and around a wonderful, big rock with a great, gushing fountain behind it. The plaza, lively with people but not crowded, is surrounded on three sides by a shopping arcade with offices for the town's doctors, dentists, lawyers, and such on the second floor. To one side, and part of this horseshoe, is Tapiola's tallest tower, the thirteen-story administrative building. Looking back across the stairs, the plaza opens up to what amounts to a landscaped park dotted with tall apartment buildings. Beyond that is water, an inlet of the gulf, the Baltic, and beyond *that* Estonia and Russia. The rest of the town is all but hidden in the woods.

Alongside the plaza, clustered around a small pool that used to be a gravel pit, are the public buildings, including a theater and concert hall, a music conservatory, an art gallery, a municipal library, a church, a youth center, an indoor swimming hall and gymnasium, a hotel, the town's high school, and lushly landscaped parking places.

From this center, walkways lead to the town's three villages, each a seemingly casually grouped cluster of elevator apartment buildings, walk-up apartments, town houses and single-family houses in a variety of architectural styles, housing five to six thousand people of different income groups. Each has a neighborhood center with its own community building, elementary school and small shops and a café. Each is carefully laid out in what Tapiola's planners call "perambulator distances," so that no mother has to push her baby carriage more than some two hundred yards for milk, bread, butter, or that Finnish staple, fish. When the shops close, there is the kiosk at the bus stop, where newspapers, cigarettes, soft drinks, and cakes are sold. Buses and cars run on separate roads that never cross the walkways. Each of these villages is separated from each other and from the town center by a "green belt" of parkland.

Between two of the villages is the town's industrial area, with a number of small plants of all kinds that are not smoky or noisy. It is dominated by the central heating plant which heats and provides hot water and electricity for all homes and apartments in Tapiola. Together with the offices, stores, schools, hotels, restaurants, etc., these plants

The plaza opens up to a landscaped park

Tapiola's town center is a masterpiece of urban design . . .

. . . and its houses seem to be growing out of the woods

provide employment for the more than 70 per cent of the town's working population which does not have to commute to work. The number of blue collar and white collar workers is about even.

The ingenuity of Tapiola's planning is matched by its consistently excellent architecture. Both emerged from national competitions. The winner of the town's overall plan, Aarne Ervi, also designed the town center and acts as Tapiola's architectural coordinator. Each cluster of high and low buildings, however, as well as the public buildings were designed by different architects. The variety in shapes, colors, materials, and interior layouts is amazing. Ervi was obviously unusually skillful about encouraging creative talent and assuring the necessary visual order at the same time. Nor is there anything precious and expensive about the buildings. They are handsome in a modern, functional, livable, and simple way. Unusual creative imagination made them economical yet spacious. You can't, on the outside, tell the "social housing" (of which 40 per cent is state subsidized for low-income families) from the more expensive ones. All rents are somewhat lower than in Helsinki. Most houses are privately owned.

The wonderful thing about the place is the way it all seems to grow out of the rocks and between the trees like mushrooms, as though it had always been there. All the buildings are adapted to the contours of the softly rolling, rocky forest land, some hugging the gullies and nestling among the trees, others providing striking focal points and accents. The landscaping, too, though rich with flowers and man-made amenities such as benches and handsomely designed street lighting, signs, and the many playgrounds, never seems to interfere with the natural setting. "Tapio" is the name of an ancient Finnish forest sprite. This is surely still his *la*, or abode.

We had come to Finland from Sweden, and I had been much impressed by Stockholm's famous new satellite communities, notably Farsta and Vallingby. Farsta's bustling town center, in the midst of which you find yourself as you come out of the subway train after a twenty-minute ride from downtown Stockholm, is an urban delight equal to the most charming piazzas in Italian towns.

These Swedish communities with their well-kept parks, gardens, and abundant playgrounds and their strict separation of cars and pedestrians, make even the best of our suburbs look woefully deprived. The inhabitants of the Swedish communities, however, live almost entirely in fairly uniform high-rise apartment blocks with small apartments that rarely have more than two bedrooms. Swedes, strangely, prefer to rent rather than own their dwellings. These blocks, particularly the more recent ones, are colorful and quite well designed. The planning of these communities is exemplary. But, somehow, it shows. Much as I liked, envied, and admired Vallingby and Farsta, I never quite lost an awareness of the benign workings of a welfare state, which I have nothing against if, like some brassieres on pretty girls, it doesn't make a perfectly good thing look unnecessarily artificial.

Even the best institution, I suppose, shouldn't look and feel institutional. Tapiola certainly doesn't. It looks and feels as spontaneously lusty and natural in an endearingly well-behaved sort of way as the Finnish children that swarm all over. Yet this, I feel, has little or nothing to do with the political or economic circumstances under which it came about. Tapiola is the creation not of a socialist government but of a social concern, which is quite a different matter. It is planned, built, and run without government sponsorship or special subsidy under political and economic conditions actually far more capitalist than in the United States. There is no FHA mortgage insurance in Finland and interest rates are much higher. People are as keen to own homes as they are in America and more and more of them do, largely through an ingenious home-savings plan.

What built Tapiola, however, was not a system but a man, a man of simple beliefs, great organizational talent, civilized tastes, and great energy. His name is Heikki von Hertzen.

Prosperity came late to Finland, von Hertzen told me, as we lunched in the excellent restaurant on top of Tapiola's tower. Until 1952, the year its planning began, the country had to pay exorbitant war reparations to the Soviet Union.

"As we finally began to catch up with the West, we asked ourselves: 'What are we to do with our new affluence? We can't eat more. There is a limit to the automobiles and gadgets we really need.'

"So I started to persuade my countrymen that we should build a suitable and beautiful environment for everyone. Good housing, I found in my work as director of a welfare agency, is not enough. We have to counteract the strains and tensions of modern urban life."

Von Hertzen did his persuading with Finnish labor unions, the Family Welfare League, several women's clubs, and sundry other citizens' organizations. They formed the Asuntosäätiö, a nonprofit Housing Foundation, struggled to get bank loans, bought the land, and went to work. Their aim was, says von Hertzen, to create an environment "that would be both socially and biologically correct."

Tapiola, despite all the usual financial and bureaucratic difficulties, is now just about completed and, in all practical terms, a greater success than anyone dared hope. There are long waiting lists of people who want to live there, but rather than expand it beyond the planned size, the Foundation has begun to build several similar New Towns throughout Finland in accordance with a national plan that is essentially designed to prevent turning Helsinki into a megalopolis. Von Hertzen credits the financial and social success of Tapiola almost entirely to good, flexible but determined management.

Here in the United States there is a feeling of frustration about our urban renewal and housing efforts and, as a result, a sort of defeatism about the environment appears to be spreading. "The assumption is that the physical form of our communities has *social* consequences," the sociologist Nathan Glazer wrote recently. "This is not so."

Von Hertzen, however, is deeply convinced that it is. "Milieu," as he calls the environment, has greater significance in an age of urbanization than ever before, he believes. It determines our working and living, our free time, cultural activities, and mental health. Can anyone seriously doubt it?

Glazer and his friends, I suppose, confuse "social consequences" with economic poverty, which, of course, has social consequences of its own, though heaven knows poor people aren't the only ones who get drunk, beat their wives, make public nuisances of themselves, or produce juvenile delinquents. He is right that no town center, patio, park bench, or playground has ever alone given a man a job any more than the poverty war's social-work treatment has. But economic poverty isn't our only ailment as everyone must realize by now. In a recently published study of American city dwellers, cited by anthropologist Edward T. Hall, only 18 per cent of a representative sample were free of emotional symptoms, while 38 per cent were in need of psychiatric help, and of these, 23 per cent were seriously disturbed or incapacitated. An obvious conclusion would seem to be that there is something wrong with the environment in which these people live.

There is, if that's what bothers Glazer, scant *scientific* evidence to substantiate this conclusion, however. The psychologists concerned with these matters usually get bogged down in the quagmire of *mental* health, which in contrast to obvious mental sickness, nobody will ever be able to define. There is, however, an exception—the so-called Peckham Experiment, which Walter Gropius has often cited because of its obvious relevance to community architecture.

The Peckham Experiment began in 1926 when a group of young Englishmen, among them, Sir E. Owen Williams and Dr. Scott Williamson, opened a small health center in Peckham, a district in southeast London. They soon discovered that it was easy enough to diagnose physical sickness even before those afflicted were aware of it. They also discovered that although sick people could be cured, it was often "useless to eradicate the disorder only to return the individual to the environmental conditions which had induced it." Under these circumstances even periodic health overhaul seemed ineffective. What was needed, the group decided, was to build "instruments of health" which would provide conditions in and through which health could be kindled. To kindle it effectively it was necessary to involve not individuals but the family.

In 1935, after years of planning and fund raising, the group built such "instruments of health" into a new Pioneer Health Centre. The building was designed "to be furnished with people and their actions . . . to invite social contact, allowing equally for the chance meeting, for formal and festive occasions, as well as for quiet familiar grouping." The idea was to provide a setting for casual acquaintanceship and for the development of friendships and a setting where the family could entertain visiting friends and relations. In short, it simulated, if you will, some of the old communities, the church, the forum, the market place, the village green, the courtyard, or a place somewhat like Tapiola. The Peckham people felt that such a setting, which has so long met the needs of man's social life and the tentative adventures of his children as they grew up, might induce spontaneous activities, with a minimum of professional guidance, that would allow everyone to develop his full potentialities.

The Centre reached a membership of twelve hundred participating families of various occupations and income, most living within walking distance of the Centre. Everyone was subject to periodic health checks. At the first check 90 per cent of the almost four thousand participants of all ages were found to have something the matter with them (some physiological defect, deficiency, or aberration), although Peckham was not a slum or social problem area where poor health conditions might be expected. Most disorders were not in themselves disturbing. What was disturbing was that these people's energies could not be fully used to counter their minor disorders because they constantly expended their energy reserves on coping with ceaseless change in their environment. Even though they often retained their sense of well-being, their functional capacity was limited. Protracted periods of such limitation of function was robbing the individual, "probably forever of his potentiality for continued growth and development, i.e., health."

With the outbreak of war, the Peckham Experiment came to an end. But it was conducted long enough to lead its scientists to several conclusions. The foremost of them was that health, like sickness, is contagious. Another was that "it is the family . . . that nature places at our disposal . . . as her instrument for the cultivation of functional efficiency"—the family as a well-functioning organism. In an environment where the family could so function, minor physical disorders would either not occur or fail to develop into the grave sociopathological conditions that usually prevail in cities. Nor was it income, leadership, or capacity and goodwill that made health contagious, but personal, family, and social opportunities for knowledge and for action.

As to action, that is, all kinds of creative activity as opposed to the apathy of staring at television or the social starvation we so often find in the slums, the Peckham study found that it is the sight of it that provides the incentive. People want to be shown. "It is the sight of action that is within the possible scope of the spectator that affords a temptation eventually irresistible to him."

I don't know if von Hertzen read or even heard of the Peckham Experiment when he set out to build a town that "was dedicated to man and his home life, his leisure and his recreation," a town where traffic was to serve the inhabitants and not tyrannize them, and where man and nature were to be dominant.

But what makes Tapiola, and the other New Towns which preceded and followed it, into good environments and good communities is "the sight of it"—the sight of social action.

We have, in our affluent society, many of the opportunities for knowledge and for pleasant things to do men have craved for throughout history. With automobiles to take us afield and to where the action is, the good life is potentially more accessible to more people than ever before. But little of this potential new wealth is immediate, present, and visible enough at the place where we live. It is so scattered that it does not tempt spontaneous involvement. There is, in reality, no multiplicity of choices, since going to a museum or going to an amusement park requires distinctly different efforts, each of which takes planning and predetermination. The crowd, as a result, is lonely, as David Riesman has put it.

Department stores have learned a long time ago that they get most of their business from "impulse shopping." They cunningly put all kinds of tempting goodies in the way of the housewife who comes into the store simply to buy an apron. By the time she gets to the fifth floor and the apron, she often has bought a bagful of things she hadn't even dreamed of before. She may have spent more money than she intended, but she is happy.

Our ministers want more people to go to church. But where, other than in the old town, are churches located to invite impulse worship?

People walk in Tapiola because walking is made tempting. They drop into the neighborhood café and meet friends and neighbors in a less formal, obliging, and sometimes less irritating setting than their homes. They see the tennis courts and decide to play. They are tempted by the beach, the community arts and crafts studios, the concert hall, the library . . . by all the things that, in our large cities, not to speak of our suburbs, take predetermination and difficult decisions to go to—decisions that are often not made. Tapiola's children do not have to be driven to the playground. They hear its gay noises when they open the windows of their bedrooms.

"Let me show you something," said von Hertzen as we walked around his town. He took us into a large basement room of one of the apartment buildings. It was part automobile workshop and part bohemian nightclub. "We made several deliberately out of the way rooms available to our teen-agers," von Hertzen explained. "This one was taken over by our motorized soapbox racing club. It's one of several clubs our youngsters have organized themselves. As you can see, here the boys tinker with old engines. But they have also set up a soft drink bar and use the place for meetings and dances. They told us what tools and equipment they needed and we got them what we could."

Was there any adult supervision and management of these activities? "Of course," smiled von Hertzen. "We have a very imaginative young man on the staff. But we don't call him 'youth activities officer,' or anything like that. That, we fear, would only scare the very kids that need involvement most. His title is 'assistant town engineer.' "

In Sweden, where there are many official youth officers, there is almost as much juvenile delinquency among the upper income groups as in the United States, which has practically no youth officers. On the central plaza of Vallingby there is an information booth and after its very pretty, young attendant had thoroughly informed us, I asked her how she personally liked the place. "Oh, man, it's Dullsville," she said in perfect American slang. "All of us take off for downtown Stockholm whenever we can." Luckily they have a subway and needn't fight for the family car. In Tapiola vandalism and teen-age problems, so often the result of boredom, are unheard of.

Von Hertzen agrees that it is too early to tell whether Tapiola will, in the end, breed more gracious citizens than physically otherwise formed and designed communities in Finland or anywhere else. This may give Nathan Glazer some comfort. What struck me, though, about the difference between Tapiola and Vallingby, between the haunt of the forest sprite and the somewhat institutional airs, was that it was not,

Mental and physical health, like disease, are contagious when, as in Reston, it's easy to . . .

as many Americans hold, a question of planning per se. Tapiola is, if anything, even more planned than the new Swedish communities. But it is, in the end, better planned. It is better planned because it was not planned with self-conscious "welfare" in mind, but with joy. It is an answer to the question: *"What are we to do with our new affluence?"*

"Culture, represented by buildings, planned and produced in our cities," von Hertzen has said, "is one of the most important and visible final results of higher human activity. We value the Greek and Roman civilizations mainly on the basis of their high urban culture and archi-

. . . find a place to go to . . .

. . . do something creative . . .

. . . go shopping by canoe . . .

. . . enjoy a dance festival . . .

. . . try a little fishing right in town . . .

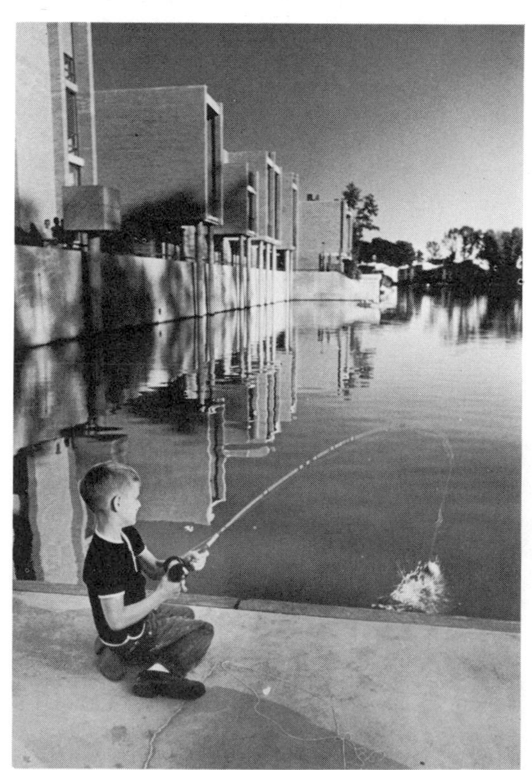

. . . and actually catch one

tecture. We know well, though, that they do not provide the only yardstick, but especially for the great masses, they are the most obvious phenomena in those cultures.

"A modern town, urban culture, and architecture, too, tell and will tell what we are and have been. They will expose the basic character of our culture. But even if it is an inspiring thought to succeed in building something that can survive our generation, the most essential thing is, however, to build for this generation and create the optimum environment we can devise for modern man."

The American psychologist-lawyer team Edna G. and Eugene V. Rostow expressed this thought somewhat differently. "In the end," they wrote, "we press for the city beautiful not because we really believe it will be the City of God, or Mumford's City of Love, or the City of Mental Health, but because we can't help doing so. We try to make cities express our ideas of beauty for the same reasons that lead us to make gardens: because it is fun to try and because such cities are a joy to behold."

August Heckscher puts it in two words. We need a more attractive urban environment, he says, for the "public happiness."

2. "A Path to Real Reform"

The sixty million Americans who settled beyond the city limits in the two decades since the end of World War II did not seek suburbia as we know it today. They sought a home of their own that they could afford with a green yard for flowers, dogs, children, and a barbecue grill in an environment that would offer them better schools and recreation, less dirt and noise, and more security than the inner city.

The government and the building industry have met a part of these demands—decent middle-income housing and good schools—but only in suburbia. White middle-class Americans therefore had no other choice than to go there. They had to take the long journey to work, the wide dispersal of community life and facilities, and the often deadening economic, racial, and even ethnic homogeneity into the bargain. This is no evidence that they like it. We must not confuse the lack of alternatives with real approval. All we know is that a majority *prefers* suburbia to apartment house living in the neglected city.

There are, however, other alternatives—a way to meet the need for reasonably priced, individually owned homes and gardens in a livable community—without urban sprawl, long commuting, and boredom. Tapiola Garden City is built on one of these other ideas which has been most forcefully advanced in recent times by the London court stenographer Ebenezer Howard in a little tract first issued in 1898 under the title *Tomorrow: A Peaceful Path to New Reform* and reissued four years later as *Garden Cities of Tomorrow*.

Howard's Garden Cities are nowadays called New Towns and they are being built or planned in most countries of the world, including the Soviet Union. The French government, for instance, hopes that by the end of this century eight new satellite towns are to be completed within forty miles of Paris. Long promoted by Lewis Mumford and his friends, the idea has also at last caught on in this country. Privately sponsored New Towns are now under construction at Reston, Virginia, Columbia, Maryland, in Arizona, Hawaii, and several places in California. In the 1966 Demonstration Cities Act we now have legislation to provide government planning assistance to New Town development. For New Towns have special significance for the United States.

They offer the only workable answer so far to counteract the disruptive effect of unlimited automobility and megalopolis. And balanced communities, where people of all kinds can find work as well as places to live, are the only solution yet advanced to disperse the low-income ghetto and thus improve the inner city both socially and physically.

Yet the New Town idea is still widely misunderstood. Perhaps because of the name "Garden City," New Towns are often confused with ordinary suburban subdivisions and then attacked because of the dullness, boredom, and tasteless uniformity associated with them. Well-planned or not, a new community is not a New Town but a dormitory unless it also includes employment opportunities along with other essentials beyond barbecue grills and shopping centers.

Others attack the New Town ideas, indeed, the whole new emphasis on building communities rather than scattered and fragmented settlements, on the ground that it is a hopelessly old-fashioned, romantic notion out of tune with the times and the real wishes of Americans. The idea of having us live "in villages," as it is often put, runs counter to conventional science-fiction imagery about living in ivory megastructure towers in a computerized pushbutton environment.

I don't believe we need worry about being old-fashioned or new-fashioned, romantic or pragmatic. What we do need to worry about is survival with a modicum of human dignity. This is endangered by the loss of identity, the addictive dependence on the automobile, the explosive injustice of the racial ghetto, and land, water, and air pollution. These are specific problems of our time. The best solution to these problems, therefore, seems to me also the most timely. If they are not entirely new, neither is the human race and its essential physical and psychological needs.

Numerous social ideas of meeting these needs have, throughout history, inspired planned communities. Many of them have been decisively influenced by American thought and experiment. A good many of these communities have actually been built and some still survive in one form or another. Ebenezer Howard's Garden City was primarily inspired by such communities in England. There is, as Walter L. Creese points out in his fascinating book, *The Search for Environment,* reason to believe that Howard was inspired by Riverside, near Chicago. Born in 1850, Howard ventured his luck in America when he was twenty-one years old. He failed as a farmer in Nebraska and before his return to England worked for a while in the courts of Chicago. He surely must have seen Riverside. If he didn't acknowledge this inspiration in his book, it may be, Creese suggests, because it had badly deteriorated after the Chicago fire and became embroiled in financial scandals.

Riverside had been planned by Frederick Law Olmsted in 1868 on a sixteen-hundred-acre tract. Though not actually called a "garden city," it was just that. Olmsted sought "the charm of refined sylvan beauty . . . and secluded peacefulness and tranquility" that would be "positively picturesque."

But Howard did not seek the picturesque. He offered instead what he called "a master key . . . to a portal through which, even when scarce ajar, will be seen to pour a flood of light on the problems of intemperance, of excessive toil, of restless anxiety, of grinding poverty—the true limits of Governmental interference, aye, and even the relations of man to the Supreme Power."

His central concern was the new lure industrialization had given the city. It is still strong. All over the world farm workers leave the country and crowd into urban slums in quest of higher pay and a better life which the city, becoming ever more crowded, is less and less able to offer. We don't talk much about it in the United States though the problem is still almost as acute here as in Latin America and Asia. In the United States the emigration of farm laborers into the city is indirectly encouraged by federal farm programs. Since 1960, 816,000 people a year have moved away from the farm—most of them into the large cities to which they are attracted by the protection of minimum wages and better education.

John Fischer, the editor of *Harper's,* recently pointed out that there were 14,500 hired Negroes employed in the cotton fields of eighteen

Mississippi Delta counties in 1965 where, for wages of three to four dollars a day, they hoed the weeds out of cotton rows. The following spring, because of the spreading use of chemical weed-killers, plus a further reduction by the government in the acreage allotted to cotton, only about 7,000 cotton-choppers were needed. The cotton-picking jobs are melting away too, as machines take over; only about half as many people were employed in the 1966 harvest than in the year before.

"What will happen to the rest?" Fischer asks. "A few, no doubt, will try to live for a while on the pitifully meager relief handouts available in Mississippi. But most will be making their way before long, toward Memphis, Chicago, Watts, and Harlem. (New York City alone took in nearly 400,000 additional Negroes and Puerto Ricans in just four years, from 1960 to 1964.) All of these places, and every other city slum, are of course already overloaded with unemployed workers. What future can they offer to still more thousands of unskilled, and often illiterate, ex-cotton-choppers?"

We can't, of course, keep unemployable farm workers on the farm. But we can and must attempt to reduce this in-migration by bringing not only industry and jobs but good schools and the urban amenities they seek out to where they are.

This was precisely Howard's idea. "There are," he wrote, "in reality not only, as is so constantly assumed, two alternatives – town life and country life – but a third alternative, in which all the advantages of the most energetic and active town life, with all the beauty and delight of the country, may be secured in perfect combination."

Starting fresh, out in the open country on a large, cooperatively purchased tract of land, Howard proposed to build his New Town in one fell swoop. Right from the start he would build into it sufficient industry within easy reach of every home to provide "for workers of every grade . . . abundant opportunities for employment and bright opportunities for advancement." He would give it "equal, nay better opportunities of social intercourse . . . than are enjoyed in any crowded city, while yet the beauties of nature may encompass and enfold each dweller therein."

Howard wanted to limit his city to about thirty thousand inhabitants, a number he thought most congenial and manageable, yet sufficient to assure a varied population able to support a varied social and cultural life. Leonardo da Vinci, in his proposal to break up congested sixteenth-century Milan into ten new towns, had advocated the same number for each. But, of course, there is nothing magical about it.

The ideal size of a city depends on what is expected of it. A regional capital should have its own theater and symphony orchestra, for example, and this obviously needs more people to support them than a satellite town, which can well get by with a couple of movie houses. Aristotle's concept that a city to be a good place to live ought to be large enough to encompass all its functions but not too large to interfere with them still holds true.

To keep the Garden City from expanding and spilling over into the countryside, Howard proposed to girdle it with an inviolate, permanent agricultural belt. This would supply the town with fresh farm products, give its residents easy access to nature and, like the medieval city walls, tighten its coherence and internal unity. Ultimately Howard envisioned that metropolitan growth would be structured by whole constellations of such distinct satellites, kept apart from each other by green open space and connected by fast transportation. Again, in the age of air, water, and land pollution, as well as desperate lack of outdoor recreation, this concept is far more vital than Howard could possibly have dreamed.

Sir Ebenezer Howard died in 1928—the knighted and honored leader of a worldwide movement—in Welwyn, near London, his second thriving New Town. His invention, somewhat updated, of course, has become national policy in England. London, to be sure, is still congested. But it is surrounded by a protected belt of lovely countryside that clearly defines where one town ends and another begins.

Since Welwyn, America has made a very vital contribution to the New Town movement. In fact modern community planning would be unthinkable without Radburn, New Jersey, which was designed in 1929 by Clarence Stein and Henry Wright, with Lewis Mumford cheering them on. Radburn adapted the Garden City to the motor age. It was the first community anywhere to put the automobile in its place, to reconcile the demands of livability with mobility. Its buildings face two directions: one toward roads and services with their noise, smells, and dangers, the other toward open green space where children can roam freely and where, in planner Victor Gruen's phrase, people can feel free to walk without attaching themselves to a dog. People and vehicles are kept out of each other's way.

Under Franklin D. Roosevelt, more than a quarter of a century ago, the United States government picked up the Radburn idea. It built three planned communities, the Greenbelt Towns—Greenhills (Ohio), Greendale (Wisconsin), and Greenbelt (Maryland). Their belts are still reasonably green. And like Radburn, they are still more pleasant places to live than most suburban areas that were to come. But they are part of suburbia and not, strictly speaking, New Towns. They never succeeded in attracting the intended industry.

But with postwar prosperity, all efforts at planning were forgotten and considered almost un-American. For the sake of quick, private gain we indulged in an orgy of scandalous public waste.

The only aspect of the Garden City concept we did adopt—with a vengeance!— was, ironically, its one serious error. Ebenezer Howard's idea of taking "people from the crowded cities to the bosom of our kindly mother earth" has contributed considerably to urban spread and the suburbanization of our cities. Revolted by the London slums at the turn of the century, the Garden City enthusiasts drank a bit too deeply at nature's bosom and intoxicated themselves with Thoreauvian ideals. Sir Raymond Unwin's slogan, in 1903, "Nothing gained by overcrowding," became the battle cry of the planner-reformers who fought for decent, safe, and sanitary housing on both sides of the Atlantic. Unwin later planned Letchworth, the first Garden City.

The low density of twenty-six people to the acre works in Tapiola because the town is small and exceedingly cleverly designed. In most larger communities and cities today, however, especially in the suburbanized cities of America, the problem is no longer that densities are

Familiar qualities recaptured in a New Town

too high but that they are, overall, too low. Yet the notion that lowering density will per se heighten livability, morality, and virtue still obsesses most of our planners and their zoning codes. They substitute compulsory open space and set-backs for creative urban design. With visions, no doubt, of deep woods, clear brooks, birds and bees, they paint green blotches on their plans. But, more often than not, they don't have the slightest idea how to make or keep them green on the actual landscape or even what people might do with them. Often they end up as nothing but a big weed patch.

This is what happened in Harlow, a 1947 vintage New Town of sixty thousand located twenty-three miles from London. The center is a bit drab, though the development corporation has tried its best to decorate it with opulent flower boxes and a number of handsome modern sculptures. I visited on market day when the vendors who travel to all the New Towns around London set up their colorful stalls, and the center was lively enough. But the rest of Harlow is utterly dull, and the faces of the mop-topped teen-agers show it. The reason, it soon dawns on you as you drive around, is precisely that you *are* forced to drive around. The unkempt green spaces that wind through the town are too large to negotiate on foot. This keeps those Beatle types from making much use of the sports fields, clubs, and activities that the planners have thoughtfully provided for them. I suspect the posters offering five pounds reward for information leading to the arrest of vandals may be one result. The automobile traffic and positively American clutter of parked cars everywhere certainly are another. Nothing gained by *over*spacing, either!

But the British have learned, and subsequent New Towns have become increasingly more compact. Their most exciting one, Cumbernauld, near Glasgow, will house seventy thousand people within a third of a mile of its center when it is completed in 1980. Architect Hugh Wilson's design points the way to the urban community of the future. Some people will live in apartment towers but most in two- and three-story town houses that are ingeniously stacked, much like a Mediterranean hilltown, on fairly steep hills. Everyone will have privacy and sunlight, yet no one looks into the other fellow's garden. And designed into this cluster are the suddenly rediscovered delights of corner stores, taverns, and other amenities, the surprising vistas, the charm, variety, and bustle that recently made places like Georgetown in Washington, D.C., Beacon Hill in Boston, or Greenwich Village in New York so popular.

New Towns have become increasingly more compact

But Cumbernauld's coal miners will have one advantage over the residents of our Georgetowns. Their automobiles have been tamed. They can walk on a network of turning and twisting alleys with the schools and neighborhood stores set along the way. The street uncluttered by cars, parked or moving, has been returned to people, especially the children. They can rattle sticks as they run along the fences or walk, sit, and climb on the low walls. The streets open into paved courts or plazas, some with odd but delightful cobblestone-paved mounds with marvelous play sculptures. This open space is put to work.

Yet the automobile can also go nearly everywhere in Cumbernauld. There is parking room for one car per family, either below its home or in a nearby garage. You will be able to park right under but not in the town center, which is now being built. Escalators, elevators, and stairs take you up inside the buildings and onto the pedestrian streets, plazas, and terraces. Leonardo da Vinci, nearly five hundred years ago, envisioned such a city where all vehicles move underground, leaving man to move freely in the sun. Leonardo might also have sketched Cumbernauld's town center, a soaring citadel surrounded by meadow that sets it apart from the residences. There will be sheep grazing on that meadow, the planners promise.

As enlightened free enterprises, New Towns have at last caught on in this country, although not all builder subdivisions that have appropriated this suddenly fashionable term meet its definition. Reston, backed by the Gulf Oil Company, is almost the spitting image of Tapiola, which is the greatest compliment I can pay its designers, Whittlesey and Conklin. And Columbia, backed by the Connecticut General Life Insurance Company, also promises as happy "a marriage between town and country," to use Sir Ebenezer's phrase, as the Finnish jewel. With an ultimate population of 110,000, it is much larger, of course, and will feature a strong, entirely urban town center on the shores of one of its man-made lakes. The rest of the plans and sketches, however, look rather suburban. Columbia's designer, Morton Hoppenfeld, is a little disdainful of Cumbernauld and asserts that Americans will never go for "medieval hilltowns."

That, however, is exactly what William Pereira is designing on Santa Catalina Island, twenty-six miles offshore from Los Angeles, and at Mountain Park near Santa Monica. He took a special trip to study Mediterranean towns and sees planning "as an opportunity to make history anew." Perhaps Californians are different.

In the end, Americans will probably want both—sylvan Tapiolas

For those who don't care for Italian hilltowns

and urban Cumbernaulds. There is no sense generalizing about urban design, which must be determined by a town's natural setting, its intended function and population, and a host of other circumstances, including the designer's art. The point is precisely to give us a greater choice and variety of good places in which to live. The point is design, any good design, instead of mere urban "happenings."

The slums in the big cities are growing faster than we can clear them. Worse, clearance or rehabilitation or anything that would get rid of the rats and squalor is frustrated by the fact that we don't know where to house the slum dwellers. We can't seem to build enough housing they can afford. The main reason is that land within the city is increasingly scarce and prohibitively expensive. But neither can we build homes for the uprooted in the suburbs. It will be a good many years until established suburbia will accept people who are both colored *and* poor. Nor is it only the white middle class that no longer lives where it works. White-collar commuters on the way to the city in the morning have lately noticed blue-collar workers commuting the other way. Industrial plants are moving out to where their trucks can get to them and where they can expand. That is also the reason so many big-city poor stay poor. It is hard to find jobs that are no longer there.

As a result, our cities keep deteriorating. With taxpayers and industry leaving, the cities receive less and less tax income but must pay more and more for welfare, health, education, police protection, and all the other expenses of the growing ghetto. All this will get a lot worse. In the next twenty years the population of the United States will increase, it is estimated, from the present 195 million to 266 million; this increase will occur in the metropolitan areas where 70 per cent of the total population already lives. But the general growth will be dwarfed by the even larger increase in the number of Negroes. In twenty-five years Chicago, for instance, will probably have a million and a half more Negroes than it has today. With our present rigidly stratified social and racial pattern, the statistical explosion may well be expressed again and again by explosions of violence such as already occurred in Watts.

The only solution is to attempt to break the pattern by taking substantial numbers of low-skilled Negroes out of the big city and moving substantial numbers of suburbanites back into it. In a paper published by the Center for the Study of Democratic Institutions, developer Bernard Weissbourd has suggested that New Towns, built in accordance with regional open-space and transportation plans, "accommodate industrial workers and industries displaced by an intensified residential and industrial slum-clearance program in the core areas of our major cities. At the same time, on the land within the city made available by slum clearance, new communities can be established for middle-income families."

New Towns would conserve precious open countryside. Not everyone will want to live in them, of course. But if we were to build just 350 new towns of 100,000 inhabitants each, they would house 35 million people, or about half of the estimated twenty-year population increase.

Our present rate of urbanization is thirty acres per hundred people and these 35 million people would therefore use 10.5 million acres. Even low-density New Towns like Reston and Columbia in this country and Tapiola in Finland, despite their abundant green spaces, use only ten acres for a hundred people. The 350 New Towns would thus consume only a total of 3.5 million acres—a two-thirds saving. It is in our power to conserve seven million acres of countryside for better health and greater enjoyment not only of the New Town residents but of all the people in our metropolitan areas.

But, welcome as this might be, private developers cannot accomplish such a program without federal aid, at least not until we have a building technology that can provide housing at prices people with moderate income can afford. Both Robert Simon, the developer of Reston, and James Rouse, the developer of Columbia, are, to be sure, rare idealists. Once their towns are going concerns with enough industry to demand low-skilled labor, they will be happy to welcome subsidized housing for low-income families. But what with American prejudice against living next door to poor people, that day will never dawn if they hasten it unduly. They would be fools to risk their investment and the whole noble idea. They are in business for profit.

Only federal assistance and state involvement, such as President Johnson has proposed, can get the big population switch started that is needed to save the cities. We simply can't count on enough private idealists like Simon and Rouse to build enough New Towns—not as long as developers can make plenty of money without all that trouble. The best, if not the only, way to create interracial and socially balanced communities is to offer housing bargains tempting enough to overcome prejudice. That takes financial help.

Only the states, with their power to make special tax concessions, build special roads, and offer other favors, can effectively lure industry into the New Towns. And, most important, only state and local governments can coordinate New-Town planning with roads, sewers, and zoning, and make sure the towns are not engulfed by suburban sprawl.

New Towns are not, perhaps, the only answer to our urban dilemma. But as Mumford suggests, "In a period when automatic and irrational forces are driving mankind close to its self-annihilation [New Towns are] a victory for the rational, the human, the disciplined, and the purposeful."

3. Towns in the City

I sometimes read in the bathtub.

Immersed in warm water I read about the city of the future, about megalopolis, dynopolis, and ecumenopolis, about plug-in cities and cities underground, in the sky, under the ocean and in the ocean, and about cities that aren't in any of these places because you must understand that "the era of a world in movement is upon us." We will therefore include time as a new element in our lives as Einstein did in physics. That means, says a Frenchman named Michel Ragon, that we'll make only five-year marriage contracts to save ourselves the trouble of divorces. And it means that we will invent a "mobile architecture," self-powered buildings complete with radiotelephony and waste disposal by evaporation.

This brave new architecture, as everyone knows, is just around the corner. It will be built by computers and such and it will turn our messy slums and shapeless suburbs into decent, safe and sanitary bliss, just as several hundred years ago the transmutation of lead into pure gold was, as everyone knew, just around the corner.

What troubles me about reading of the prospect of pushing all those buttons and of plugging our buildings, new and old, into and out of vast raceways of service conduits, as Peter Cook has proposed, is only that it gives me a kink in the neck. We may, indeed, no longer be dependent on present systems of food distribution and transportation. I have no doubts that we will soon communicate all there is to know via television. But the kink will persist until one of these latter-day alchemists designs and produces a bathtub in which one can rest the head and read (or telecommunicate) with a modicum of comfort while stretching out and getting wet all over.

I am perfectly willing to concede that around that corner are wonderful new buildings, made, as John M. Johnsen predicts, "of interchangeable parts with different circuit patterns for various performances" which will have a great "kinetic quality." As we can already see in self-opening doors and fully programmed temperature controls, says Johnsen, we need only the help of something called Cyborg and "the building itself will eventually develop into a sensory organism with feedback and consciousness of its own performance."

I only hope the bathroom in that Cyborg building doesn't keep leaking like mine does. Believe me, I am open minded about this "computery." When I saw on television how they are now able to design very complex buildings by graphic computer, I immediately called up my friendly neighborhood IBM dealer to ask if I could see one of the things. He couldn't have been nicer about it.

A few days later a crewcut young man arrived in my leaky, old house with a screen and movie projector and showed me a half-hour movie of the gadget, the thing itself being too heavy for a home demonstration. The film was a bit scratchy, but I got the idea: You sit a man in front of an IBM 2250 Display console and hand him a Light Pen, a kind of magic wand. With it he draws the rough outlines of a house, say, on the cathode ray tube which looks like an ordinary TV screen. It looks a bit scraggly and sketchy at first, of course. But all the man has to do is push a button and the sketch straightens itself out and the rough line becomes thin and crisp.

If our man thinks his drawing is too big, he can fiddle with the 2250 and reduce it; if it's too small, he can enlarge it. He can make it round or oval or otherwise shape, squeeze, stretch, condense, twist, and contort it at will. He can somehow get the drawing to turn so the house shows from the side or from above or in any other position. He can push another button and see it in perspective. He can draw in one window and, upon pushing still another well-programmed button, that window will automatically duplicate itself all over the facade in given intervals.

Anytime he doesn't like a line in his handiwork he can erase it or add to his drawing with his Light Pen. Every phase of the work is recorded and, again, at a push of a button, the 2280 Film Recorder will produce a print to take home and show the kiddies or the client. Every phase can also be put back on the scanner and changed. Once you tell the machine what you need, it does all the work itself.

The movie demonstrates, for instance, how one can add to a very complex drawing of an electronic wire circuit with this graphic data-processing system. It is quite a trick to add another connection in such a way that at no point the new wires would cross any of the existing ones in the intricate maze. Without the gadget, the man said, it would take a battery of draftsmen several days to figure and redraw the circuit layout with considerable risk of human error. On the machine he only has to touch two points, the beginning and the end of the new wire, with his magic wand. Once the button is pushed the first point just takes a walk and becomes a line, worming its way swiftly through the labyrinth like a long caterpillar in a Walt Disney trick film. The problem is solved in seconds.

The prospects that this or any other electronic device will produce a caulking that would stop my bathroom from leaking are, however, remote. I didn't pursue the matter with my crewcut friend from IBM after, upon a casual mention of the problem, he gave me a silent, incredulous stare. I am resigned to have the plumbers visit every eight months or so, fiddle helplessly, and make their promises. I will also continue to believe these assurances that they have finally licked the problem once and for all and call in the painters to have the wet blotches on the living room ceiling below replastered and repainted for the umpteenth time.

Nor will the computers build us megastructures, "mobile architecture," or plug-in cities. Men will build them, if they are foolish enough to do so. Graphic data-processing and other gadgets will undoubtedly help them immeasurably to rationalize building technology, the chaotic time sequence of the construction process, the standardization of building components, the development of new building materials, the mathematics of engineering, and the tedious preparation of working drawings. And if—with or without computers—the politics and economics of city planning are also correspondingly rationalized, this may gain us more economical and faster building. That would, indeed, be a tremendous gain.

The greatest gain, I suspect, however, will derive from the possibility that automation of technical design and building construction will free the creative talents of the designer.

The idea, for instance, of placing telephone and electric wiring, water and gas mains, and other utilities inside precast curbstones, seems to me to hold far greater promise than all the Marshall McLuhan gobbledegook about "cool kinetic" architecture. The hollow curbstone, of course, is a very simple idea that needed no computers at all to dream up. It will take all those dangling wires out of the sky and keep men from digging up the roads. "Cool" or hot, "kinetic" architecture, on the other hand, like five-year marriage contracts, sounds like an awfully complicated idea to me. And I'm not sure that it wouldn't be better if we tried to make life less rather than more complicated. I'm for clear, wireless skies and good design—with or without computers.

The focus of such good design, to be helpful, cannot be some "era of the world" in which alchemists may or may not succeed in making gold and the computerists may or may not succeed in making golden cities. The focus must be the real life of people.

It may, indeed, soon be possible for people to migrate about all their lives, and some people already live in trailers, or mobile homes, as they are now called. But all we are beginning to learn about people lately indicates that, for all its hallucinogenic effects, a migratory life has a good many side effects, particularly on the young. The same is true of other radical changes in human behavior that are technically possible. Man himself, it appears, changes far more slowly than his environment is now capable of changing.

Konrad Lorenz, the animal psychologist, deals with this phenomenon in his book *On Aggression*. Man's fidelity to all his traditional customs, he says, is caused by creature habit and by animal fear at their infraction. His rituals have originated in a natural way, largely analogous to the evolution of social instincts in animals and man. But everything which man by tradition venerates and reveres does not represent an absolute ethical value. It is sacred only within the frame of reference of one particular culture. This, however, does not in any sense derogate from the unfaltering tenacity with which a good man clings to the handed-down customs of his culture. "His fidelity might seem to be worthy of a better cause," Lorenz says, "but there *are* few better causes! If social norms and customs did not develop their peculiar autonomous life and power, if they were not raised to sacred ends in themselves, there would be no trustworthy communication, no faith and no law."

My point is that our place to live must take this reality about people into account, that it must accommodate our life and our desires as they are, and not as the machine might change them if we let it. So, in building our place to live, design, as Edmund N. Bacon has said, must be used as an instrument of leadership.

In other words, you can't create good design by Gallup poll, because people don't know what they want. You have to create something and show them. Then, in the give and take of the subsequent discussion, the design evolves. Bacon calls this "structuring the dialogue" and there is a place in this process, he says, for the architect, and for the engineers, and for the League of Women Voters—and, if need be, also the computers.

As a major element in his plan for the center of Philadelphia, Bacon has related, it was necessary to create a new entity to bind together the business focus and the retail focus. Out of this came Market East, a plan to rebuild Market Street east of City Hall. Bacon produced a design for the development of a great transportation and pedestrian center on three levels. "We put this out to the public and at first they said it was terrible. We then went back and worked two more years. We came back with a project twice as big and four times as expensive, and most people said it was great. Then the economic analysts began working on it, and they said it was impossible because there is not that much shopping."

Instead of throwing out the idea, however, Bacon went back and laboriously reworked the design in a way which he thought would please the department stores. He took it with joy and pride to the department stores, and they said it was a terrible plan because it wrecked

A transportation and pedestrian center

. . . which creates a new entity

the whole system of department store sales. So again, instead of sulking, he went back and restructured the design, working with architect Aldo Giurgola, and came back with a fourth idea.

If Market East is built as designed in this fourth go-around—the project, as I write, is in the hands of Skidmore, Owings, and Merrill—it will be a marvelous new achievement in sensible urban design. "The whole point is," Bacon said, "that we have very little reason for complaining about society until we develop people who can produce designs which can serve a potent function properly structured in relation to the feedback process of contemporary society." And that is what we need rather than an architecture shouting in isolation.

The dialogue, of course, must have a common language which, like the language of words, cannot be willfully invented every Monday morning by some beguiling technocrat or playboy architect. It must, obviously, evolve out of cultural continuity and social concern. It must be concerned—to repeat it once more—with building communities, rather than self-expressions, individual monuments, or works of art. The great and evident value of striving for community planning, building, and design is what Samuel Johnson found in the prospect of being hanged—it focuses the mind.

If, for instance, we approach the problems of the city as a whole in terms of creating communities all else would seem to fall in place. Deliberately or accidentally, the city already divides itself into more or less viable, more or less coherent, more or less self-sufficient neighborhoods—Harlem, Greenwich Village, Georgetown, Nob Hill, and so forth.

If we set out to strengthen and consolidate these neighborhoods and communities again—in an effort that the planning consultant Harvey S. Perloff calls building New Towns Intown—most of our current planning hassles would resolve themselves. There would be no question, for instance, where to build highways. We would use them to structure and define, rather than disrupt neighborhoods. We would know where to put schools, shopping centers, low-income housing, industry, offices, recreation parks, and all the rest. For our aim would be to make each community a harmonious balance between work places and homes and of people of diverse income groups, interests, and vocations.

The idea, as a conscious effort at least, of breaking up the anonymity of the existing big city by nucleating it into identifiable neighborhoods is still new. But it is already finding promising architectural expressions.

One small example is the attempt to give life to the dead spaces we have built into our housing projects. The KEEP OFF THE GRASS signs on these mangy green expanses are beginning to disappear. At the Jacob Riis Houses, a public housing project in New York City, the forbidden lawn has been replaced by a handsomely landscaped recreation plaza designed to invite people in instead of ordering them out.

A mangy lawn gave way to a fun place to play

Between the project's tall apartment towers there is now a complex of brick walks, raised planting beds, play sculpture, climbing walls, cobblestone mounds, concrete steps, hanging greenery, fountains, and pools.

There are places for children to play and for grown-ups to sit and to chat as people used to sit and chat on the stoops in the old neighborhoods. There is an amphitheater for all manner of entertainment and edification. People are really taking to all this. The idea is catching on.

As architect Charles M. Goodman and I have proposed in our book *Life for Dead Spaces,* we needn't stop with recreation malls in housing projects. We could, perhaps, even with well-designed prefabricated pavilions, provide little neighborhood centers on vacant corner lots, on streets closed to traffic, on "social bridges" across freeways, or even on the parking lots of suburban shopping centers.

The pavilions would house meeting places, particularly for teenagers, all manner of stores, craft and hobby shops, restaurants, refreshment stands, exhibits—whatever the people in the neighborhood would need and want.

But we can and should go further, much further than rejuvenating old projects and building new ones better. We can, with understanding, planning, and teamwork between architects and social planners, turn the existing "gray areas" of our cities into complete neighborhoods. Like the New Towns out in the country, the first thing a town in the city needs is a heart.

In the past our approach to urban renewal has been to clear slums, to take housing away from people because it was in bad repair. The New Town Intown would *give* the poor in the slums the facilities and institutions they need—jobs, education, communication, stimulation and, in terms of the Peckham Report, contagious health. Let's get rid of the ratholes and worry about the housing later! A peeling ceiling or a shared bathroom doesn't hurt nearly as much as a life of frustration.

As the New York Citizens' Housing and Planning Council has suggested some time ago, the New Towns Intown might begin with a board of citizens who would take care of both local planning and local administration, leaving to distant city hall only those functions that make central authority essential. The Council argues that a feeling of community requires that the community itself look after its welfare and development.

Eventually each community would develop its own civic center—complete with health and welfare facilities, a police station, a library, a courthouse, a high school whose facilities would, after school hours, serve everyone in the community. There would also, of course, be shopping and recreation. This center would be a visual symbol of the community's identity.

A new school can be the ideal starting point. When, with a Ford Foundation grant, Chloethiel Smith was asked to design a prototype for an urban school (which, of course, lacks the abundant space suburban children enjoy), she came up with just such a design.

Unable to focus her thinking on some theoretical and abstract prototype, she worked on the practical problem of designing a replacement for Washington's Shaw Junior High School, a shamefully decrepit and overcrowded old building that should have been replaced many years before. She proposed to solve the problem of play space by building a one-and-a-quarter acre playground over Rhode Island Avenue. This would also reunite the Shaw area which is badly divided by this busy traffic artery. On one side would be the gymnasium which with little enhancement was to become a community sports center, serving adults as well. It was to be flanked by a small tower where various health and welfare services in the community were to be concentrated.

On the other side of the avenue was to be the school proper. Its auditorium, again with little additional space and furniture, would double as a community theater. The library was to be a separate building housing a branch of the public library in addition to meeting school needs. The school workshops for arts, crafts, and home economics, were to be open for adult courses at night. They were to have large windows toward the street so people would see these evening activities and feel drawn in. Outdoor spaces would invite open air concerts and other activities and function as little recreation parks. Under the playground, along Rhode Island Avenue, were to be shops providing life and bustle.

At first the School Board was enthusiastic. Then, suddenly, there was dead silence about it. With the arrogant social irresponsibility which, I am afraid, is typical of the leaders of the architectural profession today, Gordon Bunshaft, in his capacity as member of Washington's Fine Arts Commission, had scared everyone, it turned out, with one snide remark. Though the model was merely the preliminary schematic illustration of an idea, Bunshaft gave it one quick look and termed it "a non-design." This unnerved the School Board's Superintendent and encouraged the Highway Department to discover that it would be impossible to move houses under the Rhode Island Avenue span. No one could remember when, if ever, a house was moved down that road.

Ironically, Bunshaft's firm, Skidmore, Owings, and Merrill, designed

A school building can serve the whole community

a most attractive community school, though not as extensive in concept, for New Haven. The Conte School is the new center of New Haven's Wooster Square, the first, and so far best, realization of the New Town Intown idea to date.

The rehabilitation and conversion of this area began in 1950 as an idea of New Haven's city planner Maurice Rotival and a student project of Yale's Planning Department under Christopher Tunnard. But it did not get going in earnest until four years later, in 1954, when Mayor Richard C. Lee was elected. Edward J. Logue, now in Boston, took over as chief planner, and the Federal Housing Act was amended to provide funds for rehabilitation as well as cataclysmic renewal. Lee, with the help of Mary Small, insisted that all planning be done in dialogue with the people of the community.

That year Wooster Square was a badly run-down area with terrible slums and cold-water flats and smoking factories, cut off by the railroad from the rest of New Haven. Today it is a well mixed and integrated neighborhood with many of its nice old houses handsomely spruced up and remodeled, some new, well-designed modern town houses, well-screened corner parking lots, well-kept little parks, spanking new factories and industries, and many strong links with the city's renewed downtown area. The Italian shops and the shops on Wooster Street give the neighborhood a special character, attracting customers from the entire area. The Conte School has not only helped to revitalize a neighborhood but, with its adult education programs, various services, sports and recreation programs, also helped to revitalize people. Elderly Italian men who were determined to spend all their spare time playing cards at first, signed up for trips to the United Nations. Elderly Negroes, who weren't sure they were wanted, now go to parties and mix freely. The area is thriving.

There are other examples—Washington Park in Boston, Harlem Park in Baltimore, neighborhoods and fractions of neighborhoods in San Francisco. The best, in terms of design, but also the most expensive, is Society Hill in Philadelphia.

Here Ed Bacon and architect I. M. Pei have successfully achieved the incredible feat of imposing modern skyscrapers onto an old eighteenth-century neighborhood, and it works. It is difficult enough to mix high-rise buildings with town houses as San Francisco's Golden Gateway, where both are perched on a plaza atop a parking garage, demonstrates. The Golden Gateway, though a bit precious, is pleasant to look at, but the mental jump from very high to relatively ludicrously low is awesome. Besides, the Golden Gateway doesn't relate to the rest of the city at all. You can, of course, walk from your apartment to a good many places in downtown San Francisco. But nothing *invites* you to do so. You climb down from that plaza platform and look around where you want to go. Nothing draws you—least of all the Bay, which is blocked off by that hideous elevated Embarcadero freeway. The new neighborhood is imposed upon but not woven into the fabric of the city.

Society Hill, in contrast, is very much part of central Philadelphia. And now that the Delaware Expressway is to be bridged by a park as the citizens have advocated and not put into an open trench as the highway people insisted, the center of Philadelphia will have a riverfront again. Thanks to Bacon's splendid green walkways I find myself hiking all over the place—not only to Independence Hall but clear up to City Hall—every time I visit. Society Hill has all of the charm and few of the drawbacks of Georgetown which, with its traffic jams and jampacked parked cars, is an impossible place for children. Society Hill gracefully separates people and cars.

More important is how at last Pei's uncompromising new architecture blends with the old (the new town houses by another architect, however, strike me as most unfortunate). Here, growing out of a real concern for continuity, seems to me a significant departure for a decent modern architecture, an architecture of livability.

What Society Hill lacks, though, is a community focus. It is a nice, new, swanky section of the city, but not a real neighborhood. There should be more restaurants, shopping, community life, and most of all, a school. There is still a chance for some of this on Washington Square. But it is a shame that Head House Square, the natural agora for the area, was turned into a phony Colonial Williamsburg-type tourist trap with cutee, oldee shoppees. It should have had a living purpose—if only a laundromat.

But cutee, oldee Williamsburg seems the fate of our old city districts, particularly if there are Federal Style remnants around. As Mumford has put it, "The great danger comes from the Colonial restorationists who do not realize that one Williamsburg is enough for even a big country. . . . Nothing could do more to make national shrines seem commonplace and undistinguished than to surround them . . . with dubious approximations of Georgian architecture. . . . What our historic buildings need, if they are to stand out in their brave uniqueness, is just the opposite of this: the benefit of the contrast provided by a modern setting, whose fresh comeliness and order do justice to what Colonial and Federal Philadelphia bequeathed to us. The lovers of the old demand too little by asking only for red brick and classic moldings, white trim and graceful urns when a new building goes up in this area." Philadelphia surely got too little when they put those silly Benjamin Franklin street lamps up in Society Hill. They add a touch of saccharine to what otherwise gives us a very pleasant and promising taste of what a New Town in a restored old Intown area can be like.

There is so much we could do with old buildings! A New Town Intown provides wonderful opportunities to put charming old buildings to new use. Unfortunately we are so far rather stuffy and unimaginative about their preservation—if, indeed, we don't bulldoze them into parking lots. The thing to do is to "Ghirardelli" them, as they say in San Francisco, where a charming, century-old Victorian chocolate factory was turned into a most delightful and sophisticated shopping center.

The old Ghirardelli factory, at the foot of Russian Hill not far from the Fisherman's Wharf, was bought in 1962 by an enterprising businessman, William M. Roth. He wanted to put the lovely old castle with its clock tower to some good use. But what? He called a few bright people together, among them Justin Herman of the redevelopment agency, architects Wurster, Bernardi, and Emmons, and landscape architect Lawrence Halprin. Halprin's doodles at the brainstorming are preserved for posterity. "It's quite clear," he scribbled, "that much of the old brick stuff should stay. But some should come out!!!" All over the "brick stuff" he drew terraces, a fountain, lanterns, trees, and people dining under them. Under it he sketched three levels of parking garages. And under this doodled fairyland he wrote in big letters: "A Beehive of Excitement!"

That's just what Ghirardelli Square turned out to be. There are three restaurants (one Mexican, one Italian, and one "waterfront café"), a children's art studio, a store for modern interior accessories, a bookstore, two flower shops, and other elegant stores. In the old clock tower is a radio station and, with part of the building still used for its

Halprin's doodled fairyland . . .

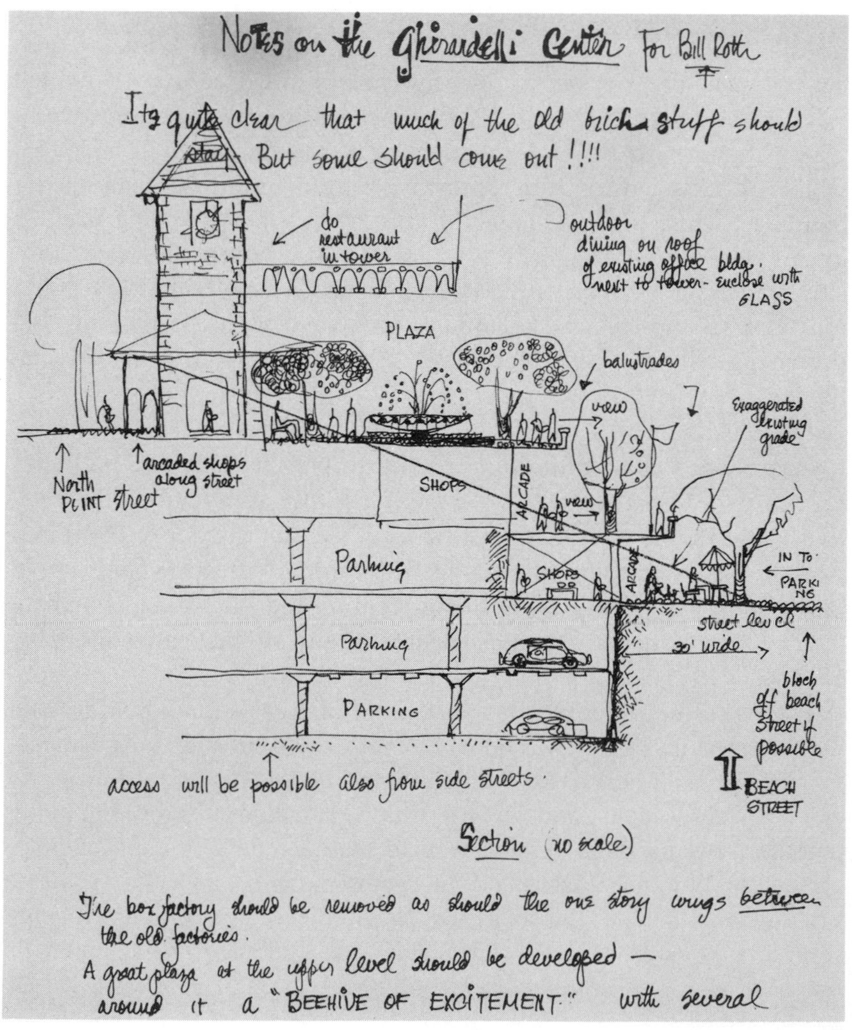

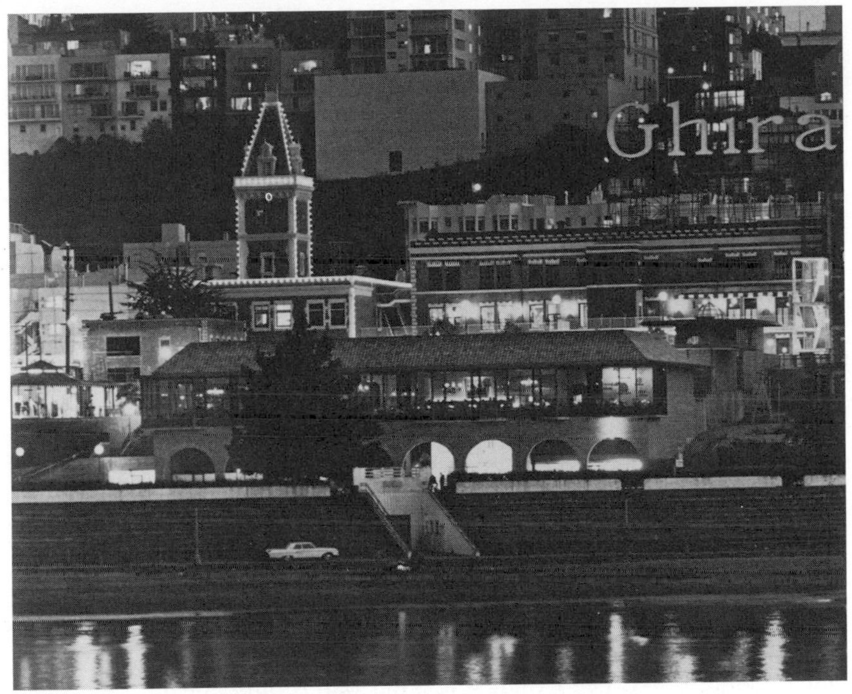

. . . becomes reality . . .

. . . in a converted chocolate factory

original purpose, the whole center is deliciously permeated with a chocolate scent. It's one of the nicest places in all San Francisco. Over the whole complex, seemingly shining all the more joyfully for its metamorphosis, is the enormous old Ghirardelli sign.

We could so easily have this kind of place almost anywhere in our cities. Louisville turned its old Illinois Central railroad depot into an Actors Theater. In St. Louis a group of architects has drawn up plans to turn the Old Post Office into a kind of Ghirardelli. But bullheaded federal bureaucrats seem intent on tearing it down. In *The Grapes of Wrath* John Steinbeck pictures a group of Oklahoma farm wives loading their goods into an old truck for the long trip to California. There wasn't much room, even for their few possessions. "The women sat among the doomed things, turning them over and looking past them and back. . . . 'No, I guess we can't take that. Here is a letter my brother wrote the day before he died. Here's an old time hat. These feathers—I never got to use them. No, there isn't room. . . . How can we live without our lives? How will we know it's us without our past?'"

How, indeed, "will we know it's us without our past," without our old buildings? We need them—leaking bathrooms and all. We need them as much as new structures. For building a good place to live is a process connecting man, nature, and society—it is continuous. No single man creates an architecture. The new architecture will grow out of the new urban community which America must create or perish.

It will grow as Benjamin Thompson, the architecture dean at Harvard, has written, in harmony only if those who work on it show respect. Thompson quotes Herbert Read, who wrote that "the act of constructing cooperatively is the groundwork of a peaceful community."

"Can we create in our own times," asks Thompson, "an architecture alive with the harmony, tranquility, and repose of the lovely New England greens—I wonder. Today's version of 'simplicity' and 'honesty' would not be the primitive stuff of early colonial villages populated by unsophisticated folk. Nor would simplicity derive from the 1920's primers of geometric forms following dubious functions. True simplicity comes at the end of an exploration of complexity, from a concise summing up of all that really needs to be said.

"To my mind no good contemporary solution is a simple spontaneous act—those Greeks with their delightful villages were simpler in living by two thousand years. And while there may be action painting, I see no action architecture without the greatest discipline, control, and education. In the end, won't the demand for greater internal discipline leave us with more freedom to search for appropriate expression outside the passing style parade?

"Our generation has been frightened by the word anonymity, which we equate with conformity. Certainly harmony will only come if egotism and upstage-itus are overcome, leaving the designers the confident self-assurance to plan for humans other than themselves. The importance and lure of the New England green is not alone the elegant white houses around the edge or the smooth rich grass between them. It is the sum total—a social concept of all the human things that happen here. The village green had unity and diversity, held together by a common theme. And when we finally find the common themes of our own times, we will create a significant civilized architecture."

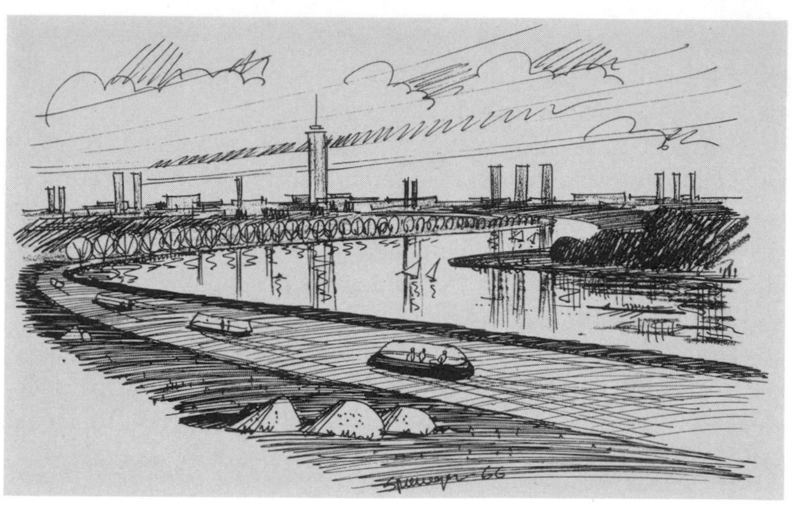

Epilogue: Tocqueville's Return

Monsieur Tocqueville, the great, great, great, great grandson of the famous author of *Democracy in America,* arrived on his first visit to the United States in the spring of the year 2003. He was delighted by the speed with which the mobile lounge attached itself to the door of the super-sonic aircraft as soon as it stopped out on the airfield. Invented by Eero Saarinen for Dulles Airport in Washington back in 1960, the year Tocqueville was born, the comfortable lounge on wheels still struck him as a marvelous convenience.

The customs formalities were attended to in the mobile lounge while it moved smoothly to the terminal. Within minutes the taxi, whose number he had been given by the stewardess on the plane, pulled up with his luggage already in the trunk. It drove him slowly through the park that surrounded the airport, its trees planted densely to screen the fearful noise of the jets. Then his taxi swung onto the radarmatic speedway, and Tocqueville got his first glimpse of an American city far in the distance.

It was a beautiful day, and the skyline was breathtaking. The glistening clusters of offices and apartment towers beyond the green-edged river truly scraped the sky. These towers, Tocqueville mused, symbolized the Promethean spirit of a world which to him, a European, still seemed new. In just about two hundred years this spirit had turned a virgin continent into a bright hope for the good life.

In the Greek legend, of course, Zeus had punished Prometheus for stealing fire from the gods by chaining him to a mountaintop where horrible vultures fed on his liver. In his childhood, Tocqueville recalled, ominous vultures, in the form of nuclear mushroom clouds, had indeed often darkened the sky. As he grew up, however, so did America. Slowly, he thought, paraphrasing his ancestor, this cumbrous democracy began to turn from its vain attempts to make a great world toward trying to make great men.

What was more, when a Congressional investigation committee returned from a brief trip to the moon and reported that there was nothing up there worth going to, expenditures for space exploration were drastically curtailed. With an arsenal of weapons capable of destroying all enemies several times over readily at hand, the country could at last devote its astounding wealth and technology as well as its Promethean spirit towards the solution of pressing problems at home.

Foremost among them, in fact the key to all others, was its man-made environment. "Our society will never be great unless our cities are great," Lyndon Johnson had said. America, toward the end of the twentieth century, acknowledged that it had become an urban nation.

Hitched to the radar device, the taxi now cruised automatically along at a comfortable 120 miles per hour. The driver swung his seat around for a chat.

"Where ya from, Mac?" he asked Tocqueville who, though a product of France's Seventh Republic, still flinched a little at such democratic familiarity. Once he had his answer, however, the driver proceeded in fair French which, along with two other optional languages, every American now learned in school by the "total immersion" method. He told Tocqueville that the last of the slums in the city had now been cleared, the ghettoes finally abolished. Their residents, he explained, had their choice of living either in rehabilitated old areas close to their former slum dwellings, in downtown apartment towers, in New Towns, or in suburban neighborhoods such as those Tocqueville could see on both sides of the speedway.

They were small communities, not unlike the ancient villages of France, clusters of houses and town houses separated by open fields, woods, playgrounds, golf courses, tennis courts, and parks. Each cluster was different, though, again like old villages, each was harmonious

Suburban cluster separated by open fields

in architectural character. Every cluster had its public square, surrounded by a small shopping center. Above the stores were offices for the local professionals and health clinics. There were also a school, churches, a town hall for community meetings and community administration, a library, public workshops for arts and crafts, and halls for teen-age dances, adult education classes, and other activities. Each square was marked by one or two high-rise apartment buildings for couples either too young or too old to live with children. Most single persons, the driver explained, preferred to live downtown, where the more varied social life afforded them a better chance of finding a mate.

The squares, like the parks and playgrounds, were bustling with people. The outdoor cafés were full. Children played and splashed around the fountains and man-made brooks. There were puppet shows and tents for storytellers and jugglers. On one square Tocqueville noticed an outdoor, traveling market with colorful canopies. Everywhere benches were filled with old folks feeding pigeons, and some sat on single chairs which could be more easily turned to the sun or grouped for games and chats. Tocqueville saw young people on bicycles and, in the parks, riding horses. He remarked on the absence of automobiles on the squares or in front of the houses.

"After the Big Traffic Standstill of 1975 we finally got wise," said the driver in his instant French. "For us kids it was the same traumatic experience the Great Depression must have been for our parents. Millions of cars stuck for a week. Imagine! Thousands of people died. Then they discovered we'd made the same mistake our grandparents had made about flood control. They used to build dikes at the mouths of the rivers, and when the rivers persisted in overflowing them, they just built the dikes higher. More floods. When I was a kid they'd build more and more highways. Same thing. More traffic jams, air pollution, nothing left in the cities but concrete ramps and parking lots. Our parents finally saw the light and went upstream and stopped some of the water from coming down by afforestation, erosion control, and gully-plugging. We finally saw the light, Congress passed NEPA, the National Emergency Planning Act, and we rebuilt our suburbs. Did it in less than ten years. Most of them had turned into slums, anyway."

"I have read about that," said Tocqueville. "'When men living in a democratic state of society are enlightened they readily discover that they are not confined and fixed by any limits which constrain them to take up with their present fortune,'" he quoted his ancestor. "But what about automobiles?" he inquired. "Have Americans lost their passion for your mechanical mistresses?"

"No, monsieur, we love them as passionately as ever, every bit as much as you French do. But many people don't own cars any more. They rent them for vacation and pleasure trips. It's cheaper, and you don't have to bother with upkeep. Some people have a special affection for fancy cars of all kinds and keep and pamper them themselves. Other car owners join garage clubs. These have a mechanic for every ten members. That means every member's car gets automatically checked and overhauled every ten days. On the day the car is in the garage you use the club's car.

"But hardly anyone drives to work or to shopping any more. Most people live where they work. If they live in the suburbs but work downtown, the commuter bus picks them up at the street corner. Everyone has a reserved seat. As you enter the bus the stewardess hands you your newspaper and coffee. You are usually at the commuter train station before you've finished your cup. The train never takes longer than five or ten minutes, so from your bed to your desk seldom takes more than twenty minutes. There is no waiting because an electronic regulator sees to it that there are always as many cars and seats as there are passengers."

Just then a silver train passed them on the center strip of the speedway.

Just then, too, a red light flashed on the taxi's dashboard. There was a buzz, and the driver's seat swung forward to driving position again. They passed through a tunnel that was brightly lighted, its walls decorated with bold, gaily colored mosaics. The design suggested an aquatic theme to let people know they were under the river. Then Tocqueville heard the click as the cab was automatically released from the radar guide. The driver steered up a ramp and along a sunken expressway, lined with a colorful pattern of sound-absorbing tile, which led through a few buildings, and came to a stop in the car entrance of the hotel. Tocqueville thanked the driver; he learned that tipping had been abolished in the United States as undignified since the taxi drivers' union, back in 1977, had won a guaranteed annual wage.

He had expected the hotel to be much larger, considering America's famous propensity for giganticism. But this too, he found, had changed somewhat with the resurgence of the new humanism at the end of the twentieth century.

The huge corporate entities, the ever larger and taller office buildings, cultural and commercial centers, Americans discovered, were as inefficient as they were ugly. Like their cities, these huge buildings with their large concentrations of people, and with them, of course, their cars, their feeding stations, and the other services they needed, had simply become unmanageable.

In the 1960's, it had been considered efficient to house a big government agency like the Federal Bureau of Investigation in Washington all in one building on Washington's Pennsylvania Avenue so that all facets of the operation would be easily accessible to everyone. When the monster had been completed in 1969, it was discovered that this concentration made the various departments and files not more but less accessible. It would have been far more efficient to house the machine operations and the big file rooms outside the city where trucks could get easily to them, and their operators and clerks could live nearby. Data might have been transmitted to the desks of all who needed them at a push of a button by closed-circuit television and other devices.

As it was, much time was wasted in endless walks up and down miles of tedious corridors, standing in line in the crowded cafeterias for lunch, not to speak of parking the car. No one got to know his fellow workers in the anonymous crowd. The work halls were too huge and the constancy of air-conditioned temperature and artificial lighting, without the relief of so much as a glance at the sky, proved tiring and irritating. The breakdown of just one mechanical device—an elevator, say—had a disconcerting falling-domino effect on the entire agency.

It was the same with the big culture centers. People found that the spell a splendid concert cast over them was prematurely dispelled by the anguish and irritation of being pushed by the huge crowds that spilled out of the center's opera and theater at the same time. Everyone was pushing to retrieve his car, and after a long wait in the dismal underground parking garage, had to fight traffic congestion to get out of the place.

Nor did anyone particularly enjoy standing in line at the reception desk and then again at the elevators of the ever larger hotels with their ever longer corridors and ever more abominable service.

If the giant structures were unpleasant and inefficient for the people who used them, they proved even worse for the city as a whole. After the FBI building was closed at night, Pennsylvania Avenue was dead and deserted so that not so much as a shoeshine parlor or drugstore, let alone a restaurant, ventured to open anywhere in its vicinity. What with far too many other government offices already on the avenue, it now became a graveyard after five-thirty and over the weekend. The authorities even threatened to shut off the new fountain since there was no one to enjoy it after office hours.

The culture center, on the other hand, was dead during the day. The artists decided to rehearse and meet in livelier parts of town where they would find the little workshops for sets and costumes, different restaurants for their meals, or little bars for a drink and a discreet rendezvous. The supersized hotels lost business because they began to repel their guests. Even Shriners decided that their conventions had gotten far too big to be fun.

So what Tocqueville now saw, as he looked out the window of his room on the top floor of his twenty-five story hotel, was quite different from what mid-twentieth-century utopians had envisioned. The sky was not screened from view by some gigantean Buckminster Fuller dome, under which people would breathe only mechanically conditioned air and never see a bird. The air he breathed was clear and natural, and Tocqueville could feel a breeze from the river. Swallows were playfully gliding and diving in the sky, chirping contentedly, and now and then turning their white bellies to the sun.

The most prominent of the towers was city hall, a noble structure with numerous terraces. It was lunchtime and the office workers enjoyed their break. Girls munched sandwiches under gay umbrellas by the terrace pools, watching their friends diving and swimming. Others played badminton.

Some of the smaller office towers had their outdoor recreation decks on the roof. Most apartment buildings had large private balconies and terraces in addition to their roof gardens. In fact, in most of them the terraces were punched right through the building so that, from the

The traffic standstill of 1975 brought change

elevator, you would step out onto a sort of open loggia with potted shrubs and flowers from which you entered your apartment as through a front yard in the sky. All these terraces and balconies were swarming with people. In many instances whole families were eating together outdoors, father having walked home from the office for lunch.

The city, Tocqueville perceived, had become the managerial, cultural, commercial, and residential center for its region. Way in the distance, beyond the busy river port, he could see the industrial district with its manufacturing plants and warehouses in what seemed like a park. There were some stacks, but the smoke was clean; the law saw to that. Factories had, in fact, become so tidy in all respects that pleasant residences, parks, and playgrounds wound right through the industrial district.

All around the downtown center, amidst a forest of trees and defined by partly sunken highways—most of them with a rapid-transit rail line in the center strip—Tocqueville could clearly discern the city's neighborhoods, or nuclei, that made up the bulk of the city. Each was marked by a distinct high building or tower, at times a church steeple, more often an administrative or apartment building. But they did not sprawl endlessly.

He had landed not in New York, like the other Tocqueville, but in a medium-sized city of a million inhabitants. Thanks to the clear weather, he could see the city limits beyond the beltway, a parkway, really, which surrounded the city much as walls did in the middle ages. Along this road were lakes, a golf course, and sport fields, and, at one point, a large amusement park under the trees, that reminded him of Tivoli in Copenhagen. Beyond, in the haze, was open country, or what seemed like it, with its rolling hills. Only the roads and the scattering of peaking towers betrayed the fact that this area was rather densely populated.

This green belt was to remain green, the talkative taxi driver had told Tocqueville. Though nationally the population explosion was at last leveling off, the population of this city was still growing. But rather than let it expand in sprawls and dribbles, as cities did before NURA, America's successful National Urban Reform Act of 1976, the city fathers had already commenced the construction of a new metro center some forty miles away. The place had been long in the planning, the driver assured him. The transportation lines and industrial parks were ready, and it would now take only the consolidation of several New Towns and some Detsubcoms (Detached House Suburban Communities, the driver had explained, pointing to what they saw on the way from the airport) to forge a viable, new metropolis for which two opera houses and several concert halls and theaters, a baseball stadium, and three universities were already under construction.

Tocqueville looked down. Here, too, what he saw did not at all resemble the utopian visions of "the city of the future" he had seen in the magazines in his childhood. The view of the central city plaza, actually a sequence of paved plazas as he remembered them in Verona, was nothing like the narrow canyons of Wall Street, let alone like Sant'Elia's futuristic drawings at the turn of the twentieth century or Le Corbusier's a little later. For one thing, he was amazed to see so many old structures—churches, office and apartment buildings, and even mansions and houses—interspersed with the new. Few of these old buildings were of the mid-twentieth century, for at that time buildings were often too shoddily built and too unattractive to be rescued. Most were of the nineteenth and even eighteenth century. Historic building preservation, he was to learn later, had become not only legally mandatory under NURA, but the preservation of worthy old structures was quite generally deemed as obvious as the preservation of worthy old books in a library—how else was one to experience history?

The old buildings were not only lovingly restored to immaculate condition, but also well fitted into the new design of the contemporary city. The new buildings, handsome in the unpretentious manner of a really well-dressed person, politely accommodated themselves to the old in scale, by either harmonizing or deliberately contrasting textures, colors, and materials. None, however, imitated the style or decorations of their older neighbors as so many rude pseudo-Colonial buildings did in the 1950's and '60's. Tocqueville also learned later upon somewhat closer inspection that many of the old buildings had been converted to new purposes and completely remodeled within. A lovely Victorian post office, for instance, had become a community center, a handsome factory was turned into a lively agglomeration of small shops and restaurants, an old church had become a youth center. Not one of them was made into a museum.

Among the new buildings, only the important ones, the landmarks, stood out. One of them was obviously the municipal opera house. Another was the ecumenical cathedral. A third was the handsome communications tower. The rest of the buildings appeared as but one element of what Tocqueville thought a charming and lively city. Its designers had obviously placed the emphasis of their ingenuity not on forms and facades, but on the streets and plazas with their colorful and richly textured pavements and furniture, on the shopping arcades, the little parks and playgrounds, and the variety and harmony of all the many details that, far more than its actual structures, determine the quality of the urban environment.

Spotting an empty table in an open-air restaurant on the plaza directly below, Tocqueville suddenly felt hungry. Abruptly he hurried downstairs.

Much to his surprise he found the moderately priced lunch every bit as good, indeed, perhaps even better than what he might have gotten in Paris.

The waitress was most attentive, since lately Americans had also rediscovered the joys of both giving and receiving good personal service. The time was passed when Americans, as the elder Tocqueville observed, had "scarcely time to attend the details of etiquette." Not only waitresses but also store clerks, gardeners, garage mechanics, handymen, and even civil servants, were polite and, working short shifts, seemed to thoroughly enjoy their work. It seemed to them far more interesting and creative than pushing buttons in an automated factory, and the wages were good. Service jobs, furthermore, were considered no more, nor less demeaning than industrial or clerical ones. Practically everyone continued to pursue some form of study and education, not for a specific purpose so much as to meet the need of the mind, much as physical recreation meets needs of the body. Status was generally measured by academic accomplishment rather than by what you happened to do to earn a living.

Tocqueville's restaurant table was along the skating rink which was frozen all year around. He delighted in watching people whirl around to the music while he ate. He loved the plaza where people hurried to and fro, clustered to have their pictures taken as in Venice, or listened to students serenade with their guitars. There were also secluded areas where people sat quietly and mothers absentmindedly rocked their baby carriages while they read. There were display areas of art and educational exhibits and glass vitrines which served as showcases for nearby stores.

The attractive design of these goods, from kitchen utensils to small furniture items (large, standard furniture items such as beds, couches, big tables, and bookshelves now came generally with the house since people refused to tote such heavy items around with them when they moved), was now leading in the world. It was, thought Tocqueville, every bit as good as Scandinavian design had been in his childhood. The reason, he had been told, was due not only to an improvement of popular taste. It was also due to the discovery that America's poorly designed products could no longer successfully compete on the world market. The discovery began with the disastrous drop of foreign sales of American automobiles. This improved at once when worried Detroit manufacturers replaced their "stylists" with real designers, stopped listening to their dealers, and threw their market surveys out the window.

The Frenchman was even more impressed with the quality and abundance of the beautiful and well-kept planting of trees, shrubs, and flowers everywhere, with the many gushing, spurting, and dripping water fountains, with the abundance of sculptures, stabiles and mobiles, murals and mosaics all around him, and with the cleanliness and air of excitement of it all. Not only the plazas but also the streets and shopping arcades he now explored seemed like one big outdoor museum in a park that almost put Versailles, his beloved Versailles, to shame.

The store fronts and advertising signs complemented the art, landscaping, and endless variety of handsome benches, bollards, and kiosks. There was amazing variation within their overall harmony. You couldn't miss a one, but none tried to outshout the other. Many stores relied on symbols rather than on a lot of outdoor literature. Where lettering was used, it was legible and dignified. Some signs were clever and witty. They were gaily illuminated at night, for the inner city was humming with activity almost around the clock and the city prided itself in being as gay and attractive and bustling after dark as during the day. The Fine Arts Council, which strictly controlled such matters, allowed advertising signs, however, only in the streets and arcades devoted to amusements, bars, and night life of which there were many, for all tastes and pocketbooks, in various parts of the city.

Public signs and maps to tell people not only where to find streets, bus and subway stops, and landmarks, but also such necessities as public toilets, attended playgrounds for the children of shoppers, pharmacies, post offices, and the like, were discreet and handsome yet prominent, instantly recognizable and legible. Most were consolidated with street light standards, trash baskets, and public telephones to avoid needless clutter on the streets.

Near one of the public telephones Tocqueville spotted a young lad chalking some rhymed wisdom on the sidewalk and being rewarded not with coins, as sidewalk poets used to be in Europe, but with the appreciative laughter of his friends. A cop, swirling his nightstick, smiled at the group. The chalk would do no damage and the city was for people.

"Nothing conceivable is so petty, so insipid, so crowded with paltry interests, in one word, so anti-poetic, as the life of a man in the United States," the earlier Tocqueville had written. Recalling this sentence, his descendant burst out laughing. "How this has changed!" he said out loud. The policeman gave him a surprised stare. Tocqueville quickly jumped onto a passing electric bus. Even in the twenty-first century a cop was, after all, a cop.

The bus rode along unencumbered because, needless to say, there were no private automobiles in the inner city, even though the poisonous, noisy gasoline engines had been replaced by much handier electrically powered vehicles, gliding on cushioned air. Supply trucks and emergency vehicles had access to the buildings on subterranean alleys, loading and unloading in their basements. There were frequent subway stops with escalators and moving sidewalks for the lazy. Above ground the inner city was crisscrossed by a constant stream of little electric buses, some moving slowly enough for the nimble to get on and off at will, others stopping frequently for the elderly or people with packages. If you insisted on driving downtown you left your car in a garage along the tunneled freeway closest to your destination. It was parked by an automatic device. Upon paying your fee you received a plastic punch-card ticket which you stuck into a gadget upon your return, and the device that had stored your car would spit it out again, ready to go. But, as the taxi driver had said, few commuters used their automobiles to go downtown. Parking was expensive and public transportation fast, convenient, and free. The authorities had finally learned that transportation, like sewers, was a public necessity which the public must support collectively. It was found not only more efficient but also far cheaper to provide subway and bus rides free of charge, than to keep building more and more expensive highways and parking garages, let alone using up precious urban land with ugly and open parking lots.

Tocqueville got off the electric bus in a residential neighborhood adjoining the river park that, embracing the harbor, ran the whole length of the city. For a while he sat in the neighborhood square, listening to a not very good high-school band. Behind the band shell was the neighborhood center with the health clinic, school, shopping, welfare services, bowling alley, movie house, cafés, amateur theater, and all the other public facilities he had so fleetingly observed in the suburban centers. Ahead of him was the river park. People were swimming in the unpolluted river; a few were horseback riding along it. Kids were chasing each other on bicycles. The young animals' zoo was teeming with small children who squealed with joy. Most benches here were occupied by young lovers, and a number of elderly people were browsing among the open air bookstalls. "Paris' contribution to the American city," he thought. Then he walked off to explore the neighborhood.

Its outward appearance, it seemed to him, did not differ much from residential neighborhoods in the city of a hundred or two hundred years ago. Here again there were an amazing number of painstakingly renovated and often gaily painted late nineteenth- and early twentieth-century structures among the new buildings. But there were also important differences. One was the fresh, clean, colorful cheerfulness of it all, from the sparkling, ever varied pavement patterns and textures to the vigorously blooming little parks at every corner. Many had gay little greenhouse pavilions where people would sit in the winter.

There were several reasons, Tocqueville decided, for this radiant health of the city and its people. Waste disposal had now been solved without leaving the pound a year of largely toxic dust that the average American city accumulated on its every square foot in the 1960's. Both heating and air conditioning of all buildings in the city was, furthermore, piped in from two big power plants on the outskirts, a development that began in Warsaw back in the 1950's, and at Farsta,

Sweden, in the 1960's. City dwellers, of course, had at last been freed of the irritation, noise, and confusion of motor traffic. The planners had rediscovered the difference between a street and a road, and the difference was decisive. Unless both roads and streets function properly, the city dies.

Tocqueville now walked down a neighborhood street. All the houses opened up to it. There were no machines to interfere with people—with the women who sat on the stoops to gossip, the prim little girls who paraded up and down the center walkway, the little boys who scared them with their scooters and soapbox buggies as they rushed down to the ice-cream and soft-drink kiosk at the corner. This street was surely for people who wanted to be where they were.

Between every four or five blocks was a road with vehicles moving swiftly along it. The houses, however, understandably turned away from them. They would show them no more than a bathroom window, perhaps; certainly not a front yard. The front was toward the green inner court with its small private gardens and public walkways and playgrounds.

There were four kinds of roads: the capillaries which fed transportation into the living cells, short ceremonial boulevards for parades and processions that included vehicles, the arteries which pumped larger numbers of people and goods in and out of the neighborhood centers, and the freeways which moved private cars, buses, and trucks to distant points in a hurry, all of them out of sight, sunken, or underground.

Another reason for the remarkable renaissance of urban America, as the Frenchman saw it, was not technical, however, but social. "If ever America undergoes great revolutions, they will be brought about by the presence of the black race on the soil of the United States; that is to say, they will owe their origin, not to the equality, but to the inequality of condition," his famous ancestor had prophesied in 1835.

In the mid-twentieth century the Negro revolution had, indeed, come to pass and, in the end, it had accomplished even more than racial equality. "Forgetful of the public," American society had, as the elder Tocqueville warned, passed "through strange vicissitudes." In the industrial revolution and well into the twentieth century streets had been unsafe and the people in them became alienated and irritable. But now, a generation later, another Tocqueville could note that all Americans were not only proclaimed equal in their humanity and material opportunity, but also had equal physical access to the good life the city had to offer. Indeed, they all lived together, and among the simple homes on the street he walked there were also more ostentatious and spacious ones. The difference between them was more a matter of interior spaciousness and furnishings than outward appearances since the notion that housing for the poor must also look aesthetically deprived had been abandoned even by Congress. The requirements of good shelter, like those of clothing for people who share the same climate were, after all, the same. And conspicuous distinction in dress between social classes had, of course, disappeared already in the nineteenth century.

All this combined had wrought, Tocqueville mused, the last and most important change of them all since *Democracy in America* was written. Conceived by landed gentry, born as a rural nation, America had not only learned to accept its urban fate but somehow suddenly began to love its cities. Just how and why this came about, Tocqueville decided to ponder at some later time. For the moment he only noted that the new love had sparked new ambition. Again a quotation from his ancestor came to his mind. "I confess that I apprehend much less for democratic society from the boldness than from the mediocrity of desires. What appears to me most to be dreaded is that, in the midst of the small incessant occupations of private life, ambition should lose its vigor and its greatness; that the passion of man should abate, but at the same time be lowered."

The misery of the city had kindled strong, new desires. The challenge was eventually met with boldness. Perhaps the little playground enclave for toddlers our visitor now entered contributed little to the cause of democracy in the rice paddies of Asia or the prairies of Africa. Or did it? he wondered as he sat down on a chair that was, alas, reserved for young mothers.

But the pretty young girl in the blue smock who was in charge of the place gave him an encouraging smile. She was an apprentice kindergarten teacher who, in the employ of the city, tended the playground, its manifold toys and equipment, and whatever children were informally and without charge entrusted to her care. It was an idea the Americans had borrowed from Sweden where attended playgrounds existed since World War II. Absorbed in the goings-on, he forgot all about just where and how one starts building a better world. Some of the dozen or so children he watched were climbing all over a colorful jungle gym. Others explored a big, hollow, sculptured animal. Still others were bent over a table, intensely occupied with their painting.

Tocqueville marveled at the agility of the pretty attendant who with one hand kept producing ever more building blocks out of a

Not forms and facades, but streets and plazas

toy shed, and with the other alternately wiped noses and gave new impetus to a small overcrowded merry-go-round.

"What's your name?" asked a little three-year-old who had suddenly noticed the entranced stranger. Tocqueville was too startled to respond with anything but the straight truth. The attendant overheard his reply, and, being conversant with the book that made the name sound so familiar to her, soon had him engaged in a long conversation. It gave him the opportunity he yearned for to share his impressions of the day.

"What do you believe turned the trick?" she asked after they had discussed the blight and plight of American cities before NURA.

"Americans," he replied, "have forever sought new frontiers. When they had reached the Pacific and had tamed their wild continent, they sought to conquer the frontier of self, of self-expression in art and architecture, of the 'small incessant occupations of private life.' It was a noble endeavor but led to a severe crisis in American society. For the self they so intently sought did not, as they had hoped, lead to the assertion of the individual in the mass. It was as theologian Robert E. Fitch put it, 'a narrow self which has made the soul sick by shrinking down the scope of its concern to a focus which is no longer part of a field.' Finally, however, they pulled themselves out and heeded philosophers like Aristotle and Saint Paul and Martin Luther and John Dewey. American man discovered what it is to find himself by losing himself. 'For man,' to quote Fitch again, 'is saved, not by self-control but by self-surrender, provided the surrender be to some thing of excellence. The excellence of an ideal can then draw out the excellence of the man; and the two may collaborate in the creation of innovations in excellence.' "

"I was talking about cities, not philosophy," said the girl, as she wiped another little nose.

"So was I," said Tocqueville. "In a word, Americans one day discovered a whole new frontier, not in the Pacific, nor in the self, but in the public realm. That's how they began to spend their devotion, energy, and money on their place to live and to build lovely playgrounds like this one in every city block."

Unsure how he might gracefully steer the conversation towards her plans for the evening, Tocqueville added one more thought: "Actually," he said, "there is nothing in the city of the year 2003 that architects and planners hadn't thought of and, in places, even begun to build in the year 1967."

Then, in his most charming French manner, he blurted out what he had on his mind. There was a long silence. At last the girl said: "You never know. Even the most wishful daydreams might come true if one wishes hard enough."

We shall never know whether she referred to this optimistic fantasy of the American city a generation hence, or the proposed dinner date.

What Can We Do?

In England, not long ago, some citizens got angry about ugly new architecture in general and a proposed scheme for London's Piccadilly Circus in particular. They formed a group called the "Anti-Uglies," staged protest marches, and organized picket lines.

Perhaps this seems extreme.

But neither does it do any good merely to view with alarm and to deplore the hucksters, vulgarians, politicians, bad architects, and special interests who ruin our place to live. It misses, as Peter Blake has pointed out in his *God's Own Junkyard,* one important point: "the point that the 'intellectual elite' in America has failed miserably to accept its basic responsibility" for a more livable environment.

The trouble with the English "Anti-Uglies" and with our own viewers-with-alarm is, of course, that they have little popular support. Most voters don't quite see what they are talking about.

The first step toward more handsome and livable communities is to create community awareness. That means nothing more or less than arousing people to the fact that ugliness is ugly and that a nation which is capable of hurling tons of hardware at Mars can surely eliminate the ugliness of the American city.

Your letters to newspaper editors, your mayor or county manager, your council or commissioners, your state legislator, governor, member of Congress, and United States Senator can add impetus to this awareness.

So do discussions about city planning and urban design in your local civic, service and business groups and arts council. Members of your planning commission, local chapters of the American Institute of Architects, the American Institute of Planners, and the American Society of Landscape Architects, local preservation groups affiliated with the National Trust for Historic Preservation, and local planning and housing associations will be happy to furnish guidance, make presentations, furnish films and pamphlets, and recommend speakers.

Awareness, of course, should lead to action—specific action. It is time all of us—citizens, government leaders, businessmen, labor unions, civic and service organizations, and educators—insisted on good community design and sound planning for orderly growth and development. It is time we became very specific about it and informed ourselves about local plans and ordinances, about the design for that proposed new school or freeway or housing project. The crisis of the American city is right at our doorstep.

To resolve that crisis we should insist that planning and design enhance not only property values but human values; that our public-works programs add not only to the tax base but to the amenity, livability, and beauty of the community. That means not only big buildings and roads but also small parks, plazas and pedestrian walkways and malls, controlled billboards and store-front signs, benches, trees, flowers, buried utility lines, the preservation and restoration of handsome old buildings and historic areas, good maintenance of public spaces, and all the rest.

It is, to cite Peter Blake once more, still possible to create some degree of order in America—and with it a chance of civilization—by demanding such things as more up-to-date and better enforced zoning and building codes, by taking the profit out of land speculation, by using tax policy to encourage good building and discourage bad building, by ridding the country of bureaucrats who have strait-jacketed most government-subsidized architecture, and by getting rid of their moribund agencies. And, I might add, by insisting on transporting *people* rather than bringing more automobiles into the city.

But we had better start demanding and insisting right now.

Acknowledgments

Many people have indirectly helped me to write this book. But I would be less than grateful if by acknowledging their help I would not also fully exonerate them from any responsibility for its accuracy and validity.

There are first of all the anonymous jury and officials of the Ford Foundation, which, in the much needed effort to encourage and assist critics and writers in the arts, gave me a lovely grant to travel in this country and abroad to see and experience architecture and urban design, particularly that of New Towns.

There are further the editors of *Harper's, The New Republic, Saturday Review, Horizon,* and the *Journal* of the American Institute of Architects, whose assignments and guidance helped focus my thinking. They also allowed me to use, mostly in different form, some of the articles I have written for them. Then there are my bosses at the Washington *Post*, notably Ben Gilbert, who share my belief that people ought to know and think more about how well we build our place to live and who are not only paying me a salary for doing what I like to do but also granting me the freedom and forbearance to do it in my own erratic way.

Mrs. Susan Norwitch and Mrs. Lois Craig have helped me more

than they know (and than I was able to remunerate them for) with research and all those often burdensome little chores that go into putting a book together. Mrs. Dorothy Sutton did an impeccable job of typing the manuscript. Pat Patterson helped with the bibliography.

Hugh Jacobsen, a most erudite Washington architect, Alan Fern of the Library of Congress, Wilhelm von Moltke and Jacqueline Tyrwhitt of the Harvard School of Design have generously lengthened their busy waking hours to read parts or all of the manuscript and offered valuable comments and suggestions that I am most grateful for even if I, to my peril, did not always heed all of them.

My publisher, Seymour Lawrence, and his savvy editor, his wife, helped greatly both with their encouragement and their practical criticisms.

I should also acknowledge that I must have been an ornery pest to both my family and my friends at the Washington *Post* during those frequent moments when I wondered why on earth I ever got myself into this venture. I trust they forgive me.

And now that the book is done, I find in retrospect that it was really fun to write. I hope you find it as much fun to read.

Bibliography

ABRAMS, CHARLES, *The City Is the Frontier.* Harper & Row, New York, 1965.

_____ *Man's Struggle for Shelter in an Urbanizing World.* M.I.T. Press, Cambridge, 1964.

Alvar Aalto. Wittenborn & Company, Scarsdale, 1963.

ANDREWS, WAYNE, *Architecture in America: A Photographic History from the Colonial Period to the Present.* Atheneum, New York, 1960.

ARNAU, FRANK, *Brasilia: Phantasie und Wirklichkeit.* Prestel, München, 1960.

BABCOCK, RICHARD F., *The Zoning Game: Municipal Practices and Policies.* University of Wisconsin Press, Madison, 1966.

BANHAM, REYNER, *Theory and Design in the First Machine Age.* Frederick A. Praeger, New York, 1960.

BAYER, HERBERT, GROPIUS, ISE, and GROPIUS, WALTER, eds., *Bauhaus: 1919-1928.* Charles T. Bradford Company, Boston, 1959.

BLAKE, PETER, *God's Own Junkyard: The Planned Deterioration of America's Landscape.* Holt, Rinehart & Winston, New York, 1964.

_____ *The Master Builders: Le Corbusier, Mies van der Rohe, Frank Lloyd Wright.* Alfred A. Knopf, New York, 1960.

BLASER, WERNER, *Mies van der Rohe: The Art of Structure.* Frederick A. Praeger, New York, 1965.

BOESIGER, W. and GIRSBERGER, H., eds., *Le Corbusier. Complete Works, 1910-1960.* George Wittenborn, New York, 1960.

BOYD, ROBIN, *Kenzo Tange: Makers of Contemporary Architecture.* George Braziller, New York, 1962.

BREUER, MARCEL, *Buildings and Projects,* 1921-1961. Frederick A. Praeger, New York, 1962.

BURCHARD, JOHN, *The Voice of the Phoenix: Postwar Architecture in Germany.* M.I.T. Press, Cambridge, 1966.

——— and BUSH-BROWN, ALBERT, *The Architecture of America: A Social and Cultural History.* Little, Brown & Co., Boston, 1961.

BUSH-BROWN, ALBERT, *Louis Sullivan: Masters of World Architecture.* George Braziller, New York, 1960.

CHERMAYEFF, SERGE and ALEXANDER, CHRISTOPHER, *Community and Privacy: Toward a New Architecture of Humanism.* Doubleday & Company, Garden City, 1965.

CHOAY, FRANÇOISE, *Le Corbusier: Masters of World Architecture.* George Braziller, New York, 1960.

CHURCHILL, HENRY S., *The City Is the People.* W.W. Norton & Company, New York, 1962.

CICHY, BODO, *The Great Age of Architecture from Ancient Greece to the Present Day.* G. P. Putnam's Sons, New York, 1964.

Cities: A Scientific American Book. Alfred A. Knopf, New York, 1965.

COLLINS, GEORGE R., *Antonio Gaudi: Masters of World Architecture.* George Braziller, New York, 1960.

CONANT, JAMES B., *Slums and Suburbs: A Commentary on Schools in Metropolitan Areas.* McGraw-Hill, New York, 1961.

CREESE, WALTER L., *The Search for Environment: The Garden City Before and After.* Yale University Press, New Haven, 1966.

CROSBY, THEO, *Architecture: City Senses.* Reinhold Publishing Corp., New York, 1965.

CULLEN, GORDON, *Townscape.* Reinhold Publishing Corp., New York, 1961.

DANZ, ERNST, *Architecture of Skidmore, Owings & Merrill,* 1950-1962. Frederick A. Praeger, New York, 1963.

DREXLER, ARTHUR, *Ludwig Mies van der Rohe: Masters of World Architecture.* George Braziller, New York, 1960.

DUHL, LEONARD J., ed., *The Urban Condition: People and Policy in the Metropolis.* Basic Books, New York, 1963.

Editors of FORTUNE, *The Exploding Metropolis: A Study of the Assault on Urbanism and How Our Cities Can Resist It.* Doubleday & Company, Garden City, 1958.

EVENSON, NORMA, *Chandigarh.* University of California Press, Berkeley, 1966.

FITCH, JAMES MARSTON, *Architecture and the Esthetics of Plenty.* Columbia University Press, New York, 1961.

——— *Walter, Gropius: Masters of World Architecture.* George Braziller, New York, 1960.

FUTTERMAN, ROBERT A., *The Future of Our Cities.* Doubleday & Company, Garden City, 1961.

GALBRAITH, JOHN KENNETH, *The Affluent Society.* Houghton Mifflin Co., Boston, 1958.

GANS, HERBERT, *The Urban Villagers: Groups and Class in the Life of Italian Americans*. Free Press of Glencoe, New York, 1962.

GIEDION, SIGFRIED, *Space, Time and Architecture: The Growth of a New Tradition*. Harvard University Press, Cambridge, 1942.

GORDON, MITCHELL, *Sick Cities: Psychology and Pathology of American Urban Life*. Penguin, Baltimore, 1965.

GOTTMAN, JEAN, *Economics, Esthetics, and Ethics in Modern Urbanization*. Twentieth Century Fund, New York, 1962.

——— *Megalopolis: The Urbanized Northeastern Seaboard of the United States*. Twentieth Century Fund, New York, 1961.

GOWANS, ALAN, *Images of American Living: Four Centuries of Architecture and Furniture as Cultural Expression*. J. B. Lippincott, Philadelphia, 1964.

GROPIUS, WALTER, *Die neue Architektur und das Bauhaus*. Florian Kupferberg, Mainz, 1965.

——— *Scope of Total Architecture*. Collier Books, New York, 1962.

GRUEN, VICTOR, *The Heart of Our Cities, The Urban Crisis: Diagnosis and Cure*. Simon and Schuster, New York, 1964.

GUTHEIM, FREDERICK, *Alvar Aalto: Masters of World Architecture*. George Braziller, New York, 1960.

HALL, EDWARD T., *The Hidden Dimension*. Doubleday & Company, Garden City, 1966.

HALPRIN, LAWRENCE, *Cities*. Reinhold Publishing Corp., New York, 1964.

——— *Freeways*. Reinhold Publishing Corp., New York, 1966.

HANDLIN, OSCAR and BURCHARD, JOHN, eds., *The Historian and the City*. M.I.T. and Harvard University Presses, Cambridge, 1963.

HARRINGTON, MICHAEL, *The Other America*. Macmillan, New York, 1962.

HITCHCOCK, H. R., *Architecture: Nineteenth and Twentieth Centuries*. Penguin, Baltimore, 1958.

——— *World Architecture: An Illustrated History*. McGraw-Hill, New York, 1963.

HOLLAND, LAURENCE B., ed., *Who Designs America?* Doubleday & Company, Garden City, 1966.

HOWARD, EBENEZER, *Garden Cities of To-morrow*. Faber & Faber, Ltd., London, 1960.

HUXTABLE, ADA LOUISE, *Pier Luigi Nervi: Masters of World Architecture*. George Braziller, New York, 1960.

JACOBS, JANE, *The Death and Life of Great American Cities*. Random House, New York, 1961.

JACOBUS, JOHN, *Philip Johnson: Makers of Contemporary Architecture*. George Braziller, New York, 1962.

——— *Twentieth-Century Architecture: The Middle Years*, 1940-1965. Frederick A. Praeger, New York, 1966.

JOHNSON, PHILIP C., *Architecture* 1949-1965. Holt, Rinehart & Winston, New York, 1966.

——— *Mies van der Rohe*. Museum of Modern Art, New York, 1953.

JORDAN, R. FURNEAUX, *The World of Great Architecture from the Greeks to the Nineteenth Century*. Viking Press, New York, 1961.

JUSTER, NORTON, *The Phantom Tollbooth*. Random House, New York, 1961.

KAUFMANN, EDGAR and RAEBURN, BEN, *Frank Lloyd Wright: Writings and Buildings*. Meridian Books, New York, 1960.

KELLY, BURNHAM, *The Prefabrication of Houses: A Study by the Albert Farwell Bemis Foundation of the Prefabrication Industry in the United States*. M.I.T. Press, Cambridge, 1951.

LE CORBUSIER, *Creation Is a Patient Search*. (James Palmes, trans.), Frederick A. Praeger, New York, 1960.

——— *Towards a New Architecture*. (Frederick Etchelis, trans.), Frederick A. Praeger, New York, 1963.

——— *When the Cathedrals Were White*. (Francis E. Hyslop, Jr., trans.), McGraw-Hill, New York, 1964.

LYNCH, KEVIN, *The Image of the City*. M.I.T. Press, Cambridge, 1960.

MARKS, ROBERT W., *The Dymaxion World of Buckminster Fuller*. Southern Illinois University Press, Carbondale, 1966.

MCCOY, ESTHER, *Richard Neutra: Masters of World Architecture*. George Braziller, New York, 1960.

MCHALE, JOHN, *R. Buckminster Fuller: Makers of Contemporary Architecture*. George Braziller, New York, 1962.

MCKELVEY, BLAKE, *The Urbanization of America,* 1860-1915. Rutgers University Press, New Brunswick, 1963.

MEYERSON, MARTIN, et al., *Face of the Metropolis*. Random House, New York, 1963.

MITCHELL, ROBERT B., ed., "Urban Revival: Goals and Standards," The Annals of the American Academy of Political and Social Science, Vol. 352, Philadelphia, March, 1964.

MUMFORD, LEWIS, *The City in History*. Harcourt, Brace & World, New York, 1961.

——— *The Culture of Cities*. Harcourt, Brace & World, New York, 1938.

——— *The Highway and the City*. Harcourt, Brace & World, New York, 1963.

——— *Roots of Contemporary American Architecture*. Grove Press, New York, 1959.

NAIRN, IAN, *The American Landscape*. Random House, New York, 1965.

NERVI, PIER LUIGI, *Aesthetics and Technology in Building*. Harvard University Press, Cambridge, 1965.

NEUTRA, RICHARD, *Life and Shape*. Appleton-Century-Crofts, New York, 1962.

——— *Survival Through Design*. Oxford University Press, New York & London, 1954.

——— *World and Dwelling*. Universe Books, New York, 1962.

OSBORN, SIR FREDERIC and WHITTICK, ARNOLD, *The New Towns: The Answer to Megalopolis*. McGraw-Hill, New York, 1964.

OWEN, WILFRED, *Cities in the Motor Age*. Viking Press, New York, 1959.

—— *The Metropolitan Transportation Problem*. Brookings Institution. Washington, D.C., rev. ed. 1966.

PAPADAKI, STAMO, *Oscar Niemeyer: Masters of World Architecture*. George Braziller, New York, 1960.

PEARSE, INNES H. and CROCKER, LUCY H., *The Peckham Experiment: A Study in the Living Structure of Society*. George Allen and Unwin Ltd., London, 1943.

PEHNT, WOLFGANG, ed., *Encyclopedia of Modern Architecture*. Harry N. Abrams, New York, 1964.

PELL, CLAIBORNE, *Megalopolis Unbound: The Supercity and the Transportation of Tomorrow*. Frederick A. Praeger, New York, 1966.

PERLOFF, HARVEY S., *Planning and the Urban Community*. University of Pittsburgh Press, Pittsburgh, 1961.

PETER, JOHN, *Masters of Modern Architecture*. George Braziller, New York, 1958.

PEVSNER, NIKOLAUS, *Pioneers of Modern Design from William Morris to Walter Gropius*. Museum of Modern Art, New York, 1949.

RANSOM, HARRY S., *The People's Architects*. University of Chicago Press, Chicago, 1964.

RASMUSSEN, STEEN EILER, *Experiencing Architecture*. Technology Press of the Massachusetts Institute of Technology and John Wiley & Sons, New York, 1959.

Reports of the Steering Group and Working Group Appointed by the Minister of Transport: "Traffic in Towns: A Study of the Long Term Problems of Traffic in Urban Areas." Her Majesty's Stationery Office, London, 1963.

REPS, JOHN W., *The Making of Urban America: A History of City Planning in the United States*. Princeton University Press, Princeton, 1965.

RITTER, PAUL, *Planning for Man and Motor*. Pergamon Press, Oxford, 1964.

SAARINEN, ALINE B., ed., *Eero Saarinen on His Work*. Yale University Press, New Haven, 1962.

SCHNAIDT, CLAUDE, *Hannes Meyer: Bauten, Projekte und Schriften*. Arthur Niggli, Teufen, Schweiz, 1965.

SCULLY, VINCENT, JR., *Frank Lloyd Wright: Masters of World Architecture*. George Braziller, New York, 1960.

—— *Louis I. Kahn: Makers of Contemporary Architecture*. George Braziller, New York, 1962.

SIMONDS, JOHN ORMSBEE, *Landscape Architecture: The Shaping of Man's Natural Environment*. F. W. Dodge Corporation, New York, 1961.

SMITH, NORRIS K., *Frank Lloyd Wright: A Study in Architectural Content*. Prentice-Hall, Englewood Cliffs, 1966.

SPREIREGEN, PAUL D., A.I.A., *Urban Design: The Architecture of Towns and Cities*. McGraw-Hill, New York, 1965.

STÄUBLI, WILLY, *Brasilia*. Universe Books, New York, 1965.

STEIN, CLARENCE S., *Toward New Towns for America*. University Press of Liverpool, and Public Administration Service, Chicago, 1951.

SWEENEY, JAMES JOHNSON, and SERT, JOSÉ LUIS, *Antoni Gaudi.* Frederick A. Praeger, New York, 1960.

TEMKO, ALLAN, *Eero Saarinen: Makers of Contemporary Architecture.* George Braziller, New York, 1962.

TUNNARD, CHRISTOPHER, and REED, HENRY H., *American Skyline,* Houghton Mifflin Co., Boston, 1955.

——— and PUSHKAREV, BORIS, *Man-Made America: Chaos or Control.* Yale University Press, New Haven, 1963.

UDALL, STEWART L., *The Quiet Crisis.* Holt, Rinehart & Winston, New York, 1963.

VON ECKARDT, WOLF, *The Challenge of Megalopolis.* Macmillan, New York, 1963.

——— *Eric Mendelsohn: Masters of World Architecture.* George Braziller, New York, 1960.

WACHSMANN, KONRAD, *The Turning Point of Building: Structure and Design.* Reinhold Publishing Corp., New York, 1961.

WEAVER, ROBERT C., *The Urban Complex.* Doubleday & Company, Garden City, 1964.

WHITE, MORTON and LUCIA, *The Intellectual Versus the City: From Thomas Jefferson to Frank Lloyd Wright.* Harvard University Press, Cambridge, 1962.

White House Conference on Natural Beauty, May 24-25, "Beauty for America." U.S. Government Printing Office, Washington, D.C. 1965.

WHYTE, WILLIAM H., *Cluster Development.* American Conservation Association, New York, 1964.

WINGLER, HANS M., *Das Bauhaus,* 1919-1922: Weimar, Dessau, Berlin. Rasch & Company, Bramsche, 1962.

WOOD, ROBERT C., *Suburbia, Its People and Their Politics.* Houghton Mifflin Co., Boston, 1959.

ZUCKER, PAUL, *Styles in Painting: A Comparative Study.* Viking Press, New York, 1950.

Picture Credits

These credits refer to the page on which the picture appears; each includes a brief description of the illustration, and, when pertinent, the designer, as well as the source of each photograph.

p. 3: Peter Agostini, *The City*, plaster sculpture, 1960; Don Cook, courtesy Stephen Radich Gallery.
p. 7: American living room, ca. 1870; Wolf Von Eckardt.
p. 10: Charles Luckmann, Prudential Tower, Boston, Mass., 1964.
p. 12: North Central Avenue, Phoenix, Ariz., ca. 1965; Del E. Webb Corp.
p. 16: Mills, Petticord & Mills, Capitol Car Distributors Office and Warehouse, Washington, D. C., 1965; Capitol Car Distributors, Inc., Lanham, Md.
p. 18: Wurster, Bernardi and Emmons, DeMars & Reay, Golden Gateway Center, San Francisco, Calif., begun 1962; Dickey & Harleen Studios.
p. 20: Alberto Giacometti, *The Square*, bronze, 1949; Pierre Matisse Gallery, New York.
p. 22: Henry Rohland, © 1963 The Washington Post Co.
p. 24: Zuoz, Switzerland; Wolf Von Eckardt.
p. 27: Andy Warhol, *Suicide*, silkscreen on paper, 1962; Leo Castelli Gallery.
p. 34: Freiburg, Germany, marketplace; Bild-Archiv Stadt, Verkehrsant Freiburg (Burschel).
p. 35: Old Courthouse and Federal Building, Chicago, Ill.; Hedrich-Blessing.
p. 37: Mies van der Rohe, Lafayette Park, Detroit, Mich., 1963; Hedrich-Blessing.
p. 38: Philip Johnson, Glass House, New Canaan, Conn., 1949; Alexandre Georges
p. 39: Crofton Village Green, Crofton, Md., 1965; Robert de Gast.
p. 43: Whittlesey and Conklin, Reston, Va., 1966; William A. Graham, Arlington, Va.
p. 45: Philadelphia street before urban renewal, 1960 (900 block N. Marshall); Philadelphia Redevelopment Authority.
p. 47: Farragut Square, Washington, D. C.; William A. Graham, Arlington, Va.
p. 49: Skidmore, Owings, and Merrill, University of Illinois in Chicago, Ill., Administration Building; Alan M. Fern.
p. 51: Raymond Hood, Rockefeller Center Plaza, New York City, begun 1931; Rockefeller Center, Inc.

p. 53: Top—Chloethiel Woodard Smith, LaClede Town, St. Louis, 1965; W. F. Jud. Bottom—Chloethiel Woodard Smith, LaClede Town, St. Louis, 1965; W. F. Jud.

p. 56: Top—Mies van der Rohe, Crown Hall, Illinois Institute of Technology, 1956; Mies van der Rohe, Architect, Pace Associates, Associate Architects. Bottom—Paul Rudolph, Art and Architecture Building, Yale University, New Haven, Conn., 1963; Yale University News Service.

p. 59: Skidmore, Owings, and Merrill, University of Illinois Chicago Circle Campus, 1965; Orlando R. Cabanban.

p. 60: Skidmore, Owings, and Merrill, University of Illinois Chicago Circle Campus, 1965; Orlando R. Cabanban.

p. 61: Skidmore, Owings, and Merrill, University of Illinois Chicago Circle Campus, 1965; Orlando R. Cabanban.

p. 65: Lyonel Feininger, cover for Bauhaus leaflet, woodcut, 1919.

p. 69: Ludwig Meidner, *Listener into the Epoch*, lithograph, 1919.

p. 70: Walter Gropius, Adler automobile, 1930; Dr. Franz Stoedtner, Düsseldorf.

p. 75: J. Knau (Bauhaus), samovar and tea pot, silver-bronze, 1924; Dr. F. Stoedtner, Düsseldorf.

p. 78: Grain elevator in Chicago before World War I; Dr. F. Stoedtner, Düsseldorf.

p. 79: Frank Lloyd Wright, Robie House, south facade, 1909; Richard Nickel.

p. 80: El Lissitzky, *Cloud Props Project*, constructivist drawing, 1924; Dr. F. Stoedtner, Düsseldorf.

p. 81: Van Doesburg, University Auditorium; Dr. F. Stoedtner, Düsseldorf.

p. 83: Walter Gropius, Bauhaus, Dessau, 1929; Dr. F. Stoedtner, Düsseldorf.

p. 84: Walter Gropius, Fagus Shoe Last Factory, Alfeld an der Leine, 1911; Dr. F. Stoedtner, Düsseldorf.

p. 85: Walter Gropius, house in Dessau, 1929; Dr. F. Stoedtner, Düsseldorf.

p. 89: Mies van der Rohe, Barcelona Pavilion, 1929; courtesy Mies van der Rohe.

p. 91: Karl Friedrich von Schinkel, Die Neue Wache, Berlin, 1815; Dr. F. Stoedtner, Düsseldorf.

p. 92: Mies van der Rohe, design for an office building on Friedrichstrasse, Berlin, 1920; Dr. F. Stoedtner, Düsseldorf.

p. 93: Mies van der Rohe, design for a brick villa, 1923; Dr. F. Stoedtner, Düsseldorf.

p. 95: Mies van der Rohe, design for a concrete villa, 1924; Dr. F. Stoedtner, Düsseldorf.

p. 96: Mies van der Rohe, Crown Hall, Illinois Institute of Technology, 1956; Hedrich-Blessing.

p. 98: Le Corbusier, Villa Savoye, Poissy-sur-Seine, France, 1930; courtesy The Museum of Modern Art, New York.

p. 100: Le Corbusier, Carpenter Center for the Visual Arts, Harvard University, Cambridge, 1963. Copyright by the President and Fellows of Harvard College.

p. 101: Le Corbusier, Government Center, Chandigarh, India, 1956; Peter Blake.

p. 103: Le Corbusier, Brazilian Pavilion, University City, Paris, 1959, detail; Peter Blake.

p. 105: Le Corbusier, *Unité d'Habitation (Cité Radieuse)*, Marseilles, France, 1952; Lucien Herve, courtesy The Museum of Modern Art, New York.

p. 106: Weissenhofsiedlung, Werkbund Exposition, Stuttgart, Germany, 1927; courtesy The Museum of Modern Art, New York.

p. 107: Ludwig Hilberseimer, houses for the Weissenhof Exhibition, Stuttgart, 1927; Dr. F. Stoedtner, Düsseldorf.

p. 109: Hansaviertel, Berlin, 1957, partial view; Der Senator für Bau- und Wohnwesen, Berlin.

p. 113: Walter Gropius, prefabricated house, 1932; Dr. F. Stoedtner, Düsseldorf.

p. 115: R. Buckminster Fuller, Dymaxion House (original model), 1927; Fuller Research Foundation, courtesy The Museum of Modern Art.

p. 118: Carl Koch, Techbuilt House, ca. 1955; copyright by Techbuilt, Inc., Architect —Carl Koch.

p. 121: Moshe Safdie, Habitat '67, Montreal, under construction; by permission of Keith Oliver, photographer.

p. 122: Skidmore, Owings, and Merrill, Chase Manhattan Bank, 1961; Eric Locker, courtesy Chase Manhattan Bank.

p. 123: Eliel Saarinen, Cranbrook Foundation, Bloomfield Hills, Michigan, ca. 1940; Carl Milles, sculpture; Harvey Croze.

p. 124: Richard Neutra, Lovell House, Los Angeles, 1929; Dr. F. Stoedtner, Düsseldorf.

p. 126: William Lescaze and George Howe, Philadelphia Savings Fund Society Building, Philadelphia, 1932; George Howe and William Lescaze, Architects.

p. 129: Skidmore, Owings, and Merrill, Lever House, New York, 1952; Ezra Stoller (ESTO).

p. 131: Le Corbusier, modular on the *Unité d'Habitation* "Type Berlin," Berlin, 1954; Peter Blake.

p. 133: Skyscraper frame, 1895; Dr. F. Stoedtner, Düsseldorf.

p. 134: Thomas Kelley, *The Washington Post.*

p. 136: Thomas Cole, *The Architect's Dream*, oil on canvas, 1840; gift of Florence Scott Libbey, The Toledo Museum of Art, Toledo, Ohio.

p. 141: Caudill, Rowlett, Scott, Roy E. Larsen Hall, Harvard Graduate School of Education, Cambridge, Mass., 1965; copyright by the President and Fellows of Harvard College.

p. 143: Top—San Giminiano, Italy, 14th century. Italian Government Travel Office—ENIT. Bottom—Louis I. Kahn, Richards Medical Research Building, University of Pennsylvania, Philadelphia, 1960; Robert Lautman.

p. 146: Bottom Left—Aubrey Beardsley, Preliminary Drawing for *Salome* by Oscar Wilde, 1893; Gallatin Beardsley Collection, Princeton University Library. Bottom Right—Victor Horta, Van Eetvelde House, Brussels, 1895; Dr. F. Stoedtner, Düsseldorf. Top—Antoni Gaudi, Church of the Sagrada Familia, Barcelona, Spain, 1926; courtesy The Museum of Modern Art, New York.

p. 147: Frank Lloyd Wright, Civic Center, Marin County, Calif., Ken Edler, Area West Photography.

p. 148: Top—Frank Lloyd Wright, Larkin Company Office Building, Buffalo, 1904 (destroyed 1950); Dr. F. Stoedtner, Düsseldorf. Bottom—Paul Rudolph, Art and Architecture Building, Yale University, New Haven, 1963; Yale University News Bureau.

p. 152: Antonio Sant'Elia, sketch for a new city, 1914; Dr. F. Stoedtner, Düsseldorf.

p. 153: Eric Mendelsohn, Einstein Tower, Potsdam, 1919.

p. 154: Top—Eric Mendelsohn, fantasy, 1917. Bottom—Eero Saarinen, Dulles International Airport Terminal, Washington, D. C., 1962; Balthazar Korab.

p. 155: Top—Eric Mendelsohn, pencil sketch of an imaginary textile plant, 1926. Bottom—Skidmore, Owings, and Merrill, United States Air Force Academy Chapel, 1962; Stewarts Commercial Photographers, Inc.

p. 157: Experimental dome for the Zeiss Planetarium, Jena, 1922; Dyckerhoff & Widmann.

p. 158: Robert Maillart, Val Tschiel Bridge, Canton Grisons, Switzerland, 1926; courtesy The Museum of Modern Art, New York.

p. 161: Concrete hyperbolic paraboloid built as a classroom project by Cornell University architecture students; Cornell University.

p. 163: Pier Luigi Nervi, Exhibition Building, Turin, 1949; Ricardo Moncalvo, Turin, Italy.

p. 164: Oscar Niemeyer, Church of St. Francis of Assisi at Pampulha, Belo Horizonte, 1942; School of Architecture, University of Minas, Gerais, Brazil.

p. 166: Eero Saarinen, TWA terminal, Kennedy International Airport, New York, N. Y., 1962; Ezra Stoller for TWA.

p. 167: Hugh A. Stubbins, Congress Hall, Berlin, 1957. Der Senator für Bau- und Wohnwesen, Berlin.

p. 168: Top—Harrison and Abramovitz, First Presbyterian Church, Stamford, Conn., 1959; Joseph W. Molitor. Bottom—First Presbyterian Church, Stamford, Conn., 1959; Ezra Stoller.

p. 170: Bertrand Goldberg, Marina City, Chicago, 1964; Orlando R. Cabanban.

p. 171: Le Corbusier, Notre-Dame du Haut, Ronchamp, 1954; Bernhard Moosbrugger, Zurich, Switzerland.

p. 173: Le Corbusier, Notre-Dame du Haut, Ronchamp, 1954; Bernhard Moosbrugger, Zurich, Switzerland.

p. 174: Pablo Picasso, *Guernica*, mural, oil on canvas, 11′6″ x 25′8″, 1937; on extended loan to The Museum of Modern Art, New York, from the artist; courtesy The Museum of Modern Art, New York.

p. 175: Le Corbusier, *Unité d'Habitation*, Marseilles, France, 1952; Lucien Herve, courtesy The Museum of Modern Art, New York.

p. 176: Top—Le Corbusier, La Tourette monastery, Eveux near Lyon, 1957; Bernhard Moosbrugger, Zurich, Switzerland. Bottom—Le Corbusier, La Tourette monastery, Eveux near Lyon, 1957; Bernhard Moosbrugger, Zurich, Switzerland.

p. 178: Mies van der Rohe, Lake Shore Drive Apartments, Chicago, 1951; Hedrich-Blessing.

p. 179: Victor Gruen Associates, City National Bank, Palm Springs, Calif.; Gordon Sommers Photography.

p. 184: Kallmann, McKinnell and Knowles, new City Hall, Boston, model, 1962; courtesy Kallmann, McKinnell and Knowles.

p. 185: Kenzo Tange, Kurashiki City Hall, Kurashiki, Japan, 1960; Fumio Murasawa.

p. 186: Hellmuth, Obata & Kassabaum, National Air and Space Museum, renderings, Washington, D. C.; courtesy National Air and Space Museum, Smithsonian Institution.

p. 188: Sert, Jackson, Gourley, Francis Greenwood Peabody Terrace married-student housing, Harvard University, Cambridge, Mass., 1963; William Tobey, Harvard News Service, photo by Photion Karas.

p. 189: Sert, Jackson, Gourley, Fondation Maeght, St. Paul de Vence, France, 1964; Wolf Von Eckardt.

p. 191: Oscar Niemeyer, Alvorada Palace Chapel, Brasília, 1958; Suzy P. de Mello.

p. 192: Oscar Niemeyer, Alvorada Palace, Brasília, 1958; Suzy P. de Mello.

p. 193: Oscar Niemeyer, Executive Palace, Brasília, detail, 1958; copyright 1966 Luis Humberto M. Martins Pereira, all rights reserved.

p. 195: Victor A. Lundy, I. Miller Showroom, New York City; George Cserna.

p. 196: Keyes, Lethbridge & Condon with Pietro Belluschi, Cedar Lane Unitarian Church, Bethesda, Md., 1964; J. Alexander.

p. 199: The Salk Institute, La Jolla, Calif.; D. K. Miller, The Salk Institute.

p. 201: Top—Hans Scharoun, Berlin Philharmonic Hall, Berlin, 1964; Berlin Bild. Bottom—Mies van der Rohe, Gallery of the Twentieth Century, Berlin (under construction); Hedrich-Blessing.

p. 202: Eero Saarinen, Concordia Senior College, Fort Wayne, Ind., 1958; Alexandre Georges.

p. 205: Philip Johnson, Museum of Modern Art, East Wing, 1964; Alexandre Georges.

p. 206: Philip Johnson, New York State Theater, Lincoln Center, New York City, 1964; Ezra Stoller (ESTO).

p. 208: Eero Saarinen, Vivian Beaumont Theater, Lincoln Center, New York City, 1965; sculpture by Henry Moore; Wolf Von Eckardt.

p. 210: Eero Saarinen, Columbia Broadcasting System Headquarters Building, New York City, 1965; courtesy CBS.

p. 212: Salvador Dali, *The Sacrament of the Last Supper*, oil on canvas, 1962, National Gallery of Art (Chester Dale Collection); courtesy National Gallery of Art, Washington, D. C.

p. 213: Harold E. Wagoner, design for National Presbyterian Center, Washington, D. C., 1966; National Presbyterian Church and Center, Washington, D. C.

p. 214: Edward Durrell Stone, Huntington Hartford Gallery of Modern Art, New York City, 1959; Joseph Heiberger, courtesy *The Washington Post*.

p. 215: Edward Durell Stone, U. S. Embassy in New Delhi, 1958; Rondal Partridge; Edward Durell Stone, Architects.

p. 216: Edward Durell Stone, model of National Cultural Center, Washington, D. C.; Louis Checkman, courtesy The John F. Kennedy Center for the Performing Arts.

p. 218: The Perkins & Will Partnership, United States Gypsum Building, Chicago, Ill.; Hedrich-Blessing.

p. 219: Minoru Yamasaki, Conference Center, Wayne University, Detroit, Mich.; Hedrich-Blessing.

p. 224: The Architect's Collaborative (Walter Gropius), U. S. Embassy, Athens, Greece, 1961; Emil.

p. 225: Top—Skidmore, Owings, and Merrill, Banque Lambert, Brussels, 1958; Ezra Stoller (ESTO). Bottom—Skidmore, Owings, and Merrill, Beinicke Rare Book and Manuscript Library, Yale University, New Haven, Conn.; Ezra Stoller (ESTO).

p. 227: Marcel Breuer & Associates, Research Center for IBM France, La Gaude, near Nice, 1960; IBM-France Research Center, La Gaude, 1960–1961, Marcel Breuer, architect, Robert Gatje, associate, Richard and Michel Laugier, supervising architects.

p. 228: Top—Harry Weese & Associates, Hyde Park Town Houses, Chicago, Ill.; Bill Engdahl, Hedrich-Blessing. Bottom—Harry Weese & Associates, Arena Stage, Washington, D. C.; Balthazar Korab.

p. 230: Society Hill, Washington Square East, Philadelphia; Alois K. Strobl, Philadelphia Planning Commission.

p. 233: Alvar Aalto, Town Hall in Säynätsalo, Finland, 1952; Heikki Havas.

p. 234: Louis Sauer, townhouses, Reston, Va., 1966; William A. Graham, Arlington, Va.

p. 237: Top—Hugh Newell Jacobsen, Cafritz House, Georgetown, Washington, D. C., rear view; Robert Lautman. Bottom—Winthrop Faulkner, Faulkner House, Washington, D. C., 1965; Norman McGrath.

p. 238: Chloethiel Woodard Smith, townhouses, Reston, Va., 1965; William Graham, Arlington, Va.

p. 245: William Penn's plan for Philadelphia, 1682; courtesy Philadelphia City Planning Commission.

p. 247: So-called Frenchman's Map by unidentified delineator, showing plan of Williamsburg, Va., 1782; Earl Gregg Swem Library, The College of William and Mary in Virginia, Williamsburg, Va.

p. 248: Broadway and the City Hall, New York, aquatint engraving, colored, by R. Varin, 1819, National Gallery of Art, Washington, D. C., Rosenwald Collection; courtesy National Gallery of Art, Washington, D. C.

p. 252: Piranesi, Veduta della Piazza del Popolo, engraving; reproduced from the collections of the Library of Congress.

p. 254: Leonardo da Vinci, proposal for tunneling under cities; reprinted from *Leonardo da Vinci* by permission of Istituto Geografico de Agostini, Novara, Italy.

p. 255: Leonardo da Vinci, proposal for street system over waterways and for early tunnels and traffic separation; in addition, the scheme for a skyscraper in the city; reprinted from *Leonardo da Vinci* by permission of Istituto Geografico de Agostini, Novara, Italy.

p. 257: Piranesi, Veduta di Piazza Navona, engraving; reproduced from the collections of the Library of Congress.

p. 259: Skidmore, Owings, and Merrill, proposal for the improvement of the Mall in Washington, D. C., 1966; courtesy National Park Service, U. S. Department of the Interior.

p. 263: World's Columbian Exposition, Chicago, 1893; Dr. F. Stoedtner, Düsseldorf.

p. 264: World's Columbian Exposition, Chicago, 1893; Dr. F. Stoedtner, Düsseldorf.

p. 271: Skidmore, Owings, and Merrill, model of Pennsylvania Avenue Plan, Washington, D. C.; Dwain Faubion.

p. 272: Le Corbusier, The Radiant City, sketch, 1922; Dr. F. Stoedtner, Düsseldorf.

p. 273: Stuyvesant Town, New York City, 1947; Thomas Airviews.

p. 275: Le Corbusier, The Radiant City, 1922; Dr. F. Stoedtner, Düsseldorf.

p. 277: Ludwig Hilberseimer, Skyscraper City, 1924; Dr. F. Stoedtner, Düsseldorf.

p. 278: Jacob Bakema, shopping street, Nagele, The Netherlands, 1957; Wolf Von Eckardt.

p. 280: Oscar Niemeyer, National Congress, Brasília, Brazil, 1960; Wolf Von Eckardt.

p. 289: Wolf Von Eckardt.

p. 295: Top—Downtown Philadelphia, 1949; Skyphotos, Philadelphia. Bottom—Downtown Philadelphia, 1965; Skyphotos, Philadelphia.

p. 297: The western addition urban-renewal area, San Francisco, Calif.; Karl H. Riek.

p. 301: Chloethiel Woodard Smith & Associates, Capitol Park Townhouses, Washington, D. C., southwest urban-renewal area, 1961; architects: Chloethiel Woodard Smith & Associated Architects, Washington, D. C.; photographer: Jorgen Gravgaard.

p. 302: Charles M. Goodman, River Park, Washington, D. C., southwest urban-renewal area, 1963; J. Waring Stinchcomb Photographic Services, Inc.

p. 303: Keyes, Lethbridge & Condon, Tiber Island, Washington, D. C., southwest urban-renewal area, 1965; J. Alexander.

p. 305: I. M. Pei, shopping center, southwest urban-renewal area, Washington, D. C.; Wolf Von Eckardt.

p. 306: Charles M. Goodman, Hawthorne School, Washington, D. C., southwest; Wolf Von Eckardt.

p. 308: View of the St. Louis Arch from the Mill Creek urban-renewal area; George McCue.

p. 314: Top—Court Street, Wooster Square Project, New Haven, Conn.; New Haven Redevelopment Agency. Bottom—Hideo Sasaki, landscaping and street furniture, Church Street Project, New Haven, Conn.; New Haven Redevelopment Agency.

p. 316: Marquis and Stoller, St. Francis Square, San Francisco western addition urban-renewal area, 1963; Karl H. Riek.

p. 317: Charles Du Bose, coordinating architect, Hideo Sasaki, landscape architect, Constitution Plaza, Hartford, Conn., 1964; Ralph H. Hutchins, Jr., Hutchins Photography, Inc.

p. 323: Copenhagen, Strøget; Wolf Von Eckardt.

p. 325: Planning Commission of Stockholm, Sergelgatan, 1963; Wolf Von Eckardt.

p. 327: Werner Hasper, Treppen Strasse, Kassel, Germany; Heinz Pauly, Kassel.

p. 328: Victor Gruen Associates, pedestrian mall, Fresno, Calif., 1964; all copyrights to this photo are retained by The Tidyman Studios.

p. 329: Victor Gruen Associates, pedestrian mall, Fresno, Calif., 1964; all copyrights to this photo are retained by The Tidyman Studios.

p. 332: Planning Commission of Stockholm, Sergelgatan, 1963; Wolf Von Eckardt.

p. 333: Top—Planning Commission of Stockholm, Sergelgatan, 1963; Wolf Von Eckardt. Bottom—Planning Commission of Stockholm, Sergelgatan, 1963; Wolf Von Eckardt.

p. 336: Central Skyway and James Lick Freeway intersect in downtown San Francisco; Wide World Photos.

p. 347: Henry Moore, *Family Group*, stone, Harlow New Town, England, 1956; Harlow Development Corporation.

p. 348: Aarne Ervi, Tapiola, Finland; Lehtikuvah, Helsinki.

p. 349: Top—Aarne Ervi, Town Center, Tapiola, Finland, 1963; Pietinen, copyright by Asuntosäätiö Housing Foundation. Bottom—Markus Tavio, Apartment Houses, Tapiola, Finland, 1963; Pietinen, copyright Asuntosäätiö Housing Foundation.

p. 356: Top—Social activities at Reston, Va.; William A. Graham, Arlington, Va. Bottom—Social activities at Reston, Va.; William A. Graham, Arlington, Va.

p. 357: Top left—Social activities at Reston, Va.; William A. Graham, Arlington, Va. Top right—Social activities at Reston, Va.; William A. Graham, Arlington, Va. Bottom—Social activities at Reston, Va.; William A. Graham, Arlington, Va.

p. 358: Top—Social activities at Reston, Va.; William A. Graham, Arlington, Va. Bottom—Social activities at Reston, Va. William A. Graham, Arlington, Va.

p. 360: Cumbernauld New Town, near Glasgow, Scotland; Cumbernauld Development Corp.

p. 365: Harlow Market Square, Harlow, England, 1947; Wolf Von Eckardt.

p. 367: Cumbernauld New Town; Cumbernauld Development Corp.

p. 368: William Finley and Morton Hoppenfeld, model of town center, Columbia, Md.; Ezra Stoller (ESTO).

p. 372: Whittlesey, Conklin and Rossant, Lower Manhattan waterfront concept for the New York City Planning Commission, 1966; courtesy New York City Planning Commission.

p. 376: Romaldo Giurgola, Market East—Study, Sectional Perspective; courtesy Philadelphia City Planning Commission.

p. 377: Romaldo Giurgola, Market East—Study, Interior Perspective; courtesy Philadelphia City Planning Commission.

p. 378: Jacob Riis Houses, New York; courtesy New York City Housing Authority.

p. 381: Skidmore, Owings, and Merrill, Conte Community School, Wooster Square Project, New Haven, Conn.; Cunningham-Werdnigg, courtesy New Haven Redevelopment Agency.

p. 384: Wurster, Bernardi and Emmons and Lawrence Halprin & Associates, Ghirardelli Square, San Francisco, 1965; design: Lawrence Halprin & Associates, architect: Wurster, Bernardi and Emmons.

p. 385: Top—Wurster, Bernardi and Emmons and Lawrence Halprin & Associates, Ghirardelli Square, San Francisco, 1965; Ernest Braun; design: Lawrence Halprin & Associates, architect: Wurster, Bernardi and Emmons. Bottom—Wurster, Bernardi and Emmons and Lawrence Halprin & Associates, Ghirardelli Square, San Francisco, 1965; design: Lawrence Halprin & Associates, architect: Wurster, Bernardi and Emmons.

p. 388: Sketch by Paul Spreiregen, AIA.

p. 390: Sketch by Paul Spreiregen, AIA.

p. 394: Sketch by Paul Spreiregen, AIA.

p. 402: Sketch by Paul Spreiregen, AIA.

Index